Aging
&
Ending

A first-year baby boomer
looks back and ahead

Michael N. Marcus

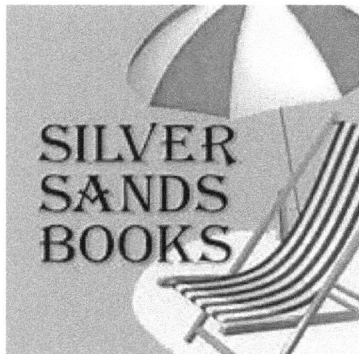

SILVER
SANDS
BOOKS

Connecticut
203.780.8118

www.SilverSandsBooks.com
SilverSandsBooks123 (at) gmail.com

Author's Notes:

a.   It's said that you know you're old when you talk more about what you've done than about what you're going to do. I'm writing this a few months after my 78th birthday. Some people think that's old. Maybe it is. I'm way past the likely midpoint of my life. That's why more of this book looks back than looks ahead. Some chapters don't look in either direction.

b.   Some material in this book was previously published in my other books, blogs and on Facebook. It's been updated and augmented where appropriate.

c.   Some things are mentioned in multiple chapters. This is deliberate, not sloppiness.

d.   You can read this book from beginning to end, or just poke around and read what seems interesting. Most chapters are not arranged in a specific sequence. However, some chapters *should* be read sequentially, as is apparent from the chapter titles.

e.   To save space, time and work, this book has no "headers," other than page numbers. A header is a bit of text on the top of a page that shows the book's title, author's name and maybe the chapter title. If you've forgotten this book's title or who I am, please look at the cover.

f.   I guarantee that this book is at least 96% true.

g.   Some names have been changed.

h.   Traditionally, short words like "a," "to", "and" and "if" start with *lowercase* ("small") letters on book covers and in chapter titles. That's how I designed previous books, but I never liked the look. The mix of upper- and lowercase letters was disconcerting, jarring and disturbed my peace. It reminded me of hills and valleys on a roller coaster. So, in this book, each chapter title begins with an Uppercase Letter, followed by lower-case (mostly). I might be damned for flouting tradition, but I'll live with damnation if I think I'm right.

i.   I type "antisemitism," not "anti-Semitism." I try to avoid hyphenated words, especially if they include uppercase letters. Please don't complain that this is demeaning to my fellow Semites.

j.   I spell out numbers up to ten. It's traditional to use digits starting at 10, but ten is such a short word that I like to spell it. *The New Yorker* magazine, in contrast, spells everything—even "*one thousand, six hundred, forty-seven.*" Yuck.

k.   I do not Uppercase "The" in "*the New York Times.*" That's not an error. It's *my* book.

l.   I do, however, Uppercase "The" in "*The New Yorker.*" I know it's inconsistent, but it's an indicator of respect for an esteemed and venerated medium. (Maybe I didn't need both adjectives, but WTF.)

m.   If I seem irreverent and cynical, it's because I am.

n.   Just as actors and musicians are motivated by applause, and chefs may be inspired to cook even better if you shake their hands after great meals, authors need the reinforcement of compliments from readers. Good reviews also help sell more books, and most authors need money. If you find a book useful and/or entertaining, please tell others and please leave a nice review on booksellers' and readers' websites such as *Goodreads.com*, *Amazon.com* and *Barnesandnoble.com*.

o.   I put text in *italics for emphasis* and to indicate that a term is esoteric, not in English, a website (sometimes) or the title of a song or publication.

p.   I usually put names of **people** and **businesses** in **boldface type** to make it easier to find the names.

q.   The book frequently shows the tiny word "I", but not due to sloppiness or egotism. It's just appropriate.

r.   Some chapters, particularly those that deal with religion, have many details and strange names. I will not be offended if you skip those chapters.

s.   I use the academic abbreviations "BCE" (before the common era) and "CE" (common era) instead of the Christian "BC" and "AD."

t.   In the printed book, some photos have poor contrast. For them to look great, the book would cost much more.

u.   There are multiple pictures of egg creams in the book. I love egg creams.
     [photo from Max Falkowitz. Thanks!]

Reader Reactions

"Michael N. Marcus delivers a whimsically profound exploration of life's quirks and quandaries, weaving together nearly eight decades of keen observation and humor, making it a delightful read for anyone seeking to reflect on the complexities of existence with a smile." — NewInBooks.com

"You made me SPIT FOOD OUT OF MY MOUTH while reading things you wrote. Not one of my better moments, Michael! Thanks to you, some people now prefer to sit next to me rather than across from me while I am eating and reading your words! You are indeed THE ENTERTAINER!!" —Cindy Dorman Genis

A few favorites from previous books:

- "This book is so funny that I nearly peed in my pants. My girlfriend didn't think it was funny, so I got a new girlfriend." —*Nicholas Santiago*
- "A hoot" —*Rosemary Garcia*
- "Every time I start laughing, there's my husband peering over my shoulder wanting to know what's so funny. This book is! Michael, your wife is a saint!" —*Deborah Slutsky Samuels*
- 'Fucking brilliant! Who knew that you had this much sexual depravity in your past? I'll never look at you the same way." —*Christy Pinheiro, author & publisher*
- "This may be the funniest book ever! I laughed so hard reading it that the dogs got out of bed and left the room. They forgave me when I read the Cat Lasagna story to them. I haven't had this much fun in the sack since, well, we won't go there. Thank you for making the dirty parts easy to find. That saved me a lot of time. You are a wise man and a wiseass: a winning combination." —*Barbara Barth, author of "The Unfaithful Widow"*
- "I loved the chapter with the three-way sex scene. It seemed very familiar. Was I there?" —*Name withheld by request*
- "The book is hilarious... really, really funny. I did a spit take and laughed so hard I could barely breathe when I read the 'cockroaches with lobster costumes' line."—*Christy Pinheiro*
- "I knew the lesbian painter. She was a lousy painter but an excellent lesbian. When does the movie come out?" —*Wendy Liu*
- "Marcus has been threatening to publish this for years. When you read it, you'll remember when you were young and insane, and you won't stop laughing. Don't write to Marcus to share similar experiences. He's going to be put away where he can't get email." —*Ted Foti*
- "A perfect combination of silliness and seriousness. You remember everything. I'm glad you didn't see me doing anything illegal or stupid." —*Susan Weiss*
- "I didn't realize what an A-hole I was then. If this book wasn't so funny, I'd sue you for libel. I'll settle for an autographed copy. Thanks for changing my name." —*Marty Gilbert*

PLEASE NOTE: Most of the comments on this page are printed exactly as submitted by readers. Some have been slightly edited. A few are complete fabrications written by the author in an effort to entice people to buy books. Please don't feel deceived. He promises only that the book is at least 96% true. If you do the math, you'll know that up to 4% could be bullshit.

Words to ponder from a Nobel Prize winner and Rock & Roll Hall of Fame member

"May you stay forever young."
"The times, they are a-changing."
"Don't think twice. It's alright."
"Don't look back"
"Enough is enough"
"I'll get where I'm going someday"
"It's all over now, Baby Blue"
"It's alright, Ma (I'm only bleeding)"
"Long and wasted years"
"Most likely you go your way, and I'll go mine"
"Ah, but I was so much older then. I'm younger than that now."
"Tomorrow is a long time"

Bob Dylan (born Robert Zimmerman in Minnesota in 1941) is probably the only member of the **Rock & Roll Hall of Fame, Nashville Songwriters Hall of Fame** and **Songwriters Hall of Fame**—who also was awarded a **Nobel Prize for Literature**.

In 1997, American president **Bill Clinton** presented Dylan with a **Kennedy Center Honor**, saying: "He probably had more impact on people of my generation than any other creative artist. His voice and lyrics haven't always been easy on the ear, but throughout his career Bob Dylan has never aimed to please. He's disturbed the peace and discomforted the powerful."

In 2008, the **Pulitzer Prize** jury cited Dylan for "his profound impact on popular music and American culture, marked by lyrical compositions of extraordinary poetic power."

Dylan received the **Presidential Medal of Freedom** in 2012 from **President Barack Obama**. He said, "There is not a bigger giant in the history of American music." Obama praised Dylan's voice for its "unique gravelly power that redefined not just what music sounded like but the message it carried and how it made people feel."

In 2013, Dylan was awarded France's highest honor, the **Légion d'Honneur.** In 2015, Dylan accepted the **MusiCares Person of the Year award** from the **National Academy of Recording Arts and Sciences**, in recognition of his philanthropic and artistic contributions.

Rolling Stone ranked Dylan first on its 2015 list of the 100 Greatest Songwriters of All Time, fifteenth on its 2023 list of the **Greatest Singers of All Time**, and placed *Like A Rolling Stone* first on their list **of greatest songs in 2004 and 2011**. He was listed second on the magazine's list of the hundred greatest artists. *The Rolling Stone Encyclopedia of Rock & Roll* says that "His lyrics—the first in rock to be seriously regarded as literature—became so well known that politicians from Jimmy Carter to Václav Havel have cited them as an influence."

[Dylan photo from Alberto Cabello, Vitoria Gasteiz. Thanks.]

Contents

You can read this book from beginning to end, or just poke around and read what seems interesting. Most chapters are not arranged in a specific sequence. However, some chapters should be read sequentially, as should be apparent from the chapter titles.

Here's some foreplay,
to get you in the mood.

- "Laugh, and the world laughs with you. Weep and you weep alone."
  —Ella Wheeler Wilcox (author and poet)
- "Laugh alone and the world thinks you're an idiot."
  —Alfred E. Neuman (gap-toothed symbol of *MAD* magazine)
- "Over? Did you say 'over'? Nothing is over until we decide it is! Was it over when the Germans bombed Pearl Harbor? Hell, no!"
  —John Belushi as Bluto Blutarsky in *Animal House*
- "Women need a reason to have sex. Men just need a place."
  —Billy Crystal as Mitch Robbins in *City Slickers*
- "Everybody deserves to get laid."
  —Patricia Arquette as Avery Ryan in *CSI Cyber*
- "Foul-mouthed? Fuck you!"
  —Eddie Murphy as Axel Foley in *Beverly Hills Cop*
- "Opinions are like assholes. Everybody has one."
  —Clint Eastwood as "Dirty" Harry Callahan in *The Dead Pool*
- "She thinks I'm a pervert because I drank our waterbed." "Stop whining and eat your shiksa."—Woody Allen as Miles Monroe in *Sleeper*
- "There was a moment last night, when she was sandwiched between the two Finnish dwarves and the Maori tribesmen, where I thought, wow, I could really spend the rest of my life with this woman."
  —Ben Stiller as Derek Zoolander in *Zoolander*
- "I have a penis and a brain and only enough blood to run one at a time."
  —Robin Williams on the *Tonight Show*
- "Listen, let's get one thing straight. In the hours you're here taking care of my mother, no ganja."
  —James Gandolfini as Tony Soprano in *The Sopranos*
- "Sex without love is a meaningless experience, but as far as meaningless experiences go, it's pretty damn good."
  —Woody Allen
- "The country runs better with a good-looking man in the White House. I mean, look what happened with Nixon. No one wanted to fuck him, so he fucked everyone."
  —Samantha in *Sex and the City*
- "Men cheat for the same reason that dogs lick their balls, because they can."
  —Samantha in *Sex and the City*
- "I've been around so long, I knew Doris Day before she was a virgin."
  —Groucho Marx
- "Fuck 'em if they can't take a joke."
  —Many people, including Michael N. Marcus

Marcus's Maxims
(Some are original. Some are borrowed.)

o   Don't put off 'til tomorrow, what you can put off 'til the day after tomorrow.
o   It's just as easy to fall in love with a rich person as with a poor person. In fact, it's easier.
o   If you are the top dog, don't treat people as if they are fire hydrants.
o   The early bird may get the worm, or a bullet.
o   Money can't buy happiness, but it makes misery much nicer.
o   Nothing is worth waiting for.
o   Never buy less than a pound of anything good.
o   Everybody lies. (Dr. Gregory House)
o   If you act like you belong, you *do* belong.
o   If you act like you have *have* authority. And most people would rather accept authority than challenge it. (The author's father)
o   The Internet never forgets.
o   Trust your mother but cut the cards. (Jean Shepherd)
o   Everything is debatable.
o   If you want your bullshit to be believed, add some cow.
o   When someone tells you about a problem, listen.
o   When someone does something good, compliment the person.
o   When someone makes a mistake, forgive and correct.
o   If you're in Connecticut or Florida and don't like the weather, wait five minutes.
o   If you want rain, wash your car, get your hair done or water your lawn.
o   No car looks better than a clean black car or a clean white car.
o   Nothing is harder to keep clean than a black car or a white car.
o   Cleanliness is next to impossible.
o   Clean mind, clean body, choose one.
o   It's always the wrong time for a vacation. So just go and enjoy.
o   Always know what you're doing and why you're doing it.
o   Focus!
o   Public opinion is overrated. If you don't care what others think of you, you can get a lot accomplished and have a lot of fun.
o   You were born with a unique package of talents and there are people and businesses that will pay for what you can do. Find them.
o   If it's not fun, either don't do it or make it fun.
o   Outside your home, always assume that someone is photographing or recording you—whether you're doing nothing, shoplifting, having sex or picking your nose.
o   Many things make a difference but very few things actually matter.
o   Sometimes good enough really is good enough, and if you strive for perfection, you'll never complete anything.
o   Always make sure your underwear and socks or stockings are clean and have no holes in them, so you won't be embarrassed if you are unexpectedly taken to a hospital.
o   Lost time can't be found.
o   Nothing lasts forever.
o   Write it down.

- The only way to win the game of life is to die while owing lots of money on insured debts.
- People who live in glass houses shouldn't.
- Garbage in, garbage out.
- A watched pot never boils.
- Buy low and sell high.
- Cave canem.
- Caveat emptor.
- In vino veritas.
- Carpe diem.
- Carpe punum. (the Fugs)
- Quidquid praecipies esto brevis.
- Aegroto dum anima est, spes est.
- Arcem ex cloacâ facĕre.
- Auctoritas non veritas facit legem.
- Audaces fortuna iuvat.
- Audi, vide, tace, si tu vis vivere.
- Cito maturum cito putridum.
- Illegitimi non carborundum.
- Faber est suae quisque fortunae.
- Semper in excretia sumus solim profundum variat.
- E pluribus unum.
- E pluribus ossefogva (*MAD* magazine)
- Nolita bis putare, bonus est.
- Life without clams is not much of a life.
- We don't get to keep our animals. We just get to borrow them. Make every moment as perfect as possible, and you will be repaid a thousand times over.
- If you fall into a sewage treatment tank, a cesspool or the space under an outhouse, yell "FIRE!" If you yell "SHIT," no one will try to rescue you.
- Don't shit where you eat. (Edward Cappiello)
- Loose lips sink ships. (U.S. War Advertising Council)
- Keep calm and carry on. (U.K.)
- If you think you are too small to make a difference, sleep with a mosquito. (Dalai Lama)
- When you're dissatisfied and want to go back to youth, think of Algebra. (Will Rogers)
- Don't eat the yellow snow. (Frank Zappa)
- Smile!

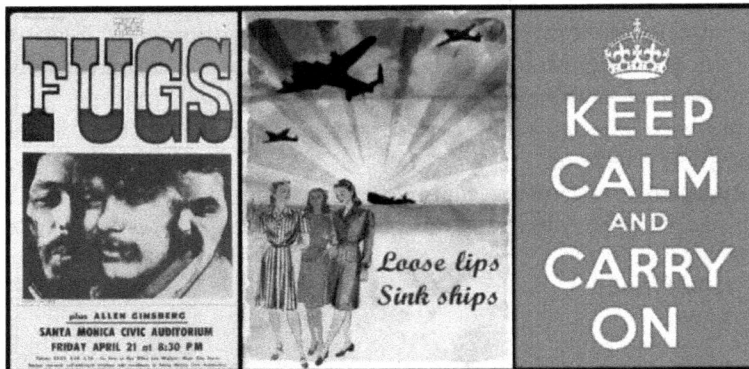

Dedications & Thanks

This book is dedicated to my parents Rita and Bud Marcus, my wife Marilyn, our dog Hunter, my siblings Meryl and Marshall, nieces, nephews, cousins, friends and classmates.

Special Thanks go to the following buddies, idols, allies and co-conspirators (approximately alphabetically, some I know online only, some I communicate with almost daily, others I've had no contact with in decades, some are deceased but fondly remembered, and some I'm just kidding about). If you're on the list, I'm glad I've known you. If you're not on the list, it's because if I included everyone, this list could fill the book):

Art Abrams, Ian Abugov, Karen Albert, Don Alderman, Charles Alpert, Gary Alpert, Jaymee Alpert, Mark Z. Alpert, Debbie Wasserman Alonso, Barbara Anderson, Ellen Angus, Len Aronow, Larry Arredondo, Andrea Avrutis, Michail Azarniyouch, Gary Babad, Joan Baez, David Barry, Joseph Beim, Jeff Berg, Jeffrey L. Bernstein, Porter Bibb, Andy Borowitz, Stephanie Brand, Corey Bandes, Desiree Bapple, Laurie Barnett, Cyn Bell-Moores, John Belushi, Judy Dimenstein Berger, Jeff Bezos, Jade Blackmore, Cheryl Lynn Blum, Jeff Blum, Marilynn S. Barry Boeker, Fred Bova, Adrienne Greenstone Brimlow-Lynch, Elliot Bronstein, Allison Cafarelli, Joseph Cafarelli, Robert Cafarelli, Shasta Cafarelli, Phyllis Caplow, Sue Chang, Vanessa Charette, Gary Cherpakov, John Coltrane, Seth Chodosh, Joe Civisca, Sheila Clark, Ed Cohen, Gary Cohen, Stu Cohen, Stephen Colbert, Judy Collins, Phil Collins, Joe Consiglio, Cathy Switkes Cooley, Eva Coombes, Philip Cutler, Deb Dahbour, Leonardo da Vinci, Miles Davis, Sheila Simon Derrwaldt, Michael Devaney-Salman, Chukwudi Dikko, Margo Portnoy Dinniman, Alan Disler, Howard Duchan, Marilyn Teitelbaum Dworkin, Deborah Edery, David Eisikovits, Gary Elkies, Donna Baxavanes Elkin, Gavi Elkind, Dave Evans, Carol Faber, Herb Feder, Judy Feinberg, Enzo Ferrari, Linda Fields, Bonnie Blumenthal Finkelstein, Cheryl Fleming, Earl Foote, Fred Forscher, Howard Fox, Ben Franklin, David Freedgood, Joel Friedland, Amy Friedman, Kinky Friedman, Annette Funicello, Felix KM Galanti, Joel Galvin, Dov Gabriel, Sherrie Galvin-Santiago, Bill Gates, Maggie Gel, Rosie Genao, Cindy Dorman Genis, Felix KM Galanti, Phyllis Gambino (but not mobster Joe Gambino or singer-rapper-comedian Childless Gambino), Yolanda Garfield, David (Tribble) Gerrold, Patricia M. Glazer, Ceil Gold, Fran Goldberg-Cohen, Judith N. Goldberg, Marty Goldberg, Stephanie Goldenhersh, Betty Fried Goldglantz, Ronnie Goodheart, Roxy Gordon, Lou Gottlieb, Myron Graff, Sarelle Green, Arthur Greenwald, Joyce Gurevich-Uvena, Stu Gurton, Adrienne Gusoff, Steve Hackmyer, Paul Hilcoff, Arlene Schwartz Hoffman, Ileine Hoffman, Lester Holt, Allan F. Hyatt, Perry Iles, Ken Irsay, Bette Isacoff, Richard Isacoff, Marty Jacobson, Larry R. Johnson, Marvin Kabakoff, Michelle Kabat, Nic Kabat, Donna Kanter, Howard Kaplan, Jonathan Kaplan, Jeffrey Karp, David Katz, Jo Yona Kelvin, Jack Kennedy, Jennifer Kern-Kaminsky, Laura Kessler, Danny Kischel, Mary Kissane, Brian Kittrell, Eric Knieling, Mark Knopfler, Gary Knowles, Vaughn Knowles, Hillary Anne Kotler, Jerome Kowalski, Harry Krause, Marty Kravitt, Howard Krosnick, Julie-Bob LaCroix, Donald Langella, Rich Lawther, Jim Lemkin, Lawrence S. Lerner, Jennifer Blum Lerner, Stewart Levine, Charlotte Libov, Abe Lincoln, Linda Howard (Hi, Howie!) Lippman, Meat Loaf, Jim Luscher, Marc Lyman, Rachel Maddow, Mike Markowitz, Jerry Marder, David B. Margolis, Dick Margulis, Michael Marmitt, Alexa Marott, Fred Marotti, Richard Martel, Howie Mayo, Debrosha McCants, Alan Melnick, Harry Mena, Karen Mender, Symie Greene Menitove, Miriam Metzinger, Joanne Milazzo, Ed Modell, Dawn Cafarelli Montemarano, Diana F. Moore, Jeff Mossman Moss, Debbie Florek Muller, Bertha Myers-Ashe, Jerry Newman, Harry Newton, Leonard Nimoy, Annette Obrasky, Joann Omisore, Harriet Otis, Roger C. Parker, Marian Paroo, Barbara Blitfield Pech, Joan Spencer Petrillo, Gerri Plante, Harry Platcow, Janice Simpson Podsada, Brad Pomerance, Mindy Portnoy (no complaint), David Presley (but not Elvis), Billy Priestly, Steven Radin, Gilda Radner, Gary Lee Radzin, Betsy Gimbel Ratner, Edith Rawls, Linda Giorgilli Rice, Nitai Riegler, Dawn Marie Rizzi, Jason Roberts, Ralph Romaniello, Renee Romaniello, Mick Rooney, Lynn Rosen-Noffsinger, Jack Rosenberg, Irina Rosewater, Deborah Zee Rubin, Jane Israelson Rubin, Emma Ruff, Jean Marie Rusin, Joshua Salkind, Bryan Salz, Jacky Sambolin, Mark Schecter, Thomas Schechter, Janice Sedaka (but not Neil), Jessica Botia Shea, Frannie Sheridan, Mike Shiner, Deborah Slutsky Samuels, Marilyn G. Scarl, Arline Greenblatt Scheinzeit, Pinky Schmeckelstein, Glenn Selwitz, Howie Shrobe, Anita Liberman Silver, Judy Dziamalek Smith, Joel Solkoff, Steve Sosensky, Deborah L. Sparks, Jan Spector, Mike Spindell, Mark Spires, Lenore Stelzer, Artie Stepanian, Slade Stephenson, Barry Tenin, Pat Mennone Trenchard, Laura Truxall, Charlie Liebman Turfboer, David Turok, Jennifer Uzzo-Bellantese, Amy Sennesh Vastola, Michael Wagner, Gil Wald, Evelyn C. Walsh, Debbie Weinberg, Donna Lyn Gerl Whitlock, Harry Whitney, Daniel Whitten, Dan Wiener, Rod Williams, Corey A. Wolf, Daniel Wolf, Volodymyr Zelenskyy, Ernie Zelinski, Louise Zingeser, Diane Ziomek, Zorro, Mark Zuckerberg, Janet Zweiback.

Special Thanks go to the girls and women I liked, loved and lusted for—but did not marry (in approximate chronological order, starting in first grade): Susan B., Phyllis C., Annette F., Alana F., Donna C., Albie L., Lynne M., Janice W., Stephanie B., Debbie L., Rosemary G., Vicky E., Nancy H., Nancy K., Forgot-Her-Name, Virginia ?, Sofia V.

Special Thanks go to my aunt, **Fanchon Kessner**. She's my mother's sister, the source of my first sexual urges, and was a big help in providing some history of the maternal side of my family.

Special Thanks go to my cousin, **Jill Marcus Lawther**. Jill is the daughter of my father's brother Arnie and helped fill in some gaps in the history of the paternal side of my family.

Special Thanks go to legal aid attorney **Toni Esposito**. She solved a BIG problem—for free!

You all helped me become what I am (whatever that is). If I left anyone out, including girlfriends whose names I've forgotten, maybe I'll include you in a revised edition. If you're not on the list, I apologize for my imperfect memory and limited space.

And Special Thanks go to the developers of **Microsoft Word** software, which I've used to write and design this book and many other books. "MSW" helps me identify and correct countless errors. Sometimes the amazing software *causes* errors. I fix them. That seems fair.

And Big Thanks to **Wikipedia** for providing valuable information and insights.

And Super Thanks to the doctors, nurses, chefs, food sellers, therapists, firefighters, ambulance drivers, hospitals, pharmacists and drug developers who kept me alive much longer than I expected.

And last, but not least, Big Thanks to the few superb teachers and professors who stimulated, inspired, directed, educated, befriended, enlightened and tolerated me.

If I told you the secret of life, it would no longer be the secret of life.

The older we get, the more 'ologists we have.

Laughter is the best medicine.

Whatever you do, do well.

Live long and prosper.

What, me worry?

Que será, será.

Michael's Literary Gods

I thank them for entertainment, stimulation and setting very high standards for me to aspire to.

Dave Barry is a Pulitzer Prize-winning humor columnist and author, and the funniest writer I know of. Dave is so funny that I had to stop reading his column because I got so jealous. No one packs more laughs into a paragraph than Dave does. He used a picture of my late dog, Hunter J. Marcus, in one of his books. It's called *Dave Barry's Money Secrets*. Here's his money secret: Dave didn't pay me any money for the picture, but I did get a free book. I'll let Dave read my books for free, too.

Jean Shepherd (1921-1999) was a radio and TV raconteur, and he probably ties with Mark Twain for storytelling ability. Shep's books include *In God We Trust—All Others Pay Cash*, *Wanda Hickey's Night of Golden Memories* and *A Fistful of Fig Newtons*. Twain was a great writer, but Shep was much funnier.

Jack Douglas (1908-1989) was an Emmy-winning comedy writer for *The Jack Paar Show*, *The George Gobel Show*, *Laugh-In* and other programs. I remember him most for his book titles, including *My Brother was an Only Child*, *Shut Up and Eat Your Snowshoes*, and *Never Trust a Naked Bus Driver*.

Michael Solomon and David Hirshey edited and provided witty headlines for *Esquire* magazine's annual Dubious Achievement Awards in the 1990s. Why is this man laughing?

Don Martin (1931-2000) was an extraordinary cartoonist, best known for his work in *MAD* magazine. Don created such notable characters as **Fester Bestertester** and **Freenbean Fonebone**, and *printed* sound effects like "FAGROON klubble klubble." Don's books are available at Amazon.

"Uncle" Tom McCahill (1907-1975) was an automotive journalist who wrote for *Mechanix Illustrated* magazine in the 1950s and 60s. He rated car trunks by the number of dogs they could hold and described the ride of a 1957 Pontiac as "smooth as a prom queen's thighs." Tom was a Yale graduate and knew classic literature as well as cars. When a reader asked how to pronounce "Porsche," Tom answered, "Portia." Some of us understood. Another reader asked, "How much is the parts cost and how much do the car?" Tom answered, "Sure."

Tom Lehrer claims he "went from adolescence to senility, trying to bypass maturity." Tom graduated from Harvard, Magna Cum Laude at age-18 and made Phi Beta Kappa. He taught at MIT, Harvard, Wellesley and the University of California; but is best known for hilarious songwriting, much of it political satire in the 1950s and 60s. His musical career was powerful but brief. He said he performed a mere 109 shows and wrote only 37 songs over 20 years. Britain's Princess Margaret was a fan and so am I. I can still sing Tom Lehrer lyrics I first heard in seventh grade.

Matt Groening created *The Simpsons* and *Life in Hell*. *The Simpsons* has been the longest-running comedy show in American television history. Because it's a cartoon, some people make the mistake of assuming it's for kids. It's not, but kids love it.

Jay Ward created *Rocky & Bullwinkle*, *Dudley Do-Right*, *Peabody and Sherman* and *Crusader Rabbit*. The Rocky show was filled with literary allusions and magnificent puns (or horrible puns, depending on your outlook on such things). Unless you're an old fart who watched TV in the 1950s and know that **Durward Kirby** was the sidekick on *The Garry Moore Show*, you would not appreciate the pun in "Kerwood Derby." It was a hat that increased the intelligence of its wearer.

Bob Dylan is a new addition to my list, and the addition is overdue. His messages and lyrics are unmatched, and he is well-worthy of his Nobel, Pulitzer and countless other awards and honors. In case you missed it, there's a page about him earlier in this book, and some of his lyrics are up ahead.

Preface

The word above is pronounced <u>preff</u>-iss, not <u>pree</u>-face.

This is my 42nd book. I hope it's not my last book, but maybe it's my best book. I've enjoyed writing and reading it—and I am hard to please.

It's a BIG book, much bigger than I planned it to be.

After nearly eight decades spent observing, analyzing and evaluating human and animal behavior, I have *a lot* to say. I have *wide* interests. I've learned a lot and I remember a lot (but not everything).

Like life itself, I can be both serious and humorous.

Much of the book is very personal. I talk about me—but I also talk *to* my readers.

Since you are reading this, I assume you were not discouraged by the book's length. I hope you'll find my words interesting, useful and entertaining. If you do, please tell others. Thanks very much.

Michael
Hamden CT, 2024

Introduction

I was born on April 15th, 1946. I am a **proud member of the *first cohort* of the Baby Boom** (along with Dolly Parton, Donny Trump, Billy Clinton, Georgie Bush, Stevie Spielberg, Patty Duke, Timmy Dalton, Jimmy Buffet, Gianni Versace, Candy Bergen, Davy Lynch, Dicky Wolf, Johnny Crawford, Peggy Lipton, Denny Kucinich, Hayley Mills, Reggie Jackson, Cher, Tommy Lee Jones, Danny Glover, Freddie Mercury, Barry Gibb, Keithy Moon, Eddie O'Neill, Cheechy Marin, Linda Ronstadt, Pat Sajak, Diane von Fürstenberg, André the Giant, Liza Minnelli and Sly Stallone).

I always thought there was *something special* about this cohort. Most of my contemporaries in school were very bright kids. Someone suggested that we benefited from *powerful sperm* stored up by our future fathers during World War II, which fertilized our mothers' eggs when the men came home from war.

"Renaissance man" **Leonardo da Vinci** has always been an inspiration to me. Although I lack his talents, I share his abundant interests. Someone said that the 21st century is too complex for anyone to now be a renaissance man—but I try.

When I was a young teenager, I felt *invincible*. I thought I could live FOREVER, or at least to a "hundert und zwanzig" (to 120, from a Jewish blessing for long life). Later, I thought I'd take my "dirt nap" before my 60th birthday. I assumed I would be killed by an overdose of brownies or by someone I pissed off.

Now, at age-78 (in 2024), I know that I won't last forever. I had two lens replacements a few years ago, and other body parts don't work as well (or as frequently) as they once did. I briefly contemplated cosmetic surgery for my wrinkled old-man's neck, and I watch TV commercials for items that I previously ignored. I pee a lot.

As a teenager, I was *focused forward*. I anticipated getting a driver's license, getting laid, going to college, voting, drinking legally, making money, seeing a new century, seeing the world, and maybe even seeing other worlds.

At 78 there's not that much to look forward to. I already collect Social Security, I'm retired, and I've downsized from a huge house to a right-sized apartment. Unless politicians mess it up, Medicare should keep paying for a big chunk of my growing medical bills.

I like to travel, but I walk with a walker—so there's little in my likely itinerary. I've had a fascination with Morocco since I watched *Captain Gallant of the Foreign Legion* TV show. I've been to Canada, Mexico and England; but I want to see Spain, Italy, Greece, France, Israel, Egypt, India, China, Japan, Austria, Antarctica, Chile, Brazil, Alaska, Hawaii, Mexico and South Africa. I'd like to go back to Medicine Bow National Forest in Wyoming to take a picture I missed in 1961. Our station wagon was overheating, and my father said we had to quickly drive to a lower altitude.

I have no children or grandchildren to see graduating or marrying. My four-legged son, golden retriever Hunter J. Marcus, died seven years ago at the age of 16.

I probably won't go back to school. There are no foods I haven't tasted yet that I want to taste. 3-D TV didn't impress me, and it flopped. But I did pay over $1,000 for my first Blu-ray video player, and it was worth it! I'll probably never own a Ferrari or go sky diving, bungee jumping or water skiing. I've done enough snow skiing, and even went SCUBA diving under the ice, twice. I have been married to a wonderful woman for a long time.

So... it seems like the next big event after my 65th birthday will be my *death*.

Based on an online calculator, I'll die when I'm 88. My father died in 2009, at 87. Supposedly we should live five years longer than our same-gender parent, which should give me 92 years.

Expecting to last beyond 90 seems a bit piggish, so I once said I'd settle for 89 years and die in 2035. Back in 2010 I started a blog called "My final quarter-century above ground." The "quarter-century" seems overly optimistic now.

Every day I read about people dying who are younger than me. I've somehow outlived two younger, apparently healthier, cousins.

About 45 years ago I met a guy whom I thought was a few years older than I was. Later I found out that I'm 3-1/2 years *older than he is*. That means I was older than him 45 years ago.

Lately I've realized that lots of people I thought were older than me are really *younger* than me. Cops, teachers, politicians, rabbis and priests used to be older than me. Now they usually are not.

As time passes, there are fewer and fewer people older than me.

However, as I grow older, I still refuse to grow "up."

Like **Tom Lehrer**, I plan to pass from adolescence to senility without passing through maturity.

Like **Peter Pan** I don't want to wear a tie.

Years ago, when our ancestors were gored to death by saber-toothed tigers or toasted and eaten by fire-breathing monsters before they reached their 21st birthdays, there was little chance of developing our 21st-century maladies. Now we have much more time to develop maladies and malfunctions, and there are many more ways to get killed. Cavemen had no nukes nor assault rifles.

I've heard of many people dying of "natural causes" at around age-75. And, of course, there are plane crashes, car crashes, tsunamis, pollution, food poisoning, terrorists and murderers.

In reality, unless we plan on suicide, none of us know how much time we have left.

I don't expect to be reincarnated (but if I could, I'd like to be my dog).

I used to say that middle-age lasts until they shovel dirt onto you. I can still say that, but with a bit less conviction. I do everything with a bit less conviction. Especially climbing stairs.

Nine years ago, I went to a doc with an office sign that said, "geriatric and adult care." I asked the receptionist how old one must be to be considered geriatric. She said 40. Ouch.

I don't always "feel old." Maybe that's because lots of my body parts have no feelings at all.

I certainly don't "think old." I have a 14-year-old brain imprisoned in a 78-year-old body. Every so often, I'll play *Honky Tonk Women* and *Gimme Shelter* by the **Stones**, turn the volume up to infinity, dim the lights, and BOOGIE like a teenager.

Maturity is overrated, and if I have not yet achieved it, I probably never will. My next stage of emotional development will likely be bewilderment.

A family physician and friend told me that "medical science can keep a body functioning long after the mind stops, but what's the point?" There is *no point*, except as a source for organ harvesting.

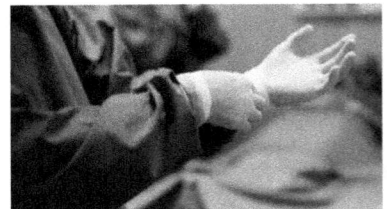

Within the past few years, I've been hospitalized and in rehab more times than I can remember. I've been diagnosed with a long list of malfunctions, but medicine and my growing list of 'ologists keep me going.

I cut back on pizza consumption to twice a month, and ice cream to once a week. I actually read food labels to minimize sodium.

I can spell the word "exercise," even if I don't engage in it; but typing is tough because I often tap the wrong keys and forget and substitute words. A while ago I wanted to type "Wendy's" but typed "Wednesday." Have I lost it? When did I lose it? Where did it go? What is *it*, anyway.

I recently drove to **Firestone** to get new brakes. The better brakes have a lifetime warranty. How long is that?

I still enjoy life and will still do almost anything for a joke. I have no idea how much time I have left. I've started to dispose of my collections and acquire less.

I tasted my first cup of coffee on my 70th birthday. I will probably never go to bed with a prostitute, smoke another joint, nor give a bronski to Sofia Vergara. Maybe it's best to not empty my bucket list just yet. It gives me something to look forward to, just in case I get a second chance.

I got good marks in English in high school. I majored in journalism in college. I've been an advertising copywriter and a magazine editor, and have written more articles, blog posts, Facebook posts, website pages and Tweets than I can count. I've also written dozens of books and have edited books for others. I have not won a Nobel Prize nor a Pulitzer, but I know how to write, and I usually do it pretty well.

I think I can write about almost anything and have not suffered from the dreaded "writer's block" since the early 1970s. On the contrary, although I was a shy teenager and young adult, now I sometimes write and say *too much*. Blame my loquacious father.

On TV's *The Honeymooners*, **Ralph Kramden** told his loquacious mother-in-law: "You are a blabbermouth, a blabbermouth, out, out, out!" A shrink once told me that my mouth was "out of control." A hate-filled woman on *Facebook* said I am a bore and should "STFU."

I'll STFU when I'm dead.
Until then, I'll talk and I'll type.

The wife and I were sitting at the breakfast table one Sunday morning. I said to her, "When I die, I want you to immediately sell all of my stuff."

"Now why would you want me to do that?" she asked.

"I figure that you would eventually remarry, and I don't want some asshole using my stuff."

She looked at me and said, "What makes you think I'd marry another asshole?"

[Thanks to **Harry Newton**, who published my second book.]

Chapter 1
Remembering

The advantages of being old, or older

I noticed something interesting in photos of writers' groups in California and England. I noticed the same thing in a meeting of writers I attended here in Connecticut. There were *no young people.* The age range seemed to be from about 40 to 85. I don't know why this is so. Are the kids' literary output limited to Tweeting and texting? Are they incapable of writing 30,000 words or more?

Despite deficiencies in appendages and sensory organs, we old farts have definite advantages over the young 'uns. We may not remember where we put the car keys or what we ate for breakfast, but we have *long-term* memory and we have PERSPECTIVE. We can look back, remember, analyze and compare. We remember things that kids have merely read about or heard about. And, because we remember when things like cellphones did not exist, we can APPRECIATE—and MARVEL at—things that younger people take for granted.

After walking around the planet for four to six decades, we've seen, heard, smelled, tasted and done a lot.

Today, a burger at Mickey Dee's can cost seven bucks. I remember the commercial that chanted "Forty-five cents for a three-course meal? Sounds to me like that's a steal." (A burger, fries and a shake cost 15 cents each.)   [Photo by Michael Kempf]

o   I remember when one-gig hard drives and plain-paper fax machines finally became available for less than $1,000.

o   I remember when, finally, more than 50% of Americans were opposed to the war in Viet Nam, and when LBJ decided not to run for re-election.

o   I remember when Ronald Reagan co-starred in *Bedtime for Bonzo*—with a chimp.)

o   I remember when most kids had married parents, and few mothers worked.

o   I remember when men were not nurses and did not teach at elementary schools.

o   I remember being shocked when politicians and priests were involved in sex scandals.

o   I remember seeing two movies, seven cartoons and a newsreel for 25 cents.

o   I remember cars that rusted and overheated and had wind-up windows and no AC.

o   I remember when it was unusual to see an imported car in the USA. Or Ikea or Aldi.

o   I remember people crippled from polio.

o   I remember presidential candidates selected at conventions, not in primaries.

o   I remember penny candy that actually cost a penny.

o   I remember when pregnant girls left high school.

o   I remember typewriters and correction fluid.

o   I remember when people were shocked by *Playboy* magazine.

o   I remember newspapers that did not print color pictures.

o   I remember having to choose from three TV channels.

o   I remember a TV that could select channel-one.

o   I remember measles and mumps.

- I remember the discoveries of sushi, burritos, quiche and fondue.
- I remember when most women used hair spray, and only strippers wore thongs.
- I remember when it was weird for a woman to run for political office.
- I remember door-to-door salesmen, and notebooks that were not computers.
- I remember shotgun weddings, people going to Europe for abortions and sex-change surgery, and to Nevada for divorces.
- I remember an early demo of stereophonic sound. We needed a radio a few feet from the TV. The TV played the left-channel audio, and the radio played the right.
- I remember when headsets were for pilots and telephone operators.
- I remember when people rented telephones and answering machines.
- I remember when answering machines were actually machines.
- I remember Pennsylvania Station, Bethlehem Steel and phone numbers with letters.
- I remember when a doctor made home visits for five bucks, drove a $5,000 Cadillac and lived in a $25,000 house.
- I remember paying a nickel for a ride on the Staten Island Ferry and for a bag of chips.
- I remember life before Amazon, email, websites, Starbucks, Keurigs, plastic shopping bags, *Star Trek* and *Star Wars*, bungee cords, The Pill, cordless phones, cellphones, reality TV, color TV, recycling bins, ZIP Codes, word processing, sports bras, $200 sneakers, unisex salons, apps, Silly Putty, The Czech Republic, Trumps, Palins, Kardashians, Lohans, Kims, networking, self-realization, permanent press, videos, value propositions, airplane hijacking, Lojack, GPS, VCR, DVR, LSD, HIV, ATMs, PDFs, FAQs, sex surrogates, texting, sexting, Nigerian scams, men going to weddings with neckties, and cars without seatbelts.
- I remember when *Howdy Doody* was "live." (I was on the show twice!)
- I remember soda vending machines that squirted liquid into paper cups.
- I remember paying for long-distance calls and keeping them short.
- I remember TV antennas (not dishes) on the roof.
- I remember when it was weird to buy water.
- I remember when an expensive college cost $3,000 per year.
- I remember when 1950s music was not "oldies."
- I remember when the USA had 180 million people and 48 states.
- I remember TV commercials for "your DeSoto-Plymouth dealer."
- I remember co-features.
- I remember mink stoles.
- I remember *Tom Corbett, Space Cadet*.
- I remember when Johnny Carson replaced Steve Allen on the *Tonight Show*.
- I remember people being concerned about 1984 and Y2K.
- I remember when it was unusual for women to wear pants to work.
- I remember pizza selling for 25 cents a slice.
- I remember when Dick Clark was young.
- I remember *Kukla, Fran and Ollie*.
- I remember 10-cent coffee. Maybe even 15-cent, although I never drank it.
- I remember when "gay" merely meant "happy."
- I remember preparing for World War Three. "Duck and Cover!"
- When our family drove cross-country in 1959, gas cost less than 25 cents per gallon.
- I remember when TVs had knobs and no remote controls.
- I remember when color TV was exciting.
- I remember having a $1,000 VCR with a wired remote control.
- I remember wristwatches with tiny LED displays.
- I remember mailing letters.

- I remember when there were just three Radio Shack stores, and when there were thousands, and no Best Buys or Circuit Cities.
- I remember when most men didn't wear necklaces and most women didn't have tattoos, or piercings other than in their ears.
- I remember tube testers at Radio Shack, being able to select either mono or stereo LPs, when mobile phones cost $3,000, and when going online could cost $20 per HOUR.
- I remember when color TVs, touch-tone phones and microwave ovens were luxury items.
- I remember open-reel tape, 78s, 45s, 33s, 4-track, 8-track, cassettes, Elcassettes, videodiscs, quadraphonic sound, and record players in cars.
- I remember cars with just three-speed transmissions. (The first Corvette had just two!)
- I remember calling relatives to let them know we arrived safely—after a 50-mile drive.
- I remember when there was no President's Day, but there was a Decoration Day.
- I remember when it was unusual to see nude bodies, or hear dirty words in movies, on TV or radio.
- I remember when tacos were exotic, and pizza was not available with eggplant.
- I remember when a science magazine said that it would never be possible to produce a color video camera that could be sold for less than $25,000.
- I remember predictions of helicopters in every driveway, flat-screen color TVs, pocket-size phones and the end of war and disease.
- I remember when cigarettes cost 27 cents per pack, had no cancer warnings, and were advertised on TV. "More doctors smoke Camels than any other brand."
- I remember when magazines cost a quarter, paperback books cost 35 cents, computers cost millions, and homes had one phone and one TV.
- I remember when milk and eggs were delivered to homes, mommy was home to cook lunch for the kids, and freezers had to be defrosted.
- I remember hearing about nickel lunches, but I remember drinking nickel Cokes.
- I remember when schools, public lavatories and water fountains got integrated.
- I remember when we couldn't buy liquor with credit cards, or many things on Sunday.
- I remember when there was a Disneyland but no Disney World.
- I (sadly) remember life without Ti-Vo, Alexa, and satellite radio.
- I remember when turbocharging was exotic.
- I remember paying to have new cars rustproofed by Ziebart.
- I remember when pocket calculators were exotic and expensive.
- I remember when people stayed home to watch TV.
- I remember when football games could end in a tied score.
- I remember when kids walked to school, and it was up-hill in both directions.
- I remember when KFC was called Kentucky Fried Chicken.
- I remember when females were not supposed to like sex.
- I remember when my computer screens and printers were monochrome.
- I remember when most cameras used film.
- I remember floppy discs, and laser discs.
- I remember changing spark plugs.
- I remember buying snow tires, even studded snow tires.
- I remember when radar detectors were illegal in some states.
- I remember when you had to get phone service from the phone company.
- I remember when nobody used lasers at home.
- I remember when most pens and batteries leaked.
- I remember the appearance of the Magic Marker.
- I remember when "Protestants" became "Christians."
- I remember the iron curtain and iron lungs.
- I remember fallout shelters.

- I remember when Ivy League schools had quotas for Jews, and fancy hotels did not allow Jews or dogs to stay in them. I remember when few Jewish people bought German cars and when few WW2 vets bought Japanese cars.
- I remember Montgomery-Ward, Gimbel's, Caldor, Bamberger's, Korvette's, Newmark & Lewis, Bradlee's, Crazy Eddie, The Wiz, Modell's, Sam Goody, Tower Records, Two Guys, Bombay Co., Service Merchandise, Woolworth's, Grant's, FINAST, Food Fair, Pathmark, Waldbaum's, Robert Hall, Thom McAn, Toys R Us, CompUSA, 47th Street Photo, Tweeter, Tech Hi-fi, Audio Exchange, Lafayette Radio, Spiratone, Sharper Image, J & R, Channel Home Centers, Blockbuster Video, Incredible Universe and Computer City.
- I remember when cable TV was unusual. So were shopping malls. And wearing jeans and sneakers to school.
- I remember when Howard Johnson's restaurants were ubiquitous, sold 28 ice cream flavors, and McDonald's signs bragged: "Over One Million Sold."
- I remember stores that let people charge without using charge cards, and when Macy's started accepting American Express.
- I remember the switch from steel to aluminum SCUBA tanks, from dual-hose to single-hose regulators, and from ski boots with laces to ski boots with clips.
- I remember back in the 1950s when banks paid less than three percent on savings. Hmm. Now two is considered high.
- I remember hearing about the Great Depression and that it could never happen again.
- I remember when there was no East Timor or South Sudan, but there were both West Germany and East Germany.
- I remember Triumphs, MGs, Simcas, Trabants, Plymouths, DeSotos and Ramblers.
- I remember bench seats in the fronts of cars and "three on the tree."
- I remember when bright lights were controlled by buttons on the floors of cars.
- I remember when the station wagon was the standard suburban motor vehicle and Jeeps were for soldiers and farmers

- I remember when Negroes became Blacks and then Afro-Americans.
- I remember when Black people started using the N-word.
- I remember when it was unusual to see Black people in commercials.
- I remember when Mormons were considered weird.
- I remember when it was shocking for a Catholic to be president.
- I remember Americans going to Cuba for vacation—but not to China.
- I remember my Diners' Club card and receiving telegrams.
- I remember when McDonald's began selling breakfast, and bagels.
- I remember when banks closed at 3 PM and on weekends.
- I remember when mail-order items were ordered and delivered by mail.
- I remember when people without legs did not compete in sports.
- I remember when Saturn was not a car, but Mercury was. Now Saturn's not a car, again.
- I remember when Pluto was a planet and a cartoon dog.
- I remember when "under God" was added to the *Pledge of Allegiance*.
- I remember the USSR and the "Cold War."
- I remember when Alaska and Hawaii were not states.
- I remember when Alexa was a woman's name, not a smart speaker.
- I remember ancient advertising jingles and slogans. "You'll wonder where the yellow went..."

One big disadvantage of all this perspective and memory is that that no young person wants to hear it.

Chapter 2
Why do I remember what I remember?

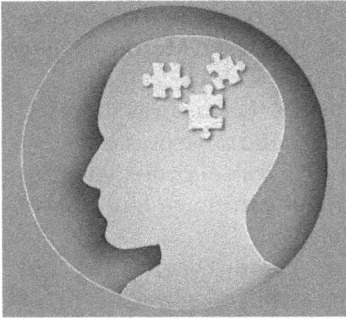

Like many people of my age, my long-term memory is often better than my awareness of recent events. As this book demonstrates, I remember a lot of my ancient history—but I sometime forget the name of someone I met a week ago or where my keys are.

My strongest memories are probably song lyrics and things I memorized for school, work and fun. Sadly, much of my brain's memory space is filled with *absolutely useless* information. It's too bad that we human beings can't selectively delete old memories to make room for new ones, as with computer files.

oI still remember the multiplication tables, laboriously learned in third grade. I know that nine times six equals fifty-four. But I could use a computer, a calculator or a phone like today's kids.

- I remember the phone number for **Susan**, a girl I had a crush on from first grade through sixth—but never had the guts to call.
- I know that the abbreviation for sodium chloride (common salt) is NaCl—but so what?
- I know most of the American state capitals—but so what?
- I can easily recite the "rainbow" colors: red, orange, green, blue, indigo, violet—but so what?
- I remember "CK722" and "2N107"—the part numbers of transistors I built things with when I was a young teenager. Does anyone care?
- I remember the **Fram** oil filter part number (PH7) for my 1974 FIAT. Does anyone care?
- I can recite at least part of the Prelude to *Evangeline*, an epic poem by **Henry Wadsworth Longfellow**, published in 1847 CE, which I studied in junior high school. **"This is the forest primeval. The murmuring pines and the hemlocks, Bearded with moss, and in garments green, indistinct in the twilight, Stand like Druids of eld, with voices sad and prophetic, Stand like harpers hoar, with beards that rest on their bosoms."** Of course, the horny young boys in my class were excited by "hoar" and "bosoms"—which probably enhanced the learning.
- I still remember the plant and animal "phyla" from biology class in seventh or eighth grade. I devised terrific mnemonic devices to help me remember the flora and fauna. For the plants, I used "Too Bad Poor Schmuck," which reminded me of **"Thalophyte, Briophyte, Pteridophyte, Spermadophyte."** For the animal phyla, my gimmick was "Pea Picker, Cotton Picker, No Room Any More At My Exclusive Athletic Club." That let me ace my bio exams by listing **"Protozoa, Porifera, Coelenterata, Platyhelminthes, Nematoda, Rotaliida, Annelida, Mollusca, Arthropada, Micrognathozoa, Echinodermata, Arthropoda, Chordata."** I hope you're impressed. (There are now more on the list.)

I've discovered and devised other excellent memory aids over the years. For example:

- I could easily recite telephone wire colors (white, red, black, yellow, violet) by remembering "**W**omen **R**eally **B**elieve **Y**ou're (a) **V**irgin."
- The maritime terms for a vessel's left and right sides are "port" and "starboard." "Left" and "port" both have four letters. "Starboard contains an "**R**" like "**r**ight."
- For plumbing: "righty tighty, lefty loosey."
- The first 12 places for Pi are 3.141592653859. It rhymes.
- "Desert" has one "**S**." Dessert has two. The "ess" in "de<u>ss</u>ert" is part of the German word "<u>ess</u>en," meaning "eat."
- I still need to devise a device to spell "pickel" properly. It's "<u>pickle</u>." But "<u>nickel</u>" is correct. Why?
- I sometimes confuse "hyper" and "hypo." (I have orthostatic **hypo**tension, but used to be **hyper**sensitive to bright light.) "Hyp**O**" has the letter "**O**"—like "l**O**w."
- I need a gimmick to help me decide between "weird" and "wierd."

I was employed as a shoe salesman while in high school and college and I still remember some stock numbers from eons ago. Number 3660 was a white buck from **Stride Rite**. Number 3778 was a scotch-grain from **Gerberich-Payne**. Big deal?

I was never a sports fan, and my knowledge of players was minimal. My brother **Marshall** often used my lapse to beat me when we played *Trivial Pursuit*. I generally answered "**Joe Namath**" or "**Mickey Mantle**" even if the question was about boxing or hockey. One time the correct answer really was Joe Namath—and I won!

Mon Dieu, je peux compter en français.

While watching the opening ceremony of the 2024 Paris Olympics, I realized that I could count to ten in French: *un deux trois quatre cinq six sept huit neuf dix.*

I never studied French in school, so I assume that my polyglot papa taught me to count in French when I was *un petit enfant*. The foreign numerical sequence still occupies a chunk of my brain many years later.

I can also count in German, Hebrew, Spanish, English and *Igpay Atinlay*! But not Chinese, Japanese, Arabic or Russian.

None of this is important or useful, but it's amusing. Like my father, I've always been a language fan, and I know bits of many languages.

I still remember *lots* of Latin vocabulary from high school, but I can't count in Latin. I don't know if I ever could. Latin is both important and useful, and I wish it was still a mandatory subject in America.

Eiffel Tower photo from *Newsweek*. Merci!]

Chapter 3
Peering ahead

Another one gone, and fewer left

Holy shit!

I just looked at my appointment book.

It's late-Sepember in 2024. There's less sunlight each day. Winter is coming.

This year has been a blur.

I can remember assorted minutes and hours, maybe even half-days. But not weeks or months.

Where did July go? And August? Where did my life go?

This will be my approximate 60th summer of unfulfilled fantasy.

I'll need a second life to check off the remaining items in my to-do-list. I'd really like to visit some countries and cities.

Damn.

Kids look forward to birthdays because age implies freedom, status and empowerment. Later on, it just means one less year left.

My tank of life is emptying

I had my 78th birthday on 4/15/24. I hope to have another birthday in 2025. It's not a "milestone" birthday to be marked by celebration, it's just one of many innocuous numbers that mark a decrease in the years I have left until what's left of me gets put away to rot.

When we are young, we are excited, maybe even proud of reaching ages 5, 10, 13, 16, 18, 21, 25, 35—because each of those numbers indicates added privileges and authority.

Later on, 65 means money from Social Security and Medicare, and senior discounts at unexciting restaurants.

After 65, each new number means that there is less left in the tank of life. Time is speeding up as it passes by. Sometimes years feel like they have only about five or six months in them.

My predicted death year of 2035 is approaching quickly. It's a mere 11 years away, now. But there are many unforeseen horrors that could move my exit date closer. I'm taking things off my bucket list as I realize they are unattainable fantasies. I am buying less and giving way more.

I watched both of my parents—both previously super-smart and vigorous—fade away to become barely animated collections of atoms.

Damn. Shit. Hell. Fooey. I'm not depressed. I'm just pissed off.

Is living long really better than dying young?

If you know me online or in the real world, you may know that I enjoy pointing out the imperfections of others. However, I am not reluctant to point out my own shortcomings—especially if they are funny.

I now present some of my most memorable mental malfunctions:

o I sometimes stand in front of my residential door and press a button on my electronic car key and get pissed off because the door doesn't open. I hope this is not an indicator of an imminent end-of-life downward spiral. How many brain farts (senior moments) do I need to have in one week before I officially have Alzheimer's?

o I once went to a Halloween party—a week early.

o A few years ago, I had an appointment to see my nephrologist (kidney doc) but instead I drove to my neurologist (brain doc). Another time, I was supposed to see my neurologist, but went to my urologist (dick doc). That makes sense because, allegedly, men think with their penises.

o I went to a gas station. Instead of paying at the pump I paid inside because I also wanted a drink. I paid $25 for fuel at pump #3. I got my drink and went out to pump the gas. No gas came out. I looked around and discovered that I was at pump #4. Someone more observant than I was, got $25 of *my* gas at pump #3 and drove away without even thanking me. A mind is a terrible thing to lose. So is gasoline.

o One morning my wife, the lovely Marilyn, asked me to carry some laundry upstairs. I was wearing a pair of stupid sweatpants made *without pockets*, and I stuck a cordless phone into the waistband. When I got upstairs, I felt the phone slip downward and I thought I heard it hit the floor. I put the laundry away and then went to the spot where I thought I heard the phone hit the floor, but it wasn't there. I checked the room where I put the laundry. It wasn't there, either. We then looked all over but could not find it. I then tried the obvious trick. I called the cordless from another phone. It rang. No matter what room Marilyn and I searched, the phone sounded close—but we never, ever saw it. We looked high and low, cleared away some crap, checked wastebaskets and moved furniture. We checked to make sure the dog had not grabbed it. Nothing. Marilyn then offered a bit of brilliance that solved the mystery. She said the ringing sound seemed to be *following us around*. I looked down and noticed a lump in my sweatpants above my right ankle. The phone had slipped out of the waistband and down my leg, but the elastic cuff prevented it from falling on the floor. The phone was still *in my pants*! The ringing did indeed follow me around!

o I recently got into my car, sat in the driver's seat, and reached around to grab the seatbelt on the left side. I couldn't find it. I even opened the door, figuring that the extra space would make it easier to grab the belt But, no. It turned out that I had *already* put on the belt. Safety first, I suppose.

o When I was a young kid, I thought that a sign that says, "**Post No Bills**" means that the mailman should deliver letters, but not invoices.

Chapter 4
Am I losing my mind already?

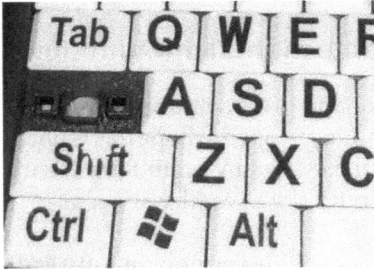

My mother lived for more than 90 years. She was super-smart. Like my father, she attended a high school for the "gifted," and she earned multiple college degrees.

In her last year or so, she had trouble with conversations. Like many people—even young adults—she sometimes couldn't think of a word she wanted to use. Instead of merely hesitating, Mom sometimes substituted words that made no sense to others. [More in chapter 28]

When she was younger, Mom read three or four books a week. At the end, she stopped reading. When she was in high school, Mom won an award for penmanship. At the end, she had trouble writing a check.

Although I am "just" 78 years old, I've lately been concerned that I might develop my mother's condition.

I never learned how to type the "real" way, but about five years ago I degenerated from being the world's fastest eight-finger typist to be a pretty-good two-finger typist. (I actually have ten fingers, but I've never used them all for typing.)

Now I'm a *terrible* two-finger typist. I produce a lot of typos—often pressing an adjacent key, like "v" instead of "c." I frequently hold down the shift key as I press the key to insert an apostrophe and end up inserting a colon. I often type "i nthe" and "fro ma." Until I removed it, I often tapped the Caps Lock key by accident, and the semicolon instead of the apostrophe, and the "Page Down" key instead of "delete." I seldom produce an error-free sentence. [The first time I typed that sentence, I typed "arror," and then I corrected it to "errror."]

A more recent—and much scarier—sign of degeneration is that I sometimes substitute words at the keyboard, usually with the same initial letter, like "party" for "path." Sometimes I use the wrong letter sequence, like "nad," "shuold" or "writign."

TRhis is an uncorrected sample of my typign. Anr here is another sample senterncer, and some moer. Today is Sunday and I havelots of newsapers to read. I wnatto spend some time writing.

This is really scary. Is it an early sign of dementia? Is part of my brain DEAD?

I can tolerate the loss of my hair, but I don't want to lose my mind!

(at top) Aging Baby Boomer's Low-Tech Secret Weapon:
If you remove the Caps Lock key, you can't tap it accidentally.

Chapter 5
The ultimate indignity

Years ago, when young nieces and nephews wanted to stay at our house, **Marilyn** and I established a simple rule: "If you want to sleep here, you have to learn how to wipe your own ass. We don't change diapers." (We have no children to practice on.)

The kids learned fast.

I am now in my 79th year. Lately, as I've visited elderly friends and relatives who are on the downward slope of life, and are in nursing homes and wear diapers, I've contemplated my own inevitable decline.

If I ever become unable to wipe my own ass, and must display my private parts to strangers in order to obtain assistance for a very basic human function, will I have lost my humanity as well as my dignity?

Will I be willing to go on? Is there living without wiping?

I don't know.

Chapter 6
Contemplating suicide
(just an intellectual exercise)

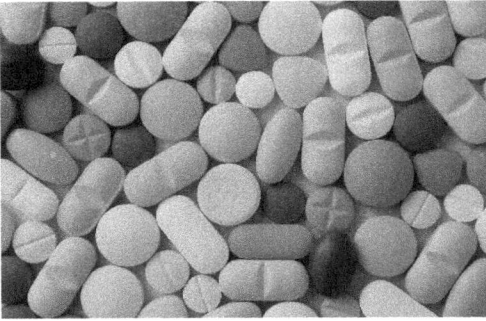

A wise person once said that when you talk more about what you've done than about what you want to do—you're old.

Based on that, I suppose I'm old. I'm scheduled to become 79 years old on 4/15/2025.

I've gone SCUBA diving under ice, I've skied, experimented with various pharmaceuticals, been arrested, had a threesome, eaten raw clams and been to three foreign countries. I've survived long enough to collect Social Security and Medicare. I've written and read many books. I have many friends on Facebook and a few in real life. I've earned and spent lots of money. I've voted in almost every election I was eligible to vote in. I was invited to the White House (Bush One) and was nominated to be *Hispanic Businessman of the Year* (a long, silly story).

I live with a wonderful woman and had a wonderful dog, and both seemed to like me.

I am unlikely to visit the moon, become president, earn a PhD, or win an Olympic medal for jumping. At this stage, it's extremely difficult for me to stand up after being on the floor.

I have no human children to provide grandchildren. I probably won't buy a 3-D TV. My current home is smaller and less grand than my previous home.

I am almost prepared for the end. My will needs to be updated—but I've written the text for my headstone and planned the music for my funeral.

My bucket list is pretty much empty. It contains a few unrealistic fantasies (time travel back for a weekend in 1967, read every book I own, own a Ferrari, get an honorary PhD from Lehigh and ride a fast camel across the dunes in Morocco).

There is just one semi-realistic item on the list. For years I've had a vision of staying in a cabin next to a lake in the **Adirondack Mountains** in upstate New York. I'm writing this in the summer of 2024, but *winter* is coming. I'm both pissed and relieved. This summer, like most summers, has been extremely frustrating, even annoying. Many things on my to-do-list remain undone. I want summer to just *go away*.

My mind sees my body asleep in a chair near a cabin on the shore of a lake in Adirondack State Park. **Dave Brubeck's** *Blue Rondo a la Turk* is playing, but not too loud. A breeze is tickling my face. Blue Rondo, blue sky, blue water, my dog and a boat are waiting for me to awake.

Maybe next summer.

Maybe next life.

So, with health declining, money waning, discomfort increasing and little or nothing to look forward to... why should I bother to stay alive until my anticipated death in 2035?

Is there any good reason to not kill myself right now?

There are a few:

- My wife needs me.
- I have to sort out, throw out, and give away lots of stuff.
- I want to finish writing a few books that I've started or planned.
- I actually enjoy large parts of most days.
- Suicide is not reversible.
- There is probably no pizza or ice cream after death. Or miso, gyoza, gyros or burritos.
- I'd like to get back to Maine at least one more time.
- Some people would probably miss my blogging and Facebook postings.
- I expect that someone will give me a really good 80th birthday party if I stick around.
- I probably won't hear what people will say at my funeral.
- I have some things to return to Amazon.

Chapter 7
Not enough time to read all my books

I first typed this chapter in a room filled with books, in a house filled with books. A quick estimate indicated that I had about 400 linear feet of books (40 feet more than the length of a football field), with the books standing up, not lying in the grass.

With an average thickness of one inch, and 12 books per foot, those 400 feet mean that I had a frightening total of about 4,800 books. That can't compare with the Library of Congress's collection of several million books, but it's pretty good for an amateur bibliophile.

And that 4,800 number doesn't include hundreds of other books on my iPad, Kindle Fire, desktop, laptop and smart phone, and on the trucks coming from Amazon. Or what I might pick up at Barnes & Noble.

I'm what is called an *avid reader*. I'm also a collector. That can be fun—or a danger. I read *everything*. I read labels, cereal boxes, signs and even magazines that I should have no interest in (including one for tow truck operators, two for poultry farmers, one for appliance dealers, one for tool distributors, one for pizza makers and another one about air compressors).

When I was a young teenager, I subscribed to about two dozen magazines—about science, cars, cameras, electronics, politics and skin diving. Plus *MAD* magazine, of course. They took up a lot of space. One summer I decided that instead of going to the beach club every day, I would devote three days each week to going through my magazine collection. I'd cut out the interesting articles and file them for future reference.

This was actually a problem—not a solution.

At the age of 14 I could not afford to buy a photocopier and therefore could not resolve the dilemma caused by pages with important articles on both sides—but about different subjects that should go into separate folders.

But even worse was the depressing realization that the magazines were coming in faster than I could read, cut and file them. I stopped being a librarian—and I swam more.

And that brings me back to 2021.

I assumed that I'd finished reading about half of my books. To simplify, I assumed I had about 2,500 p-books and e-books to go. According to my theory, I had about ten years left. I acquire about 80 books a year. I read about 100 books a year. I figured that as I age, my acquisition rate may diminish, and my reading speed may also diminish. However, I'll probably have more time to read.

Although my College Board scores in "verbal" were much better than in math, my quick computation made me think I'd die with about *2,400 unread books*.

SHIT! What should I do?

Should I read faster, live longer, stop buying, or get rid of a lot of books? None of the options appealed to me; but before I moved in 2021, I did give away *lots* of books.

Chapter 8
When is it time for a nursing home?

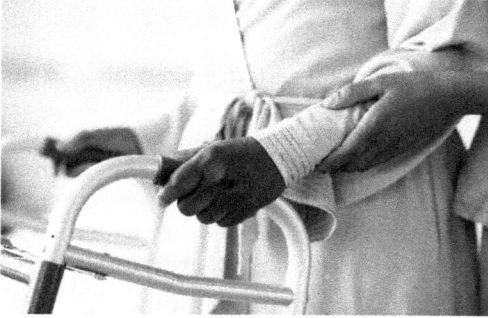

During a visit to one of my doctors, I asked him, "How do you determine whether or not an older person should be put in a nursing home?"

"Well," he said, "we fill up a bathtub. Then we offer a teaspoon, a teacup and a bucket to the person to empty the bathtub."

"Oh, I understand," I said. "A normal person would use the bucket because it is bigger than the spoon or the teacup."

"No," he said. "A normal person would open the drain. Do you want a bed near the window?"

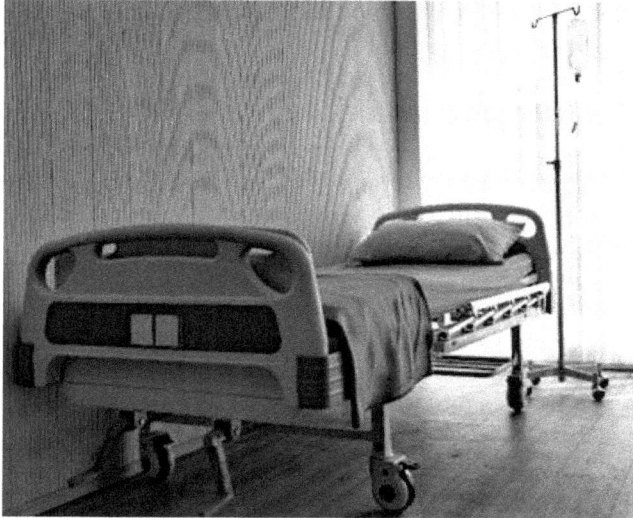

Chapter 9
What remains for my remains?
My cremation dilemma

A man I knew died about 25 years ago. He had seldom visited his parents' graves, and assumed his own children would seldom or never visit his.

He therefore announced that he wanted to be cremated, with his ashes divided into three piles and distributed to his wife and kids, so the survivors would always be nearby.

I've never felt a strong bond with the dead, whether they have been reduced to box of rotting flesh or a pot of powder. I can think about my dead relatives whenever I want to, without visiting a cemetery or running my fingers through their ashes.

I would probably feel pretty weird if a long black car or a big brown truck showed up at my door, and the uniformed driver handed me an urn with a packing slip announcing the arrival of Great Uncle Benny. I'd probably stick the urn in a closet along with a bowling trophy won by my late father-in-law in 1957.

I know that burial space near big cities is being rapidly used up. Some people are buried head-up/feet-down to save space. Obviously, reduction to ashes would save significant real estate, but I thought that cremation is cheating the system.

We are all part of the food chain.

Every time we inhale microbes or bite into a burger, we implicitly agree to a contract. We get to eat and absorb other life forms now, to support our bodies as long as we need them. When we're dead but still fresh, our bodies should first be scavenged for any useful parts. Eyes and skin and a pancreas and heart may improve the lives of other human beings.

The leftovers become the equivalent of *compost*, and life goes on. The rejected pieces should be buried in a rot-able container—so we can become worm food. Then the worms help grow plants, which absorb carbon dioxide and emit oxygen which supports the life forms up above our carcasses. If cows or other creatures munch on "our" grass, trees, flowers or bushes, we earn extra points. It's kind of like trading carbon credits. In a tentative obituary, **Benjamin Franklin** described his destiny as becoming "Food for Worms."

However, at the advanced age of 78, I've been re-evaluating my termination options. I realize that I could probably save thousands of bucks by being cremated instead of having a conventional funeral. The money saved could go to relatives and charities. A recent issue of *Consumer Reports* said that about 60% of corpses now are being cremated.

I did some checking. I was surprised and disappointed to learn that the foundation that granted me a free final resting place does not permit the burial of "cremains." So, I had to do some research, comparison shopping and serious thinking.

o   The nearby cemetery where my parents are buried would charge me $3,000 for a spot. YIKES!

- I've always liked the water (my "favorite toy"), so sprinkling my ashes in the ocean has some appeal. However, my ego demands that there should be some kind of *permanent structure* to remind people that I once existed. I'm not a pharaoh or ex-president, but a grave marker would be nice. It should outlast my books, blogs, magazine articles and *Facebook* posts. In 2013 **Donald Trump** wrote, "Show me someone without an ego, and I'll show you a loser—having a healthy ego, or high opinion of yourself, is a real positive in life!"

- I like the idea of providing my unneeded body parts to people who could use them, or medical students who might learn something by exploring my innards. But I'm fundamentally modest, and don't like the idea of people cutting up my naked body.
- If there is a funeral or memorial event for me, I'd like it to be *festive*, not morbid. I want someone to play my collection of a dozen versions of the happy-and-peppy klezmer song *Rumenye Rumenye.*

It might even wake the dead.

Chapter 10
I can't take it with me, but I'm not ready to throw it out

When I moved from an apartment to my first real house in 1977, I felt that for the first time in my life, I had enough storage space for all of my shit.

Unfortunately, I failed to realize a basic fact of life: *shit expands to fill the available space, and then it overflows.*

The move to our second house in 2001 required FIVE MOVING VANS, plus about 70 trips in our own minivan, plus disposal or recycling of about FIFTY CUBIC YARDS of crap, junk, stuff, things and trash.

o   Shit is stuff with value that is mostly sentimental.
o   Crap is stuff that can be eliminated with little debate or tears.
o   Junk can be eliminated with no debate or tears.
o   A collection is a bunch of junk which can be classified and displayed.
o   Trash should have been thrown out, not stored for later debate.
o   Garbage usually is disposed of promptly because it starts to stink.
o   A husband's shit may be considered junk by a wife.
o   And, vice versa.

One good way to classify stuff is by applying the 90-day rule (or one-year or five-year rule, or whatever time interval you select). If something has not been used in the last year (or other time interval), there's a good chance that it will not be used in the next year and can be eliminated.

Unfortunately, if you have enough space, the 90-day rule can be easily extended to become a 30-year rule.

Our second house was *huge,* a B.F.H. (big fucking house). Most people who saw it thought it was much too big for two people and a dog. It was *not.* A house can never be too big. Not even Buckingham Palace.

Well, we lived in the house for over 11 years. The house contained a lot of both shit and crap (plus lots of stuff and things). The formerly cavernous attic was almost impenetrable. The three-car garage became a storage space. It had about ten cartons that had not yet been unpacked from the 2001 move. (A shelf in our laundry room had a carton containing a silver serving thing which was packed for a move in 1975 but never unpacked.) A guest room had no room for guests.

In the summer, it was time for spring cleaning. It's always time for spring cleaning.

In 2012 we had 14 huge bags which were supposed to go to **Goodwill** by the end of 2010. Now, in 2024, I live in a right-sized apartment, I now divest instead of acquire, I go to Goodwill about once a week, and sell things online.

I'm faced with a major decision. I have a growing stack of early versions of my books which were marked for corrections. I don't want anyone to read them, so I can't sell them or give them away. I can't junk them, because destroying books is one of the few sins (or maybe the only sin) I recognize.

Sometimes, when overcome with egomania, I have a vision that some future literary critic will analyze the book stash and proclaim to the world, that "AHA! In version 3.68, Marcus changed a comma to a semicolon in the last sentence on page 254."

I realize that there is little likelihood that this will happen. But just in case, I'll keep the books. Besides, retention is better than sinning.

The next time I move, I want to go horizontal, feet first, in a zipper bag, with a tag on a toe.

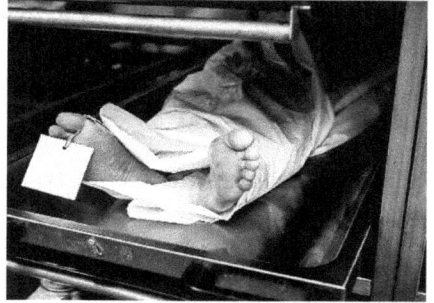

I'll let the next generation decide what is valuable shit and what is mere crap or junk.

Chapter 11
Text for my gravestone

When I was young, I had delusions of immortality. I honestly thought that if I was on a plane with 393 other people and the plane crashed, I would be the sole survivor. It was probably a combination of innocence, ignorance, egomania and utter lack of confidence in others.

I also felt that if I went into a jungle alone and had to face hostile tigers, alligators or Viet Cong I would survive; but if I was part of a huge army, someone else would fuck up, and we would all get killed. I didn't like teamwork.

Now, decades later, I have a more realistic assessment of my future. I know I won't live forever. And since I don't want someone else to mess up my epitaph, here it is:

OK, what's next?

I like "**Rockwell Bold**" for the typeface. Someone just has to fill in the final date and pick a nice piece of rock.

As for the words, yes, I'm an incurable optimist. I've always been resilient. I recover quickly from setbacks and disappointments and I'm always looking ahead. On freezing days in January, I know that the Earth gets more sunlight each day and is warming up. Spring is coming. I used to say, "Soon my dog and I will be in the pool and my ancient FIAT Spider will be out of the garage." Sadly, the car and dog are both gone.

Someone, please make sure my stone is done right. My words are important to me. If you fuck up the stone, I'm gonna come back and bite your neck. Thanks very much.

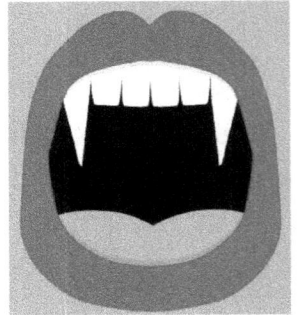

Graves and monuments for famous people can be revealing, creative, intriguing or bland.

Mel Blanc, ("the Man of a Thousand Voices") spoke as Bugs Bunny, Daffy Duck, Tweety, Sylvester, Yosemite Sam, Foghorn Leghorn, Tasmanian Devil, Porky Pig, Elmer Fudd, Barney Rubble, Dino, Mr. Spacely, Secret Squirrel, Speed Buggy, and Captain Caveman. Mel's stone displays a signature line from Porky Pig: "**That's all folks.**"

Mel provided voices, sound effects and acting in countless movies, radio and TV shows, including *The Abbott and Costello Show* and *The Jack Benny Program* (my favorite).

The gravestone for super-funny **John Belushi** shows a dismal skull and crossbones, and this line: "**I may be gone, but Rock and Roll lives on.**"

Notorious gangster **Alphonse Capone** does not use his nickname, "**Scarface**," and his stone is surprisingly religious, and ungrammatical. It says, "**MY JESUS MERCY.**"

The gravestone of noted author **Mark Twain** is disappointing. There is zero creative writing on it, just his real name, pen name and birth and death dates.

Benjamin Franklin was an important statesman, inventor, writer, printer and publisher. His gravestone, which he shares with his wife, has very few words. It says simply: **BENJAMIN AND DEBORAH FRANKLIN 1790.**

It's common for visitors to cemeteries to leave little tokens of remembrance for the departed. Many people leave flowers. Jewish people usually put small stones on graves. Fans of Mel Blanc have left small stuffed cartoon characters. Visitors to Mark Twain's grave have left coins. I'm surprised that nobody left bullets for Al Capone. `

Chapter 12
My un-bucket list
I'd rather be pushing up daisies than pulling up weeds.

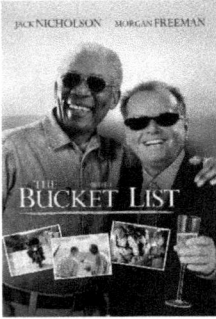

The Bucket List is a terrific 2008 movie in which **Morgan Freeman** and **Jack Nicholson** play two old guys who leave a hospital's cancer ward to accomplish the things on their "bucket list." That's the list of things they want to do before "kicking the bucket," and includes race car driving, skydiving, climbing the Pyramids and going on a lion safari.

I don't have a bucket list. There's not much that I want to do that I have not yet done in 78 years—other than see a few countries, jump from the George Washington Bridge, pilot a plane, know that one person who really pissed me off endures an extremely painful death, and maybe travel back to one amazing weekend in 1967. Oh, and it might be nice to re-grow the hairs that used to be on my head, arms and legs, and to be able to buy Indian nuts, Uneeda Biscuits and Zwieback toast. And to go through 24 hours without any body part aching.

One morning several years ago, in my miserable role as suburban husband and home-owner, I was once again reminded of all of the things that I ABSOLUTELY HATE to deal with, and presumably will not have to deal with after I croak.

So, here's the beginning of my UN-BUCKET list of things I hope to avoid:

- Pulling up weeds
- Cleaning the pool
- Cleaning a fish tank
- Unclogging ice cubes stuck together in the freezer
- Painting
- Writing checks
- Mailing anything
- Packing to move
- Picking up plastic peanuts
- Mopping
- Hanging tools back up on the Pegboard
- Searching for keys and eyeglasses
- People who ask me what to do and do something else
- Returning things to Sam's Club without a receipt (Costco is MUCH better)
- Returning empty bottles to get the deposits back
- Taking bags of stuff to Goodwill
- Taking crap to the municipal transfer station
- Sorting out papers for Income Tax
- Sorting out mixed screws and other small hardware
- Picking up the wrong screwdriver
- Trying to get a dog to drop a shirt or shoe
- Making small talk, especially in a hospital
- Being pressured to taste something I know I'll hate
- Christmas music in stores
- Political commercials
- Clearing a toilet clogged with someone else's shit
- Indecision
- Airplane "food"
- Sloppy painters
- Off-brand crappy soda
- Bad bagels
- Requests for my opinion when I don't give a shit
- Cleaning out the car before paying for cleaning
- Thinking about painting

- Buying a tool to replace a lost tool and then finding the lost tool
- The Tea Party, The Palins, Joe the alleged plumber
- Blue laws
- People who insist that Apple computers are easier to use than Windows computers
- Junk mail
- Wearing a tie
- Newspaper sections I pay to receive, sort out, schlep for recycling—but NEVER read
- Duplicate copies of *Parade* magazine. One is too many.
- The *New York Post*
- Errors in newspapers, magazines and books
- People who buy a bankrupt restaurant, spend six months and a million bucks redecorating, and then open and quickly go bankrupt. They could've done fine with new paint, menus and tablecloths.
- Too-small napkins
- Too-small beverage glasses
- Overpriced eyeglasses
- Paying 40 cents more for a medium cup of tea instead of a small one.
- Waiting for a table in a restaurant
- Waiting for a doctor
- Waiting for people who are late
- Being late for an appointment
- Waiting in line at the Post Office
- Waiting for my turn to pick up a prescription
- Waiting for anything
- Waiting for anyone
- Unavailability of clam chowder except on Fridays
- Unavailability of Manhattan clam chowder—even in Manhattan
- Too-salty anything
- Intermittent malfunctions
- Cars that won't start
- Shoppers with full carts ahead of me in the express lane
- Parking lots with too few handicapped spots
- Doors that take too much work to open
- Assholes on the radio
- Assholes
- Diarrhea
- Stomach aches
- Pains and problems that doctors can't diagnose or cure
- Computer fuckups
- Bad toupees
- Gefilte fish
- People who don't show up, or call if they're going to be late
- People who change phone numbers more than once in a lifetime
- Going shopping with my wife
- Going shopping for my wife
- My wife going shopping with me
- My wife going shopping for me
- Stupid names and names that are not pronounced the way they're spelled
- Shitty movies
- Shitty TV shows
- Hearing sloppy speech ("So, I was like, 'how the fuck are you?'")
- People who say "y'all"
- Negotiating anything
- Bending over for anything
- PMS
- Post-MS
- Fat people in tight pants
- Plumbers' butt
- Un-dyed hair roots
- Slow gasoline pumps
- Gasoline pumps that require holding the trigger
- Getting rained-on while filling my tank
- Too-low toilets
- Single-ply toilet paper
- Crabgrass
- Soda with no carbonation
- Crab legs (they taste good but are too much work).
- Yogurt
- Bottled water from Dannon ("Yogi water")
- Most soft cheeses
- Tzatziki sauce (I eat *gyros* with tomato sauce).

- Dumb holidays that force me to pay employees to skip work and go shopping or get drunk
- Medical insurance
- Rebates
- Forgetting to do things
- Forgetting how to do things
- Forgetting names
- Misplacing keys
- Misplacing important papers
- Cleaning swimming pool filter cartridges
- Buying things that have to be returned
- Pizza with too much cheese
- White "pizza" (if it doesn't have tomato sauce, it's not pizza, Goddammit!)
- Pens that run out of ink too soon
- Having too many of the wrong-size batteries
- Having too many of the wrong printer cartridges
- Printer cartridges that go out-of-date before use
- Getting inappropriate "cold calls"
- Recycling
- Restaurants with a huge selection of good ingredients, but nothing good on the menu
- Store salesmen who assume I want to bargain when I just don't want to buy the ugly piece of crap
- Late airplanes
- Snow (it was fun when I was a kid)
- Sunburn
- Rain
- November
- Las Vegas water
- Bad pistachios
- Bad pickles
- Bad pizza
- Bad waiters
- Too-wet coleslaw
- Ice cream that has defrosted and refrozen
- Power failures
- People who are sure they won't like something that they have never tried
- Typos
- Senior moments (a.k.a., brain farts)
- Forms that have to be filled out with a pen on paper, not on the web
- Forms that have spaces that are too small for the info that has to go in the spaces
- People on the phone who ask for an account number a few seconds after I keyed-in the account number
- Football
- Soccer
- Hunting
- Golf
- Boxing
- Wasting taxpayers' money
- Crooks in pulpits and politics
- Picking up broken glass
- Tech support people who repeat my question but don't understand it
- Tech support people with "heavy" accents
- Under-cooked eggrolls
- Exotic lettuce
- Our non-metric system
- Converting Fahrenheit to Celsius, and vice-versa
- Learning to use a new camera
- Forgetting how to use a camera
- Losing remote controls
- Ugly cars
- Chinese restaurants that don't understand what NO SCALLIONS means
- Doggie drool on a book
- Picking up dog shit
- People who fear dogs
- Changing flat tires
- Ice cream joints that don't make ice cream sodas
- Forgetting what day it is
- People who misspell my name
- Errors in take-out or delivered food
- Misdirected mail
- Dentistry
- Rectal exams
- Waiting for results of a prostate biopsy

Chapter 13
Devolution from daredevil to drunk to disabled

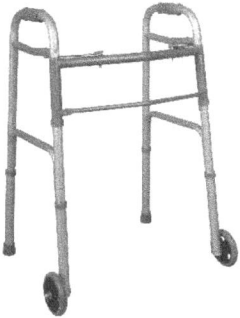

For the last few years, I've used a walker—not just for walking, but even for safe standing in one place for more than a few seconds. In 2023 I briefly held onto the walker with just my left hand as I used my right hand to reach something in my pantry. The walker slipped away from me, and I fell and broke my friggin' elbow. My arm was immobilized for months!

I was never *mucho macho*, but I was also never a wuss, a sissy or a scaredy-cat. Now I am *very* timid, and I *hate* my condition.

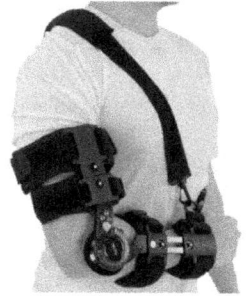

Because of physical impairments, if I bend down to pick something off the floor, I risk falling. I've fallen several times, requiring firemen to pick me up!

In July of 2024 I was showering, and I dropped a slippery bottle of "body wash" in the tub. It stayed there until a visitor picked it up for me.

I thought that a bar of soap might be better, so I got a six-pack of "Dove Men+Care Body Soap and Face Bar" from Amazon. I tried it out and, of course, I dropped it.

I needed something more secure, with a *tether*, and I searched Amazon for "soap on a rope." I did not place an order immediately because I was overwhelmed by the many choices.

I could get roped soap that looks like a penis, testicles, a turd, a fish, a Death Star, a rock, brass knuckles, a boot, a bagel, a marijuana leaf ("Dope on a Rope"), a dumbbell, an alligator, a pirogi, napalm and more. Even ordinary soap bars.

I could select designers and scents, and get soap apparently endorsed by **Leonard Nimoy** ("Spock") or singer **Freddie Mercury**; and there's a two-piece set conveniently labeled for face and ass. It's hard to decide—and easy to stay stinky.

It was easier for me to select a wife back in 1971. There were just three contenders. They all smelled good—and none had ropes attached.

I started going "deep-sea fishing" with my father when I was just three years old! While in elementary school, I collected bumble bees by grabbing them by the ass!

A shocking experience: When I was in junior high, we were assigned to do "research" for science class, and I was curious to see if it was possible to build up immunity to electric shocks. I had no expectation of being tried for murder and facing two kilovolts in the chair in the Big

House, but I wanted to see how much juice I could take. [I almost killed myself. Details are in another chapter.]

Frigid fun: On New Year's Day of 1964, I went *ice diving*. It seems like a stupid thing to non-divers, but divers think it's a great adventure. You find a lake with thick ice on top. You use a chain saw to cut a big hole in the ice and put a long ladder across the hole. A rope is tied to the ladder and the other end is tied to the divers to connect them to potential rescuers.

On this day, it was *brutally* cold out, something like six degrees Fahrenheit at Bolton Lake in north-central Connecticut, with a wicked 50MPH wind whipping across the ice. The good news was that it was so fucking cold that there was little danger that the ice would melt and we would get dumped into the lake. The bad news was that it was so fucking cold that we were freezing our asses off.

[Details are in another chapter.]

Horsing around: The sister of a girl I dated in college was given a horse for her birthday. She named the horse "Vida," in honor of the **Iron Butterfly** song *In-A-Gadda-Da-Vida*. The family didn't have much money and couldn't afford to hire a professional trainer, so I volunteered to try. I had generally been successful with animals. One of my tropical fish, a Kissing Gourami named Carl, grew huge and lived for six years. I liked dogs. Most dogs liked me, and some dogs obeyed me. And a horse is just a tall dog, right?

Besides, 15,000 years ago, the first Cro-Magnon who rode a horse didn't read any horse books or watch a horse DVD, and probably didn't know any more about horses than I did. I decided to walk into the corral with an apple and a smile and see what would happen. I got kicked. I got pushed. I got knocked over. I got bitten. Vida stomped on my foot and pushed it deep into the mud. Vida wouldn't even take the apple from me.

I have a new appreciation for Cro-Magnons.

First job, last drunk: I've been drunk exactly twice in my life. The first inebriation was at a bar while in college in 1967. Somehow, I managed to ride home on my motor scooter, but when I got there I had *absolutely no memory* of the trip. I must've been guided and protected by **Dionysus**, the Greek god of wine, festivity and frenzy. My second drunkenness happened while working at my first post-college job, assistant editor of *High Fidelity Trade News* in Manhattan in 1970.

My first big assignment was reporting on the 1970 **Consumer Electronics Show** at the **Hilton Hotel**. I had to wander around the show, ask what's new, take pictures, shake hands and kiss the behinds of advertisers who made my pathetic $115-per-week job possible.

As a "trade magazine" that didn't charge for subscriptions, our only source of revenue was advertising from companies that made hi-fi equipment. It was vital that every actual and potential advertiser be given the impression that they were VERY IMPORTANT to us.

The real boss of the magazine was not the editor or publisher, but Ken, the ad manager; and he directed a steady stream of reporters, editors and photographers to each manufacturer.

We had an intense rivalry with *Audio Times*, and it was important to provide more coverage of advertisers than they did—or at least create that appearance. Our editorial staff consisted of the editor, me, and a few freelancers who would write for anyone for a nickel or a dime per word.

For important events, we were augmented by shills. At one press conference, we had two real editorial people, the production manager pretending to be a reporter, and an ad guy pretending to be a photographer. He flashed his strobe light at dramatic moments—but had no film.

There was a lot going on in electronics in 1970. Cassettes were challenging both 8-track and open-reel tapes. Pre-recorded video was starting. Different varieties of quadraphonic sound were competing. Speakers were shaped like end tables, conga drums, ears and sculpture stands. The color of audio components was shifting from silver to black. "Solid State" was the hot label.

There was a social shift along with the changes in technology. This was the era when electronics makers first noticed the "youth market." Hippies who once were thrown out of stores were now invited to spend big bucks on audio gear. Equipment ads talked about rock instead of Bach.

I had invited my college buddy, Dave, to see CES with me. We spent about eight hours, cruising the show floor over and over and over again, with little rest and no food.

When the show closed at 5 PM, the action shifted upstairs at the Hilton and across the street to the **Hotel Americana**, where manufacturers welcomed retailers, journalists and even competitors to their hospitality suites. In most cases, a hospitality suite was an ordinary room, with a full bar and the bed in the bathtub so products could be displayed in the bedroom.

Dave and I worked our way through the Hilton and the Americana, stopping in dozens of suites and drinking in each one. By ten PM, Dave and I had probably walked ten miles, and each of us drank three gallons of liquor and eaten two shrimp, a pretzel and a celery stalk.

We could barely stand up, but we were commanded to go to a party for the launch of a hi-fi store franchise chain. This event called for more hand-shaking and strobe-flashing, a lot more drinking and a little more celery, pretzels and shrimp. I don't remember what happened during the next few hours, but the editor said that I sat in the lobby of the hotel, embarrassing our company by reciting fake Japanese poetry; and one guy reported that I tried to crawl up Fifth Avenue, towing my camera case behind me.

I remember waking up in a strange bedroom, with no knowledge of where I was or how I got there. The phone had familiar letters and numbers on it, so I figured I was in a friendly country.

After a while, my spinning head slowed down enough so I could stand up, and I noticed a door. I walked out, and discovered I was in the suite belonging to **Pickering**, the phonograph cartridge company. I found another door and discovered Dave, starting to wake up.

Dave told me that Tom, the Pickering sales manager, had rescued us from somewhere, taken us out to eat at **BrewBurger**, and then got us upstairs in the Hilton and put us to bed.

It was now about 6:30 AM. Going home was out of the question since I had to be at my desk at 8:30. I threw some water in my face, left the hotel, and started walking, taking a very long route from 56th Street to 45th Street and sobering up a little bit more with each step I took.

I got to work on time and managed to type a few pages. I later ran into Tom from Pickering, and Dave called me on the phone and we reviewed the night's activities.

Tom said I was too drunk to walk to BrewBurger, so he and Dave had gone to eat without me. But Dave insisted that I was at the restaurant with him, when I was really in bed.

He must have been drunker than I was.

In the beginning, according to the Bible, God created Heaven and Earth. In the beginning of my life as a book publisher, I created a memoir. A memoir is often written near the end of a life. I didn't know when I'd die, so I wrote my memoir when I was 62, back in 2008. Now I'm 78. I'm still alive—and I still don't know when I'll die. Maybe I won't finish writing this book, or this chapter or this page.

I've lived my adult life as a Jew and a non-believer, but I'm open to well-thought-out disagreement. In 2019 I explored various religions, and beginnings and ends. A book was the result. I don't expect to have a deathbed conversion, but if it happens, you may read about it in the end of this book.

At my age it's common to think about THE END (which may occur at any moment). Some evil people suddenly become nice people, hoping to spend eternity in Heaven instead of the warmer alternative. Others, who have not been particularly evil, start thinking ahead.

Jewish theology doesn't deal much with the "afterlife." Christians constantly think and talk about it. I've thought about it a lot lately. If I go to Heaven, will I be reunited with my wonderful dog who died a few years ago? Will I spend eternity as a pained, crippled old man—or as a vibrant 20-year-old, laughing, eating fine foods, listening to my favorite music, reading good books, hanging out with great people, and getting laid a lot?

I have a long list of physical ailments, and a long list of "ologists" who attempt to limit the damage and extend my life. Lots of my body parts don't work as well as they once did, or as often; and many previously insignificant functions are difficult and/or painful. It's tough to type accurately, or to use a screwdriver or stairs. I pee a lot, I have Parkinson's Disease (fortunately no tremors), I have diabetes, and my heart does not supply enough blood to my lungs. I have perpetual pain from arthritis, plus atrial fibrillation. My left pinky has been numb for years. Because I use a blood thinner, small cuts take *forever* to heal. I have "diabetic ulcers" on both lower legs that periodically bleed and require hospital visits. A fall in my kitchen caused a concussion and a fractured clavicle. In another fall in another kitchen, I broke an elbow. My knees and hips are weak and will probably need to be replaced with artificial joints if I live long enough. I once asked my orthopedist if I could get an entirely new skeleton to accept my skin and brains. He replied, "Not yet, but check back next week." I'll keep checking.

I sometimes think it would be nice to be in a nursing home where I would have zero obligations—or merely to not exist. I have made some medical progress, however. I've had Bell's Palsy and Diabetic Palsy but so far, no Cerebral Palsy. I almost never have migraine headaches, which plagued me as a teenager. I no longer suffer from gout or sleep apnea (a disorder that causes you to stop breathing while asleep. Your brain tries to protect you by waking you up enough to breathe, but this prevents restful sleep. Eventually, it can cause serious complications). I never had a heart attack or a venereal disease or been shot or mugged or addicted to drugs. I have not smoked in many years and drink "adult beverages" just a few times each year.

Wife Marilyn and I suffered from simultaneous sleep apnea, and we both slept with annoying "CPAP" (Continuous Positive Airway Pressure) machines. Our intimate foreplay devolved into tangling our air hoses together. Some limitations can be funny (if I suppress my pride). I had to call a neighbor to help lift me off the toilet. I've also needed neighbors and firemen to lift me off the floor after slipping.

Being pathetic has advantages, however. My handicapped parking tag usually gets me excellent spaces, and when I walk with my walker, people often carry trays for me in restaurants and hold doors open for me. I used to hold doors open for others.

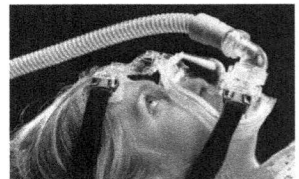

I wish I could be as polite as I once was.

Chapter 14
Redecorating myself

I became 65 years old back on April 15th, 2011.

That's still middle-aged. I used to say that middle age lasts until they shovel dirt onto you. I can still say that, but with a bit less conviction. I do everything with a bit less conviction. Especially climbing stairs.

I was thinking of getting a tattoo to assert something. But I don't like pain or infections—and it would really piss off my wife. Marilyn was sure I would get AIDs, toxic shock or typhoid.

I made an appointment with a local tattooista. I planned on something subtle: "**TA-2**." The tattoo guy didn't get it.

On the morning of my birthday, wife thought I was going to the urologist ("dick doc"), but I actually went to a hair salon for a cranial redecoration.

In lieu of tattoo, I settled for a shaven head and a trimmed beard.

I'd been married since 1971, but my wife had never seen my cheeks before. Not those cheeks, anyway. I was not sure if I'd keep the new look, but I did like it. (DAMN—my nose looked huge, and I never realized my head was so thick.)

Shortly after my trim, I was due to rendezvous with Marilyn at the snack bar at **Costco**. She was already on the line. I got behind her. I bumped my cart into her cart. She turned around and SCREAMED.

A few days later, we planned to meet another couple at a local restaurant. Marilyn got a ride with them, and I drove alone. I saw Marilyn approach the restaurant door. I ran and opened the door for her. She said, "It's nice to know there are still some gentlemen left." Then she turned around, saw me, and said, "Oh shit, it's you!"

A few weeks later, I dyed the beard dark brown, like it was years ago. This time Marilyn screamed again—and ran away.

However, our golden retriever Hunter loved the taste of the hair coloring and tried to lick it off.

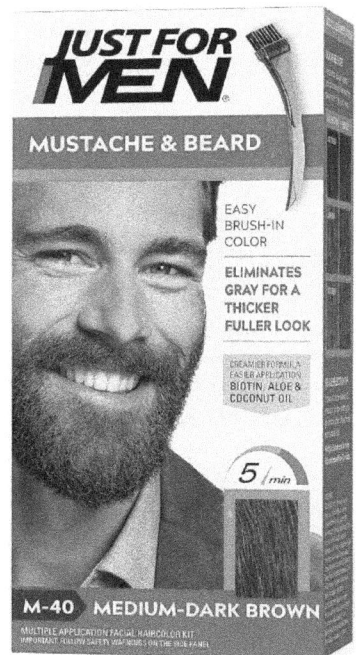

Chapter 15
Will work keep you alive?

"*Arbeit macht frei*" is a German phrase that can be translated as "work will make you free." The phrase was posted at the entrances to several Nazi concentration camps, most notably Auschwitz.

Most of the slave workers who avoided the ovens, gas chambers, bullets and deprivation were freed by the Allied armies—not by the work they were forced to do for Hitler.

However, some of the workers who had special skills—ranging from singing to missile-making and forgery—were kept alive by their important work, and ultimately freed when the Nazis surrendered.

Even outside concentration camps, work can keep people alive. And, perhaps the lack of work hastens death.

I turned 65 in 2011 and thought I'd be retiring—not running a new book publishing firm.

OTOH my father's father sold his shirt-making business to another company when he was 80. He was forced to retire at age 85, and within a few months he was in a nursing home, and then *dead*.

He told us he had no reason to get up in the morning.

In 2008 my father announced that there was nothing left on his to-do list, and he was ready to die, and he did (at 86).

It's important to have a reason to get out of bed—and I think writing and publishing are great reasons. I often get out of bed to start my workday at 3:30 AM—but that's probably not right for normal people.

Arbeit macht mich lebendig (work makes me alive).

Chapter 16
The weirdest experience of my life

One summer, my wife and I were in Maine, driving south to Bar Harbor after a visit to Quebec, Canada. Beautiful mountain vistas surrounded us and beckoned us—but we wanted to reach our hotel before dark.

Besides, I'm a water boy more than a mountain man, and it seemed that every 500 feet we'd encounter a sign indicating that the next turn would take us to beautiful Lake Bigfish, Lake WeWeHaHa or Lake Dip-yer-toes.

It was becoming increasingly difficult to ignore the water pressure. I took the next turn at an appropriate sign and salivated over the prospects of getting wet in the cool, clear waters of some random but authentic Maine lake.

While looking for the lake, I thought my eyes were playing tricks on me. Perhaps the weird Canadian food had warped my brain. *Poutine* is a disgusting Québécois snack consisting of French fries topped with slimy cheese and gravy.

I thought I saw a sign that said *Telephone Museum*.

This made no sense because there was no reason for any museum to be in very rural **Ellsworth, Maine**. It also made no sense because I collect telephones and would have loved to visit a telephone museum.

I looked again and saw that the sign was real, not an illusion. I thought I had made a random turn, but maybe I had made an involuntary response to something my wife did.

Maybe Marilyn poked me at the intersection. Maybe she also had made advance arrangements for some Maine woodsman to hang up a phony sign to mess with my mind. We drove a few minutes deeper into the woods, and then on my left appeared **The Telephone Museum**.

Really! I'm not kidding. I swear it happened.

Chapter 17
How I became semi-famous

BUGLER IN BROWN. French pattern, smooth mixture Eton suit with suspender shorts, white whipcord, lettuce on blouse, green and brown bow pattern self-tie, green socks, brown shoes.

I'll probably never become world-famous. It's unlikely that I'll be elected to be president or win an Oscar, Emmy, Grammy, Pulitzer or Nobel prize.

I was a shy kid, but I am not now a "shrinking violet."

In fact, I have a big ego and admit to being a "publicity whore."

In a biography published in *Smithsonian* magazine, **Adam Smythe** said that **Benjamin Franklin** was an "eternal self-promoter... even in the image of death." I have long admired Franklin, and I'm pleased to emulate him.

Here's some of what I've done to achieve fame and infamy:

o   My birth was announced in a publication for retailers, like my father.
o   When I was just three years old, I modeled clothing in a book called *Right Dress*, published to help parents properly clothe their kids.
o   A little later I was in the "Peanut Gallery" on the *Howdy Doody* TV show—twice! In one episode, **Clarabell the clown** took my handkerchief, put it into a zipper banana and refused to return it. I don't remember if I cried.
o   My picture was published in the *New Haven Register* after I raised money for the "Fresh Air Fund" with a stand that sold drinks and candy at a bus stop.
o   Years later, my picture was taken by an FBI agent at an anti-war protest.
o   I was invited to the White House to have my picture taken with **George H. W. Bush**.
o   I had my picture taken with Mouseketeer **Annette Funicello**!

o   I was nominated to become "Latino Businessman of the Year." (I'm not Latino, but someone thought my last name was "Marcos" or "Marquez.")
o   I won an **"ANDY" award** for my copywriting from the Advertising Club of New York.
o   I won several contests for my Halloween costumes.
o   I was president of the New Haven Finsters, a SCUBA-diving club. (The two other members were also presidents.)
o   I won trophies in sports car rallies (but never first place).
o   I beat two "intellectual property" lawsuits against professional lawyers representing big companies.
o   I kissed three lesbians.
o   I got a rent reduction for my room in the Grand Central YMCA because I wrote a powerful fundraising letter.
o   I lived long enough to start collecting Social Security.

- I passed the Red Cross tests to become an "Advanced Swimmer," "Senior Life Saver" and "Water Safety Instructor."
- I passed two SCUBA-diving tests.
- I gave blood to the Red Cross.
- I've met both **Paul Newman** and **Robert Redford** (they played *Butch Cassidy and the Sundance Kid*, and Henry Gondorff and Johnny Hooker in *The Sting*.)
- I picked up hitchhikers and hitchhiked.
- I once held my breath underwater for over three minutes.
- I had mononucleosis ("the kissing disease") TWICE, when it was supposed to be just once-per-person.
- I was temporarily blind in one eye.
- I had Covid-19 *three* times.
- I still remember the plant and animal phyla, the Prelude to *Evangeline*, multiplication tables, and Pi to a dozen places.
- I never learned to whistle or snap my fingers properly.
- I was a pretty good mechanic, electrician and carpenter.
- I still remember song lyrics from the 1950s.
- I won the "Marketing Executive of the Year" award from Junior Achievement.
- I was a millionaire (on paper).
- I started several successful businesses.
- I've written over 40 books, including several bestsellers.
- I've written dozens of articles for newspapers and magazines.
- I've started over a dozen Facebook groups and I post a lot.
- I discovered a glitch in word-processing software made by Lotus (then part of IBM). Someone in Lotus told me that the glitch was named to honor me—and fixed. Oh well. Fame is fleeting.
- I lost my "coffee virginity" at a 70th birthday party hosted by **Dunkin Donuts**. It was covered by newspapers and TV stations.
- One time I was at Dunk and ordered a delicious hot chocolate. I drank some of it in my car on the way home and put the remainder in my freezer for future consumption. I later partially defrosted it and loved the icy drink. I told the manager about my discovery, and eventually "frozen chocolate" was on the menu. You're welcome.
- While in college, I had a summer job working in a shitty shoe store. Most of the employees ate at a nearby **Burger King**. At one time I wanted a big cheeseburger, which was not on the menu. I asked for a "Cheese Whopper" and got what I wanted. Eventually the "Whopper with Cheese" was added to the menu. You're welcome.
- Another time at the King I wanted just a basic, simple, unadorned cheeseburger. I ordered a "shitless cheeseburger." The order-taker looked puzzled, and I explained that I wanted my burger "without all of the shit on it." I got what I wanted, but sadly, the "Shitless Cheeseburger" did not appear on the menu. You're welcome.

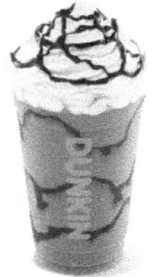

Chapter 18
Ways to go

Here's a list of the 15 most common causes of death in the United States, provided by CDC/NHS, National Vital Statistics System. Pick a good one.

Cause	Percent of Total
1. Diseases of the heart	28.5
2. Malignant tumors	22.8
3. Cerebrovascular diseases	6.7
4. Chronic lower respiratory diseases	5.1
5. Accidents (unintentional injuries)	4.4
6. Diabetes mellitus	3.0
7. Influenza and pneumonia	2.7
8. Alzheimer's disease	2.4
9. Nephritis, nephrotic syndrome and nephrosis	1.7
10. Septicemia (blood poisoning)	1.4
11. Suicide	1.3
12. Chronic liver disease and cirrhosis	1.1
13. Primary hypertension and hypertensive renal disease	0.8
14. Parkinson's disease (tied)	0.7
15. Homicide (tied)	0.7

And for the entire world (from World Health Organization):

Cause	Percent of Total
1. Ischemic heart disease	12.6
2. Cerebrovascular diseases	9.7
3. Lower respiratory infections (e.g., pneumonia)	6.8
4. HIV/AIDS	4.9
5. Chronic obstructive pulmonary disease	4.8
6. Diarrheal diseases	3.2
7. Tuberculosis	2.7
8. Malaria (tied)	2.2
9. Cancer of trachea/bronchus/lung (tied)	2.2
10. Road traffic accidents	2.1
11. Childhood diseases	2.0
12. Other unintentional injuries (tied)	1.6
13. Hypertensive heart disease (tied)	1.6
14. Suicide (tied)	1.5
15. Stomach cancer (tied)	1.5

Chapter 19
You know you're old when...

Here are some benchmarks of aging:

- At age-5, you love playing on the floor. At age 50 you hate getting down on the floor because it's hard to get up.
- At age-6, a nap is a punishment. At age 40, a nap is a mini-vacation.
- At age-8, you need help with complicated things. At age 18, you provide help to others. At age 58, you need help again.
- At age-10, you're insulted if a waitress calls you "honey." At age-30 it feels nice. At age-50 you call the waitress "honey."
- At age-16, you hate needing a parent to drive you in the car. At age 60, it's nice to have a driver.
- Around age-20 in rural areas, or 22 in more developed areas, you first notice cops who are younger than you are.
- By age-24, you notice teachers and bus drivers who are younger than you are.
- By age-30, you notice doctors and clergy people who are younger than you are.
- By age-32, you notice elected officials who are younger than you are.
- By age-35, store clerks and restaurant servers start calling you "sir" or "ma'am."
- By age-40, you notice college presidents who are younger than you are.
- By age-45, you realize that some people whom you always thought were older than you, are really younger.
- By age-47, you start getting asked if you have a senior citizens' discount card.
- By age-50, there are heads of nations who are younger than you are.
- By age-52, you talk more about what you've done than about what you want to do.
- By age-55, you realize that that "new" restaurant has been around for 50 years.
- By age 57, you start watching TV commercials you never cared about before.
- By age 58, you realize that some of your contemporaries have retired—or died.
- By age-59, some old friends don't recognize you—or you don't recognize them.
- By age-60, you look forward to hitting 65 and collecting Social Security.
- By age-61, you realize that you are not immortal.
- By age-62 you stop making long-term investments for retirement.
- By age-63, you attend more funerals than weddings.
- By age-64, you start giving away more than you buy.
- By age-66, you decide that wearing a hearing aid wouldn't be so terrible.
- By age-75, you stop buying fruit that needs time to ripen before eating.
- By age-80, you don't give a shit what anyone thinks about you.

Chapter 20
Alternatives to "dying"

- o Pushing up daisies
- o Buying the farm
- o Taking a dirt nap
- o Passing away
- o Going to the great beyond
- o Departing
- o Shuffling off this mortal coil
- o Exploring the afterlife
- o Meeting Saint Peter
- o Knocking on Heaven's door
- o Terminating with extreme prejudice
- o Heading for the pearly gates

Chapter 21
Law & disorder

I'm a law lover—or a law fan, law geek or law groupie. I've been one for many years. When I was a kid, I often hiked up **West Rock**, a mountain in New Haven, to visit the "**Judges Cave**," and ate at the nearby **Three Judges** restaurant. New Haven has important streets named to honor those judges. The Torah has an important *Book of Judges*.

John Dixwell, Edward Whalley and **William Goffe** were three of 59 English judges who sentenced **King Charles I** to death in 1649. They charged him with attempting to "uphold in himself an unlimited and tyrannical power to rule according to his will, and to overthrow the rights and liberties of the people."

The trial led to the end of the monarchy. Statesman, politician and soldier **Oliver Cromwell** became "Lord Protector of the Commonwealth," and there was no king for a while.

When **Charles II**, son of the executed king, became king in 1660, he sought revenge on the judges. He ordered that they should be hanged, drawn and quartered. To avoid this grisly fate, Whalley, Goffe, and Dixwell fled to North America.

Judge Dixwell stayed in New Haven, and Whalley and Goffe went to Boston. Even far from England, the judges were far from safe. Soon after arrival, a warrant was issued for their arrests, and they hid.

Local Puritans, mostly Cromwell supporters, helped the fugitives. At first, the judges were hidden in the home of **Reverend John Davenport**. (New Haven has an avenue named for him.) When that wasn't safe enough, Whalley and Goffe were hidden in the woods of what is now **West Rock Ridge State Park**. (New Haven has another mountain, **East Rock**.)

West Rock has a huge rock with huge cracks in it. The two judges started hiding there on May 15, 1661, and ate food brought by locals. A panther scared the judges from the woods, and they fled to Hadley, Massachusetts, where they remained. In honor of the infamous fugitives, the hideout was named "*Judges Cave*" and the path leading up to it is "**Regicides Trail**."

The cave displays a plaque which reads, "Here May Fifteenth, 1661, and for some weeks thereafter Edward Whalley and his son-in-law William Goffe, members of the Parliament-General, officers in the army of the Commonwealth and signers of the death warrant of King Charles First, found shelter and concealment from the officers of the Crown after the Restoration. 'Opposition to tyrants is obedience to God,' 1896."
[Adapted from *Atlas Obscura*. Thanks.]

Family Law. My brother and two nieces are attorneys. One niece teaches law at Harvard. My father had a law school scholarship, but never used it because he fell in love with retailing.

As a store owner, Pop often knew more about leases than his landlords did. I won two *pro-se* cases (acting as my own lawyer) in New York City's Landlord & Tenant Court. Before one session, because I was wearing a tie, other litigants assumed I was a Legal Aid attorney and asked *me* for advice. I had taken a few law courses in college but was not prepared to advise anyone.

I like the online abbreviation: "INALB" (I'm not a lawyer, but...).

I'm not a lawyer and will never be a judge on TV or the Supreme Court. However, I've generally done well at *pro-se*. I defeated two highly paid pros in intellectual property cases and was successful in traffic and small claims courts. I had a great victory when I wanted to break an apartment lease. But, so far, no *pro-se* capital cases (where execution is possible).

I did well in those law courses in college, but I realized I did not have the patience to learn and remember all that would be necessary to pass a bar exam. I do love legal research and negotiating. So, I've remained a mostly successful amateur, and an addicted observer.

LAW & DISORDER

I've probably seen each episode of each variety of TV's *Law & Order* at least three times, plus *Judy Justice, Judge Judy, Judge Jerry, Judge Mathis, Judge Ross, Judge Hatchett, Judge Jeanine, Judge Karen, Judge Wapner, Judge Cristina, Judge Mablean, Hot Bench, Couples Court, Divorce Court, Night Court, LA Law, Boston Legal, Texas Justice, Perry Mason, Matlock, Court TV, The Verdict, The Verdict is Yours, We the People, Harry's Law, How To Get Away With Murder,* and more.

My favorite TV cop is **Lenny Briscoe**, played by **Jerry Orbach** on the original *Law & Order.* I love his sarcastic "Lenny Lines" delivered after discovering a corpse early in each show.

I was sorry to see the departure of **Christopher Meloni** who played **Olivia Benson's** partner **Elliot Stabler** in *Law & Order: Special Victims Unit.* After leaving SVU, Stabler was the main character in another of L&O creator **Dick Wolf's** spinoffs, *Law & Order: Organized Crime.* I like Meloni, but thought this series sucked. I initially thought the remake of *Matlock* with Kathy Bates sucked, but became a fan.

I like the evolution of characters. **S. Epatha Merkerson** first appeared as an office cleaner. Then POOF!—she was a lieutenant. **Olivia Benson,** portrayed by **Mariska Hargitay** (daughter of muscle man/actor **Mickey Hargitay** and actress/singer/Playmate **Jayne Mansfield**) rose from mere detective to Captain and Commanding Officer of the SVU.

I like most of the characters, but can't stand a few, particularly **Arthur Branch,** played by presidential candidate **Fred Thompson,** and **Ben Stone,** played by **Michael Moriarty. Amanda Rollins** (played by **Kelli Giddish**) often annoys me, but not nearly as much as her sister **Kim.**

A few faves are **McCoy, Munch, Stabler, Cutter, Barba, Carisi, Carmichael, Lupo, Bernard,** the leaning-over **Goren,** Judges **Ian Feist** and **Stanley Gollub**—both played by

Merwin Goldsmith, alte-kocker **DA Adam Schiff**, and **Fin Tutuola**. It was always weird seeing **Dann Florik** as **Captain Cragen** because he looked like my father, who also looked like **Yoda**.

The *L&O* shows had frequent guest stars, including **Jerry Lewis, Philip Seymour Hoffman, Allison Janney, Martin Short, Angela Lansbury, Whoopi Goldberg, Tovah Feldshuh, Marlee Matlin, Joe Piscopo, Carol Burnett, Edie Falco, Michael Tucker** and **Robin Williams**. The guest star was seldom a perpetrator, and the first suspect never was guilty.

Some of my trials

Of course, cops lie. Around 1998, I got a ticket for making an illegal right turn in Queens, New York. It was late in the afternoon, when the sun was low and caused so much glare that it was impossible to read a sign that said that right turns were not permitted between 4 PM and 6 PM.

I pointed this out to the cop, and he said, "That's what everyone tells me." A young nephew was with me, and I thought he could be a good witness for me in traffic court.

I did some research before going to court. I checked the printed regulations and spoke to a *traffic device maintainer* who worked for the city. I determined that in situations where sun glare is a known problem, cities are *supposed* to provide additional signs farther from the intersection and/or large shields around the affected signs.

I went to court and cited chapter and verse to the judge. I also asked the cop if others had complained about difficulty in seeing the sign, and the lying SOB denied it.

My 14-year-old witness disagreed with the cop but was deemed to have less credibility. Or maybe truth just doesn't matter when the city needs to grab every buck it can.

The judge admired my research and said he'd give me an "A for effort," but I still had to pay the fine. My nephew learned that cops can be liars, even in court, and even under oath. That's an important lesson. I'm glad he learned it when he was just 14.

When is a room not a room? My second Bronx apartment was a big bargain. Because of New York City's weird rent control system, my monthly rent in 1971 was just $95.22. I had 'inherited' the apartment from cousins of my maternal grandmother, who were the apartment's original tenants. The law allowed rent increases only when someone new moved in, and I was just the second tenant. The place was conveniently located, in good condition, and had some luxury touches including wooden parquet floors. The kitchen, however, was both ancient and tiny. I installed new flooring, a new countertop, a stainless-steel sink and the first and only dishwasher in the building.

Several years after I moved out, I was reading the rent control rules and discovered that for an apartment's room to be considered to be an official room, it must have a minimum of a certain number of square feet, which my kitchen did not have. I complained to the former landlord, who said that *regardless of its puny size*, the kitchen qualified as a room because it had a *window*. I sued him and received a refund of about a thousand bucks, and applause from some of the folks in the courtroom. It was my debut performance as an unofficial lawyer. The victory was very sweet and motivated me to play **Perry Mason** some more.

The lawyer was a liar. I once had a customer with a very expensive apartment in Manhattan. **Sheila** was a mistress, a kept woman, being kept by **Harold**, a lawyer with a wife and kids on Long Island. Harold seemed to treat her well, at least in terms of spending money—except for one time.

Sheila ordered an expensive, ornate (and I thought ugly) Italian phone, made with onyx and gold-colored metal. It cost about $400, which was a lot of money in the mid-1980s. It's a lot of money now, too, especially for a *really ugly phone*.

When I delivered it and plugged it in, she liked it and gave me a check. No problem, I thought. A few days later, she called and said she wanted to return it because it was not what she ordered.

This didn't make any sense. She had no complaint when she first saw it. She had ordered from a color catalog page, and that page and my order form and the phone's package and the label on the phone's bottom all showed the same model number as the one she had ordered.

I figured that hubby Harold blew up when he saw her checkbook. Four hundred bucks was a lot of money for a really ugly phone.

I refused to take the ugly phone back. I had done nothing wrong. I could not return that onyx monstrosity to my supplier and it was extremely unlikely that I could sell it to anyone else.

Harold was not happy, and he stopped payment on the check. I sued him in small claims court. The court was inconveniently located near the bottom of Manhattan, and Harold and Sheila missed the scheduled court session. They, the defendants, got an automatic postponement to a new court date, and that *really* pissed me off.

The law was very unfair. If I, the plaintiff, didn't show up, the case would have been dismissed and the defendants would have gone home victorious. They could have kept the phone for free. It's not so ugly if you don't pay for it.

Harold and Sheila *did* show up the second time. Harold was used to trying cases in fancy venues like the **Supreme Court of the State of New York.** Snooty Harold had a **Harvard** law degree and clearly thought my small claims case and the appointed referee were several strata beneath his exalted stature. (There was a six-month wait for a *real* judge, so I got a "referee.") Harold expected an easy victory and to keep his four hundred bucks.

As "Defendant's Exhibit A," Harold showed the referee the catalog page from which Sheila had ordered the phone. With excruciating detail, worthy of a forensics expert tracing blood spatter, he pointed out what he insisted were significant differences in the grain pattern of the onyx in the photograph, and of the actual onyx in "Exhibit B," the telephone which he showed to the referee.

The referee, a graduate of **Brooklyn Law School**, was as streetwise as **King Solomon,** as knowledgeable as a Nobel scientist and not impressed with highfalutin' Harold from Harvard.

The referee pointed out that onyx was *not* molded plastic, and it was therefore unrealistic to assume that two pieces of stone that came out of the Earth would look identical.

I easily won Round One.

Harold then shifted strategies to portray evil me as unresponsive to his complaints. He told the referee that he left a message with my answering service when he first saw the phone, and that I did not return his call.

It seemed like I should have already won the trial after the referee's lecture about the earthly origins of onyx and that this move by Harold was—as **Perry Mason** often said in court—"incompetent, irrelevant and immaterial."

But, rather than objecting to the testimony, I decided to take advantage of it—and maybe have some fun.

Harold was accustomed to being the attorney who questioned witnesses and not being a witness himself, so he got careless. I was now the sharp-toothed legal shark. I smelled blood in the water as my turn came to examine the witness.

I had what seemed like a simple and innocent question—almost a time waster—but I was really hoping to set Harold up to commit perjury and *lose the case.*

I asked Harold if he spoke to a man or to a woman when he called my answering service.

Without hesitation, this esteemed officer of the court and professional bullshit artist told the referee that he spoke to a *woman.*

I then shifted from being an attorney to being a witness. I said to the referee, "Your honor, I don't use an answering *service.* I use an answering *machine,* and it answers in my own, obviously *male,* voice."

I got paid for the phone *and* I recovered the court costs. I wasted a lot of time, but I *loved* playing lawyer.

My only regret was that Harold was not disbarred for perjury in a courtroom. But eventually, he did get paid back many times over, for fucking with me.

You see, Harold's wife, **Lorraine**, found the apartment lease and discovered that he had been shacking up with Sheila; and Lorraine beat him up in a very costly divorce.

And, by then, Sheila didn't want him either.

She got pissed off at him because he didn't want to pay for the onyx phone that she liked so much. She moved out of their love nest and started dating others. Eventually she married the referee from Small Claims Court and went back to college and became a divorce attorney.

Justice usually does prevail. Sometimes it just takes a while. Sometimes, verdicts are reversed after years of imprisonment. Sometimes, defendants are pardoned *after* they're executed.

It took me over 50 years to write about mymacy' horrid my sixth-grade teacher.

I lost the trial but won the case.
In the mid-1970s, I lived in a brand-new, luxury high-rise apartment building in Queens, New York. My wife and I planned to live there for three years and then buy a house. The building was filled with lots of other young couples who had similar plans and dreams.

Unfortunately, we all soon realized that each month that we stayed in the building meant that the prices of houses we might want to buy were going up, while we were paying about $600 to the landlord instead of us-ing the money to build equity in our own real estate.

Some of the other couples broke their leases early but had to pay *huge* penalties, often agreeing to keep paying rent until a new tenant moved in. The building still had virgin apartments, so there was no incentive to the rental agents to steer prospective tenants to previously occupied apartments.

I, however, had an advantage over my peers.

I was a *big* pain in the landlord's ass.

The landlord hated me and wanted me *out.*

I was active in the building's tenants organization, and became reporter, editor and publisher of the *Tenants Times.* My neighbors loved it. Our landlord hated it.

Every time the landlord announced a new rule or claimed that some activity was a violation of the lease, I'd do some research and publish a special issue to point out that the landlord was full of crap. I knew the lease better than he did—a lot better. This was a talent I inherited from my father, a retailer who was a master lease negotiator and knew the contents of his landlords' leases better than the landlords or their attorneys did.

My landlord once tried to ban cookouts on our balconies, claiming that they violated the lease *and* were a terrible fire hazard.

I was pleased to point out that the lease *didn't even mention* outdoor cooking. I also interviewed the local fire chief, who said that, in the last 40 years in the entire Borough of Queens, there was no record of any fire being caused by cooking on a balcony. I published this information, along with some advice about minimizing annoying smoke, and keeping a bucket of water or a fire extinguisher handy.

After this, the landlord changed the lease for new tenants to specifically outlaw balcony barbecues and was determined to find a way to get rid of me.

He discovered that I had erected a huge Citizens Band radio antenna on the roof and snaked a cable down seven floors through a ventilation shaft to my apartment.

This, he was certain, was a violation of the lease and grounds for my eviction. Eviction sounded pretty good to me, because I could move out without penalty and then pay my money towards a mortgage for my dream house, instead of as apartment rent.

When we went to court, the landlord's attorney showed the judge several pictures of my huge antenna on the roof of the building as well as a yellow-highlighted page from my signed lease, noting the prohibition of the installation of exterior antennas without permission.

Now it was time for me to launch my *secret weapon* and win the war.

I opened my briefcase, removed a manila envelope and took out a neatly typed letter on the landlord's expensive engraved stationery.

It was dated on the same day that my lease was signed.

It was signed by the landlord's rental agent—who also happened to be his *son*.

The letter, which was written as an enticement to get me to sign the lease for the apartment, gave me explicit permission to erect the CB antenna on the roof!

The landlord's attorney turned white and gulped.

The judge and stenographer tried hard not to laugh.

The lawyer made no effort to dispute the letter. He just wanted to find a way to get me out of the building ASAP.

He was engaging in pest control.

I negotiated the right to end my lease with no penalty or payment and to move out at any time within the next 12 months. The landlord paid the court costs.

It was only years later, when I was examining some old papers, that I realized that I was officially evicted.

I *still* think I won the case.

After years of dealing with the public, I learned that certain stereotypes apply most of the time:

- ○ Lawyers were the crookedest (often wanting to avoid paying sales tax).
- ○ Interior decorators were the nuttiest.

Mrs. Statler was a decorator, married to a lawyer, and together they drove me *nuts*. Details are in Chapter 82.

A lawyer wanted to eat my liver. **Ron** was a lawyer, married to **Sharon**, a famous soap-opera actress. They moved into a beautiful, huge, custom-built house on Long Island that I wired for phones, audio, video and computers.

Ron's personality ranged from a kindly Dr. Jekyll to a vicious Mr. Hyde. Apparently, his mood swings were triggered by Sharon, but I never saw what she did to make him change.

She was always cold to me. On the day after they moved in, I was chatting with them in the kitchen, and I asked how the unpacking was going. Her highness replied, "Do I look like someone who unpacks?"

When Ron was in a "nice guy" mood, he'd chat pleasantly about music or politics, give me presents, serve me meals and trust me to watch his young daughter. But twice, when there were problems with equipment I had installed, he threatened to *cut open my chest and rip out my liver and eat it.*

No other customer ever said that to me. Ron sure had a flair for the dramatic.

Later on, he and Sharon divorced. Ron's mood swings stopped, and he was nice every time we spoke after their split. Divorces are unpleasant and I don't know the details of this one, but I think Ron was lucky to escape with his mind intact. I blame her—not him—for his viciousness. Although he is on my worst-customer list, it's only the pre-divorce Ron.

I skipped the trial but won the case.

I once got a ticket for an illegal left turn at a particularly confusing intersection in Scarsdale, New York. I thought the conditions might be ambiguous enough for me to avoid a fine—if I got to speak to the right judge.

However, the maximum fine was only $45, and it would not jeopardize my license or raise my insurance; so, it was quicker and simpler to just visit the court clerk and deliver a $45 check.

When I got to the court, I was horrified to learn that fines had to be paid in cash!

This court was in fancy-shmancy SCARSDALE, and they wouldn't trust a $45 check.

When I lost a traffic court case in crappy Jamaica, New York, they were quite willing to accept my check. I told the snotty Scarsdalian bureaucrat that, as long as I had to waste my time by coming back a second time, I wanted to change my plea to Not Guilty and have a trial. She modified the record and put my name on the court calendar for trial a few months later.

On the scheduled day, I went to court. I had $45 in cash in my pocket because I assumed I would lose, and I dressed a little better than I normally did.

When my case was called, I said something like "Defendant ready, Your Honor," just as I'd seen on *Perry Mason*.

However, no one showed up to represent the Village of Scarsdale. The Plaintiff was apparently too busy giving tickets to other drivers to come to court.

The case was dismissed, and I got to keep my cash.

On the way out of Town Hall, I couldn't resist stopping by the court clerk's office for some immature gloating.

I held up the $45 and said, "If you accepted checks, this money would be yours!" I was tempted to call her a stupid bitch, but, with great effort, I controlled my glee.

But when is the trial? My company was once sued by an annoying customer.

He invented a lot of phony complaints, even alleging fraud because there was one name on my initial proposal and a different name on the final invoice.

There was *no fraud*. My business had changed its name to get a better position in the Yellow Pages and we went from being a company to being a corporation.

The real reason for the suit was the all-too-common "buyer's remorse." The customer had agreed to spend too much money and was now looking for a legally sanctioned way to avoid paying his bill.

The summons listed about a dozen complaints that I could easily challenge. When we got to court, our case was called, and the judge invited both parties into his private "chambers" for a pre-trial conference.

The plaintiff went through his bogus complaints, and I made a half-hearted effort to refute them, saving my stronger arguments and abundant evidence for the later courtroom appearance.

After a few minutes, the judge said, "Thank you very much; you'll be notified of my decision by mail."

I was shocked, and replied, "But, Your Honor, when is the trial?"

His Honor said, "You just had it."

Verdict for the amateur professional, or the professional amateur

In the 1990s, I lived in a townhouse condominium in Westchester County, New York. I was one of the original residents, having moved there in 1978.

When the place was built, its builder, like other builders, needed to establish rules and regulations. He apparently went to an office supply store and paid a few bucks for an all-purpose document written by a lawyer who never lived in our condominium, never knew the people who would live there and certainly had no idea how society would evolve over the following decade.

One important way that society evolved was the new popularity of the "home office." Once home offices were limited to doctors, but, by the mid-1990s, inexpensive computers and the Internet enabled a wide range of occupations to be carried out in underwear or pajamas at any hour of the day or night.

Some professionals:

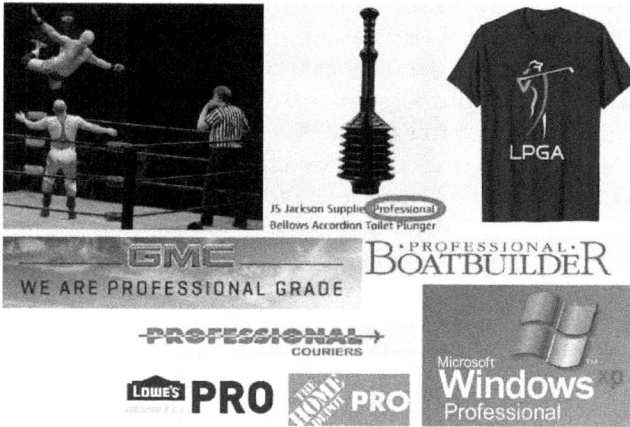

Our condominium's bylaws specifically outlawed carrying out any occupation other than "professional" activities on condominium property. The attorney who wrote the rule in 1970 knew what he had in mind, just like the folks in 1792 who wrote that "...the right of the people to keep and bear arms, shall not be infringed" knew what *they* had in mind.

But, in both cases, there has been a lot of disagreement and interpretation over the years, selective prosecution, perhaps some persecution, and ample income opportunities for attorneys.

In my condominium, plenty of occupational activities were carried out in apparent violation of the rules. Schoolteachers corrected exams and read term papers. Salespeople wrote proposals. Bartenders mixed drinks. The ice cream man sold pops. Landscapers planted, mowed and trimmed. Lifeguards at the pool guarded lives. Carpenters remodeled kitchens. Doctors prescribed medication. Plumbers replaced water heaters. Cops and insurance agents investigated burglaries. Our managing agent managed. Our maintenance men maintained.

Lots of people—residents, visitors and even employees of the condominium—worked there every day in flagrant violation of the holy writ, and life went on just fine.

But, one day—and I don't know why—the Board of Managers decided to sue me for violating the rules against operating a "non-professional" business on the premises.

My main business at the time was installing business phone systems. I installed them at the premises of my customers. Many of them were in Manhattan, New Jersey, Long Island or Connecticut—but certainly *not* in my own living room.

I made most of my money outside the house, but I did have a few business visitors each month. Some were salespeople showing me new products, some were prospective customers, and a few were customers picking up phones.

I certainly had no store. There was no showroom, no sign in the window, no bright lights, no factory with loud noises or noxious odors that would have violated the bylaws or zoning regulations. I had no employees. My business certainly drew less traffic than a perfectly legal doctor or a 17-year-old girl.

The traditional examples of permitted "professional" occupations, as envisioned by the ancient unknown lawyer who wrote our rules, were doctors, dentists, architects and—of course—other lawyers. I had to prove to the judge that this group was much too narrow and an unrealistic interpretation for the late 20th century.

I told the judge that many occupations were widely recognized as professions and deserved to be included, starting most obviously and in chronological order, with "the world's oldest profession"—prostitution. Wasn't a hooker as worthy as a dentist?

I then told the court about professional wrestlers, professional golfers, professional tennis players, professional musicians, professional divers, professional gamblers and professional assassins. GMC makes professional trucks. I showed the judge a copy of *Professional Boatbuilder* magazine and *Professional Hair Salon* magazine and told him about magazines called *Professional Woman* and *Quilting Professional* and *Christian Professional.*

I also told him about the Professional Drivers Association and the Association of Professional Body Piercers, and I showed packages labeled "professional screwdriver," "professional duct tape," and "professional toilet plunger."

The judge ruled that "professional" was now synonymous with "business" and merely meant the opposite of an amateur or non-business activity. Unless condo rules were rewritten to include or exclude specific occupations, neither the oldest profession, nor mine, was a violation.

Who's a professional?

IMPORTANT: A delayed trial usually helps the guilty and hurts the innocent.

Chapter 22
Parental issues

Which came first:
the chick or the driver's license?

I turned 16 in 1962, during my sophomore year in high school.

Connecticut let people drive when they were 16 years old, but my parents had different rules.

Mom said, "You don't need a driver's license because you don't go out with girls."

Hey, Mom! Did you ever think that maybe the reason I wasn't going out with girls was because I didn't have a driver's license?

Good kids who are old enough to drive should not have parental chauffeurs.

Which is worse: mom & dad
or moo-goo-gai-pan?

When I went home from college, I frequently got really bad migraine headaches.

My parents often brought in Chinese food as a treat for me. It wasn't available where I went to school.

Around this time, a theory started circulating that migraines were triggered by the monosodium glutamate ("MSG") used as a flavor enhancer in many Chinese dishes.

To experiment, I avoided Chinese food when I next went home. I still got a migraine. **Unavoidable conclusion: parents, not MSG, made me sick.**

Who was right?

One afternoon, when I was about 14, I sat at our kitchen table, reading and snacking. My mother was in the adjacent dining room with a neighbor. They talked about their kids.

My mother said, "I knew that Michael was right, but I couldn't let him know it."

That incident affected me for as long as my mother lived. **Warning: Distrust may never be reversed.**

Chapter 23
Low-tech and no tech
(This may piss off Walmart.)

A while ago, I returned something to a Walmart store in Middletown, New York. I did not have a receipt, so they said they would send me a refund check.

After 30 days, I got nothing and called the store. The customer service lady said she couldn't find any record of my return. I offered to read the numbers off the return receipt, but she needed to see the numbers, not hear them.

Silly, but no big deal, I thought.

I then uttered one of the most common four-word phrases of that era: "What's your fax number?"

I was shocked at the four-word reply: "We don't have one."

Yuck!

I like Walmart, but this was absurd. They'll sell me a fax machine but won't receive a fax.

Walmart is the world's retailing giant, a zillion-dollar-per-year behemoth that brags about its efficiency and technology. It's a success story that sells zillions of pieces of merchandise each year—including fax machines—and they didn't have a fax machine for use by their own staff or customers.

And, no, I couldn't send a fax to a demo machine in the electronics department. And, no, I couldn't send it to the fax machine in the garden department. And, no, I couldn't send it to sibling Sam's Club in the same building.

I even offered to give them my credit card number so they could sell me a fax machine, set it up, receive my fax and then pack up the fax machine and issue a credit to my credit card.

But, no.

The grand temple of technology, the world-beater and Sears-beater, the company that sells almost everything to almost everyone, the biggest retail business in the universe insisted that I *mail* them a copy of my receipt.

I never mail anything. I hate the mail. Mail doesn't work for me. I can't cope with mail. If something can't be phoned, faxed, e-mailed, FedEx'd, or UPS'd, *it just doesn't go.* I send electronic birthday cards, not paper ones. My desks have stacks of stuff that should have been mailed weeks, months or even years ago.

My wife learned not to ask me to mail anything. I pump out faxes and e-mail all day long; but things she asked me to put in the mailbox are still stuffed above the visor in my car. They'll stay there until she reads this.

C'mon, Walmart. Get connected! I know where you can get a good deal on a fax machine. Try aisle seven.

But wait! There's more! When Walmart was finally ready to send me the refund, an employee had to make a trip to the local post office to purchase a money order, because *the store didn't have a friggin' checkbook!*

Chapter 24
Reading is living & living is reading

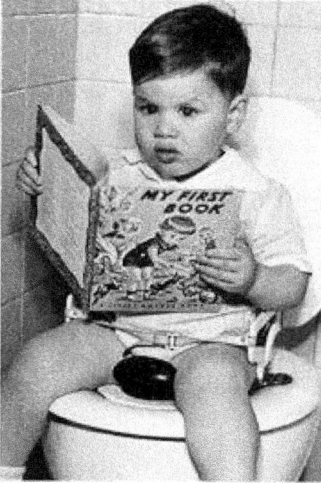

My parents were both avid, addictive readers. They'd read anything, anytime, anywhere. They often referred to our bathroom as "the library" (or the "throne room"). I was affected by their genes and their examples.

I started reading at an early age. As the photo shows, I also read in the bathroom. I have no idea why I was wearing a diaper while on the toilet, but it apparently did not limit my enjoyment of books.

As a young child with an early bedtime, I read books under my blanket with a flashlight. When my technical talent grew, I got creative. I attached a tennis ball to a string and attached the other end to the pull chain that activated my closet light. If I heard Mom or Dad approaching, I'd yank the string to kill the light and toss the ball and string into the closet—and feigned sleep.

Later, and to this day, I eagerly look for and digest text in almost any form. I enthusiastically read books, magazines, newspapers, web pages, signs, coupons, political mailings and even product labels and cereal boxes.

I've subscribed to lots of "trade magazines" that had *nothing* to do with my business, such as publications for sellers of health foods, furniture, pizza and air compressors. I learned that I could learn something useful from *anything* I read, even if the subject seemed to be absolutely irrelevant. All knowledge has value, but it can take years for the value to become apparent.

I may have picked up my irrelevant reading habit from **Bud Marcus**, my father. Years ago, he was able to get a free picture frame with a free subscription to a pair of farm magazines. I eagerly read every issue of *Poultry Journal* and *Chicken Gazette* that appeared in our mailbox and learned much more than I needed to know about egg incubators and rooster castration!

The phrase "avid reader" could have been invented for **Rita Jacobs Marcus**, my mother. Despite needing time to go to graduate school, teach, be active in community affairs and be mother and wife, Mom seemed to devour a book each day. I remember making many trips to the public library with her, and to a drug store to rent scarce new books; and she influenced me to read and to write.

Thanks, Mom.

People start to read at different ages and for different reasons and with different talents.

My nephew **Joe** was initially motivated by searching through *TV Guide* for wrestling broadcasts. When we were in my car, he eagerly studied store signage. At appropriate times he'd yell, "*Toys R Us, Uncle Michael, Toys R Us!*"

Joe's sister **Allison** was an autodidactic (self-taught) reader. As soon as she learned the sounds associated with each letter of the alphabet, she figured out how to read. When she was just a few years old, she'd perch on my shoulders and read the *New York Times* with me. I think that when Allison started kindergarten, she was reading on a third-grade level. In high school she worked in the local library.

Younger sister **Michelle** is supersmart like her siblings and is now an attorney. She revealed that she did not become a reader until she was in first grade. She said her father Robbie (my wife's brother), had lots of books and often told stories to his children. That's important, but I don't remember *my* folks ever telling stories or reading to me. Michelle told me that her father wanted his kids to stay sharp over the summers. "He worried that we lost too much being out of school, so he encouraged us to read during the summers by paying us $5 for each book. The books had to have 150 pages or more and we had to give a good summary of the book to him. He recently made the same offer to his grandsons."

Speaking of siblings:

o After retiring from teaching, my sister **Meryl** often visited the elementary school we both attended, to read to the kids.

o When our younger brother **Marshall** started to read books, he was initially confused by the "headers" on the tops of the pages, which usually displayed the title of the book and the title of the chapter. He thought that all of the left-hand pages were one story, and the right-hand pages were another story. Apparently, he wasn't bothered by pages that ended mid-sentence, and he read all of the lefties, and then all of the righties. I straightened him out.

Can dogs read?

Our golden retriever **Hunter J. Marcus** was very smart. He understood spoken words and silent gestures. In this photo he seems to be reading the *Times* upside-down, but he wasn't.

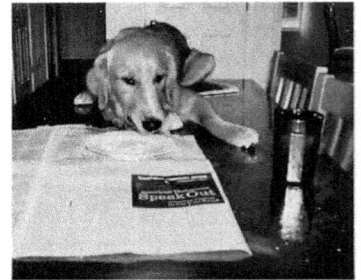

My own reading history has an unusual twist.

In high school, tests routinely showed that I was in the "99th percentile" for reading speed, comprehension and retention. Somehow, despite my superstar reading status, in September of 1963, I inexplicably found myself in a *special education remedial reading class* surrounded by kids who could be charitably described as "slow learners."

This class made the **Sweat Hogs** on *Welcome Back, Kotter* seem like Rhodes Scholars.

I knew there was a mistake, and as soon as the teacher came in, I went to his desk to attempt to arrange for my prompt exit. But, before I could speak, the teacher held up his hand between his face and mine and commanded me to "**shut the fuck up and sit the fuck down.**"

Our relationship got worse after that.

The first classroom assignment was intended to assess our degree of reading retardation. The teacher distributed neatly printed pages, bearing four simple paragraphs with short words in large type.

It looked more like an eye chart than literature.

We were instructed to read the paragraphs, and then turn over the paper and answer the questions on the back of the page. Once we started writing our answers, we were not supposed to turn the page over again to the front.

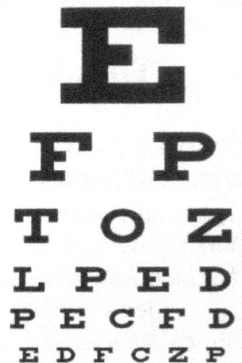

The stories were only slightly more complex than the "Oh, Sally, see Dick" adventures we read in first grade. I finished the assignment in approximately 14 seconds and then noticed that my classmates were laboriously sounding out each syl-la-ble.

The teacher noticed that I had stopped reading, and said, "What's the matter, dumb ass? Too tough for you?"

I meekly said that I had finished the test.

But he refused to believe me. Eventually, he looked at my paper and saw that I had answered the questions—and answered them all correctly.

At this point, most of the kids had flipped over their papers, and were trying to copy answers from each other.

Their overt and clumsy cheating led our teacher to the only logical conclusion: I must have *stolen* a teacher's copy of the test and copied the answers onto my paper.

I was escorted to the principal's office, and then I eventually got to see my guidance counselor, and she uncovered a scheduling error. I was given three free periods a week to swim or hang around the library, and someone else got a chance to "shut the fuck up and sit the fuck down."

Sadly, the ability to read and the affection for reading often fade.

Both of my parents stopped reading as death approached, with severe dementia. I sure hope dementia is not my destiny.

And, about "the book"

While in college in Bethlehem, Pennsylvania, I rented a room from a local family. The Websters had two pieces of 'literature' in their home. One was the local newspaper. The other—which all three called THE BOOK—was not the *Holy Bible*. It was *TV Guide*.

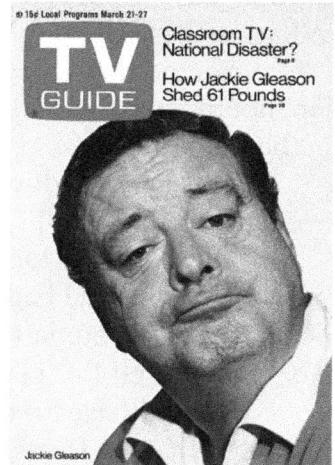

Chapter 25
Does a miscarriage count as a dead child?

And: Why a dog can be better than a human child.
Who will visit the nursing home?

Once a pregnancy is confirmed, the future parents—and the extended family and community—focus on the future delivery.

Paint colors or wallpaper are picked out. Names are evaluated. Toys and clothes are accumulated. Jokes are told about preschools and colleges.

And then, a few months early, the doctor delivers a blood clot instead of a child. It's flushed or bagged and burned. There is not even enough to "deserve" a funeral and a gravestone.

After, there are tears, testing and finger-pointing. Is it her fault or his fault or their fault? Could she have done something differently to "hold onto" the baby? What do they tell people?

Should they try again? How many times should they try again? Sex becomes a job, not romance, when scheduled with a calendar and thermometer? ("I'm really not in the mood but we have to do it today.")

What about adoption? Are they bad people if they don't want to adopt? Heck, even gay couples adopt.

What are the long-term effects of childlessness?

My wife and I had two misses. I sometimes feel that by not reproducing, by not being part of the human continuum, I've never really grown up and I became *my own kid*. I buy myself lots of big boy's toys.

We did have a wonderful and loving golden retriever. I scooped up dog shit instead of paying for weddings and college.

We have wonderful nieces and nephews, but as we get older, we wonder who will be available to wipe up our drool when we're in the nursing home. I paid for a year of college for one nephew and told him that he owes me a year of drool-wiping. He thought I was joking. I smiled when I said it, but I wasn't joking.

I'm sorry if this depresses anyone, but maybe it will provide a push for someone to write a book about men and miscarriages.

I don't think I can do it.

Chapter 26
Avoiding idiocy at funerals

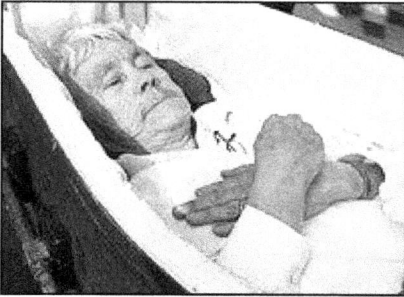

When a Jewish person dies, the funeral is scheduled very quickly—often the next day if family members can arrive quickly enough.

There is no wake, viewing or visitation spread over several days before interment.

The coffin is CLOSED, with no need for fine clothes and bling, and makeup or posthumous plastic surgery. The lasting memories of friends and family can be of a person—not of a corpse.

I'm Jewish but have attended a few non-Jewish funerals. People approach and study the tarted-up corpse (that may be wearing clothes that would never have been selected or tolerated in life, and perhaps with hair parted improperly, dirty eyeglasses, or some other failure in "preparation"). The DB (dead body) usually looks more like a manikin than a person, and much less lifelike than a DB provided by a prop house for *Law & Order*.

Inevitably, there will discussion of the DB's appearance, and some idiot will remark that "Uncle Willy sure looks fine."

It has taken me great restraint to not respond, "You fucking idiot! Your uncle is as DEAD as a damn lamb chop in a case at the supermarket. Willy is now a piece of meat!" What the hell does it matter what a piece of meat looks like—if you are not considering buying and eating it?

I've never said it in person, but I have to say it here.

Keep the box *closed*. It will save some money, avoid some tears, and avoid some idiocy.

[The photo shows a LIVE person at a protest about health services, from BBC.]

Chapter 27
My Genealogy

I can't claim that I know my genealogy (family history) going back multiple millennia, or to the Mayflower's reaching Cape Cod in 1620. We are much more recent arrivals to the USA.

Our family name has been **Marcus** only since the early 20th century. It used to start with "Dzm" and end with "ski" and had many more consonants than vowels.

The Marcus name sounds Roman (more about the name in another chapter), but the paternal side of my family originated not in Rome but nearly 1,000 miles northeast in *Sopotskin*. Or Sopotkin, Sopochkinye, Sopokotzky, Sopockinski, Sopochani or any of many name variations.

Sopotskin was in an area called *Suwalki Guberniya*. "Guberniya" is a Russian word that means "governorate." It's similar to an American state. In 1897, the population was 52% Lithuanian, 23% Polish, 10% Jewish, and there were smaller percentages of other ethnic groups.

Sopotskin's location changed a lot, although the town didn't physically move. Since 1991, it's been in Belarus, near the borders with Poland and Lithuania. When my paternal grandfather's family left town, Sopotskin was in Poland.

It's also been in Lithuania, the Belarusian People's Republic, White Russia, the Byelorussian Soviet Socialist Republic, the Lithuanian-Byelorussian Soviet Socialist Republic and the Union of Soviet Socialist Republics. It depended on who had the most powerful army and made the map.

When **Grandpa Walter Marcus** (born in 1896) was in grade school in Poland, there was a picture of **Russian Czar Nicholas II** on the wall. Walter's father, **Isaac**, was in the leather business, supplying the Czar through Christian intermediaries because the Czar would not do business with Jews. Sopotskin was becoming a lousy place for Jews to live, so Isaac moved the family to the U.S. in 1906 and chose our fine American-Roman name.

The Czar had a Russian-Roman name: Romanov. **Nicholas Romanov** abdicated in 1917 at the start of the Bolshevik (Communist) Revolution and was shot in 1918.

The killing was ordered by **Vladimir Lenin** and **Yakov Sverdlov**. Yak was Jewish. Vlad had a Jewish grandfather. Russian antisemites *play down* the Jewish origins of Communism. American antisemites *play it up*. Antisemites also complain about Jewish capitalists. Our tribe gets blamed for *everything*—except for Jesus. It seems very strange that so many Christian antisemites think God had a Jewish son and pray to him. No Christian antisemite calls Jesus a "kike."

Romanov was busy. He hurt lots of Jews and non-Jews. His nickname was *Bloody Nicholas*. His official titles were Emperor and Autocrat of All the Russias, King of Poland, and Grand Duke of Finland. Bloody Nick is now the Russian Orthodox "Saint Nicholas the Passion Bearer."

Walter's wife, my **Grandma "Gee"** (**Genevieve**, actually) was, like **Bruce Springsteen**, born in the USA—but on Long Island, not in New Jersey. I don't know much about her history, but she was born in 1898, her maiden name was **Goldstein** and she had several sisters. When she and

Walter met, they were approximately the same height (about five feet tall). According to family lore, Walter went into the army, and when he returned, Grandma had become *much taller*. They reminded people of *Mutt & Jeff* in the comics. Walter drove cars with blocks on the pedals to help him reach them. Grandma seemed like a giant, but her tall genes did not reach future generations.

Also, according to family lore, Grandma Gee was very ill when she gave birth to her second son, my **Uncle Arnie**. She was diagnosed with a heart defect and warned that having sex could kill her! Walter used this as an excuse for decades of adultery. He said he fooled around "to save Grandma's life" and his fooling around was not a secret. Once a neighbor told Grandma that she had seen Walter with a beautiful woman. Grandma replied, "well, I wouldn't expect him to be with an *ugly* woman!"

Walter had a lengthy relationship with a woman, probably his secretary. She sometimes served as his driver, probably without those booster pedals. One time the illicit couple visited our family in New Haven. My mother was really pissed off at the public display of philandering.

Walter owned a successful shirt business, called "**Yorkshire**," the source of his nickname "**Yorky**." Actually, his birth name was "**Velvel**," later Americanized to "Walter." He was a great salesman, selling high-class shirts to prestigious menswear stores throughout the eastern United States. He spread his seed as well as his shirts, and allegedly there are men who look like me in Pennsylvania and Florida.

I spent a few vacations in Brooklyn and sometimes went to work with Grandpa. He took me to nice restaurants and even to a bar for a non-alcoholic drink with lots of cherries. But I was expected to *work* for the nourishment, even during vacations! He had me assemble shirt boxes and even use an industrial sewing machine to attach labels to shirts. I wonder if that was legal.

As the first grandchild I had some special status. Grandpa Walter got me custom-made shirts to wear for my bar mitzvah in 1959. None of my friends had custom shirts.

Walter and Gee were "snowbirds," with a nice apartment in Miami Beach, where Walter had some shirt customers. I knew that he had hosted my cousins and brother for vacations, and wife Marilyn and I were excited when he finally invited us. Walter viewed himself as the unofficial mayor of Miami Beach. He knew *everyone* (and allegedly had a secret son there—my unknown uncle). He took us to fancy restaurants and introduced us to many of his pals.

Apparently, he bragged about my tech talent. One day he took me to a menswear store where he had arranged for me to replace some faulty fluorescent-light fixtures. Vacation? Hah!

The **Sagamore** hotel where we stayed had a great location, right on the beach and near the famous and delicious **Wolfie's Deli**. The hotel had the classic Miami Beach "art deco style" but its glamor had ended decades earlier.

Our room was plain and tiny and hot. Instead of genuine air conditioning there was a small opening in one wall that periodically emitted small puffs of air. Marilyn and I didn't complain or ask for a better room. After all, it was a freebie—we thought. At checkout time we were shocked to get a *bill*. We surmised that Walter was punishing us for an inadequate tip to a cabana boy. Apparently, he had spies watching over us!

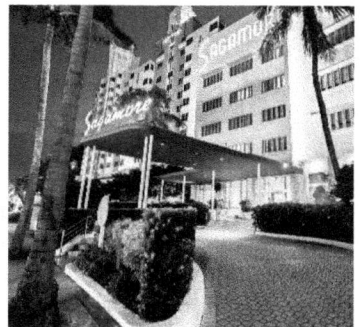

Late in life, Grandpa sold his company to a competitor and went to work for them. When he was forced to retire, he had nothing to do. Walter had no hobbies and no diversions other than sex. He was horny 'til the end, even paying for genital manipulation in his nursing home.

Walter was an expert observer and perceptive analyzer of people, and a *very* funny guy. When he was asked "How are you?" by people who definitely didn't care and didn't even listen to his answer, he used to say, "Sick in bed, thank you." They never noticed. Try it yourself. It's *really* funny.

One of his other classic comedy bits was to ask someone about the weather, while indoors. If the reply was, "it's nice out," Grandpa would quickly respond, "so take it out."

One time Walter had a lapse in perception. I drove to his apartment in Brooklyn to take him and Grandma Gee to visit my folks in New Haven. As we drove along Ocean Parkway, I saw him in the rearview mirror, looking panicky. He yelled at me to "SLOW DOWN." I was not driving too fast. Grandpa saw the digital display on the radio, which was playing WCBS ("88"). He thought that the radio was the speedometer, and my speed was 88!

I never told this to anyone before, but I'll tell you a family secret. Grandpa Walter once said this about his sons: "Arnie is nicer." That may be right, but since I didn't spend much time with my Uncle Arnie, I can't agree or disagree—but he was always nice to me. Like Grandpa and my father, Arnie could be a funny father.

My father was frequently sarcastic, and his humor could be cruel, especially to my mother. I wondered why Mom did not divorce him. She sometimes called my father "**Little Hitler**." Other nicknames were "**The Human Garbage Disposal**," and, when darkly tanned from golf or fishing trips, "**Little Black Marcus**." (That's derived from the *Little Black Sambo* book.)

Sadly, I suppose I thought my father's personality was OK and normal. I inherited some of Pop's worse traits and could be nasty to my wife.

Neumann Jacobs (the source of my middle name, **Neuman**) was born in Germany and came to the United States around 1870. His son, **Julius Jacobs**, my mother's father, later renamed **Jay**, was born in upstate New York in 1896 (the same year Grandpa Walter was born in Sopotskin). Jay married my grandmother **Adele, ("Grandma Del")** Schwartz, who was born in 1900. As a little kid, Grandma Del sometimes affectionately called me "Noony," derived from my middle name. I loved her but hated the nickname (more elsewhere).

Grandma Del was older than sister **Dorraine** and brother **Milton**. I don't think I ever met Milton, but our family visited "Aunt Dorraine" in Long Beach, California when we drove cross-country in 1961. She lived in an apartment building near the Pacific Ocean shore, along with other Navy wives who fruitlessly waited for their husbands to come home from World War II in the Pacific. I don't remember much about her, other than that she frequently sat on tissue paper, which she pronounced, "tiss-yoo." My sister and I referred to her as "**Aunt Tissyoo**."

Grandma's father, **Harry Schwartz**, was an "ambulance chaser" who tried to get clients for local lawyers, and an unsuccessful gambler. He sometimes could not afford to pay the family's tiny rent. They were evicted and their furniture was put on the street in **Hell's Kitchen**.

Although the family was Jewish, young Grandma went to a local church for piano lessons. She told me that once she arrived early for her lesson and saw a priest and nun kissing!

Now that I've typed this chapter, for the first time I've realized that my lineage is mostly Germanic. Maybe that explains why I get *so pissed off* at people who are always late, like my Italo-Czech-Jewish wife. I also get pissed off at myself when I'm late.

I was Grandma Del's first grandson, and she told me I was her favorite grandchild. Maybe she told my siblings and cousins the same thing. She was my favorite grandparent. I saw her more often than the other elders and she spoiled me and was sometimes *too* affectionate. I remember sitting in the back seat of a car and she fondled my fingers. Yuck. It was weird and creepy and bothered me. It seemed to go beyond a normal grandmotherly gesture, but I don't remember if I asked her to stop.

A great many years later, there was a reprise after both my grandfather and her later boyfriend had died. Whenever I visited her, she'd kiss me on my lips. My special status with Grandma Del lasted until she died.

Once when I was a little kid in the Bronx, I spoke to Grandma on the phone. Of course, she asked how I was. I responded that I was "all right now." That was a *big* mistake. Mom told me that Grandma was a "big worrier" and that I should *never* reveal any illness.

Later, when I was in college, I called her to have the usual grandmother/grandson chat. I said, "Hi, Grandma," and asked how she was. She told me about a few aches and asked how I was. She asked about my folks, my brother and my sister. I asked about some relatives. She asked about school. I asked about her neighbors. She asked me about Uncle Steve and Aunt Judy.

I said, "Who?"

She repeated, "Uncle Steve and Aunt Judy."

I said, "I don't have an Uncle Steve or Aunt Judy. I must have called the wrong grandma." She said, "That's OK. I enjoyed our talk. Please call again. My own grandson never calls."

Although Grandma was generous to her grandchildren, as a victim of childhood eviction and survivor of the Great Depression, she remained *extremely frugal*. During the Depression she sometimes gave Grandpa Jay after-work snacks of saltines and water. To save money, sometimes Grandma's sole "nourishment" was coffee. I once went shopping with her in a Woolworth's "five-and-dime." She needed two ballpoint pen refills, priced at a dime each. Grandma explained that if she bought two at once, the total price would come to 20 cents, and she'd have to pay a penny tax. But if she made two separate ten-cent purchases, there would be *no sale tax*.

Grandpa's first optometry office was in their Bronx apartment, and his daughters were not allowed to play when patients were present. Later, when Grampy could afford a separate office, he had a little workshop where he prepared eyeglasses. It was filled with terrific tools and became my "laboratory" during school vacations when my parents were in Florida.

Grandma Del went to secretarial school and worked as a secretary for Grandpa Jay after they married. I don't remember them being obviously affectionate, but she was a devoted wife and took pride in caring for his business shirts. A favorite color was light pink.

When they lived in the Bronx they slept in twin beds, like Lucy and Ricky Ricardo on TV's *I Love Lucy*. After Grandpa died, Grandma moved to an adult condominium community in Delray Beach, Florida. There she had a double bed, which she shared with Irish-American Catholic boyfriend, **Michael Killeen**. He wanted to marry her, he made her happy, but she said she'd prefer to marry a younger and healthier man.

Grandma was far from the "picture of health." She had a bad leg (as did Mr. Killeen) and badly twisted toes. Despite these infirmities, she climbed up high in the **Statue of Liberty** with me.

Grandma Del was an excellent wheeler-dealer. She once sold an old piece of furniture for the same price she had paid for it years earlier. It was in perfect condition, of course.

Grandma Del could be a money-maker. During the Depression she helped support her family by selling beautiful items she had crocheted or embroidered, and she was even a "wet nurse" (although I don't know if she got paid). In later years she worked for **Macy's** (and was paid to march in the Macy's Thanksgiving Day Parade), and in the office of a restaurant chain.

Grandma Del was an early recycler, even *ironing used wrapping paper* to remove the creases for reuse. She horded shopping bags and refused to pay a few bucks extra rent to have a modern refrigerator. Her vintage fridge often contained delicious cherry Valentine's Day hearts for the grandchildren. When walking from her apartment to the elevator, she'd always enter the tiny incinerator room. She didn't always have refuse to throw out, but she always looked at what "treasures" her neighbors might have left on the floor for others.

Grandma Del was an excellent cook, and my favorite meal was her pot roast. Sadly, she did not pass the secret recipe to my mother, but my wife Marilyn came close to duplicating it.

Grandma Del was immaculate. Her kitchen floor was *really* clean enough to eat off. But her apartment showed exposed electrical cords that I would've found a way to conceal. Later in life she was less fastidious. I remember her baking a delicious chocolate cake for me, but it contained little bits of aluminum foil. It looked pretty—but was hard to digest.

Grandma "Gee" and Grandpa Walter Marcus often took me to nice restaurants, both in Miami Beach and Brooklyn. Grandpa called Italian restaurants the *luksch* (Yiddish for "noodle"). I remember going to a Brooklyn pizzeria. I was shocked that the place did not offer meatball as a topping, which was common on New Haven's "ah-beetz." The cook made me a meatball-topped pie as a special favor for Grandpa, and it was later added to the menu. I guess I was the "Johnny Appleseed" for meatball pizza. My father had a similar role, introducing the egg cream to New Haven.

I never liked Grandma Gee's cooking. One of her specialties was roast duck, which I despised. **Cousin Jill Marcus Lawther** said she "really enjoyed" Grandma's flanken (short ribs). I don't think I ever tasted it.

Jill's mother, my **Aunt Bea**, cooked spectacular scrambled eggs, with a secret ingredient she wisely refused to reveal to me. I think it was cottage cheese, which I would normally cross the street to avoid.

[Egg cream photo from Max Falkowitz. Thanks!]

A brochure promoting
my first Bronx home

200
East 205th
Street

And the real thing

Chapter 28
My mommy

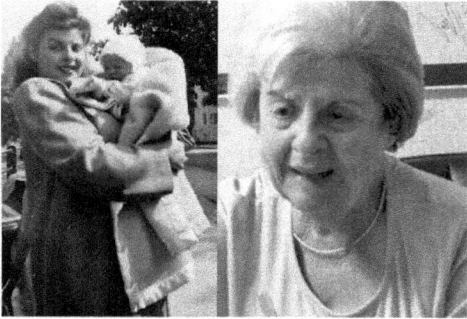

My mother, **Rita Jacobs Marcus**, died in 2015. She was 93 years old.

I'm the oldest of three siblings, and was "the bad kid," often getting in trouble, and the "under-achiever" who disappointed my parents.

Mom and Dad were New Yorkers who went to high schools for very smart kids. Mom (born in the Bronx) went to **Hunter High School**, Dad (Brooklyn-bred) went to **Townsend Harris**. Later, Mom went to **Hunter College**, Dad to **City College**. More years later, Mom earned a master's degree and sixth-year certificate.

While I was in high school, Mom and I attended *Sunrise Semester* on television at 6 AM. She got academic credit. I did it for joy. I got special permission to sit with her in a class on teaching the "new math" that she needed for her master's degree at **Southern Connecticut State College** (now "University").

The degree also required a Phys-ed class. One hot summer in the 60s my perennially overweight mother played touch football with a class of super-fit male Viet Nam vets. She was a good sport, even about sports. Not me. In intramural softball, when asked what position I wanted to play, I'd ask to be "left-out."

Mom never learned to type but won a penmanship award and got special permission to submit her master's thesis in longhand. My own writing is barely legible—even to me.

Mom was always reading. She seemed to read every new bestseller and was in a book discussion group in her late 80s. I ignore fiction.

My parents did a lot of travelling, both in the USA and in Europe. Our family drove cross-country in 1961, and we often took Sunday drives. However, sometimes Mom preferred to lie on her bed with a book than to get into the car with the family. I remember Mom saying to Dad: "You want to go for a ride, *you* go for a ride."

Mom never drove a car while we lived in New York, but she did get her license shortly after we moved to New Haven in 1952. I won't say that my father was a sexist, but he drove Chryslers and Mom drove less expensive Plymouths.

She was a fine driver, and very protective. I remember that if she was driving and I was in the right-front seat, she'd always put her right arm in front of me if we were going to make a sudden stop. I learned that and did the same for my dog when he was in the front. (My wife usually sat in the back.)

Mom and I, like Bill and Ted, had an *excellent adventure* during the summer between my junior and senior years in high school. We visited several colleges—even as far away as Pittsburgh. I did not have my license at the time, even though I was old enough, so Mom drove us.

Later on, I did get my license, and sometimes used Mom's car without authorization. I once made a minor miscalculation while trying to get her Plymouth out of the garage and bumped into the side of the garage. The damage to the fender and the wall was minor, but visible. Since my parents couldn't imagine that I had driven the car, my father blamed my mother for the damage, and she accepted responsibility. Sorry, Mom. Sorry, Dad. Sorry, Plymouth.

Mom had a strong sense of outrage against social injustice and was in the civil rights movement in New Haven. She gave money to important causes.

She was a great planner and, with Dad, a firm believer that "if you're not ten minutes early, you're late." Greeting cards were signed and put in stamped, addressed envelopes a week before they had to be mailed. I've always been a procrastinator. ("Don't put off 'til tomorrow, what you can put of 'til the day after tomorrow" is one of my mottos.)

Dad was a great joke-teller and prankster. Mom was more stoic, "not the funny parent."

Mom was active in various Jewish organizations, and an officeholder. Our home was not kosher. Mom taught her children that "religion is for the brain, not the belly."

Mom was a great baker and "company cook"—but family meals were often disappointing. I cook and reheat, but don't bake.

When I was in elementary school, I had a traditional stay-at-home mother who cooked lunch on school days. Later, Mom became a teacher, and babybro Marshall went to restaurants for lunch on school days.

The lunches served in our high school cafeteria cost us 35 cents a day. And as you might expect of food supplied by the lowest bidder, it usually sucked.

As an alternative, sometimes we'd have bags of mommy food, or go to nearby Chuck's or Al's restaurants after school. Sometimes we'd go to one of the kids' houses and raid the fridge.

My mother was getting pissed off about the fridge raids. She didn't mind us eating the leftovers, but she didn't like the mess we usually left on the stove and in the sink. Mom gave me specific instructions to terminate the after-school cooking.

One day some friends were at my house, and, of course, we were hungry. I didn't expect my mother to get home for a couple of hours, so I thought we could safely reheat some spaghetti, eat it and clean up any trace of it before she came home.

Unfortunately, Mom's plans changed, and she walked in while the pot of pasta and sauce was still on the stove. She got REALLY pissed off. She grabbed the pot and flung it at us.

Mom was no Tom Seaver, Cy Young or Sandy Koufax. She'd never be a major league pitcher. She missed us, and the spaghetti hit the ceiling. The individual noodles hung like stalactites on the ceiling of a damp limestone cave.

Every so often a noodle would wriggle out of its saucy adhesive and go "bloop" and hit the floor. Mom didn't laugh. We did.

She had multiple injuries over the years, with so many parts replacements that I referred to her as "Bionic Rita." Her internal pieces of stainless steel set off the terrorist alarms at airport gates. Despite physical limitations, she once toured Europe in a wheelchair.

My mother had a powerful brain, but her body suffered greatly over the years. She even had a broken neck. She fell from her bed (or maybe her wheelchair) and broke a leg. Mom had many falls in her last decade and had not been able to stand up for several years. One time she slipped in her bathroom and spent the night on the bathroom floor because she couldn't get to the emergency pendant that she had left on the nearby night table.

Mom knit, crocheted and made nice ceramic tchotchkes after retirement. At the end she couldn't hold a fork or spoon or release her grip from a handkerchief without assistance.

(OK, it's time for a humorous interlude: Mom once broke a toe by kicking my brother Marshall in the ass.)

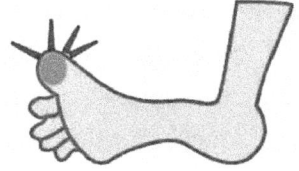

My father's last year was spent in a nursing home in Florida and Mom drove to see him almost every day. Determined to be a loving, supportive wife despite her own physical limitations, Mom walked across a huge parking lot—with a walker—to get into the building.

Mom wrote lots of letters and she loved to talk, in-person or on the phone. There were times when she paid the phone bill partly by check and partly with cash—so Dad would not see the canceled check and realize how much she was spending to call from New Haven to New York. (Update: my bro-in-law Alan Alpert insists that my father *did* know.)

In her last years, Mom's communicating, and her brilliance, slipped away. She stopped writing and reading. I visited her in her nursing home and in a common-but-sad role reversal, I fed her chunks of fruit. She could not stand, but she had a strong bite, and her eyes sparkled while she chewed pineapple and melon.

When she was more lucid (even a few months earlier), she sometimes articulately described hallucinations, such as that my father climbed out of his grave and married another woman. She told of the three mechanics who were working in her bedroom and left through the back door (there were no mechanics and no back door), and she insisted that her name was written on the ceiling above her bed. She also told me that a noisy family moved into her guest room.

Mom often substituted words: almost any noun for another one, or used a general term like "device" for "seatbelt" or "clock." Other times the substitution made no sense, like "marshmallow" for "checkbook." Sometimes she'd mix baby-talk with substitution, like "toidy sheets" for "toilet paper." She sometimes merely substituted a word that was the right part of speech, but made no sense, like "produce" for "bank check" and "poster" for something I never figured out. Some sentences were complete mysteries. At other times, Mom's conversations seemed normal.

Mom often answered the phone upside-down and yelled, and neglected to hang up.

I once noticed that Mom had exchanged eyeglasses with another resident of the nursing home. Neither woman noticed. More recently she lost a lens from her glasses—but the lens was from in front of her blind eye. She no longer read, so the glasses were put away.

She shared a room with a slightly older old lady. They had two TVs, a few feet apart. Sometimes they silently displayed two different programs, but neither woman seemed to notice.

Those were the good old days.

Near the end, Mom did not recognize her children or grandchildren.

She said almost nothing. Her favorite word was "no"—even if she meant "yes." But Mom could be responsive even without words.

One time I showed my mother her wedding picture. I pointed to my father and asked if she knew him. She smiled.

I asked her if she ever had sex with him (probably the first time I ever mentioned sex to Mom). Her smile got bigger, and her eyes sparkled brightly.

I asked her if the sex was fun and she started giggling.

That was a good sign.

She smiled a lot, watched television, listened to conversations intently, and had occasional moments of surprising lucidity. She could sometimes fill in words from old songs and seemed happy despite her limitations.

While I did not inherit Mom's seriousness, her handwriting, her academic achievement, baking ability or her sportsmanship; I did get some of her intelligence, her drive for fairness, her love of reading, her love of learning, her love of travel, her hatred of cooked carrots, her ability to make things by hand, and her ability to function with little sleep. I started typing this at 3:45 AM. Mom taught me that much could be accomplished while others are still asleep.

I posted this on Facebook in 2013:

My mother is almost 91.

We visited her in the nursing home today. Our dog Hunter helped pull her wheelchair and did tricks. Wife Marilyn fed her an eggplant hero. I held her glass of ginger ale. Mom still can slurp and chew very well, but no sentences came out of her mouth.

We told her things and asked her questions (e.g., do you remember our first apartment in New York, do your feet hurt?). I counted "no" 21 times and "yes" just twice. That's all she said. Just a few years ago Mom was brilliant, articulate, aware, well-read, interested in politics and re-membered everything back to around age-three. Now she's more like a two-year-old with minimal memory.

Mom doesn't complain of pain, smiles at appropriate moments, stares at me, enjoys food and TV. I wonder what she thinks of her situation—*if* she thinks of her situation.

I hope this is not a preview of me.

Years ago, Mom and I were both "walking wounded."

(Back then, I was much bigger and had dark hair. I lost nearly 150 pounds since the photo was taken. It was like losing another person who was living under my skin, clinging to my bones and sharing my organs.)

Chapter 29
Buddy Marcus was not my buddy until late in life

My father, Bertram "Buddy" (or "Budd," or most often "Bud") Marcus, was a very smart man, a wise man and often a wise guy. He died in 2009 at the age of 87, and I miss him every day. When I look in a mirror, if I ignore my beard, I see Pop's face looking back at me.

Pop skipped at least one year of school and graduated from college with honors when he was just 19. I'm 78 and am still an undergrad.

He taught at a college and was a successful and innovative businessman, a builder, a singer, a techie, a fisherman, an athlete, a polyglot, a gourmand, an avid reader, a great storyteller and more.

Pop taught me some valuable lessons:

1) If you act like you have authority, you *have* authority. And most people would rather accept authority than challenge it.
2) If you own or manage a retail store, try to hire people who previously owned successful businesses. They are less likely to waste money by writing phone numbers on expensive gift boxes instead of using scrap paper.
3) In the winter, keep plenty of gas in your car's gas tank, in case you get stuck in the snow and need to run the engine to provide heat.
4) It's just as easy to fall in love with a rich person as a poor person. In fact, it's easier.
5) Never go to a restaurant until it's been open for at least 30 days. Let the chef make mistakes with someone else's stomach.
6) Never use more than four squares of toilet paper at a time. (I often disobey this.)
7) If you have multiple appointments scheduled on one day, and you're running late for the next one, cancel and re-schedule it—rather than change all the other appointment times.
8) Although I never heard my father say "think outside the box," he was often an unorthodox problem solver. Once, a big stuffed teddy bear was in high demand, but a truckers' strike halted deliveries. Pop contacted the manufacturer. Bears were transported to a bus terminal and got tickets to *ride on seats in a Greyhound bus* to New Haven.
9) The toy departments in my father's stores normally charged just 81 cents each for popular toys that other stores sold for 99 cents. To make extra "margin" at the low price, Pop created a wholesale distribution company at home called the **Marshall Novelty Company** (named after my brother). Soon, our garage was filled with toys, allowing my father's stores to make a decent profit at 81 cents.

10) Pop sold **Trimfit**-brand nylon socks with a *lifetime guaranty*, provided by the store—not the maker. If a customer returned an old worn-out sock, my father was *thrilled* to replace it, knowing that the shopper would tell her friends about the wonderful store.

11) Most stores restricted the use of their restrooms to customers, only. Pop would let *anyone* use the john. The risk of vandalism or theft of toilet paper was small, and people might buy something after using the facilities.

12) In stores, salespeople often approached prospective customers and asked "May I help you?" That question can easily be answered with "No." Dad taught his salespeople to engage the public with a friendly introduction. If I said to a visitor, "Hi, my name is Michael," I usually learned the name of the person, had a pleasant conversation, and made a sale.

One time I asked Pop if he thought a new business idea that I was considering would be successful. He said he did not know what would happen in the future, but he *did* know that if I didn't try out my idea, for the rest of my life I'd wonder what could have been. My father said **Just Do It** before **Nike** said it. They're both right.

I felt sorry for Pop when he taught me the facts of life. My old man was obviously and uncharacteristically nervous. He badly messed up my sex lesson.

He skipped the fun part.

He never told me how the "pollen" got from the daddy to the mommy. I first thought it flew through the air and I couldn't figure out how it reached the right mommy. I eventually figured it out.

One of Dad's best jokes involved a transaction between a prostitute and the great Yiddish actor **Boris Tomaschevsky** of the famed **Second Avenue Theater** in Manhattan.

After their physical encounter, the beautiful young woman asked Boris for her money, but he gave her a ticket to see his show.

She was greatly upset and said, "But Mr. Tomaschevsky, I need money to buy *bread*.

He responded, "I am the great Tomaschevsky, star of the Second Avenue Thee-a-ter.

I am an actor.

I pay with tickets.

If you need bread, *fuck a baker*."

This reminds me of a line frequently attributed to Marie-Antoinette (1755-1793 CE, queen and bride of France's King Louis XVI). In the late 18th century, when told that her subjects had no bread, Marie allegedly responded, "*Qu'ils mangent de la brioche*" ("Let them eat cake"). With that heartless remark, the queen became hated and spurred the French revolution that led to her beheading with a *guillotine*.

Dad spent the end of his life in a nursing home in Florida, where he sadly declined from brilliance to dementia.

Some years ago, he was anticipating his last day.

Pop said that he wanted to get drunk on **Canadian Club**, smoke a **Garcia y Vega** cigar, and make a tape recording to be played at his funeral.

I don't know if he wanted to reveal a secret or tell people off. Maybe he just wanted to sing some songs and tell some jokes to ensure that we would be properly entertained.

I don't think he ever made the recording.

My father had a very full life. It was so full, in fact, that after 87 years, Pop had done all that he had wanted to do. He had checked off every item on his "Honey Do" list and had simply run out of things to look forward to.

He had seen it all, done it all, heard it all and read it all. He probably even ate it all.

Pop was tired, worn down and worn out. Life was seldom fun anymore, and he frequently upset those of us who loved him, by telling us that he had lived long enough. His greatest pleasures seemed to be singing to the nurses, and farting. He stopped using his hearing aid and once nearly fell out of bed when he used the remote control for the bed instead of the remote for his TV.

It was always hard to argue with Dad about anything, and extremely hard to win.

When I last visited my father, he asked what day it was. I said it was Saturday. Dad responded that Sunday would be a nice day to die. He asked me to hire a hitman to shoot him. I couldn't argue with that. I couldn't even find words to say to him.

I left the nursing home bewildered, frustrated and in a daze. I got into my car and just drove. I didn't know if I was heading for the Gulf of Mexico or the Atlantic Ocean or Key West or New York. I just *drove*. Eventually I ended up at my Aunt Fan's home, and just sat on her patio until I regained my composure.

We could not convince Dad to hang on a while longer. A brand-new pill or a new injection or new exercise wouldn't help. There was no cure for my father's feeling that "enough is enough."

In his jokes, Dad frequently spoke of "taking a dirt nap." And he did that.

For my first few years I was Buddy Marcus's only kid, and despite his long hours at work I got plenty of attention. Dad wheeled me all over the Bronx in a huge and heavy baby carriage.

We'd hang out on an overpass to watch trains pass under us. He'd stop at a barber shop and schmooze in Italian, or talk Greek to the owner of a luncheonette, or tell jokes in Yiddish to pals and to strangers.

Starting when I was three years old, we'd schlep from the Bronx to Montauk, at the eastern end of Long Island, to go deep-sea fishing. I ate lunch and caught fish while adult men were puking into the water.

I remember the first car Dad brought home to our Bronx apartment. There was a strange noise coming from under the hood. Dad raised it and found a nearly new pliers rattling on the air cleaner.

It was an important part of Dad's tool collection until I borrowed it to build a fort in the swamp in New Haven years later. I dropped it into the ooze and we never saw it again.

Dad loved to go for rides when we lived in the Bronx. I remember trips to Jones Beach and Peach Lake, and deep into Pennsylvania. And deep into Brooklyn.

That's where I got to meet my father's grandfather, my **Great Grandpa Joe**. All I remember was that he wore long underwear with a flap in the back. Until I saw Grandpa Joe, I thought butt flaps existed only in cartoons.

In first grade, Dad and I built a telegraph, and he taught me how to splice wires to fix my bicycle horn. They were my first lessons in what has turned out to be a life-long love of technology.

Almost every sentence from the mouth of Buddy Marcus was part of a lesson. Dad was driven to explain things, but he was also driven to *keep talking* long after the point was made.

I'm the same way. I'm pedantic like my Pop. I don't like listeners who cheat and figure out the ending before I perform the finale.

With Dad's guidance, I investigated the origins of the Marcus clan in Sopotskin.

Since 1991, Sopotskin has been in Belarus. When our family left town in 1906, it was in Poland. It's also been in six other countries. Its address depended on who had the most powerful army and made the map. Back then, the name that would later be Marcus, began with DZM and ended with SKI. It has many more consonants than vowels. Today you probably can't even find one Dzmichivitski in a Google search (except for things I've written). But there are *lots* of Marcuses.

I inherited a lot of things from my father and the Sopotskin genes.

When I was in high school, Dad gave me a hard time when he discovered that I was collecting street signs. He stopped his tirades after I discovered a photo of young Buddy Marcus with *his* collection of signs. I was the bad kid who stole signs, lost or broke Dad's tools and got lousy report cards. I was the son of two super-scholars, and I was the chronic underachiever.

One time Dad said, "I know you think I'm a schmuck, but when I was your age, I was a pretty smart kid." I'm sure he was a smart kid and a smart adult, but I could not appreciate it until years later. It was like **Mark Twain**, who said, "When I was a boy of 14, my father was so ignorant I could hardly stand to have the old man around. But when I got to be 21, I was astonished by how much he'd learned in seven years."

When I was a teenager, I fought a lot with my parents. They sent me to a psychiatrist. After a while, the shrink said that he wanted them to come in so he could hear their side of the story. My father refused to go. He said, "I'm not going to pay $25 an hour to be told it's MY fault that you're messed up." I never found out whose fault it was.

Pop taught his kids wonderfully silly songs like *The Sheik of Araby*, where we'd insert the phrase "with no pants on" after every legitimate line in the song:

I'm the sheik of Araby—WITH NO PANTS ON.
Your love belongs to me—WITH NO PANTS ON.
At night when you're asleep—WITH NO PANTS ON.
Into your tent I'll creep—WITH NO PANTS ON.

And he taught us the song about a herring salesman who was frozen in the snow:

If you go to Russia, where the herring breezes blow,
You'll find a herring salesman
A-frozen in the snow.
The reason he is frozen
Is because his fish smell so,
And far above his carcass,
The herring breezes blow.

And another favorite was:

A personal friend of the tsar was I.
A personal friend of the great Nicolai.
We frequently slept in the same double bed.
I'm at the foot and him at the head.

He sang these funny ditties so often that I've remembered the lyrics for more than seven decades, even if I don't remember where I put my keys or wallet.

Despite Dad's love of singing, he never did much *listening* to music at home. Mom and Dad frequently went to New Haven's Shubert Theater for drama and musicals, but the only phonograph record (those were kind of like big black CDs) I can remember him buying was "*How Much is that Doggie in the Window?*"

It was a hit in 1953 when Dad was 31 years old. I was seven at the time. When I was 31, I listened to the Stones, Dylan and the Doors. Now my iPods have the Stones, Dylan and the Doors, a dozen versions of "*Rumenye, Rumenye*," and, of course, that doggie in the window. Thanks, Dad.

In addition to music, Dad shared discoveries in language, history, science and math.

He showed me how the digits in the nine-times table always add up to nine. Nine times three is 27. The two plus the seven equals nine. It's not useful—but is definitely cool.

And do you know that if you scrunch up the paper wrapper from a drinking straw in a restaurant, and then pull it off the straw, put it on the table, and let a little bit of soda drip on it, it will wiggle like a worm?

Dad's linguistic affinity helped him create knock-knock jokes that included the family. One featured his younger brother, my Uncle Arnie Marcus:

- o **Knock knock.**
- o **Who's there?**
- o **Arnie Marcus.**
- o **Arnie Marcus who?**
- o **Arnie Marcus, get set, go!**

The following is an "alphabetical conversation" in a restaurant. It may not be a "Buddy Marcus Original," but since my father taught it to me, I'll include it here:

Translation into words:

- o **Customer: F.U.N.E.M?**
- o **Waiter: S. I. F. M.**
- o **Customer: F.U.N.E.X?**
- o **Waiter: S. I. F. X.**
- o **Customer: O. K. M. N. X.**

- o **Customer: Have you any ham?**
- o **Waiter: Yes, I have ham.**
- o **Customer: Have you any eggs?**
- o **Waiter: Yes, I have eggs.**
- o **Customer: OK, ham and eggs.**

Dad also taught some more useful things. I helped him finish the basement on Brooklawn Circle in New Haven, which prepared me to finish my own basements later on.

I may have surpassed Pop's carpentry skills. When we lived in the Bronx, he drilled a hole to hang a picture on the wall in the master bedroom. The end of the drill bit came out in the middle of the living room wall. I've never done that.

Dad knew a lot about science and technology, but not everything.

- o He was stumped when I asked him why the sky looked blue and why a mirror reverses left and right, but not up and down.

- o Dad removed the training wheels from my bike when I was six years old, and I was pleased that I could ride without them. I asked him why I didn't fall. He gave me a bullshit answer: "You're going so fast that you *don't have time to fall.*" That didn't explain why I didn't fall when pedaling slowly, but I dropped the uncomfortable subject.

Despite dad's expertise, I disobeyed his instructions and examples a few times:

- As mentioned above, I sometimes use more than four squares of toilet paper.
- Dad used tooth powder, which he poured onto the palm of one hand, and then dabbed his damp toothbrush in the powder, and brushed. I use toothpaste, which I can squeeze right onto my brush. It's easy and sanitary.
- When he had soup and it was served with a pack of crackers, Pop would open the pack and then use his hands to crumble the crackers and then dump the crumbs into his soup. I crush the crackers while still in their packs, then open the pack and pour the crumbs into my soup. As with toothpaste, it's easy and sanitary.

My father's business connections gave him powers and abilities far beyond those of other kids' fathers.

I got the very first **Daniel Boone** coonskin cap in all of New York (before the **Davey Crockett** craze). I even posed for pictures in a book about kids' clothing.

Back then I wasn't such a sexy model. But the clothing manufacturers knew that if they wanted to sell pants and shirts to **McCreery's** department store, they'd better butter up Buddy Marcus by using yours truly as a model.

Dad's connections easily got me into the audience of *Captain Video* and *Howdy Doody*—something that the sons of dentists had to wait years to accomplish.

In New Haven, Dad had an endless supply of movie passes, and my buddies and I spent many Saturday afternoons at the Roger Sherman or Lowes Poli theaters.

I thought my father was important and famous.

One time when I was a kid, we went to a hardware store in New Haven. The owner, **Herman Alpert**, came over to help Dad get what he needed. Herman addressed him as "Buddy," and I was *very* impressed.

I was less impressed a few minutes later when Herman called his next customer "Buddy."

My life as the son of a retailer was different from other kids in other ways. During Chanukah, most kids got clothes on a lot of nights. Since I had an almost unlimited clothing budget throughout the year, there was no point in giving me a sweater for Chanukah. I usually did pretty well for the first three or four nights, but not for all eight.

One year on night-seven I got a beautifully wrapped pair of my old man's old underpants. On night-eight I got a roll of string.

I started campaigning for a toboggan when I was about 12. I got it when I was 17—the same time that my friend Howie got a little green British sports car.

Dad and I love hoaxes and pranks.

When I was a kid and there was a bad snowstorm, he'd call a radio station to have them announce a cancellation of the **Fafnir Society** meeting at the **Hotel Taft**. There was *no such organization*. Fafnir was the name of his partner's *dog*.

Another time Pop was in a department store in Manhattan and convinced employees to move pocketbooks from one counter to another. It wasn't his store, and he wasn't their boss.

This taught me valuable lessons (mentioned elsewhere). If you act like you have authority, you *have* authority. And most people would rather accept authority than challenge it.

Dad, like Mom, was an avid reader. He'd frequently fall asleep leaning into a book, and he had tall stacks of unread newspapers. So do I.

My father is the source of my interests in business, building things, technology, travel, history, maps, music, food, collecting, cigars, pranks, photography, law, language, tropical fish, and probably everything else I care about. He was awarded a scholarship for the University of Chicago's law school. He never went there because he fell in love with retailing.

Pop taught me a lot, but I wanted him to teach me *more*. He was my best teacher and best resource, and I felt both deprived and deserted when he retired to Florida, because I had so much more to ask him about business and about life. But it was his right to decide to move on.

Dad was one of the world's funniest storytellers and a major influence on my writing. We both include *lots* of details.

As a storyteller, I'll never be Buddy Marcus's equal. But I'll always be his student.

The Catskill Mountains—the "Borscht Belt"—are where such comedians as **Milton Berle** and **Jerry Lewis** first got famous, and where Buddy Marcus worked as a waiter.

Pop told me that if he was "waiting a table" with eight people who ordered steaks with a mix of rare, medium-rare, medium, medium-well and well-done, he'd tell the chef to make them *all medium*.

His scam made all the meals ready at the same time and made it much faster and easier to pass out the plates. He'd fake a careful inspection of each plate to ensure that he gave the right one to each person. Only a small percentage of guests would notice the error/scam and none wanted to wait for a replacement. If anyone complained, Pop blamed the chef.

Although he was hauling trays of food from the kitchen to the tables, Dad was funny enough to have been on the stage.

Like me, my father liked to be the center of attention. One time at a family gathering, my uncle "Red" was telling a joke. Dad left the room. I don't know if he had previously heard the joke, resented the competition, or didn't want to be expected to laugh and applaud. Whatever the reason, leaving was not nice.

There was a lot of laughter in our home even before we got a television, and we were one of the first families to get a television. Pop introduced me to *MAD* magazine. All fathers should do that. It's as important as teaching about the birds and the bees.

Chapter 30
I became a "new me."
It's much better than the old me.

When I was a teenager and young adult, I was often pain-fully shy (and even antisocial).

Once when I was around 16 years old, I was planning to ask a girl to go to a school dance. But I was so shy (Intim-idated? Apprehensive? Terrified?) that ultimately my mother called the girl's mother, and the two adults made arrangements for us. I no longer remember the girl's name (I think she was a neighbor) or what happened at the dance. Maybe she'll read this and get in touch.

Later I gained a bit more confidence, but not enough. My first post-college job was as the assistant editor of a magazine. Often, when I was supposed to call someone for a telephone interview, I deliberately called at lunchtime or after 5 PM, so the person would probably be unavailable. I could honestly tell my boss that "I tried."

I never went to bars, discos or mixers to "pick up chicks," but I did have dates, girlfriends and sex—and got married in 1971.

My parents grew up during the Great Depression and were taught—and taught me—to never waste a morsel of food. Our family was "comfortable," but food waste was strongly discouraged.

If I rebelled about finishing a meal that I hated, or even if I was genuinely full of food, my frugal mother would say, "You'll eat it and you'll like it and there are thousands of people starving in Europe!"

Somehow, I never quite understood how my eating every last disgusting green pea would help unfortunate refugees on the east side of the Atlantic Ocean.

My punny and funny father told his kids to "be sure to eat every piece of meat and pea (pee) on your plate."

Both of my parents were big (i.e. wide) people, and their examples and instructions caused me to eventually become "morbidly obese." *I was never as huge as I look in the photo.* My clothing was artificially inflated for Halloween. Fortunately, my dog recognized me.

In the early 1990s, I began taking a new diabetic drug that dramatically reduced my appetite. Breakfasts, which could have included two bagels in the past, were reduced to just one, or a half. My size decreased dramatically. I was constantly giving my too-big clothes to **Goodwill** and buying smaller sizes. I could buy nice jeans at **Sam's Club** for just 14 bucks, instead of paying 50 bucks at the fat man's store.

I looked much better and felt much better. I had a strange urge to "try out" my new body. I started talking to women near me on lines at the post office and supermarket and in elevators and parks. It felt good, and I was never rebuffed.

As I write this in July of 2024, my wife has been hospitalized for nearly two months. I've been living a sad, lonely, bachelor-like existence—for the first time since 1971. When I went out today, I complimented several women for their hair, eye makeup, nails, jewelry, clothing and footwear.

I was not flirting. I was not trying to start a relationship. I was not horny. I was simply attracted, seeking conversation, and thought that maybe I could make some-one realize that the effort she put into her appearance was noticed and appreciated.

Chapter 31
Jive talkin' and other verbal foibles

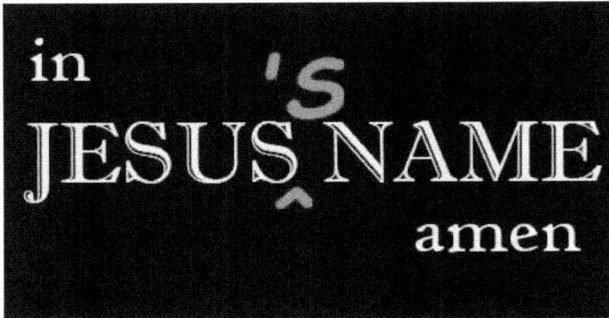

Although I aim to speak perfect American English, I have failed a few times, usually after reading but not hearing a "new" word. The first failure was such a personal shock that I've remembered it for about 70 years!

WTF? Mighty Michael admits to being imperfect
- I pronounced "synagogue" as "sy-nuh-gog-you."
- I pronounced "kiosk" as "ky-osk."
- I pronounced "acai" as "ah-ky."
- Readers of my *BookMaking* blog have likely noticed (or been pissed off by) my frequent snarking about errors made by other publishers and writers. Despite my snotty, know-it-all attitude, I readily admit to being human, and therefore both mortal and fallible. I hereby confess to several errors related to publishing. **1.** In 1976 I accused co-author **Porter Bibb** of bullshitting about the *baobab* tree. I thought he made it up, but the tree *is* real. Sorry, Porter. **2.** In my first book about publishing, I recommended using the *prime* and *double prime* to indicate quotations. That's wrong. Curly punctuation marks are proper.
- **Sheila M. Clark**, my ultra-observant editor, noticed that I had used the word "illicit" instead of "elicit" in a new book ABOUT PUBLISHING MISTAKES we were co-writing. Some of my books share material, so I checked and found the error in three books. It was also on a website and on a blog. As a renowned and committed nitpicker, I am embarrassed by this horrible senior moment (a.k.a. "brain fart"). I was greatly surprised that none of my readers caught the error. It would have been a great opportunity to dump on me for being a damn hypocrite.

However, despite my personal occasional lapses, I can be absolutely intolerant of other people's verbal foibles.

- I once stopped dating a young woman who pronounced the name of the musical group "The Association" as "The Association**s**."
- I stopped dating another young lady who pronounced "Sony" as "Saw-nee."
- Some broadcasters seem to think that the Spanish phrase "mano a mano" means "man to man." It actually means "hand to hand," a type of combat, originally between matadors.
- CBS newsman **Charlie Rose** has decades of experience in journalism. He deserved to be fined $10,000 and required to return his honorary doctorate's degree for pronouncing

"Porsche" as "Porsh" and "Audi" as "Aw-dee" one morning. Can he pronounce "Chevrolet?" How about "Jaguar?" "AMG?"

o   The agency that supervises bridges and tunnels surrounding Manhattan Island is not the "Port of Authority." It's the "Port Authority of New York and New Jersey."

o   Every autumn I have shit fits when broadcasters refer to the "Macy's Day Parade." It's the "Macy's Thanksgiving Day Parade."

o   The famous skyscraper in midtown Manhattan is the "Empire State Building," not the Empire Statebuilding."

o   The huge arena in midtown is "Madison Square Garden," not Madison Squaregarden." It's oval, not a square, and not a garden. The original structure was built in 1879 near Madison Square (named for President James Madison), at 23rd Street.

o   The town in New York state near Connecticut is "Port Chester," not "Porchester."

o   The possessive form of "Jesus" needs an apostrophe plus an "s." It's "in Jesus's name," not "in Jesus name." (Some disagree.)

o   I like money but hate "moneys."

o   I can't stand being told to have a "blest" day, not a "bless-ed" day.

o   I can't stand hearing or reading "y'all." "You" works just fine as a plural.

o   I can't stand it when people confuse "less" and "fewer," like CBS newsman **Steve Hartman**. "Less" applies to things that are measured, like apple juice. "Fewer" goes with things that are count-ed, like apples. Here's an exception: "three weeks or less" is OK, because the three weeks are considered to be *one* entity, not several. "Less than 24 hours" (*Time* magazine) is also OK.

o   I can't stand it when people confuse "farther" and "further." "Farther" refers to physical distances, like "Chicago is farther away than Albany." "Further" is the proper term for non-physical entities, like "further developments." I recently heard **Nicolle Wallace**, a news anchor on MSNBC, confuse the words.

o   I can't stand it when highly visible and influential people, like "Coach" **Tim Walz**, say "are" instead of "our."

o   I can't stand it when people don't understand the difference between adjectives and adverbs. "Feel bad" does not mean the same thing as "feel badly." "Look different" does not mean the same thing as "look differently." After the Harris-Trump debate in August of 2024, MSNBC's **Joe Scarborough** said that **Donald Trump** "looked badly." The proper word is "bad." In October of the same year, alleged genius Trump said that he "felt badly."

o   I can't stand it when people confuse "go" and "come." "Go" goes with things or people that are going away from the speaker. "Come" is the word for movement toward the speaker, like "He'll come here tomorrow."

o   I can't stand it when people and publications confuse "jive" and "jibe." And, to make things worse, we also have "gibe" and "jib." And, as the **Beatles** sang, "*goo goo g'joob*."

o   I can't stand it when **Talking Caller ID** mispronounces names or garbles abbreviations.

o   I can't stand misleading names and labels. I was born in New York City. It has a City Hall. I now live in the city of Hamden, Connecticut. Why does it have a "town" hall? For many

years I lived in the city of Yonkers, New York, but part of our condominium property was in the adjacent town of Greenburgh. We had a classy and inaccurate Scarsdale address. Nearby Scarsdale is *both a town and a village*. Don't ask me why.

o And why do highway signs at *city* borders have signs that say, "Town Line?" However, the border sign for Meriden, Connecticut says "City Line." That's a good sign. [Grin]

o I don't like it when people say or write "my mom" or "single mom." I prefer the more formal "mother," but I do refer to "Mom" as a character in this book.

o I'm not happy about gender-unspecific first names. Now there are both real and fictional woman who share my traditionally male name. I don't demand that "Mary" be reserved for baby girls and "John" belongs to newborn boys, but eventual difficulties could be lessened by more traditional parents. I went to college with a young man named "Terry." Whenever he typed his name, he added "Mister" in parentheses after the name. Now people can be named "X" or "Brooklyn" or "Dweezil" or "Moon"—which don't even hint at a gender.

^Michael Learned
vMichael Burnham

o I can't stand it when teachers and doctors mispronounce words and pass along the imperfections. I used to see a doctor who pronounced *Gabapentin* as *Gabapenteen*. I've had teachers who mispronounced the term for *Neanderthal* cavemen. The correct pronunciation is *nee-AN-duh-TAHL*. **CONFESSION TIME**: I used to think that the authentic pronunciation of *Cro-Magnon* is *Cro-man-yun*, but it's not. Except maybe in France.

o I can't stand hearing or reading "them" or "they" when referring to just one person. I write extra words to avoid this issue.

o I can't stand it when people say, "all corners of the world." Our globular planet is *spherical*, with no friggin' corners, dammit!

o I can't stand hearing or reading "tin foil" or "tinfoil." Tin foil was largely replaced in the 1940s by less expensive and more durable *aluminum* foil. The newer material is still sometimes referred to as "tin foil"—particularly for the "tin foil hats" allegedly worn by deluded people.

o I can't stand the use of obsolete, archaic terms, such as "ice box" for "refrigerator" or "home relief" for "welfare." The *New York Times* said that protesters were "filming the skirmishes on their iPhones." iPhones do not use film! Or even tape. They have solid-state memory.

o I can't stand it when people, particularly on TV, say "radio car," "patrol car," "squad car" or "cruiser car." They are all "police cars."

o I can't stand it when people use a brand name as a term for a generic product, such as "Frigidaire" for "refrigerator" and "Kleenex" for "tissue."

o I have not yet adjusted to the desire of people to select their favored pronouns—but I am evolving and becoming more tolerant.

o Other toleration evolution: I am now merely amused but not upset when I read words written by people who are learning the English language and they type what they think they heard or read, and *type with a foreign accent*. I once edited a school paper a kid wrote about **Johnny Tremain**. She stated that Johnny "main chanced" something. The real term was "mentioned." I heard an America-born kid say "bonts-uh-won-yuh." That's how his Colombia-born mother said "Pennsylvania."

- Words can be fun, and even funny. I've written about *flongs, dingbats, pilcrows* and other strange publishing terms. Now, I'd like to introduce you to the **TOMBOLO**. Although the word came to English from Italian, it's definitely not something you'd enjoy on top of your pizza or inside a calzone. A tombolo is like a sandbar, but it is *perpendicular* to the shore, not parallel to it. In Milford, Connecticut there's a famous tombolo (but everyone calls it a "sandbar"). At low tide, it connects Silver Sands Beach with Charles Island—which may contain buried pirate treasure.

- On CNN, **Bryan Lanza,** former communications director for the Trump transition team in 2016, said, "the both of them" instead of "the two of them." A communications director should communicate better.

- I can't stand puzzling or mysterious labels on packages and in ads. What the heck is a *State Farm*, and does *ranch dressing* taste like cow poop? How can a liquid be "dry," as in "Canada Dry" ginger ale? I don't like the commercials that sang and ads that stated, "My beer is Rheingold the dry beer. Think of Rheingold whenever you buy beer." Sand should be dry. Liquids should be wet.

- I can't stand it when people pronounce *February* as *Feb-you-erry.*

- Both **Dubya** and **Barack** regularly say "GUNNA" instead of "going to." That's not the way English used to be spoken at **Yale** and **Columbia**, their alma maters.

- I can't stand it when people use the wrong names for TV shows. I was annoyed by—but did not correct—a good friend who said *Face the Music* instead of *Name That Tune.* Another friend confused *What's My Line* and *I've Got a Secret.*

- And speaking of "got," I can't stand it when people say "got" instead of "have." The license plates issued by the "Keystone State" used to proclaim, "You've got a friend in Pennsylvania." In 2023 The **Pennsylvania Department of Education** established "You've Got a Friend in Pennsylvania"—an automated phone service that delivered pep talks, jokes, and words of encouragement from students. For 2026 the state's plates will state "Let Freedom Ring."

- I guess I'm a cultural/linguistic bigot, but I just can't take anyone seriously who has a *southern accent* (except for **James Carville, Bill Clinton, Jimmy Carter, Ann Richards** and maybe a few others). I'm not the only one who feels this way. I once worked with a successful and wealthy man in Manhattan, who was born and raised in Kentucky. He told me that a teacher advised his class that if they wanted to become successful, they should study and emulate the speech of northern broadcasters. A recent article in the *New York Times* said, "Studies show that people with Southern accents are often regarded as less intelligent, even by people who have those accents themselves."

- I once had a customer whom I initially spoke to on the phone. He had a slow, southern drawl. When I met him in-person, he sounded like a tough **Tony Soprano.** I mentioned this strange duality. He explained that he worked in finance, and if he "sounded southern" in negotiations, opponents would assume he was slow-witted and reveal things they shouldn't. I find it difficult to respect people who sound like they just left some "holler" in the deep south. My ears and brain shut down when someone says "poke" for "bag" or "done" for "did" or "Coke" for all brands of soda—or types "y'all" in emails.

- The beloved **Yankee Stadium** announcer **Bob Sheppard** died at age-99. He was known as "the voice of God" and was complimented for his expert elocution. Although he performed in a stadium in daBronx, he sounded like he was in Fenway "Pock" in "Bah-stin"—never pronouncing a final "R."

o I can't stand ancient Bronx/Brooklyn pronunciations such as *terlet* and *fill-um*. **Waite (not "Wade") Hoyt** played baseball during 1918-1938 and announced ballgames on radio. He was one of the dominant pitchers of the 1920s and was inducted into the **National Baseball Hall of Fame** in 1969. He was born in Brooklyn, and after an injury, Brooklynites couldn't decide whether to say, "Hoyt is hurt," "Hurt is hoyt," "Hoyt is hoyt" or "Hurt is hurt."

o I can't stand it when someone on TV says that "the following images are graphic." How can video images *not* be graphic?

o I'm particularly pissed off about the substitution of "HEY" for "hello." It seemed to have made a rapid transition from playgrounds to *CSI Las Vegas* and then to the rest of the world. When I was a child, if I used that word, my fastidious mother would scold me with "Hay is for horses—not for people!"

o I'm even more pissed off by the use of "WAS LIKE" as a replacement for "said." It seemed to start with Hollywood's dimwitted bimbettes and even spread to the White House! *Time* magazine quoted **George Dubya Bush** using that phrase.

o I'm also annoyed by what I see as the rampant infantilization (if that's not a word, it should be) of speech. Kiddie Talk and Baby Talk are creeping into adult conversations, and even book, movie and TV show titles. However, I confess that I sometimes say "boob," "pee," "poo," "poop" and "tummy" in jokes or for conversations with kindergartners; and I did say "poop" and "pee-pee" to my late dog. I cringe when I hear a doctor say "tummy." What's wrong with "abdomen?"

o I confess to sometimes ending phone conversations with "bye-bye," but I refuse to say "MY MOM" instead of "my mother."

o Southern speech is a topic for a possible future book. OTOH, northeast speech often pisses me off, such as the cliched "Pock yaw cah in Hahvid Yahd."

o By the way, Derek's last name should NOT be pronounced "Jee-tuh." The boss's last name was NOT "Steinbrenn-uh."

o Not only do many New Englanduhs (and some New Yawkuhs) drop R's, sometimes an R gets put where it doesn't belong. My ninth-grade English teacher in N'Haven said, "Ameriker."

o In Manhattan, you can meet someone at the intersection of "toity-toid and toid."

o East of Manhattan is *Lawn Guyland*, and if you travel west, you'll reach New Joisey.

o If you go far west, you might hear former **Governator Ah-nold** say "Cally-fawn-yuh."

o Bad grammar is another—but related—subject. MSNBC's **Rachel Maddow** (who has a PhD and should know better) said "less" instead of "fewer" twice in the same broadcast. She also said "between," when referring to a group of about six nations. NBC's **Priya Sridhar** said "between three vehicles" and NBC's **Dana Griffin** said "between all four..."—on the same day! "BeTWeen" goes with "TWo." BOO!

o The website for **Grimaldi's** pizzeria in Woodbridge, Connecticut, said "Join us every week day for the best Happy Hour in Woodbridge with easy access on and off the Merritt Parkway right before or after the Sleeping Giant Tunnel." **BOO!** (1) The tunnel goes through West Rock. Sleeping Giant is a different mountain with no tunnel. (2) "Weekday" is one

word, not two. (3) The restaurant is near the Wilbur Cross Parkway, not the Merritt. I would've gladly edited the website in exchange for pizza and beer, but the pizzeria closed.

- A few years ago, when the **Hibachi Grill Supreme Buffet** opened in Orange, Connecticut, its first advertising bragged about offering the biggest selection "on the peninsula." Orange is *not* a peninsula. Further reading revealed that the advertising was copied from another restaurant (maybe in Maryland).
- The **Osaka Hibachi Buffet** opened nearby in Stratford, with similar stupid plagiarism. Its advertising sheets and website proclaimed it to be "the largest restaurant in Manville and the surrounding areas." The donor of the advertising text (unwittingly, perhaps) is the **Flaming Grill & Supreme Buffet**, 110 miles away in New Jersey.
- Osaka in Stratford seemed to be able to see into the future. Before opening it bragged that "satisfied customers are what have made our restaurant so popular."
- One good thing: When the Stratford restaurant copied the New Jersey restaurant, someone was smart enough to not copy "Darty Tray."
- One silly thing: "Osaka" is a city in Japan. "Hibachi" is a Japanese cooking style. The owner of the restaurant is *Chinese*.
- Terminology can be misleading, deceptive, motivational and persuasive. Advertisers know that because the initial digit is 4, not 5, a $4.99 price seems much lower than $5. "Quarter-pounder" seems to outweigh a mere four ounces.

Foreign words can be problematical.

- If I try proper pronunciation of "Paris" or "Moscow," most Americans are puzzled.
- In ethnic restaurants, if I attempt to properly say "*zeppole*" or "*gyro*," the order-takers (often of a different ethnicity) don't know what I'm talking about.
- I frequently go to a Jewish deli. If I order a favorite, "*kasha varnishkas*," I get a blank stare from the gentile employees, so I have to translate to "kasha with bowtie noodles." Oy.
- The American military services use a "phonetic alphabet" to spell words on the radio: "Able, Baker, Charlie" etc. The letter "Q" was originally represented by the Canadian city of "Quebec." However, the proper pronunciation is "kay-bek." Eventually "Queen" became the new Q word so Canadian troops could better understand their American allies.
- (Not foreign, but it seems appropriate to include here). Shoe salesmen use names to represent alphabetical widths in shoe sizes such as "Give me a six Benny" or "This guy needs a ten triple-Eddie." The names: Albert, Benny, Charlie, David, Eddie. By now there may be a Frank and a George. Sadly, many shoes are now made in narrow, medium and wide widths, with no letters.

It's OK to call me a grammar geek, but not a word nerd.

A *geek* probably has better social skills but may be clumsier than a *nerd*, who is less single-minded than a *wonk*, less obsessively studious than a *grind*, and less pathetic than a *dork*. But the terms overlap in many respects.

Chapter 32
My most miserable memory

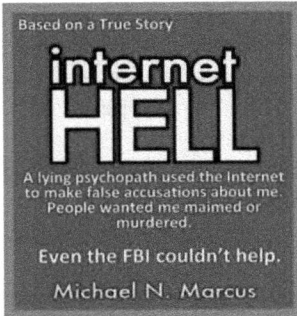

Based on a True Story

internet HELL

A lying psychopath used the Internet to make false accusations about me. People wanted me maimed or murdered.

Even the FBI couldn't help.

Michael N. Marcus

A Saturday morning in 2010 started out fine.

The weather was perfect. I had minimal obligations. I was supposed to vacuum the algae from the bottom of the pool, spray some weed killer on my front walkway, go to the Post Office, continue editing a book, and help my wife pick out a microwave oven. I also wanted to spend a few hours hanging around the house with my dog while listening to the funny programs on NPR, just like any other Saturday.

I had no reason to believe it would be *one of the worst days of my life*. And then I got a phone call from an old friend. She had gotten a *Facebook* message from an unknown "**Kevin Phillips**," saying that I am a convicted pedophile, had been in prison for child rape—and more. The message had a link to the lie-filled smear-blog that went live on June 25th. It said:

o   Michael N Marcus is a dangerous convicted pedophile and child molester who raped a young boy in California. A devious liar and scumbag, he is on the Child Sex Offenders Registry, [All false] but moved to Connecticut to start a new life. [I moved when I was six years old—an age when I was more likely to *be* molested, than to molest others.]
o   Michael N Marcus's Sleazy House (pictured) in Milford Connecticut. [It's actually nice.]
o   DO NOT ALLOW YOUR CHILD TO SLEEP OVER OR STAY AT MICHAEL N MARCUS'S HOUSE. Although he has served prison time for luring and raping a young boy in California, [Not true.]
o   Marcus is unfortunately not on the sex offenders registry in Connecticut. Since 1986 (before his 1st and 2nd sex offence convictions) [Not true.] Marcus has run a sleazy [Not true.] website
o   HOW YOU CAN HELP: Sign our petition to get the Connecticut Governor M. Jodi Rell to have the Pedophile Michael N Marcus's name added to the CT sex offenders register. We need your help to protect Connecticut's children (particularly young boys) from this dangerous pedophile. The blog pages were signed by "PROTECT OUR CHILDREN."

There are several legitimate organizations that use that name. None of them were involved in my attack. As the day went on, I started getting emails and phone calls from other people. The dishonest accuser/attacker had notified many of my Facebook friends (some are relatives and business associates, and some are in the media) of my alleged criminally perverted past, using several aliases. My favorite: "**Jonah Ark**."

I'm known for very realistic pranks, spoofs and April-Fooling, and several friends and business associates and even one employee first thought that this was one of my own gags—and then realized it wasn't. As someone who prides himself on superb bullshitting, I will admit that the work was fairly well done—but not as well

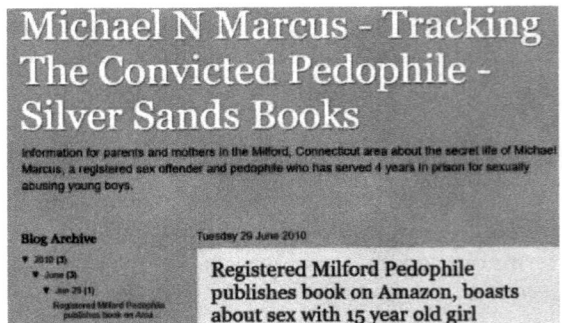

Michael N Marcus - Tracking The Convicted Pedophile - Silver Sands Books

Information for parents and mothers in the Milford, Connecticut area about the secret life of Michael Marcus, a registered sex offender and pedophile who has served 4 years in prison for sexually abusing young boys.

Blog Archive

▼ 2010 (3)
▼ June (3)
▼ Jun 29 (1)
Registered Milford Pedophile publishes book on Amaz

Tuesday 29 June 2010

Registered Milford Pedophile publishes book on Amazon, boasts about sex with 15 year old girl

done as I could have done it—but I am not crazy enough to publicly accuse myself of child rape. I like publicity, but not *that* kind.

There is no way I would accuse myself of the crimes mentioned in the sick blog.

In a blog, *anyone can say anything about anyone*. Truth and accuracy and bigotry and malice *just don't matter*. Several companies act as "hosts" for blogs, usually without charge. One of the most popular is **Blogger**, created in 1999 by **Pyra Labs** and bought by **Google** in 2003.

Blogger allows pretty much anything to be published on the blogs it hosts. Its policy is to not remove any content without a court order decreeing that certain content is defamatory, or a notice that content has been posted in violation of a copyright.

- o It is extremely easy to post something on a blog.
- o It is extremely difficult to have something removed, even if it violates the rules of the blog.
- o Bad guys—including my attacker—know this and take advantage of it.

On June 25, 2010, my attacker uploaded the first of several postings to a new blog with the horrible, dishonest and embarrassing title of <u>michael-marcus-pedophile.blogspot.com.</u> The main purpose of the blog was to get people to believe that I was a convicted pedophile, a dog rapist, a wife burner, and a variety of other despicable things—that were *completely untrue*.

The blogger warned readers to stay away from me and keep their children from entering my house. My attacker carefully examined my websites and chose items that he could easily distort to inflame readers and made other claims that were pure fantasy. His claims could easily be determined to be false by anyone who tried to verify them.

For example, he claimed that I had been imprisoned in California for child rape and was on the California list of sex offenders. Both charges can be easily disproved online or with a free phone call.

He learned that I had a dog named **Hunter** and declared that I raped Hunter. I loved Hunter—but not that way. He said that that I put "half-naked images of children on the home page" of one of my websites. The children were wearing modest bathing suits and were standing in a swimming pool (with the dog I allegedly raped). The girls' mother was at the side of the pool when the photo was taken.

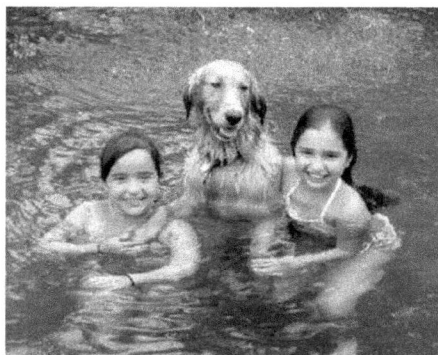

The attack blog contained my photograph (a copyright violation), a photo of my house (another copyright violation), several other copyright violations, my address, my phone and fax numbers, and a link to a map to enable people to get to my house and possibly *kill me*.

My attacker's writing style at times seems very professional, even academic, legalistic or journalistic in tone, with phrases like "aiding and abetting." Other times it was juvenile ("sleazy," "sicko," "scumbag"). His style is distinctive, strangely using the British "offence" instead of the American "offense" and skipping the period after my middle initial—regardless of which phony name he used.

Also on June 25, my attacker posted a petition on **Change.org**, "an online hub for social change." The fraudulent petition said: "Targeting: The Governor of CT, The CT State Senate and The CT State House Started by: Protect Our Children [NOT TRUE] Pedophile Michael N Marcus is a dangerous and evil pedophile who has serious convictions for pedophilia and crimes against children in CA. He's moved to Milford, CT and is NOT on the CT sex offences register.

This petition has two purposes:

1. To get Connecticut to adopt a similar Megan's Law to keep track of pedophiles like Michael N Marcus who live near schools and children's play areas after they have served jail time.

2. To petition Connecticut's governor to please ensure this dangerous pervert and child sex molester, Michael N Marcus, is made known to parents to ensure this evil monster can't ruin another family's life. Here's the pedophile's Facebook page: Join the Facebook Petition Page against Pedophile Michael Marcus. Pedophile Michael Marcus's current address is: 195 Magnolia Road, Milford CT."

The petition was addressed to my governor, **M. Jodi Rell**, and says "Michael N Marcus is a Registered Child Molester, Sex Offender and Pedophile. He is currently living in the Milford Area of Connecticut, with schools and kindergartens within a 50 mile radius of his house."

While it is true that there were a great many schools within 50 miles of my home—and within 50 miles of most homes—I am absolutely NOT a child molester. Nearly 30 people apparently believed the lies about me and signed the petition. Some added comments. **Julie G.** of Missouri signed the petition against me and wrote: "These type of human beings should be killed."

Dear Julie: Did you ever think that maybe the petition you signed has no basis in fact, and by signing it you could hurt innocent people?

The petition sought to have me put on the "Connecticut Sex Offences [sic] Register." A more careful attacker would have written "Connecticut Sex Offenders Registry." The petition page had links to the libelous phony blog, and to my real page on Facebook. Unfortunately, just like Blogger, Change goes to great effort to disassociate itself from the content it distributes and to deny any responsibility for the harm it may cause.

From the Change user agreement: "The Company is not responsible for the conduct, whether online or offline, of any User of the Site or Service." My attacker had deliberately violated the user agreement. I complained, and after a few days the petition was deleted. I have no way of knowing how many people saw it, believe it or hate me because of it.

On June 25, 2010 at 7:50 PM, my attacker started his second petition, this time on Facebook, which quickly attracted a collection of apparently like-minded folks who believed every morsel of baloney that he served up.

This time my attacker used the fake name '**Mike Josephs**' and a photo likely from a clip art gallery. The 'Mike Josephs' page on Facebook had absolutely no information about him other than he is a man. It showed 11 friends. Some were real and some were fakes—just like him.

'Josephs' wrote: "Michael N Marcus raped a young boy in California, and now he's living in Milford, Connecticut. Our children are too important to not act. By our indecision, we are risking another child's life! Marcus is a child rapist and convicted pedophile and we need to get this sicko off our streets." And: "Michael N Marcus is a registered pedophile and child molester. He holds convictions for raping a young boy in California." And: "I'm thinking this pedophile has settled in Milford due to the low crime rate.

We need a national register of perverts, as Michael N Marcus committed these molestation offences in a different legal jurisdiction, it's difficult to apply complex points of law. Every parent in Milford though, needs to know that pedophile Michael Marcus is on their doorstep."

The first fellow traveler chimed in 8:06 PM, soon followed by others. It is virtually impossible that people would have found the petition by accident or would have had a reason to search for it. The only possible conclusion is that my attacker either informed potential allies of the petition, or—more likely—*invented* the people. The fact that there was essentially no information online about any of these signers reinforces the theory that they are fakes.

A photo from Facebook showed the alleged '**Johnathan Hawking**.' There was just one bit of "basic information" shown for 'Johnathan'—his sex was listed as *female*. It is unlikely that a real person would make this error and not correct it. It is likely that my attacker, in a hurry to create a multitude of false identities, would not notice the error—and the person who invented them violated Facebook terms.

Fake
"Johnathan
Hawking"

'Hawking' wrote: "Pedophile Michael N Marcus is actually a typical example of his convicted breed of registered sex offenders who move State [sic] for reasons of anonymity. I would definitely support a change in the law enforcement or at least a review of Megan's Law. My reasoning is that there has been a dangerous trend since the late nineties of convicted pedophiles like Marcus manipulating the system to hide their crimes. One just hopes Michael N Marcus hasn't hurt another little boy where he lives in Milford, CT—as Michael N Marcus's criminal history suggests pedophiles don't get cured, they simply move on to targeting a new family."

The alliance of bloodthirsty defenders of morality wanted me butchered and dispatched to the lowest level of hell.

- Someone identified as '**Melinda Tufnell**' wanted my balls cut off. She (or he) wrote: "Pedophile Michael N Marcus is another depraved, nasty deformity who has a registered history of disturbing child sex offences and sick pedophilia convictions, parading as an 'upstanding pillar' of the community. This case exemplifies exactly why Obama needs to enact a complete overhaul of the child protection regulations in our country starting at the federal level with a focus on data handling of registered pedophiles, rapists and sex pests across the States. Castrate this sick hairy freak and put it in a cage where it belongs. I'm tweeting this to my colleagues."
- Of course, since 'Melinda' did not exist, she had no colleagues to tweet to—but real people may have read and believed her lies. That's the big problem with my attack. The web gives credibility to things that should be regarded as incredible. People believe what they read. Even liars believe that others tell the truth. '**Harry James**' (the name of a real American bandleader) repeated the other folks' lies and suggested that I may have beaten my wife. He (or she) wrote: "We as Americans need to act. Congress is going to have to start taking this problem seriously; there are too many unregistered pedophiles like Michael Marcus falling off radar. You can't get much more serious than child rape. He's registered in California as a pedophile and convicted sexual offender with a forensic history as long as my arm. Is he a wife beater as well? When are we going to wake up to the dangers of letting these pedophiles out of jail and back onto the streets!??!"
- An entity posing as '**Kendra Lay**' told the world: "A convicted criminal like MNM can defraud his way into another State—and there's no paper trail back to his original sex offences/rape crime. Please let all the local parents in Milford know about this child rapist Michael N Marcus. God bless America."

Non-existent
"Kendra Lay"

- Someone posing as '**Alice Clark**' wrote: "We've confirmed that Michael N. Marcus has a conviction for sexually abusing a young boy 15 years ago, but does anyone have any more info on his police cautions for downloading child porn?
- The nonexistent '**Victoria Owens**' proclaimed: "I read on Foxnews [sic] yesterday that Dangerous Pedophiles like Michael N. Marcus have been using *Wikipedia* to groom their child victims. In any case, Marcus is a confirmed convicted child rapist and

pedophile in CA. Just because he lives in CT doesn't change a thing, a pedophile is a pedophile. period.

o The alleged 'Billy Hamilton' didn't display a phony photograph, but instead is identified with a cartoon of a person about to draw a gun from a holster. His Facebook page said that 'Billy' is a female. He or she wrote: "With that hairy beard, Marcus looks like a sleazy creeper! I wish you all the best in getting him behind bars where he belongs—evil pedophile. You can count on my signature!" [**Hey, Billy, beards are supposed to be hairy.**]

The introduction to the *Facebook* petition page announced: "Child Molester, Michael N Marcus, is a dangerous and evil pedophile who has serious convictions for pedophilia and crimes against children in California. Now he's moved to Milford, CT and is NOT on the CT sex offences register. Please don't let pedophile Michael N Marcus destroy another child's future and ruin another family's life."

Upon simple study, it became apparent that nearly all of the people who signed the petition were FAKES. 'Melinda' and 'Kendra' use the same British spelling of "offences" as the fake 'Mike Josephs' and the writer of the original attack blog. 'Hawking,' 'Josephs,' 'Tufnell' and other phantoms all eliminate the period after my middle initial.

My skillful opponent even arranged for his fake allies to have *real friends*.

The fake 'Mike Josephs' behind the Facebook falsehoods also declared; "Folks, it's further distressing that this California-registered pedophile and child molester, Michael N Marcus, has joined a young women's social network called She-Writes.com [sic]. Why would an old man join a WOMEN'S social network? At this point it's difficult to ascertain whether this revolting beast has been grooming children/single mom's [sic] with young kids through the SheWrites.com social network."

Actually, SheWrites is open to post-menopausal and childless women, and even girls and men. As often happened through this ordeal, my attacker did insufficient research—which made him look stupid.

His apparent stupidity, however, did not lessen his impact. My attacker used the fake female name '**Caroline Harris**' to join SheWrites.

On June 27, 2010 at 6:30 a.m., he repeated the bogus accusations against me and warned the group's women to prevent their children from contacting me.

The phony Caroline wrote: "Please join our Facebook petition to the Connecticut Governor M. Jodi Rell requesting a review of Megan's Law and the status of Pedophile Michael N Marcus (a member of SheWrites) who is currently residing near schools in the Milford, CT area. IF MARCUS HAS ATTEMPTED TO GROOM YOUR CHILD THROUGH JOINING A WOMEN'S SOCIAL NETWORK YOU NEED TO CONTACT YOUR LOCAL AUTHORITIES. DO NOT GIVE ANY INFORMATION ABOUT YOUR CHILD OR FAMILY TO MICHAEL N MARCUS WHO RAPED A YOUNG BOY IN CALIFORNIA AND IS KNOWN TO GROOM CHILDREN ONLINE." I complained to the ladies at SheWrites. The phony warning about me was quickly removed and the non-existent 'Caroline Harris' lost her membership.

My active attacker also used **Yahoo, Excite, Bing, PhotoBucket** and **AOL** to smear me—in violation of his user agreements.

Sadly, the Internet has a long memory. Even after cooperative websites removed bogus claims about me, search engines retained the links, and even some cached pages—so the damage and embarrassment continue, perhaps *forever*. Has this hurt my business? Does it keep people from associating with me? Does it hurt a doctor with the same name? I'll never know.

Lightning Source is the company that printed and distributed most of the books that I wrote. My attacker sent two vicious and totally dishonest emails to Lightning, trying to get the company to *stop printing* my books. The attacker also accused the company of committing crimes and threatened to sue the company!

Incogman (i.e., incognito man) is the name used by the man behind a vicious and dishonest white supremacist hate blog that was hosted by **Wordpress** until late July, 2010.

The blog's heroes include Adolph Hitler, KKK-er David Duke and Mel Gibson. The blog had a long list of targets, including Blacks, Jews, Wall Street, the Federal Reserve System, Zionists, Israel, Hispanics, liberals, President Obama, illegal immigrants, interracial marriage, the Trilateral Commission, the New World Order, Arabs, the ACLU, the Anti-Defamation League, civil rights leaders, Russians, "corporate globalist whores," Asians, gays, transgenders, pornographers, the "brown horde," publishers, filmmakers, broadcasters, "disgusting dyke Jewess Sandra Bernhard," AND ME!

On July 20, 2010, the blog posted my name and complete address, along with this call for my murder: "We got your number and address. Its [sic] about time to get into action. Anyone who is close to this Jewboi [sic], get a gun and blow his head off. Its [sic] about time to blow up a Jewboi [sic] head and start moving to the second phase." The posting included a link to the original lie-filled attack blog. The posting was signed by 'C.S.'

Others quickly chimed in with such remarks as:

o "I just may have to do a big investigative piece on this sick Jewboi [sic]."
o "Bloatedsoontobeflyblowncorpse. Is it possible you'll be catching bullets soon? More than probable i'd [sic] say, you repulsive shit kike! Rot with your filthy family of rats, bastard jew! I expect you'll get shot in your fat arse a few times, before you get your neck snapped. Rat faced kike!"

Incogman (who sometimes used the name '**Philip Marlowe**'—a character in novels written by Raymond Chandler, first published in 1939) apparently realized that the threat against me might have gone too far. He later said he removed the call for my murder within ten minutes of its appearance.

After the deletion, Incogman/Marlowe responded to fans with messages, including: "Yes, they did shut me down. Permanently. Although I have no specific knowledge of why they did it at this time. . . . Possibly all this [Connecticut Senator] Lieberman bill business made them want to forestall any government request. I was classified as 'mature' and foolishly believed that this gave me a degree of 'invisibility.' This complete censorship came out of the blue. . . I was getting close to 4000 hits a day. . . Let me state for the record: Soon enough they'll shut down every place on the Net for White people to freely talk. Maybe even here. The White race cannot be allowed to talk freely in any public venue, if the Jews have their way. Are we going to let these people keep cutting off our balls forever?"

Since I was fairly certain where my attacker lived, my first reaction was to contact the police in Suffolk County, Long Island. I was told to first make a report to my local police, and if its investigation pointed to a Suffolk County resident, the Suffolk police would cooperate.

I followed Suffolk's recommendation and called the police in Milford, Connecticut, where I lived. An officer and a detective visited and took a detailed report. I later was contacted by the department's computer forensics expert.

After six weeks, he was unable to solve the crimes. He said my attacker had used temporary foreign internet addresses, and Milford police have no jurisdiction outside the U.S.

On the day that I first learned of the attacks, I contacted the nearest FBI office. This was a Saturday, and I was told to call back on Monday. On Monday I described the situation, and I was told that *no Federal crime had been committed*. However, if my attacker tried to extort money from me to halt the harassment, then the Feds would get involved. Later a special agent interviewed me when the attacks escalated to what might be considered "hate crime," but there was no arrest.

Although I intensely wanted "the alleged perpetrator" to be arrested, convicted and incarcerated, *none of that happened*.

His mental condition deteriorated considerably. He stopped seeing his son, was abusive to his family, trashed their basement, and his parents ultimately threw him out. Last I heard, he was living in a homeless shelter. That's not the same as prison, but it's OK.

Whodunnit?

Just as **Carly Simon** steadfastly refused to identify the subject of her *"You're So Vain"* song, I won't tell you who I think my attacker is. Some people in the publishing business think it's someone I offended in a book review. I doubt that an author would go that far, and risk so much. I'll simply say that I think my attacker is a man who had a relationship with a relative of a relative and resented my efforts to help his troubled son.

o   I thank family, friends, neighbors and business associates who refused to believe the false accusations and gave me support and suggestions. Facebook helped my attacker, but also provided comfort and a venue for friends to defend me. The Internet hurts, and heals.

o   I thank **Frank Juliano** of the *Connecticut Post*, for his interest in my case, his extensive investigation and a large and thorough article that helped me gain support from neighbors who were unsure if I was guilty or innocent.

o   I thank **Officer Billy Simpson** and **Detective Richard Frawley** of the Milford Police Department for their concern, comfort and efforts to help me.

o   I thank writer and online buddy **Tyge O'Donnell** for providing a strong defense.

o   I thank online ally and independent publishing supporter **Mick Rooney** for researching the accusations and telling the world that I am "entirely innocent."

CONNECTICUT POST

Milford man falsely branded a sex predator

By Frank Juliano
Staff Writer

MILFORD — Michael Marcus calls the experience "Internet hell." Marcus, 65, has been accused in online blogs, petitions to public officials and letters to the Connecticut Post of serving prison time for sexually assaulting a child. He had sex with an underage girl and even with his own dog, the allegations said. None of it is true, according to law enforcement officials. Marcus said Milford police and the FBI's computer crimes unit are now investigating the source of those allegations. He has had mixed success in getting the fake postings removed from websites. The owner of Phone Geeks, a telecommunications equipment company here, Marcus said that he believes a distant relative is behind the Web-based attacks. A family dispute was the likely trigger, he said.

See Milford on A5

Even I got scammed!

My smart SOB attacker lied about my books being banned by **Amazon**, which sells many of the books I've written. I believed him. On June 25, 2010, it seemed that my books were banned due to complaints by my attacker. In truth, I was a victim of a computer glitch which made many authors' books temporarily unavailable.

No credit goes to the nutjob who claimed: "Amazon removes Pedophile Michael N. Marcus's sick pedophilia book that boasts about raping a 15-year-old girl. In a victory for children's rights campaigners across America today, Amazon removed all material relating to Pedophile Michael N. Marcus from their websites. Milford pedophile Michael N Marcus was boasting about how he had underage sex with a 15-year-old minor, and 'contemplated sex with another 15-year-old girl' in the editorial review he wrote on Amazon to advertise his sick pedophilia book to fellow child molesters browsing the Amazon shopping site. In a disturbing admission, Marcus also guarantees his readers in his editorial review on Amazon, that his sex crimes are 'at least 80% true.'"

Friends, what happened to me could happen to anyone.
Be careful. Be alert. Be prepared.

I wrote a book about my ordeal. It's horrifying, informative and entertaining.
https://www.amazon.com/dp/B00AS44XS8

Chapter 33
About my names

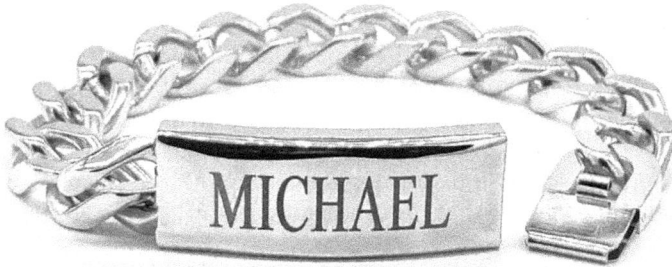

In most Jewish families it's common to name a new baby after a deceased relative. The infant's name may be the same as the old name, or similar, or merely start with the same letter.

My first name, **Michael**, was chosen to honor **Meyer Polaner**, my maternal grandmother's uncle, who was not connected to the **Polaner jelly** company. (The Polaner name just means "someone from Poland," and lots of people came from Poland.) My lack of connection to the jelly people doesn't bother me because I *hate* jelly and I'm not looking for freebies or discounts.

Meyer Polaner's children, **Helen** and **Nat**, lived together as adults. I assumed they were husband and wife, and I didn't learn that they were siblings until I was a teenager. (That's not so bad. According to *Time* magazine, half of American high school seniors think Sodom and Gomorrah were married.)

The Polaner apartment in the Bronx later became my first marital home. The Polaners were nice people, but eccentric. It's unlikely that anyone else will ever write about them, so I'll give them some paragraphs here.

Helen's favorite hobby was *hypochondria*, and she enriched many doctors, hospitals and pharmacies. After about age-50, Helen used a wheelchair, but there was doubt about whether it was a necessity or merely for convenience.

Her cousin, my cynical and sharp-tongued Grandma Del, insisted that, in a fire, Helen would stand up, run and be the first one out of a burning building. Grandma disliked Helen's frequent and disgusting medical reports and often responded, "Spare me the gruesome details."

When Helen died, I went to her funeral, expecting to be one of maybe three mourners. I was shocked to find that the place was *packed*. Apparently, her money had helped scores of World War II refugees move from Europe to the United States and start new lives here. Helen lived frugally but was a very good investor with a very good heart.

Nat was overshadowed and overwhelmed by his sister and seldom spoke in her presence. Some in the family jokingly referred to him as "gnat" and pronounced the "g," like "guh-nat," to emphasize his insignificance, despite his large size. His huge pants almost reached his nipples.

Nat never became a confident driver and Grandma Del said he drove at two speeds: "slow and stop." Like **Rodney Dangerfield**, Nat Polaner got no respect.

After Helen died, for a few years Nat's personality *bloomed*. He actually spoke, and he told interesting stories. It's intriguing to speculate how his life might have been if he didn't live with Helen, and how many others live in similar stifling relationships. When Nat died, I went through his things and found love letters written shortly after World War II. From 1947 on he was somber and almost speechless.

"Michael" has been one of the most popular male names in America since the mid-20th century. If a woman in a supermarket yells, "Michael!" half of the males in the store instantly turn around and say, "Yes, Mommy."

Michael comes from an ancient Hebrew name. It means "who is like God." It's probably a question, but, sometimes, when I'm in the mood for self-flattery, I assume my folks picked the name because I was Godlike prenatally. I like my full name, and don't like being called "Mike." I *hate* "Mickey."

David Daniel "**Mickey Marcus**" (1901-1948 CE) was an American Army colonel who helped organize war crimes trials in Germany and Japan. He was later Israel's first general and assisted Israel during the 1948 Arab-Israeli War. Marcus was killed by friendly fire and was portrayed by **Kirk Douglas** in the 1966 movie *Cast a Giant Shadow*.

"Mickey" was buried at **West Point**, with military honors. The funeral was attended by New York Governor **Thomas Dewey**, former Secretary of the Treasury **Henry Morgenthau** and **General Maxwell Taylor**, then Superintendent of West Point. Marcus's grave is said to be the only one in the West Point Cemetery for an American killed fighting under the flag of another country. He was eligible for interment there because he was a graduate of the academy and served honorably. His helmet and pistol are displayed at the West Point Museum. His gravestone reads: "Colonel David Marcus-a Soldier for All Humanity." Nice!

I am no expert on Christian theology, but I know there was a **Saint Michael** who was painted by **Raphael** slaying **Satan**, and an archangel named Michael. (Actually the saint and the angel may have been the same Michael. I haven't quite figured it out.) Strangely, there has never been a Pope Michael, but there was a **Pope Marcus** in 336 CE, and he became a saint! I think he looks like me, and like an elderly **Jerry Garcia**.

Michaels have ruled the Byzantine Empire, Bulgaria, Poland, Portugal, Romania and Russia. **Michael Dukakis** failed to become U.S. president in 1988.

The name **Marcus** was derived from **Mars**, the Roman god of war, and there were *lots of us* in ancient Rome.

Marcus Cicero (106-43 BCE) was a Roman statesman, linguist, lawyer, political theorist and philosopher. He is considered to be one of Rome's greatest orators and writers and introduced the Romans to Greek philosophy. During the dictatorship of Julius Caesar, Cicero favored freer republican government. So do I.

Marcus "the wise" Aurelius (121-180 CE) was emperor from 161 until his death. He looks like Dr. Jack Hodgins on *Bones*. This Marcus was the last of the "Five Good Emperors," and is also considered to be one of the most important Stoic philosophers. He was emperor during wars in Asia and Europe. Unlike me, he stressed discipline, virtue and tranquility.

On the other hand, evil **Marcus Crassus** (115-53 BCE) was a Roman general, politician and slave dealer who suppressed the slave revolt led by **Spartacus**. Crassus made the Top-Ten List of richest historical figures and helped **Julius Caesar** start his political career. Gen. Crassus was such a greedy SOB that it's said he was executed by having molten gold poured down his throat. COOL CONNECTIONS: In the 1960 *Spartacus* movie, **Kirk Douglas** played Spartacus, who fought Marcus Crassus. In 1966, Douglas played **Colonel David Marcus** in *Cast a Giant Shadow*. Kirk's actor son **Michael Douglas** had a bit part in the movie.

Marcus Brutus (85-42 BCE) is best known for leading the assassination conspiracy against **Julius Caesar**. "Et tu, Brute?" ("And you too, Brutus?") was said to a Marcus. Those words were supposedly Caesar's last words, as Brutus stabbed him on the Ides of March (March 15th) in 44 BCE. March 15th was the original Income Tax Day in the United States. Later it was moved a month to April 15th, my birthday. That's another cool connection. We Marcuses are all connected (if we try hard enough).

Marcus Antonius, a.k.a. "Mark Anthony" or "Marc Antony" (83-30 BCE) was "Master of the Horse" under Julius Caesar, and Caesar's cousin, so he probably could call him Julius, not Caesar. He identified his cousin's killers during a dramatic funeral eulogy. **Shakespeare** wrote his lines: "Friends, Romans, countrymen, lend me your ears. I come to bury Caesar, not to praise him. The evil that men do lives after them. The good is oft interred with their bones." This Marcus was played by **Richard Burton** in the 1963 *Cleopatra* movie (opposite **Liz Taylor**) and by **Marlon Brando** in the 1953 *Julius Caesar* movie. My mother used to say I look like Brando. Antony is immortalized in the names of countless beauty parlors and pizzerias.

Siegfried Marcus (1831-1898 CE) was a prolific German inventor who spent most of his life in Austria. He invented the internal combustion engine in 1864, installed it on a cart and successfully drove it. It was the precursor to the automobile.

Because he was Jewish, Nazis destroyed most of the records of his work. His second car, finished in 1889, was rediscovered in 1950 and *it could still be driven*. The car was stored behind a false wall in the cellar of a Vienna museum to hide it from the Nazis.

For better or worse, I'm *not related to any of them*. Our family name has been Marcus only for a little over 100 years. It used to start with "Dzm" and end with "ski" and had many more consonants than vowels.

I find it ironic that the first name of **Mikhail Poopy-Head Gorbachev**, last leader of the officially atheist USSR, is pronounced so closely to the original Hebrew mee-chai-ail, which means "who is like God." I wonder if he knows or cares. (I'm talking about the real Russian pronunciation, not the lame Americanized "mee-kale.")

My middle name, **Neuman**, has been a major burden for me. Neuman is only a teeny bit less alien than its source, Neumann—the first name of my mother's father's father, my great grandfather **Neumann Jacobs**. I never met him.

For the first quarter-century of my life, I hated and hid my unconventional and un-American middle name. I was so detached from the name that I misspelled it as "Numan" on a school registration form in second grade. Any kid who discovered my secret name compared me to **Alfred E. Neuman** from *MAD* magazine. *Time* magazine once misspelled his name as "Newman." For a while, when people asked what my middle initial "N" stood for, I'd say that it stood for "<u>N</u>one of your fucking business."

As a little kid, I was sometimes affectionately called "Noony" by Grandma Del. I loved her but hated the nickname.

In fifth grade, an obnoxious girl who lived near me heard about it and used to follow me to school chanting, "**Michael Noony Marcus**." In college, I lived with Indian students who told me that "noony" is the Hindi word for "penis," which made me feel a bit better. I recently read that "noony" is slang for "vagina." Now I'm completely confused and may need to consult a guru.

I wished my parents spelled "Neuman" as "Newman," or gave me a good American middle name like Paul. My sister Meryl's middle name sounds normal, but it's spelled "Carin." Youngest sibling Marshall escaped the curse. His middle name is "David."

All of our first names begin with "M" and end with "L." Allegedly Meryl and I were a coincidence and then Marshall made it a *tradition*. My parents didn't like Mitchell, Mendel, Muriel or Muttel so they stopped at three. I'm sure **Sarah Palin** could come up with more, like **Moosetestickal**.

I was taught in junior high school that there is no improper way to spell a proper name. I disagree. "Michael" is the only right way to spell "Michael." It's a perfect Anglicized representation of the ancient Hebrew name.

Anyone who spells it "Micheal" is an *ignorant idiot* and deserves an F. Anyone who spells it "Mykul" is being innovative and denying history but not making a spelling error. At least there's no doubt about how it's pronounced. My first name is certainly not pronounced like the letters M-I-C-H-A-E-L seem to indicate, but most Americans can pronounce "Chevrolet" with no trouble. I'll allow Mykl, Mykul and Mikal to exist, but not MiQuale, M'quil, Miquail, Mykell or Mykale.

Now there are even females named Michael. I don't like it and I want it stopped. What's wrong with Michelle or Michaela? Why do parents give kids confusing names?

The parents of basketball player **Isiah Thomas** should have paid more attention in church. They left out an "a," but their kid pronounces his first name as if the letter *is* there.

I like the look and sound of "**Michael N. Marcus**", and it helps distinguish me from all of the other Michael Marcuses out there, so it's easy to Google me. My use of the "N" may be an unconscious homage to my grandfather **Dr. Jay N. Jacobs** who used the initial to break up the alliteration. (By the way, did you notice the weird plural of Marcus? Microsoft Word thinks it's wrong, but it's right. Word accepts "buses" but not "Marcuses." Also, I think that "serieses" should be the plural form of "series.")

I used to be amazed when I found another Michael Marcus. But it's more likely that a male Marcus would be Michael, not Bill or Ted. Cosmetics maker Michael Marcus pissed me off when he registered *www.michaelmarcus.com* first. However, I did get *www.michaelmarc.us*.

For a few years when I stopped hating my middle name, I sometimes used the pretentious pen name "**M. Neuman Marcus**." That label became very useful when the classy department store **Neiman Marcus** had a branch near me. I opened an account, and my credit card had the name "M. Neuman Marcus" on it. During my annual visits to buy a few jars of Neiman's Texas Chili, I was taken *very* good care of.

Even my last name has been useful while shopping. I once went to the **Marcus Dairy Bar** in Danbury, Connecticut for a newspaper and a milkshake. When it was time to pay, I playfully showed my driver's license and asked if I could get the family discount. The cashier said, "Sure, Mr. Marcus. Everything in the store is free."

I paid the full bill and left a big tip. I didn't want to be a cheapskate and embarrass the family.

Sadly, the Marcus Dairy Bar closed in 2011 after nearly 63 years in business.

Maybe I should've spent more.

Disambiguation:

Although my initials are "MNM," please don't confuse me with **M&M** candy ("melts in your mouth, not in your hand") or rapper **Emenem**.

OK, time for something punny:

I mentioned above that **Marcus Antonius** spoke at the funeral of emperor **Julius Caesar**. **Shakespeare** wrote his line: "I come to bury Caesar, not to praise him."

A farmer grew a huge strawberry and was certain that it would be a prizewinner, so he took it to a county fair to be judged. The night before the contest he stayed with the berry in a hotel room. During the evening, there was a knock at the door, and the farmer opened it and was surprised to see a man with a drawn gun. Shocked and trembling, the farmer told the gunman, "I thought you were her to judge my berry." The armed robber replied, "I've come came to seize your berry, not appraise it."

[ID bracelet photo from Jewelry by Jose Jay]

Chapter 34
But that's not our corpse

A few years ago, my wife and I attended a funeral about 50 miles away from home, in a city we were not familiar with. The proceedings started with a religious service in a synagogue, and then a long line of about 20 cars meandered through the city streets to the cemetery for the burial.

Our car was near the end of the line and, when we reached the cemetery, we sensed that something was wrong. Instead of familiar Jewish stars, most of the gravestones were engraved with crucifixes, and we saw lots of statues of Jesus and Mary. Most of the mourners were Black, not White.

Apparently as some cars navigated through a complex intersection, we separated from the main group and merged into a *different person's procession*.

We never found the right cemetery, but we had a nice lunch at **Bertucci's**.

Rest in peace.

Chapter 35
Tie score. Psycho-drivers: 1, Michael: 1

In around 1972, I was walking along a major avenue in the Bronx where children were playing on the roadway. The traffic light turned green and a hot-rod burned rubber and leaped from the intersection as if it was in a drag race.

I was concerned about the kids, and yelled, "Slow down, asshole!" Despite his noisy exhaust, the driver heard me and got out of the car and ran toward me. I ran into a supermarket to hide. The speeder found me, punched me in my face, broke my glasses and told me to mind my own fucking business.

A little while later, while I was driving in a tough neighborhood in Queens, a driver cut me off and I gave him the finger.

The driver slammed on his brakes and blocked my car from moving. He opened his window and started waving a baseball bat and swearing at me. I yelled at him to get out of his fucking car and fight like a man.

He got out and started walking toward me. When he was a few feet away, I stomped on the gas pedal and sped down the block in reverse. By the time he got back in his car, I was far away and moving fast.

Lesson: If you *act* like a tough guy when encountering a *real* tough guy, it's good to have planned an escape route.

Chapter 36
Drilling him a second asshole

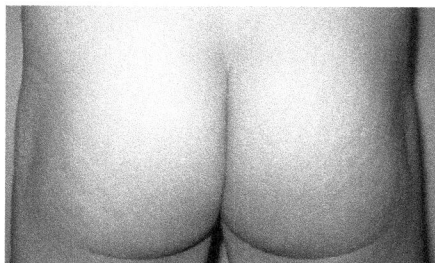

When I was a teenager, my bedroom was a former guest room in our basement. The house was a split-level and the room was above ground and had a normal window. It was nice, not a dungeon.

Late one night, I was awakened by sounds outside my door. I got out of bed, opened my door slightly and spotted a neighborhood "bad kid," going through my mother's pocketbook.

He had apparently gotten in through the unlocked back door and sneaked upstairs, grabbed the pocketbook and taken it downstairs to separate the cash from the other stuff.

A normal kid would've been scared shitless and kept silent until the burglar left. But I've never been accused of normalcy. I decided to defend my home from the invader. I had no Colt nor Winchester, but I was a SCUBA diver, and I had a powerful speargun powered by a monster-sized surgical rubber tube. According to the salesman, the gun was strong enough to penetrate a car door!

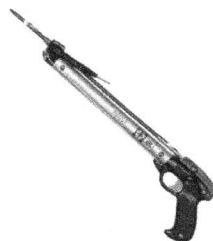

In the past, I had never aimed the speargun at a creature any more treacherous than a flounder (and I didn't catch a lot of fish) but desperate times call for desperate measures. I quietly and carefully pulled back the rubber loop and hooked it onto the notch on the steel spear. I stood by the door edge and took careful aim at the middle of the intruder's ass.

I didn't particularly want to kill him, but I hoped to punish him and keep him from running away until the cops arrived. Unfortunately, I missed his butt crack. I was sleepy and shaky and not a great shot, even from eight feet away. My spear tip approached his ass at the wrong angle and bounced off the wallet in his back pocket.

He was startled, however. And when he saw me standing in my underpants and realized that he nearly gained a second asshole, he said, "Are you fuckin' nuts? You could've killed me." Then he dropped my mother's money on the floor and ran out of the house through the back door. I don't know if he ever tried to rob us again, but we did keep the door locked from then on.

[Butt photo from Peter Klashorst. Thanks.]

Chapter 37
A platinum card is just as good as Medicaid

Years after I moved out of the Bronx, I was visiting someone who still lived in the Bronx. I saw posters and heard amplified announcements proclaiming the availability of **FREE CHEESE**, being distributed by the Department of Agriculture.

Apparently, our taxes subsidized the dairy farmers, and they overproduced—so this was a way of paying back something to the blood-sucked taxpayers. I didn't need the cheese, and if I did, I could afford to buy my own, so I ignored the announcements.

After a while, the audio announcements turned frantic. Apparently, any cheese that was not given away by 4 PM would be thrown away.

There was no provision for storing it locally or returning it to government warehouses or to the dairies that made it. Our government agents were begging us to take it away. I did not want to turn down my government in a time of need, and accepting free food was certainly less of a burden than joining the Army or paying a tax surcharge, so I went to the community center and joined the giveaway line.

When it was my turn, I was asked for my welfare card. I said I didn't have one. Then I was asked for a Medicaid card. I didn't have one of those, either. Then I was asked if I had a Medicare card, and I didn't have one of those.

The woman on the opposite side of the counter said, "Sir, we'd really like to give you the cheese, but the regulations require us to see some identification."

I smiled and asked, "Do you take American Express?" She said, "Sure." I showed my platinum card, and I got a huge ten-pound block of cheese.

Thank you, Mr. President.

Chapter 38
Unplanned chick magnetism, how rich people eat, a confession and an overdue apology

When I was in junior high school, like many Jewish kids who lived in Connecticut, I spent some February school vacations at the **Concord** resort in New York's **Catskill Mountains**, affectionately known as the "Borscht Belt" and "Jewish Alps."

The Catskills were where the movie *Dirty Dancing* took place, where such comedians as **Milton Berle**, **Buddy Hackett** and **Jerry Lewis** first got famous, and where my own father had worked as a waiter during his college vacations.

It was where teenage boys of my generation learned to ice skate and ski. They dreamed of getting laid, but a little more realistically, boys hoped to reach "second base", preferably touching a bra that contained a genuine breast, and not merely a wad of Kleenex tissue or a falsie.

In February of 1962, I was 15 years old and in ninth grade. On my third day of skiing, I was bored and feeling unjustifiably confident in my progress, and I decided to promote myself from the beginners' ski slope to the intermediate slope. It didn't look too much steeper or any more dangerous, but what I didn't notice was the ice where I expected soft snow to be. I lost control, spun around, flipped and flopped, lost my skis, heard a CRACK and I hurt like hell.

I waved my ski poles and yelled for help, and a few minutes later, I was sliding down the hill in a sled-mounted basket aided by two ski patrolmen. I was a bit disappointed that I didn't get visited by a St. Bernard dog with a keg of brandy around its neck as I'd seen in cartoons.

An ambulance transported me to a local hospital for X-rays and I was informed that I had a broken ankle. My parents were summoned, and they took me back to the Concord with a cast and crutches.

My skiing was obviously over for the week, but I saw no reason to skip the teen dance scheduled for that night. It was no more likely that I could dance than ski, but perhaps some sexy 16-year-year-old girl would notice my wound and offer to sign my cast or provide other comforts.

Although I had a brief career as a model around age-three, I was a shy teenager who never attracted much attention from girls. But when I hobbled into the teen dance that night, I was like **Carly Simon's** unnamed subject of *You're So Vain*. Like **Mick Jagger** or **Warren Beatty** or possibly someone else, I was the guy who walked into a party and all the girls wanted to be my partner.

The cast and crutches were great chick magnets. A war hero or a rock star couldn't have attracted more admirers than I had that night. Falling on my ass on an icy hill did not require any high degree of bravery or talent, but all of the girls wanted to hear how I got wounded and soon my white cast was covered with blue ink and red lipstick kisses. I also collected some names, addresses and phone numbers on pieces of paper and one of those notes led to a romance that lasted for several years.

Alicia was very smart and very pretty and the only child in a family that lived about 20 miles from me. The relationship began by mail and after my ankle healed, I started riding my ten-speed bicycle to visit her on Saturday afternoons. Unfortunately, it was mostly uphill.

Although both of our families spent winter vacations at the same Catskill Mountain resort, our worlds were different. My own family was "comfortable", but Alicia's family was *loaded*. We had a Chrysler. They had a Cadillac. All the girls I knew had plain names like Susan and Judy and Harriet. But even Alicia's Jewish friends had glamorous WASPy names like Muffy and Buffy and Sondra. They spoke WASPy, too. After a sarcastic remark from a friend of mine, Alicia replied, "You're uncouth." A New Haven teen's retort would have been, "You're an asshole."

Alicia's parents often took Alicia and me out to eat at expensive restaurants, and it was when we ate—no, better make that *dined*—that I discovered that these people were in a class above that of my own family.

I had been brought up not to waste even a morsel of precious food. If I rebelled about finishing a meal that I hated, or even if I was genuinely full of food, my mother would say, "You'll eat it and you'll like it and there are thousands of people starving in Europe!"

Under the same rebellious conditions, my usually compassionate and coddling maternal grandmother would coldly remind me of the "starving Armenians."

Even as a very young child, I detected a large gap in the dining table logic of these two women. Somehow, I never quite understood how my eating every last disgusting lima bean or LeSueur green pea that was glaring at me from my plate would help fill the gaunt bellies of unfortunate refugees in Novi Pazar, Vagharshapat, Hrazdan or Yeghegnadzor.

I'd gladly have mailed the vegetables across the Atlantic to any country where they would be appreciated and improve either the standard of living or the child mortality rate.

Confession: Mom, I often hid the despised green things under a plate or a napkin or under the table, or even stuffed them in my pocket or handkerchief for later secret disposal.

My mother bragged about the diverse foods she ate, and she apparently thrived on weird stuff like kale, okra and Brussels sprouts. But she could not tolerate even the *smell* of kasha which my father and I loved. She hated to cook it and would leave the house when Pop and I ate it.

Mom had a perverse ritual to demonstrate that she was the supreme ruler and I was a mere serf with minimal rights—but with better conditions than were provided at Auschwitz. Once each year, she'd force me to eat food that I hated: those disgusting peas and shepherd's pie.

I doubt that **Dr. Spock** would approve, but I couldn't convince Mom to ask him.

Mom was an excellent "company cook," with special recipes that would impress our visitors. But family meals sometimes included salt soup, barely defrosted French fries and burned chicken. Mom knew that I liked only the white meat of the chicken but apparently, she didn't know it was possible to buy only the white meat, or to buy additional white meat. (My dog ate only white-meat chicken, too. He'd happily eat the dark meat, but my wife wouldn't let him. She's convinced that white meat is healthier, so that's what he got.) On the other hand, Mom was a talented baker, and she did a great job with lamb chops, London broil, pot roast, chocolate pudding and fried flounder, so I hereby forgive her.

My father never complained about Mom's cooking. Although he appreciated fine foods, he gladly ate things that few other people ate (like lox "wings" which are often treats for cats) and Mom sometimes called him "the human garbage disposal."

Alicia never had to eat anything she did not like to eat. Being an only child, her position in the familial line of succession was perfectly safe and she was secure from sibling rivalry. Hers was the only face immortalized with a gilt-framed oil portrait over the marble fireplace. Not only did Alicia never have to eat food she didn't like, but she didn't have to finish *any* food.

In fact, she told me the *exact opposite* of what my mother had said. Alicia's instruction was, "You should always leave some food on your plate." According to the rich people's rules taught by Alicia's parents, finishing a meal implies that you are hungry and poor, and you actually need a meal.

I never before knew there were people who thought like that. After a great meal—which I usually finished like a famished member of the destitute lower class who didn't know the rich rules— we'd go back to Alicia's house. Her parents would go to the den to spend the evening watching TV. Alicia and I would go to the living room to spend the evening making out. She was probably 14 when we started dating, so real sex was out of the question. At least it was out of the question for "nice girls" of her age in that era. Or maybe it was just not a good idea when parents were in the next room and the TV volume was too low to mask the sounds of heavy breathing and squealing.

By one in the morning, it was time to go home. After five highly stimulating but unfortunately unfulfilled hours, I usually had a severe case of *blue balls* ("temporary fluid congestion in the testicles and prostate region in the human male often accompanied by a cramp-like ache and tenderness of the testes caused by prolonged sexual arousal and lack of orgasm").

In that condition, I couldn't ride a bicycle 20 inches, let alone 20 miles. Fortunately, Alicia's parents liked me. Her father put my bike in the trunk of his Cadillac, and he drove me home.

Eventually I got my driver's license. This solved some problems but presented another problem. You see, despite all of Alicia's wonderful qualities she did have one quality that I perceived as much less than wonderful.

Alicia had a long ponytail. No! *Wait a minute.* It was not a mere ponytail. It was more like a horse's tail, almost long enough for a giant Budweiser Clydesdale, which reached down to the middle of her behind.

I wondered if she was trying to set a *Guinness Book* record. I hated the ponytail, and I was embarrassed to be seen with her because of it. During the time that our dating involved my biking up to her town, there was little chance of our being seen by anyone who knew me. But, once I had a driver's license and the use of a car, my new mobility meant that I could take Alicia on dates anywhere.

There was now a heightened risk that we might be seen by someone who knew me, and any friend or classmate would certainly give me shit about the strange growth that emanated from the back of Alicia's head. I had to come up with excuses for why we couldn't go to the big city of New Haven for movies or concerts.

Long-Overdue Apology:

Alicia, I'm sorry. I really liked you a lot, and the reason I didn't invite you to my high school's junior prom was because I really hated that hair thing, and I didn't want to be seen with you. The girl I took to the prom had more conventional hair, but *I liked you better*. I suppose I was immature, inexperienced and insecure. I should have learned to live with the hair.

Chapter 39
What I learned in college

Good advice: In the first Phys-ed class of my freshman year at Lehigh University, the director of intramural sports, who was described as a wise and kindly "grandfather" to each incoming class, advised us well.

John Steckbeck told us how to determine when our gym suits needed cleaning: "Gentlemen, when your shorts, socks, T-shirts and jockstraps are able to stand up by themselves, it's time to wash them."

And he told us how to avoid venereal diseases and unplanned offspring: "If you're gonna take it out, and you're gonna get it wet, put a raincoat on it!"

Bad joke: Lehigh wisely recognized that freshmen were hopeless slobs, and our room and board fees included maid service. We put charts on our doors indicating our first class of each day in a futile effort to keep the cleaning ladies from barging in at six if we didn't have to wake up until nine.

In addition to dusting, vacuuming and making our beds, these substitute moms would help us start the day with a few words of encouragement, efforts to fix us up with a daughter or neighbor, and a stupid riddle or lame joke.

One day **Katherine** asked me, "What did the bathtub say to the hopper?" ("Hopper" was a Bethlehem term for "toilet." Coal was a big influence on local lingo.)

I told her I didn't realize that tubs could talk. According to Katherine, the bathtub told the toilet, "Ha-ha! I get twice as much ass as you do but I don't have to take any shit."

Chapter 40
When death can be productive

Deaths—at least deaths of good people—are undeniably sad. Even if the newly deceased suffered greatly, and the death caused suffering to family and friends, death causes not just relief, but grief.

Despite the grief, some funeral procedures—such as Irish wakes and New Orleans jazz funerals—seem downright jubilant.

The first funeral I attended was for an elderly relative. After the religious service, the "mourners" gathered in a large room in the funeral home and chatted as if they were at a cocktail party. There was little seriousness, and no tears, and I was shocked.

As I have gotten older, I have had to attend more funerals, and the behavior—despite differences in religion, ethnicity and location—has been the same.

A few years ago, I attended the funeral of a woman who was about 95 years old. Her time, clearly, was up. She died in her sleep, with no suffering. There was a mass in a Catholic church followed by a service at a cemetery. These sessions, led by priests and with words added by family, were appropriately solemn. But afterwards, we went to a very nice restaurant, and it was PARTY TIME.

The mood was undeniably jovial. There was little crying for the deceased, nor looking ahead to Heaven as touted by the priests.

Instead, it was a family reunion, and an occasion for people who were connected by the cadaver but had never met, to get to know each other.

At events like this, there are always comments like "How come we can get together at funerals, but never at happy times?"

That question made me think about a possible "purpose" of death.

Just as decaying flesh and vegetation can fertilize the fields to feed a new generation of plants, animals and people, maybe the celebration after a human death leads to a renewal and re-invigoration of the human community—the coming together of friends, relatives and even strangers who would not be in the same place if someone had not died.

Maybe it's important and useful—not frivolous and wasteful—for some of the insurance money to pay for food and drink, and not just scholarships and medical research and new clothes, cars and homes.

Party on!

Chapter 41
Sibling synergy

When I was a little kid, I could not tie my shoelaces, so younger sister **Meryl** tied them for me. (Now my shoes close with Velcro.) However, she had trouble turning doorknobs, so I opened doors for her.

If we had salad, I ate tomato but not lettuce. She ate lettuce, but not tomato. Now we both eat both.

If we were served hard-boiled eggs, I ate the yolks, but not albumin (whites).

She eats both. I'm still yolk-only.

Since I have some space to fill, here's an ancient pic of siblings Michael & Meryl from Halloween, probably in 1952:

Chapter 42
When silly words die

scrovney!

fibbling juice

Languages change. New words, like "texting," frequently appear. Old words, like "austerulous," fade away.

For a while, *Time* magazine and **Bill Buckley** made an effort to popularize ancient words (or maybe it was just intellectual snobism), and *SaveTheWords.org* was devoted to keeping old words alive.

But *SaveTheWords* was devoted to real words—words that appeared in newspapers, magazines, TV shows and dictionaries.

I recently wondered what happens to the wonderful silly words that are used within families, often for generations, but die when there is no next generation.

When I was a kid, we said "boompsie" for "fart." Does anyone else still use the word? *Urban Dictionary* says it means a behind, but that's not what it meant to us.

Sometimes these family words evolve from baby talk. When I was young, apple juice was called "fibbling juice." My little sister, **Meryl**, and I used to blow air through a straw in the juice glass to make bubbles at the bottom, and the sound of the bubbles seemed like "fibble." *Urban Dictionary* has a much naughtier definition of "fibbling."

When I was at Lehigh University in the mid-60s, an engineer from the student radio station built a primitive wired remote muting control that could be used to silence the commercials on the geek lounge TV. It was called the "scrovney."

The kid in the room with the lowest status was put on scrovney duty, and it was his job to anticipate the onset of a commercial during *Batman* or *Voyage to the Bottom of the Sea*. (We said, "bottom of the sink" to acknowledge the cheesy, unconvincing special effects and monsters.)

Scrovney Boy was supposed to press the scrovney button just-in-time to avoid the ads. If he was late—or early—by even a fraction of a second, the others in the room would harass him with loud shouts of "SCROVNEY!" and pelt him with wads of paper.

For over 52 years, my wife and I have often referred to our TV remote controls as "scrovneys." Our scrovneys are now wireless and they control fast-forwarding on our DVRs, but the term and the purpose have survived.

Before I wrote a blog post about it, "scrovney" had not been on Google, but it was listed for a while. I thought Marilyn and I would be the last people to ever shout "SCROVNEY!" But, thanks to search engines, maybe the silly word will survive on the web.

That's nice.

Chapter 43
Creative licenses

"Vanity" license plates provide a variety of benefits ranging from amusement to practicality. They can produce laughs or confusion, boost egos and promote businesses, and certainly provide funds for the states that sell them. Now it's common for vanity plates to have space for eight letters and numbers—but it wasn't always that way. When I was a kid, Connecticut allowed just four "characters," so folks had to be inventive. My favorite plate from that era was on a car driven by a urologist. It said "**PPMD**."

I knew an accountant in New York named **Louis Re**. His plates served as concise mobile business cards: "**LOU RE CPA**."

For several years my parents had boring vanity plates. Mother Rita Marcus's Plymouth had a tag that said "**RMAR**", and my father Bud Marcus's Chrysler showed "**BMAR**."

I frequently exhibited my beloved Italian 1978 FIAT 124 Spider at car shows, where it often won prizes. When people saw the car, their most common question was "what year is it." I told them to look at the plate (shown above). My present car is an unglamorous but fine Honda. My plate is uninteresting: three digits plus "**TUT**. I often forget the numbers, but ancient Egyptian **King Tut** is memorable.

My buddy **Ralph** was also a car fan and also drove an Italian car, a *Lancia*. Most Americans anglicized the brand name as "lan-see-uh." To counteract this, Ralph got plates that helpfully said "**LONCHA**." It wasn't always helpful. When Ralph's father (born in Italy!) saw the plates, he said, "Oh, Lonka." Ralph groaned.

Ralph and I often competed in sports car rallies. I drove and he navigated. Lots of teams got lost, and it was common to try to follow another competing car. One driver did not want any followers. His plate proclaimed "**IM LOST**." But a California car brags: "**IMRIGHT**."

There's a natural impulse to "talk dirty" on vanity plates, and state motor vehicle departments can use computers to detect and reject smut in multiple languages, including obvious tricks like "**GO 2 L**." Some wise asses have beaten the system by substituting similar-looking numbers for letters, such as a number one for the letter "I." **SH1T**" looks very much like "**SHIT**."

Sometimes abbreviations stand in for dirty words, such as on the car with "**2FNFAST**."

A New York plate brags, "**2 FAST 4 U**."

A driver in New Hampshire proclaims, "**I FARTED**."

Another driver in the same state advises people to "**PB4WEGO**."

An apparently Jewish driver in Maryland tells folks: "**MASLTOV**."

A New York *Star Trek* fan had plates with the Starship Enterprise number: NCC-1701.

Some plates express a sexual preference, such as the New York car with "**ASSMAN**."

Some plates combine a vanity message with a state slogan or a car brand. The plates on a Virginia car says "**EAT THE**" above the state-provided "**Kids First**."

Many plates are mysterious to folks in following cars, but some mystify *their own drivers*. I recently saw a plate that said, "**IMLF3**" and asked the driver what it meant. He said he didn't know—because he had borrowed the car.

Chapter 44
Poetic license

When I was in eighth grade, my English teacher was a miserable bitch, disliked by almost every kid in the class. We were once assigned to write essays about poetry. At the time, I hated poetry, except for funny stuff like one of the world's shortest poems, by **Ogden Nash**:

> **"The Bronx?**
> **No thonx."**

Basically, my essay said something like **I hated poetry** because it is artificial and is much less efficient than prose for delivering a message. I DESPISED faked/fudged/phony constructions like:

> **"My country 'tis of thee,**
> **Sweet land of liberty."**

I got an "F" on the essay. **Elliot**, one of my classmates, got an "A" for a few pages of bullshit about poetry "opening a golden door into the soul of the poet."

I was sent to the guidance counselor for guidance and discipline. I did not get any discipline, but I got some vital guidance: Give the bitch the same bullshit that earned Elliot the "A."

In other words, if you want to succeed in life, give the audience what it wants, even if you must lie or sell out.

I don't think it was good advice then, or now. An audience can usually determine if a performer's heart is not in a performance.

A few weeks later, we were assigned to write poems. That was even worse than having to write *about* poems.

Rhyming is probably a natural activity and source of amusement for every kid.

But going from "**Roses are red, violets are blue. Sugar is sweet, but I hate you**" to something of homework-quality would have been a major leap for me.

I was desperate to avoid a second flunk from the bitch, so with help from my father I did come up with something that I still think is pretty good. It was about a windshield wiper destroying rain drops. I don't remember it all, but it started with:

> **"Oh wiper, you viper,**
> **You snake on the glass.**
> **You strike hard and swiftly.**
> **You kill with each pass."**

I got an unexpected "A" on that one. I suppose I was a poet, but did not know it. [Grin.]

I also got an "A" on a second poem that involved some event in international relations in 1959 or '60. Apparently, **President Eisenhower** was being pressured by the dreaded commies to give in on some diplomatic negotiating. I need a word to rhyme with "now," and my father suggested the phrase "**but Ike would not kowtow.**"

I had never heard "*kowtow*" before and thought my father had made it up just for my poem. Pop explained that it came from a Chinese word meaning "submit" and I kept the word. The bitch knew what it meant and was impressed. This is probably the third time in over 60

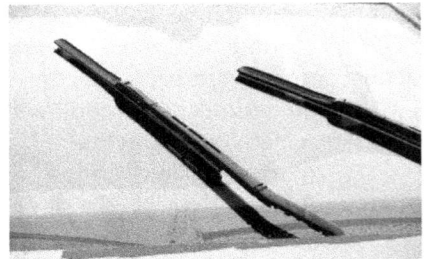

years that I used the word "kowtow." It's not part of my normal writing vocabulary, but if I encounter it, I don't need a dictionary.

In high school I became a good rhymer, often writing poems and songs about bad teachers. The worst was Bertha "Crazy" Frehse (pronounced "frayzee"). We never knew what to expect when we entered her classroom. A student could be pinched or poked on the shoulder and commanded to go to the blackboard and "write ten beautiful words," or "write 200 words about tobogganing," or "explain why striped cats are superior to spotted dogs" or "list 500 reasons why Elvis should be president" or write 500 words on "how Capri pants have been the downfall of western civilization." (Girls couldn't wear pants to our school back then.)

▶ I've never bought a poetry book, but I do have appreciation for rhyming lyrics, especially:

"Lady Madonna, baby at your breast
Wonders how you manage to feed the rest"
(Lennon & McCartney)

and: "Yesterday
All my troubles seemed so far away
Now it looks as though they're here to stay
Oh, I believe in yesterday"
(Lennon & McCartney)

and: "If you miss the train I'm on,
you will know that I am gone."
(Hedy West)

and: "When your rooster crows at the break of dawn
Look out your window and I'll be gone.
You're the reason I'm a-traveling on
I wish there was something you would do or say
To try and make me change my mind and stay
But we never did too much talking anyway
But don't think twice, it's all right"
(Bob Dylan)

and: "You would lose them
I know how to use them.
No one beside you
No one to hide you"
(Mimi & Richard Farina)

and: "My father always promised us
That we would live in France
We'd go boating on the Seine
And I would learn to dance"
(Judy Collins)

and: "And it's too late baby now it's too late
Though we really did try to make it
Something inside has died
And I can't hide and I just can't fake it"
(Carole King)

Revised Battle Hymn:
"Mine eyes have seen the glory of the coming of the Lord.
He was wearing pink pajamas and was riding in a Ford.
Glory, glory, hallelujah!"

and:
"Happy birthday to you.
Happy birthday to you.
You look like a monkey.
And smell like one, too."

Revised Nursery Rhyme:
"Roses are red-ish.
Violets are blue-ish.
If it wasn't for Jesus,
You all would be Jewish."

and:
"Trick or treat.
Smell my feet.
Give me something good to eat."

and Alka-Seltzer Jingle:
Pop, pop, fizz, fizz.
Oh, what a relief it is."

and:
"Nationwide is on your side."

and:
"You'll wonder where the yellow went, when you brush your teeth with Pepsodent."

and: "You know the day destroys the night
Night divides the day.
Tried to run. Tried to hide.
Break on through to the other side"
(The Doors)

and: It's nine o'clock on a Saturday
The regular crowd shuffles in
There's an old man sittin' next to me
Makin' love to his tonic and gin
He says, "Son, can you play me a memory?"
I'm not really sure how it goes
But it's sad and it's sweet and I knew it
complete
When I wore a younger man's clothes"
(Billy Joel)

and, from Tom Lehrer, one of my literary gods:
"I always will remember
'Twas a year ago November
I went out to hunt some deer
On a mornin' bright and clear
I went and shot the maximum
the game laws would allow
Two game wardens, seven hunters,
and a cow
I was in no mood to trifle
I took down my trusty rifle
And went out to stalk my prey
What a haul I made that day
I tied them to my fender, and I drove them
home somehow
Two game wardens, seven hunters, and a
cow
The law was very firm, it
Took away my permit
The worst punishment I ever endured
It turned out there was a reason
Cows were out of season
And one of the hunters wasn't insured
People ask me how I do it
And I say, "There's nothin' to it
You just stand there lookin' cute
And when something moves, you shoot!
And there's ten stuffed heads in my trophy
room right now
Two game wardens, seven hunters, and a
pure-bred Guernsey cow"

and: "You used to laugh about
Everybody that was hangin' out
Now you don't talk so loud
Now you don't seem so proud
About having to be scrounging
Your next meal.
How does it feel?
To be without a home?
Like a complete unknown?
Like a rolling stone?"
(Bob Dylan)

and: "Passengers will please refrain from
flushing toilets while the train
is in the station.
Darling, I love you."

When I was a kid, I was amused by:
> **"Two, four, six, eight.**
> **Now it's time to urinate."** (Or "defecate," "masturbate," "demonstrate," "masticate,"
> **"flagellate," or "fornicate")**

(I don't know if the poet was my father or me, but it's unforgettable.)

"Pi" to 12 places is also unforgettable—because it rhymes:
> **3 point 1 4 1 5 9, 2 6 5 3 5 8 9**

Every morning, when I start to boil water for my daily tea. I automatically and silently say:
> **"I'm a little teapot,**
> **Short and stout**
> **Here is my handle**
> **Here is my spout**
> **When I get all steamed up**
> **Hear me shout**
> **'Tip me over**
> **and pour me out!'"**

(Written by George Harry Sanders and Clarence Z. Kelley and published in 1939.)

Many rhymes have become powerful, unforgettable, unignorable "ear worms." The words *cling* to me. They're forever embedded in my brain and bonded to my body.

I have no plans to write serious poetry, but being forced to succeed at something I hated has probably been useful to me as a person and as a writer. I gained appreciation for those who do write poems well (especially **Edgar Allan Poe**), I sometimes insert rhymes (and alliterations) into my prose just for fun.

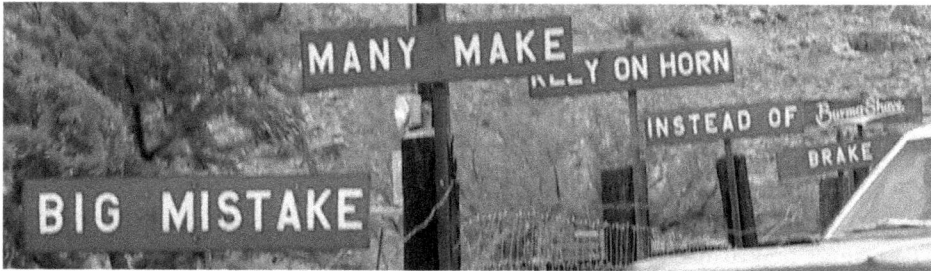

From 1926 through 1963, American highways were enhanced by sequences of red rhyming signs promoting safety and **Burma Shave** shaving cream.

I'd be neglectful if I didn't mention **limericks**, little bits of often-dirty poetry. Two classics start with "There was a young man from Nantucket" and "There was a young man from Woonsocket." Google will guide you to the complete verses and many more.

[The photo at the start of this chapter shows American poet **Edgar Allan Poe** (1809—1849) by an unknown photographer, restored by Yann Forget and Adam Cuerden. My maternal grandparents lived near his cottage in "Poe Park" in the Bronx, New York.]

Chapter 45
I envy androids

Other than people who are planning suicides, most of us don't know how much time we have left.

When I started my blog about dying, back around 2010, I did some research and calculating, and estimated that I'd die in 2035, at the ripe old age of 89. The 89 number seemed realistic: neither pessimistic nor greedy. Now I doubt that I'll hang on that long.

I've been a *Type-Two* diabetic for about 35 years, but it's under control. I've had kidney stones, but they were blasted to smithereens, and I peed out the pieces. I need a walker. I have Parkinson's Disease, but so far, I have no tremors like **Michael J. Fox**. I don't smoke and seldom drink alcohol. I don't swim with sharks, rob banks, jump on trampolines, sky dive or engage in dangerous sex.

Like many Americans I used to eat too much (now meals are an obligation, maybe a burden, and seldom a joy). I assumed that I'd have a heart attack when I was in my 40s, then 50s—but it didn't happen.

Some years ago, I lost nearly 150 pounds. I got rid of the other person who was living under my skin, sharing my organs and hanging onto my bones.

I was able to buy jeans for $14 at **Sam's Club**, not $50 at the fat man's store. I felt good, looked good and some hot chicks flirted with me. I now weigh 30 pounds less than the weight my cardiologist recommended. I can still wear the sweatpants I bought as a college freshman in 1964 (don't ask why I still have them).

Ten years ago, I was diagnosed with inadequate kidney function and atrial fibrillation (also known as coronary arrhythmia and irregular heartbeat). I was given a new drug for high blood pressure—and three days later I was diagnosed with low blood pressure, (80/60, compared to a normal 120/80).

I had a small scab on one arm from a dog scratch. Suddenly it erupted and blood started spurting. The leak was probably caused by my new blood thinner.

My heart and kidney problems were discovered while I was visiting my wife **Marilyn** in a hospital. They had not been previously diagnosed, but probably were incipient and worsened by my not eating or sleeping properly while Marilyn was away, plus stress.

I got some new drugs to take with various good and not-so-good effects. Some drugs may be the wrong drugs.

Human bodies are complex and often very confusing.
Androids don't deal with this crap.

Chapter 46
When does "old" start?

I became 78 this year (2024). I'm a few years younger than Biden, and a few months older than Trump. Am I (GASP) already an *alte kocker*? (That's Yiddish for "old shitter.") I prefer something like "esteemed, learned kvetcher." (To *kvetch* is to complain.) I do a lot of that.

I've kvetched for my whole life. My mother said that I once cried in my highchair until she realized that I was upset because a kitchen cabinet door was left open. I could not speak yet, but I *could kvetch*.

I've always had very high standards, that often do not apply to me. My wife often kvetched about my lapses. She thinks I should shower every day. That's ridiculous. I have *aroma*—not stench.

The web makes it easy to kvetch to a large audience with my blogs, websites and Facebook pages. My books are filled with kvetching (mostly funny kvetching).

When does alte-kockering begin? Maybe 75 or 80? Or 40?

Is there a Yiddish term for "pre-alte kocker?"

[Photo from www.elephantjournal.com. Thanks.]

Strange Talents, Strange Inabilities, Creative Compensations

I've been able to do some weird stuff, including balancing a broom on the tip of a finger, holding my breath for three minutes, and doing the backwards backstroke.

However, I am unable to do some very basic things. I probably should be embarrassed to admit ths, but I've revealed a lot in this book, so here's some more: *I can't snap my fingers or whistle*.

When I was 14, I stayed up until about 5 AM and finally mastered the elusive tasks, and went to sleep. When I awoke, I could no longer snap or whistle.

Dejected and ashamed, I developed creative compensations. I fake the finger snap by making a silent gesture with my fingers and a clucking sound with my mouth. I can make a passable whistle sound by sucking air *in*, rather than blowing air *out*.

Chapter 47
Rethinking "fear"

In his first inaugural address, on March 4, 1933, American President **Franklin Delano Roosevelt** declared, "The only thing we have to fear is *fear itself*."

In 1973, **Erica Jong** wrote a book called *Fear of Flying*, about female sexuality. The book supported the development of "second-wave feminism."

I never feared flying or sex.

Although I've never been particularly brave or macho, I've often said that "Fear is a useless emotion because it cripples your mind."

But now, because of a partially crippled body, I've gone from mere caution and timidity to genuine *fear*. I need to use a walker for walking, or even for standing for more than a few seconds.

I've fallen about a dozen times over the past few years, and I needed to call for firefighters to pick me up. The falls were more embarrassing than painful—but one time I broke an elbow when I fell in my kitchen (a very dangerous place). I needed help to get up from a toilet four times: twice at home, once in **Home Depot** and once on a ferry boat. The incidents would've been great for YouTube.

It's OK to laugh at me. Heck, even I laugh at me.

I have long been fascinated by euphemisms.

- Some euphemisms, like "gay," have become so common that the earlier use of the word has largely ended.
- Some euphemisms seem nastier than the words they replace. "Son of a bitch" was devised to replace "dog"—a horrible epithet in England. In the USA, "bitch" is a bad word, unless you're talking about a female dog.
- Some euphemisms, like "SOB" and "son of a B," are euphemisms for *other* euphemisms.
- Some euphemisms are just plain confusing. "Pissed-off" (sometimes hyphenated, sometimes not) is common in America, but "ticked off" and "teed off" are common, too.

Chapter 48
Am I a man or a ball?

I have:

- Too much to do that people expect me to do that I don't feel like doing
- Too much to do that I want to do but can't start or finish
- Too much that was fun but is no longer fun
- Too many books unread and unwritten
- Too many bills that I can't pay I full
- Too much news that I can't stand
- Too little to look forward to
- Too little tolerance
- Too little energy
- Too little time
- Too little joy

Is this depression, sadness, pissed-offedness? Sometimes I seem like a ball on a pool table, bouncing around and reacting, not initiating action.

For over an hour after hearing a **Bob Edwards** interview on the radio I still had a tear in my right eye.

I sometimes have to pee—but lack motivation to get up and go to the john.

Some body parts always hurt. Others have no sensation. My typing is filled with errors caused by my brain malfunctioning, not by sloppy typing.

Have I lost *it*? Where/why did "it" go?

Have I finally, at age-78, passed from middle age to old?

Why did I type this page instead of finishing three long-past-due books?

Will reading this help me?

Can I give myself a good kick in the ass?

Chapter 49
Sometimes it *is* too late

Back in 2014 I was reading an article in the *New York Daily News* about a woman who was near death after being hit by a "speed demon" on a $4,000 bicycle in Central Park.

At first her name didn't mean anything to me. But then I realized that **Jill Tarlov** was the daughter of my late father's late cousin, **Malcolm Tarlov** from Norwalk, Connecticut.

I probably had not seen Jill in more than 50 years and probably would have gone the rest of my life without thinking of her. It's sad to be reminded of people only when they are dead or nearly dead.

- o   If you have old friends and relatives whom you don't hate but have not spoken to in a long time, get in touch. You may not have another chance.
- o   Apparently, there are no bike speed limits in the Big Apple. There should be.

Chapter 50
I learned some things in 78 years

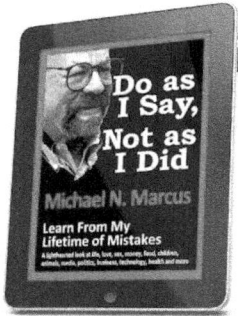

I've done a lot in my first 78 years, probably more than I'll do in my next years. I did some of the right things and many of the wrong things. I learned lots of lessons and ten years ago I put them into a book.

Do as I Say, Not as I Did

If the old me could have spoken to the young me, maybe I wouldn't have made so many stupid mistakes.

From an early draft of the introduction: "Time travel is a pervasive theme in popular culture. For something that doesn't actually exist, time travel is surprisingly popular."

Google showed about ten times as many links for time travel as for European travel.

Time travel has inspired countless books, movies, TV shows, games and comic books.

My interest in time travel has often been extremely personal. I fantasize about *interacting with myself*—not with dead presidents or great grandchildren.

I've contemplated how the 11-year-old me would have reacted to the 20-year-old me. Would the 15-year-old me think the 40-year-old me was interesting, cool, smart, boring, stupid, scary, a creep or an asshole?

More importantly—and the impetus for that book—I've thought that if the old me could have spoken to the young me, maybe I'd now be healthier, wealthier and happier.

I wish I could forcefully advise myself to "do this, not that." The ten- and twenty-year-old me might have ignored the advice of parents, teachers and doctors—but not the advice of *me*. If I talk to myself, I *have* to listen.

I've learned a lot since 1946. Many of the lessons have been difficult and some have been painful. I figured out many things myself. Some lessons were taught to me by others, especially by my father.

While technology will not allow me to go back and talk to myself, I can warn and advise anyone who's willing to pay attention. That's why I wrote that book.

And, maybe by looking back, I can influence my own future.

Chapter 51
Forgive and forget, or ignore and move on?

We've all heard the phrase "forgive and forget." I seldom forget, and if I remember evil, I seldom forgive.

At a school reunion about 30 years ago, I was approached by another man.

Years earlier, when his hair was darker and greasier, "Rick" was known as "Daddy Demon." He was probably one of just two Jewish juvenile delinquents in New Haven.

Rick smiled, said "Hi, howya been?" and raised his right hand to shake mine. I kept my right hand at my side.

I reminded Rick that in the fall of 1958, when we were both in the seventh grade, on the way home from school, he and a couple of other 12-year-old hoods ambushed me for no discernible reason. Rick poked holes in both of my bicycle tires and then he snuffed out a cigarette on my head.

A few months later, Rick's posse held me down on the ground with my mouth forced open so they could spit into it. Later on, one of them stabbed me in the pool at our country club.

I did not shake Rick's hand.

I did tell Rick to go fuck himself.

I still remembered a lot.

Fast-forward to a few years ago. Rick wanted to join an online group that I administer. My initial reaction was to ignore him—a polite way of saying "go fuck yourself" again.

I thought about my decision. I'd held a grudge against an evil, sadistic bully for many decades, the vast majority of my life, and now he wanted—or needed—something from me.

Unlike that day in 1958, I now had power over him. I was in a position to show the mercy that he and his posse did not show.

I clearly did not forget what they did—and cannot forgive it—but I could *ignore* it.

Maybe Rick on Social Security was not the same person that the pre-teen Rick was.

I've done a few crappy things in my life ('tho I was never a bully) and I'd like my transgressions to be ignored.

So, I let Rick into the group.

If I meet him again, maybe I'll be willing to shake his hand. I probably won't tell him to go fuck himself. I'd probably like to have a conversation with him. I'd like to know what diabolical influences turned him into Daddy Demon, and how he outgrew the demon.

Maybe by being nice to a former nemesis, I outgrew a demon of my own.

I definitely feel better now.

Chapter 52
I may have lost "it"—but didn't lose it

Several years ago, I prepared to take the train from Connecticut to Manhattan for **Book Expo America**. I thought I put my cellphone and two bars of **Bonomo Turkish Taffy** into my shoulder bag.

When I got on the train, I wanted to call home and tell my wife that I had made the train, but I could not find the phone. I went through the bag several times and finally gave up, assuming I had never put the stuff in the bag.

At the show I was not able to communicate properly with wife or office. There apparently were no pay phones at **Javits Center**. I was able to borrow cellphones and stay in touch minimally.

When I got back to Connecticut, I scoured the car and house. I inspected every likely and unlikely place. I called **AT&T** to determine whether anyone had used my missing phone. No one had.

A few minutes later I heard the tell-tale notes of *Louie-Louie*—my ring tone—coming from the shoulder bag I had schlepped to New York and back.

I started ransacking the bag for the umpteenth time and discovered a hidden compartment containing my phone and taffy. They'd made the round trip with me. If someone had tried to call me in New York, "Louie" would've helped me find the phone.

By the way, I deliberately bought my Nokia Lumia 920 in *red* to make it hard to misplace.

It was misplaced for a month.

Chapter 53
Am I aging gracefully, or disgracefully?

Another time at **Book Expo America**, I spoke to two smart, witty, attractive young ladies. If I was not happily married, I would have "tried something."

Somehow the topic of my age came up. One of my new companions guessed that I was 52. The other said 47.

When I revealed that I was really 67, they were *amazed*.

I was—and am certainly not—a prime specimen of American masculinity, but the reactions of these ladies gave me a good ego boost. Actually, when I see pictures of some of my contemporaries, and some of my wife's contemporaries, I think we're doing *just fine*.

I wonder if I dyed my gray beard brown or black, could I pass for 35? If I shaved it off, could I pass for 17? Probably not.

Oh well.

What language do cops speak in Georgia?

I was stopped by a cop in Georgia while driving from New York to Florida. I don't know if I was speeding, had a dead taillight or if my northern license plate marked me as a likely source of revenue. I stopped my car, lowered my window, and had my license and registration ready.

When the officer appeared, he said something that sounded like "gmrjklvot strlgnvuk papaflurbo zlot norpelaz."

In the past I had no trouble understanding Bill Clinton or Andy Griffith—but the cop's sounds were incomprehensible. I said, "what?" and he repeated the gibberish.

I again said, "what?" He just muttered and waved me away.

Chapter 54
Obsolete measurements & terminology

At one time some things were described as "the size of a Volkswagen" or "bigger than a breadbox."

But now, Volkswagens come in multiple sizes and shapes—and few people use breadboxes.

We need some new standards.
We also should abandon ancient terms.

Rotary-dial telephones have not been made in many years. But we still "dial" our modern touch-tone phones, and the latest cellphones have "redial" buttons. "Auto-redial" is a common contemporary phone feature.

"Chamber pots" were used in Ancient Greece (12th-9th centuries BCE to 600 CE), and in the Elizabethan Era (1558-1603 CE). So, why are 21st-century children taught to "go potty?"

At one time, wicker "waste baskets" were common. Today, even wooden, plastic, glass and steel trash cans and refuse receptacles are called "waste baskets."

People born before the baby boom wear "dungarees." We boomers wear "jeans."

"Tin foil" was largely replaced in the 1940s by less expensive and more durable *aluminum* foil.

At one time, a police vehicle with a two-way radio was an expensive bit of high-tech, called a "radio car." Now, every police car has a radio. Maybe several.

Not too long ago, a flat-screen television was an expensive and rare status symbol. Today, almost every TV made has a flat screen. It's no longer costly, coveted or worth mentioning.

And, of course, DVRs and other "set top boxes" don't sit on the tops of flat-screen TVs.

Until the late 1940s, many American kitchens had "ice boxes." Today we have refrigerators, but some old farts still use the old term or call any brand fridge a "Frigidaire."

There's no good reason to call a CD or a downloaded selection of songs an "album."

Making a digital recording is not "filming."

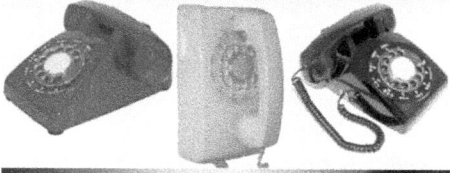

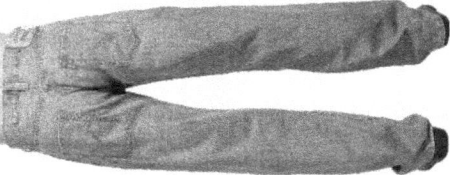

The "FLASH" buttons used for Call Waiting on modern phones do not flash a light on an operator's switchboard. Similarly, very few currently used phones are "hung up" at the end of a call.

Chapter 55
Fired, hired, fired, hired, fired

In 1971, while I was assistant editor at a magazine for hi-fi equipment dealers, I got friendly with some folks at *Rolling Stone* magazine. A while later, I wrote a major cover story for our mag about the exploding "youth market," and it inadvertently helped *Rolling Stone* to get hi-fi advertising.

Although the main audience for my article was hi-fi dealers, it also reached important executives at the manufacturers. *Rolling Stone* decided to run ads in our magazine to get even more hi-fi advertising, and they paid me to write and design the ad.

Rolling Stone then decided to make a major long-term effort to develop hi-fi advertising and wanted a regular column of education and product reviews, and I was the logical one to write it.

I wasn't sure if my company would allow me to freelance for another publication, so rather than ask and risk being turned down, I decided to go ahead with the plan, but use the pen name, *Mitchell Newman*. I wasn't deep undercover, however. Mitchell is an obvious variant of Michael, and my middle name is Neuman. *Rolling Stone* agreed to pay me $75 per column, which would appear in each issue, every two weeks.

Unfortunately, I was soon in a terrible writer's slump at my daily job. For weeks, I found it very difficult to put words on paper, and I was fired from my $125-per-week job. I quickly persuaded *Rolling Stone* to hire me full-time at a bit over $20K per year to both guide the ad staff and write my column, this time under my real name.

Rolling Stone's New York office at 78 East 56th Street was in constant turmoil. We were a remote satellite of the San Francisco headquarters, separated by 3,000 miles and three time zones, and seldom visited by the boss, **Jann Wenner**, who apparently preferred the West Coast.

In the two years I worked there, we went from trying to sublet half of our floor, to renting a second floor, to getting rid of the second floor. For several months, we published a specific New York City edition, and then closed it down. Years later, the San Francisco operation was closed down and New York became corporate headquarters.

We had an endless stream of publishers in New York, with a new one every six months or so. The first and best was **Porter Bibb**. Each new publisher would typically fire about 80% of the employees hired by his predecessor and then rehire about half of them, and then he'd get fired, and the cycle would repeat with the next publisher.

Each day, writers went to work, expecting to be fired, and eventually most of us were.

You are fired again!

I went through a particularly weird outplacement procedure. "**Larry-the-prick**" was a new publisher and an evil S.O.B. who was hated by most of the staff. He called me into his office to tell me that I was going off salary, and I'd be writing a column for each issue, which was the way I had started working for *Stone*.

This was not unexpected or frightening because there were lots of other publications I planned to write for, but I did ask for severance pay. Larry said I was not entitled to severance because I wasn't being fired. I was just changing my status.

A few months later, Larry said he no longer wanted me to write my column. I again asked for severance pay. With a sadistic gleam in his eyes, the prick explained that in *Rolling Stone's* version of *Catch 22*, freelancers do not get severance pay when their work is no longer wanted.

A bit later, Larry was canned, just like his employees. Since he wasn't a freelancer, the evil prick probably got severance pay.

People often warn others to not "say ill about the dead." I am not obligated to abide by that advice, because many dead people *deserve* ill words.

If Larry had not died in 2003 and he survived to read this chapter, I'd say, FUCK YOU!

I wish I had said it years ago. My tormented and abused coworkers would likely have applauded.

Chapter 56
Three in a bed (*Ménage A Trois*) two ways

For a while when in college and shortly after I finished, I had the hots for a kinky, lusty and loose young lady named **Nina**. We dated, but she was never my girlfriend. We even dated while she was another guy's girlfriend. Her boyfriend was 400 miles away in medical school. She sometimes said they were engaged but she wore no ring and didn't act betrothed.

I read that **Marilyn Monroe** regarded her spectacular sexuality as a gift to be given to **JFK** and others, and it often seemed that Nina felt that way.

Sometimes Nina had the hots for me, sometimes for either of two friends of mine, and sometimes she was hot for **Danny**, our art professor.

I don't know that Nina qualified as a nymphomaniac, and I wouldn't call her a slut (but others did). She just *loved* sex. She was into traditional as well as somewhat more exotic erotica, such as simultaneous salad tossing (see *Urban Dictionary* if you need an explanation), streaking, outdoor, mild bondage, flashing truck drivers and performing in personal porn; but she drew the line at girl-girl sex. Nina was not wife material, but she was definitely fun to be with—with a trustworthy prophylactic.

One night, Nina and I were at Professor Danny's apartment to look at 35mm Kodachrome slides he had taken at European museums during several summer vacations. He could not afford to have prints made from the thousands of slides and had pawned his slide projector to pay rent.

We sat around his dining room table and held up the tiny slides in front of the chandelier bulbs to see them. It was not much of an art exhibition.

After a while, Danny brought out some wine, and then some joints and put **Procol Harum** on the stereo. Pretty soon we three had a serious buzz on.

Before *A Whiter Shade of Pale* ended, Danny moved his chair so he could sit behind Nina.

He started massaging her shoulders and back and occasionally reached around to stroke her braless breasts through her thin satin blouse. He kissed her neck and her exposed shoulders. Then he took her right hand, kissed it, held it, and stood up and invited her into his bedroom.

Nina stood up, too.

She smiled at him. Then she turned her head and smiled even more brightly at me.

Nina playfully grabbed my right hand with her left hand, touched it to her right breast and invited me to come along.

This was the 60s, so I went along.

Pretty soon, one professor and two students were naked and squished together on a double bed. Since it was Danny's home and he was our professor and he had issued the first invitation, I felt he deserved to be first with Nina, and I was relegated to "sloppy seconds." I hate even typing that phrase, let alone participating in it, but horniness, wine and marijuana can overcome a lot of reservation and revulsion.

Unfortunately, Professor Danny couldn't get hard, and he resorted to packing poor Nina with Vaseline in an effort to ease his entry. It didn't help. (He didn't know enough to use K-Y Jelly.) Frustrated, Danny told me to take over. Suddenly, my position in the sexual sequence had greatly improved. I had moved up from Sloppy Second to Top Dog, Leader of the Pack, Ichi-Ban, Numero Uno... and the nutty professor started rubbing my penis to get me in the mood.

I could tolerate three in a bed, or maybe four, but not another man's hands on my private parts. And I certainly had no intention of returning the favor. Danny's effort to get me in the mood got me *out* of the mood. I quickly rolled off the bed, grabbed my clothes, and got out of that apartment as fast as I could.

Danny gave both Nina and me A's in the course. Nina was an excellent artist and a good student who deserved the top mark even without extra credit for sex.

I probably deserved a B-plus, but the embarrassed and cautious professor apparently gave me "Please-keep-your-big-mouth-shut" bonus points to boost my average into the A range.

He later married another one of his students and Nina married one of my friends. I don't know if Danny ever had prints made from his Kodachrome slides.

When my income at *Rolling Stone* was reduced from a salary of $400 per week to a freelancer's fee of $75 every two weeks, I was seriously dating three young ladies. Actually, it was more than dating. I was *auditioning potential wives*: **Marilyn**, **Virginia**, and I forgot the third one's name. I do remember that she lived in Brooklyn, and she had a southern accent. Number-Three got pregnant by someone else and had a painful abortion. She recuperated in my apartment. I was a very good friend.

Anyway, for a normal bachelor in Manhattan, a drop of over 80% in income would make a serious impact on dating. But things are different for a journalist with abundant freeloading options. There were plenty of ways to have free dates.

Writers and editors and their companions could go to free movies and concerts just by requesting "review tickets." There was even plenty of free food at lavish press conferences and sometimes invitations to check out new restaurants and bars.

Even with no invitation, it was easy to crash an event with a free meal at the **New York Coliseum** or a hotel by wearing a badge from some previous event or showing a press ID or a business card. The gatekeepers would never risk offending a member of the press, even someone with dubious credentials who was not on the invitation list. The cost of food and booze was minimal compared with the potential benefit of positive press coverage or the risk of negative coverage after turning someone away. As for gifts, there were always trinkets from trade shows and press conferences, free samples, and plenty of free records and tapes sent to us to review. When my wife-audition process had narrowed to the three leading contenders, I needed a tiebreaker, and my Marilyn was the only one of final trio who was willing to sleep with me *and* **Long John Nebel**.

No, I'm not talking about a *Ménage à trois* with three living people in the bed. Long John Nebel did a late-night talk-radio show, and I liked to sleep with the radio on. Fortunately, Marilyn accepted me and didn't object to John, and she didn't ask how much money I was making.

Even in 1971, $37.50 per week didn't go very far. 1971 was a time of granny gowns, granny glasses, going bra-less and anti-materialism; and it never occurred to Marilyn to ask about my salary. Besides, she had a *real* job with a decent salary. I knew how much she made.

Marilyn swore that, if she ever remarries, she'll demand to see the next guy's paycheck and previous year's tax return before she says, "I do."

Anti-material Marilyn didn't want an engagement ring, but she later changed her mind, and I gave her a diamond ring on our fourth anniversary. Her mother complained that the stone, selected with assistance from my brother—an alleged jewelry expert—was *cloudy*. Marilyn and I are still married after over 52 years, but now we listen to podcasts at night.

Chapter 57
Decision & indecision

Eighth grade in New Haven was decision time. Fourteen-year-old children were supposed to choose their life's path. Would they wear blue collars, or would they wear white, or maybe pink?

Inherent to the decision-making process was exposure to basic training in three directions.

To try out life in carpentry, factory-working or car-fixing, we (boys only, of course) had brief courses in mechanical drawing, printing and woodworking.

Our white-collar life sample was a short "Language Exploratory" course in an arbitrarily selected foreign language. After studying Spanish, French or Latin for five months, we were supposed to know if we wanted to go to college. For the other five months of the school year, all eighth-graders had typing class, to prepare for a career in an office or beauty salon or maybe the military. It was confusing.

I had started sort-of typing around age-ten, on a very old Remington with sticky keys that my father had brought home from his office. Like most beginners, I began with the basic index-finger hunt-and-peck method and had advanced to pretty quick two-fingered typing when I was given my very own Royal portable at age-13.

By the time we started "Business Exploratory" (a.k.a. typing), I was a very fast six-fingered typist. I didn't always use the same fingers for the same keys and had no idea where the "home position" was or why it existed, but I typed well, and seldom peeked at the keys.

My teacher (a nice lady whose name is lost to history) was faced with a major dilemma. Even though I did everything the wrong way, on the first day of class I was already typing faster and more accurately than my class was expected to type after five months of instruction.

To make it worse, the teacher knew that if she tried to force me to type correctly, I would inevitably type more slowly, make more errors and maybe sprain a wrist. Maybe I'd even sprain two wrists.

Since she recognized that I was heading for college, not a career in business or hairdressing, and would probably never need to touch a keyboard after eighth grade (HAH!), my enlightened teacher gave me an easy "A," and let me sit and read a book propped up on the typewriter until the course ended. The teacher told me, "If you won't tell, I won't tell."

But, now I've told you.

Chapter 58
Spooky story

Wendy's family paralleled mine. She was my age. Her younger brother was the same age as my sister. Our parents were friends.

Wendy and I were often in the same class. She sat next to me in first grade, where she once dropped a milk bottle. It smashed on the floor at our feet, and then she peed into the milk puddle and the vile mixture splashed on my shoes.

I got even with Wendy in third grade when I was drinking milk in class. I started laughing at something and I sneezed milk at her.

When we were young teenagers, we belonged to the same beach club. At that time, her father had a terminal illness. One night I was at a teen dance at the club, and my mind kept repeating a horrible phrase, "Hi, Wendy, is your father dead yet?" "Hi, Wendy, is your father dead yet?" "Hi, Wendy, is your father dead yet?" Those words—which I could never, ever say—were haunting me. My mouth was closed, but my brain kept speaking.

At some point in the evening, I saw Jean approaching me. She was my friend and also Wendy's friend.

Jean was crying, and when she got close to me, her face turned fiery red and she started pounding my chest with her fists, screaming and calling me horrible names.

When she eventually calmed down, Jean said that she had seen Wendy a few minutes earlier, and that Wendy's father had died two weeks earlier, and that Wendy told her that I had just said, "Hi, Wendy, is your father dead yet?"

I *had not even seen Wendy that day*, but she'd read my mind.

Years later, Wendy was killed by her husband.

Yikes!

Chapter 59
Why I became a cynical secularist

When I was a little kid in the Bronx, I had no formal religious training. I suppose I knew that I was Jewish (whatever that meant) and some people were not.

I was aware of some Jewish holidays, foods, words and rituals. My parents sometimes spoke Yiddish (the common language of Jews from Eastern Europe) when they did not want my younger sister or me to understand what they were saying. I eventually figured it out. I'm good with languages.

I received Chanukah presents, but also had my picture taken with Santa. I probably heard "JESUS H. CHRIST" as an expletive; but neither that nor Santa had religious significance to me.

My impression of God was based on images of an old guy with a long beard up on a cloud.

I had somehow absorbed little bits of religion. I'd heard snippets about God in popular culture ("God bless you," "God damn you," "God-awful," "God-fearing," "God willing," "God forgive me," "God forbid," "for God's sake," "from your mouth to God's ears," "God will get you"). But all I knew was that if I did something bad, God might punish me.

My first religious experience occurred in a park near our apartment.

When I was around four or five years old, I was sledding, lost control, and crashed into a tree. I was not injured. My sled was not damaged. But I thought I was in *big* trouble for hurting **Mother Nature**, who was *God's wife*. I started chanting "I love God, I like God, I love God, I like God, I like God, I love God." Apparently, my penance was effective because the tree did not fall on me, my sled did not go into a flaming abyss, I was not struck by lightning, and I am still alive to tell the tale. In retrospect, my ad-libbed chant may have been like the "say ten Hail Marys" often prescribed by Catholic priests to sinners.

My father's parents lived in Brooklyn and were Orthodox-Jewish. I sometimes visited them and once went to an Orthodox synagogue with pop's pop, **Grampa Walter Marcus**. It was a strange, alien environment—as strange as the Tatooine cantina scene in the original *Star Wars* movie. I saw old men with prayer shawls over their heads rocking back and forth, chanting in a language I did not understand. It was Hebrew with a Litvak (Lithuanian) accent.

As a young child in 1906, Grampa Walter immigrated to New York City from Sopotskin, a

village in what was then Poland and is now in Belarus. I saw him three or four times each year and he rewarded me with a quarter for each prayer that I mastered. I also earned a quarter for each new bicycle trick I could perform. I preferred learning tricks to prayers.

The only religious activity I recall demonstrated by my America-born paternal grand-mother, **Grandma "Gee" (Genevieve)**, was the cooking of mostly sticky and sweet kosher food. I hated it. My father loved it. My mother tolerated it.

Like many Jewish families of that era (and even now), the Marcuses of Brooklyn were selectively kosher. There was no *treyf* (non-kosher food) in their apartment on Ocean Parkway, yet when outside their home, they enjoyed vast food varieties in restaurants, hotels and non-kosher homes of relatives and friends.

My mother's parents (the **Jacobses**, both born in the USA around the beginning of the 20th century) lived in the Bronx. I don't think they celebrated any Jewish holidays. If a Jewish "high holy day" of Rosh Hashanah or Yom Kippur was on a Wednesday, when neighbors were likely to be in synagogues, my maternal grandparents were likely to be in Manhattan at a Broadway matinee.

Mom's parents were not even remotely kosher like Pop's parents were. Like many Germanic Jews of that era, the Jacobses were unobservant, secular, cynical, assimilated and borderline antisemitic. Actress **Kyra Sedgwick** described her Jewish mother, **Patricia Rosenwald Sedgewick,** as an "antisemitic Jew."

A large Jewish Community Center and synagogue was conveniently located across the street from the Jacobs apartment on Valentine Avenue, but they were not members and apparently never went there. (The building later became "**El Mundo**," a Latino-focused department store offering everything "From toothpaste to high-end furniture.")

Grandma "Del" (Adele) Jacobs was particularly hostile to recent immigrants who "speak with a heavy handwriting." When she was single, she refused to date any Jewish man with an accent. After she became a widow, however, she had a long romance with a heavily accented Catholic man from Ireland. He wanted to marry her, but she preferred to just live with him—first in the Bronx and later in Florida.

Grandma was a Yankee of sorts, born in Manhattan's "Hell's Kitchen" neighborhood west of Times Square (now gentrified as "Clinton"). She viewed herself as an inheritor of high-class Viennese culture, and initially dismissed my father-to-be as a "Polish peasant." Pop did some historical research and determined that her forbears were just as Polish as his were.

Grampy Jay did not trust Orthodox Jews in business. He warned, "The bigger the beard, the bigger the lie." Despite their cynicism and lack of personal piousness, Grandma and Grampy were very proud of their grandchildren's achievements in religious school and glad to attend bat and bar mitzvahs. (Grandma Del erroneously pronounced *bar mitzvah* as *b'mitzvah*.)

Grampy Jay was extremely anti-religion. However, he recommended religious school for his grandchildren, so they'd gain knowledge to make up their own minds about religion. Despite his theological cynicism, Grampy sometimes combined bits of Jewish pride and wit. He invented hybrid names including "Franklin Delano Resnick" and "Gina Lola Berkowitz."

My mother felt deprived because of her lack of Jewish education and in-home observation. On Friday afternoons, when her Jewish school friends were rushing home, eagerly anticipating the approaching Sabbath rituals and meals, Mom had nothing special to look forward to.

The family had no Chanukah candles or Passover meals, but Grandma did make an effort for some Jewish holidays. She had matzos on the table for Passover, but there was no praying.

As an adult, Mom was active in Jewish organizations, studied Hebrew, became a bat mitzvah when she was 60-plus, and fought antisemitism. I remember going with her to a mobile home park in around 1960 that had been accused of turning away potential Jewish residents. She posed as a customer and asked the salesman about nearby synagogues. Ironically, this was in Milford, Connecticut, where I later lived for about 20 years, and there are very few synagogues.

I don't remember my parents ever attending synagogue services in the Bronx. Our family moved to New Haven in 1952, when I was six years old. My parents joined a Conservative synagogue (**B'nai Jacob**) and I probably started attending Sunday School when I was in second grade and "Hebrew School" after regular school twice a week, likely in fourth grade.

I was mostly unimpressed and uninspired by my education. We kids were presented with a mixture of Jewish history, culture, religion and the Hebrew language. A few teachers were superb, but some lessons were dispensed by teachers of inadequate quality, with inadequate thought and inadequate explanation.

I remember being taught that, during the Holocaust, Nazi doctors sterilized some Jewish people. I thought this meant that the victims were dumped into vats of boiling water, as opposed to enduring involuntary surgery to prevent reproduction.

י	ט	ח	ז	ו	ה	ד	ג	בּ	א
Yod	Tet	Chet	Zayin	Vav	He	Dalet	Gimel	Bet	Alef
(Y)	(T)	(Ch)	(Z)	(V)	(H)	(D)	(G)	(B/V)	(silent)
ע	ס	ן	נ	ם	מ	ל	ך	כּ	
Ayin	Samech	Nun	Nun	Mem	Mem	Lamed	Khaf	Kaf	
(silent)	(S)	(N)	(N)	(M)	(M)	(L)	(Kh)	(K/Kh)	
ת	שׁ	ר	ק	ץ	צ	ף	פ	פּ	
Tav	Shin	Resh	Qof	Tsadeh	Tsadeh	Feh	Peh		
(T)	(Sh/S)	(R)	(Q)	(Ts)	(Ts)	(F)	(P/F)		

In our first year of Hebrew language instruction, we were expected to learn and remember the meanings of indecipherable strings of alien symbols. We were not taught what the individual symbols (*graphemes*) represented. We were not prepared to recognize those symbols so we could determine that several would produce the Hebrew words for "boy" or "pen." It was like being expected to recognize the English words "cat" and "dog" without knowing the sounds that the letters represent. Our class of apparently normal kids was as dysfunctional as a gathering of dyslexics.

The religious instruction was limited to learning how to read several dozen Hebrew prayers that were used in synagogue services on the Sabbath and other holidays. I remember that my father was shocked to learn that one of the first prayers we learned was the "Mourner's Kaddish," the prayer said by mourners at funerals and regular services. Perhaps Pop thought that the school was premature in preparing young children for the demise of relatives. Maybe he did not want to confront his own mortality.

I "outgrew" religion when I was 12 years old (before my bar mitzvah) and could not get a good explanation for why the Supreme Being who smote the enemies of the ancient Jewish people did not stop the Spanish Inquisition, Attila the Hun, the Black Plague, the Holocaust and the KKK.

An Orthodox rabbi explained the un-blocked mayhem by telling me that Jews did not pray enough to be worthy of rescue by God.

That seemed like baloney in 1958 and does so now. If God really did exist in the old days, then she, he or it must have been protective even before people decided to pray.

Apparently, God can be loving *or* vicious.

Another horrid justification for the Holocaust is that it was God's punishment for assimilation and Zionism. Did a Jewish infant in Europe deserve to be grabbed by the legs by a Nazi soldier and have its head smashed into a brick wall?

I think not.

From *Modern Jewish Library*: "The Holocaust also impelled many theologians to reconsider the Jewish conception of God. According to biblical theology, evil and suffering afflict the Jewish people as a result of their sins. However, the horrors of the Holocaust made this theological explanation unacceptable to many thinkers. Richard Rubenstein has articulated the most radical theological response to the Nazi atrocities. According to Rubenstein, God is dead. One cannot viably assert traditional Judaism or a belief in the Jewish God in light of the Holocaust."

I wondered if the allegedly omniscient, omnipresent, omnipotent King of the Universe was absent, distracted, no longer cared, or *never actually existed*. Maybe God was a mythological creature—created in man's image rather than the other way around.

Other people probably wonder this, too. The nonreligious population is estimated to be 16% worldwide, 76% in Japan, 21% in the USA and 1% in Iran and Uganda. Non-religion is growing in most American states, even in the conservative South. According to the Pew polling people, the percentage for Mississippi grew from 6% to 14% between 2007 and 2014.

Top 10 Countries with the Highest Number of Atheists

Country	Total Atheists (WVS 2017-2022) ⌄
China	479.7M
South Korea	28.4M
United States	27.3M
Japan	23.6M
United Kingdom	15M
Vietnam	11.9M
Germany	9.8M
Russia	8.7M
Canada	7.7M
Australia	5.3M

[Data from Cambridge University. Thanks.]

Chapter 60
You can't always get what you want, or what the doctor ordered

Although my parents were commoners (in the British sense) and I'm not a prince, I was born in the **Royal Hospital** in 1946. The hospital was on the Grand Concourse in the Bronx, when the Bronx was grand.

I was scheduled for a return visit to have my tonsils removed in 1952. Royal Hospital was overbooked, and I was instead sent farther west to **Mother Cabrini Hospital**.

Not only was it not Royal, but it provided my first exposure to nuns. I had never seen nuns before, and these were not like **Singing Nun Debbie Reynolds** or **Flying Nun Sally Field**. They had scary black clothing—like witches—and stern demeanors, and they poked needles in me! I endured the horror and pain however, by focusing on my *future sweet reward*.

I was less than happy about the prospect of being cut open to have part of my body removed. But **Dr. Casson**, our family physician, had assured me that the surgery wouldn't hurt, and that when it was over, I could have any flavor of ice cream that I wanted.

That was a deal I could live with, and Dr. Casson noted that I was to get fudge-ripple, my favorite.

Had I known when I was led to my hospital bed that his promised prescription applied to Royal but not to Cabrini, I probably would have tied bed sheets together and gone out a window and hitchhiked home.

In blissful ignorance, I kept my eyes on the prize. I endured anesthesia and surgery and awoke in the recovery room, happily anticipating my fudge ripple.

Then scary **Sister Evil** appeared, carrying a bowl. She reminded me of the wicked witch who stirred the boiling cauldron in *Snow White and the Seven Dwarfs*. That scene had scared the shit out of me a few months earlier and I made my grandmother take me out of the movie theater.

The nun-witch put the bowl of reddish glop in front of me.

I thought she was showing me the bloody tonsils that the surgeon had cut out of me. Timidly, I asked what the stuff was. She said that it was my *strawberry ice cream*.

With a very hoarse voice, but as forcefully as a frightened six-year-old who had just endured surgery could be, I tried to explain that there must be a mistake. "Please lady. Dr. Casson said I could have fudge-ripple," I pleaded.

With much more force, Sister Evil replied, "You get what you get or you don't get any!"

I've remembered her exact words for over 70 years, and in all those years I have never eaten strawberry ice cream.

[Strawberry ice cream photo from Yellowimages.com. Thanks.]

Chapter 61
Picky eater and drinker

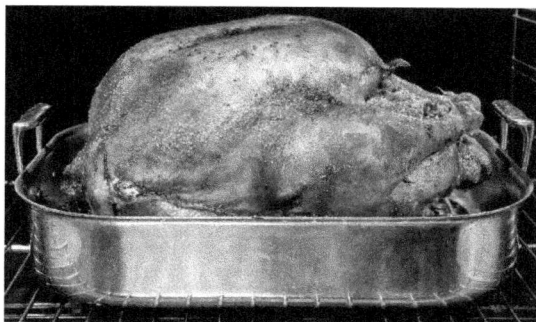

My parents, who were kids during the Great Depression, were taught to try, eat and enjoy a wide variety of foods—and to *never* waste a morsel.

My father was a voracious, adventurous and enthusiastic eater. After our family thought we had eaten all the meat from a turkey, Pop would render the carcass into something resembling a pile of sawdust and toothpicks.gld

The first time my wife met my parents, she assumed she was acceptable because my father took her plate and finished what she didn't eat. (I mentioned this in another chapter. It belongs here, too.)

My father seldom cooked, except on our backyard patio. He usually started charcoal fires by squirting on gasoline intended for our lawn-mower, rather than buying fire-starting fluid. We got used to burgers flavored with Sunoco and hotdogs enhanced with Shell.

Pop was always eager to try new foods in Europe, in local restaurants and from supermarkets and ethnic food stores. One time he brought home a jar of a strange green glop. It may have been a Mexican food. My sister and I called it **G.L.D.** (the abbreviation for "Green Loose Doody") and it remained unopened and uneaten in a kitchen cabinet for many years.

My mother also had wide tastes, eagerly devouring "weird" foods such as okra and kale (decades before it became popular. There was one veggie that she hated, however: cooked carrots.

I inherited this particular distaste, and I laboriously pluck out the little orange chunks before eating my beloved chicken-noodle soup. Sometimes my wife eats them. I also refuse to eat cooked green peas and string beans—but love them *raw*. I also love raw clams.

The potato is one of very few vegetables that are not eaten raw, at least not by most human beings. I love "taters" mashed, baked, roasted, grilled, home-fried, French-fried, julienned, hash-browned, scalloped, in pierogis, in soup, in hash, in pancakes, in rolls, and probably other ways I can't think of now.

But I *absolutely detest* sweet potatoes and potato salad. I've never tried potato pizza, but probably never will. I assume that I won't like it.

When I was a kid, I was accused by my parents of being a picky eater, and I probably was one. I strongly rejected some foods that most people enjoyed. But on the other hand, when I went to college, I found that most of my classmates refused to eat onion soup or liver, which I loved. The more they refused, the more I could eat.

Around age-six, a favorite restaurant in Yonkers, New York, not far from where we lived in the Bronx, was demolished to make room for a huge shopping center. That's when I stopped eating ketchup and coleslaw.

Nearly two decades passed before I again painted my fries red, but, at age-16 I tasted some *extremely good* coleslaw and got hooked. It was not at a gourmet restaurant, or even at a kosher deli, but at the lowly lunch counter of a **W. T. Grant** five-and-dime, next to the store where I had my first summer job. It was perfect. It was crunchy, not slushy, and the cabbage was shredded, not chopped. It had just the right bite of vinegar, and I got a decent size portion with a 75-cent roast beef sandwich that fit my $1 lunch budget.

I had tried other coleslaws since **The Adventurers Inn** closed to make way for the **Cross County Shopping Center** in Yonkers, but nothing impressed me until I tried the slaw at Grant's.

I was curious about what made it so great, but since I had no interest in making it myself, I was not sufficiently curious to ask for the recipe.

One morning around ten, I was sent to Grant's to pick up coffee and a toasted corn muffin for **Mike Deutsch**, my boss. While waiting for the muffin, I learned the secret of the slaw.

There was a huge stainless-steel vat on the back counter, filled with the coleslaw ingredients.

Elizabeth, a tiny cook who was maybe four feet, eight inches tall, was standing on a stool. She was arm-pit-deep into the vat—violently stirring, squishing, mashing and mixing by hand.

The little lady was wrestling with and almost strangling the cabbage and the carrots. She then withdrew her ungloved hands and wiped each arm off into the vat with the opposite hand.

After she cleaned herself, I could see that Elizabeth's little Barbie-Doll-size arms had a resemblance to King Kong's giant-gorilla-size arms.

The secret ingredients in the world's greatest coleslaw were *arm hair and sweat*.

I like cocktail sauce, tartar sauce, salsa and mustard, but not relish. I like sour pickles, but not sweet ones.

I never ate lettuce until after college. It seemed to be both tasteless and useless. But my father explained that the main purpose of lettuce is to hold salad dressing, and I changed my attitude. Similarly, to me the only reason to eat turkey is to support Russian dressing, when cold, or gravy, when hot.

And of course, the main purpose of chickens is to grow necks, wings and skin, and to lay eggs. I never eat the white part (*albumin*) of hard-boiled eggs—but I eat yolks. I love brownies and chocolate cake but scrape off the icing. I used to love going to vote in public schools. The PTA ladies often had homemade baked goods, and I tried to go early and buy *every* brownie.

Now, they sell **Girl Scout cookies**, which I *don't* like. My favorite cookies are soft chocolate chip (my wife prefers them hard), pizzelles and Mallomars. Mallomars are unavailable in warm months, allegedly because of possible melting in the trucks that transport them. That may have been a problem many years ago, but refrigerated trucks are now ubiquitous.

I don't eat a lot of candy. I detest peppermint. I'm both diabetic and picky and don't eat things that are very sweet. I like Hershey's no-sugar chocolate, Hershey bars, Hershey kisses, cherry licorice, caramels, Krackle, Mr. Goodbar, M&Ms, Kit-Kat bars, chocolate-covered almonds, saltwater taffy, and Turkish taffy.

But since early childhood my favorite candies are Tootsie Rolls, and the cherry hearts sold for Valentine's Day. The best thing about January can be found in chain drugstores like **Rite Aid** and **CVS**. That's where you can get **JuJu Hearts**, the magical chewy-gooey red cherry candies I've been addicted to since babyhood.

If I close my eyes when I open the package, the sweet aroma transports me to Cherry Blossom Time in Washington DC—or at least to my grandmother's apartment in the Bronx.

When I was a kid, my **Grandma "Del"** would buy many pounds from **Krum's**—the pre-eminent candy store in the Bronx, or maybe in the world.

Some years she even arranged to buy the huge pile of hearts on display in the window, at a special price after Valentine's Day. We grandchildren would get a few pounds in February, and Grandma would stash the rest in her freezer, to be gradually defrosted and doled out throughout the year. (In later years, when Grandma Del moved to Florida, I provided JuJu Hearts for her.)

Krum's was famous for its candies and ice cream sodas and used to be on the Grand Concourse between 188th Street and Fordham Road. In the front of the store was a huge display case of chocolates and other candies, and farther back you could sit and slurp. The landmark **Loew's Paradise Theater** was across the street, and before **McDonalds** and **Taco Bell** came to town, teens went to Krum's for a post-picture snack.

The Paradise was reincarnated as a mostly Latino concert venue and then a huge church. Grandma Del and Krum's are long gone, but JuJu Hearts have survived.

The price has gone from 15 cents a pound to 99 cents for a 9-ounce bag in 2009, to $1.59 for 12 ounces in 2011 to 99 cents for 6 ounces at CVS in 2012 or $1.99 for 12 ounces at RiteAid for the past few years. Rite Aid often discounts the price by 50 cents. I got a full pound for $1.99 a few years ago because I'm a good customer (i.e., registered drug addict). I even got a second bag for half-price.

Product names, prices, candy size, package size, flavor, retail availability, manufacturers and even the country of origin vary over time. Recently, **Amazon** and the drug chains sold JuJus with the

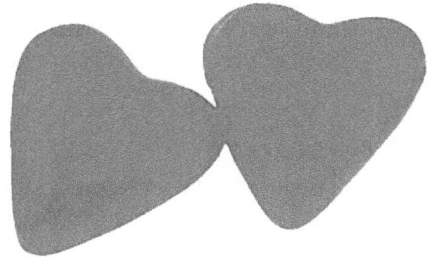

"**Brach's**" brand—which now belongs to giant **Farley's and Sathers**. F&S now supplies such vital foods as Chuckles, Jujyfruits and Jujubes.

The product name has morphed, too. It's now "Jube Jel Cherry Hearts." It gets a B-plus. The A grade is reserved for Krum's, which theoretically will never be equaled.

The Brach's taste and texture are nearly perfect—a bit chewier than the 2012 vintage and just a tad sweeter than the 2010 vintage, but not as sweet as 2011. (I have samples preserved in my freezer.) There was none of the weird smell I couldn't identify when I first opened the bag or waxy texture of 2012. 2024 is not a great year for JuJu Hearts, but is a pretty good year— and it's much better than the dreadful 2009).

Stop & Shop strangely had two very different offerings for 2013 but had none when I checked in 2024. I didn't find any at **Walgreens**, or **Wally's Mart**.

Some basics:

o   JuJu/Jube Jel Hearts' taste and texture are unique: sweeter and softer than red hot dollars, but not as sweet or slimy as Gummi Bears or Worms.
o   Strangely, the JuJu/Jube Jel Heart formula doesn't seem to be used for anything else, at any other time of year—not even for JuJubes or Jujyfruits. But that's OK. JuJu Heart season is only a little longer than the bloom of the Cherry Blossom. The rarity makes them more special, and less destructive to teeth and glucose levels... and freezers make it possible to prolong the pleasure.
o   JuJu Hearts are like pistachio nuts or sex. When they're great, they're fantastic. When they're pretty good, they're good enough; and when they're bad, they're terrible.

JuJu history:

o   The JuJu name apparently comes from the jujube, a red fruit first cultivated in China over 4,000 years ago, that can be used for tea, wine, and throat medication, or eaten as a snack.
o   A jujube tree in Israel is estimated to be over 300 years old.
o   The jujube's sweet smell is said to make teenagers fall in love, and in the Himalaya mountains, young men put jujube flowers on their hats to attract hot Sherpa babes.
o   In West Africa, Juju refers to the supernatural power ascribed to objects or fetishes. It can be synonymous with witchcraft and may be the origin of the American "voodoo."
o   Some of the first JuJu Hearts were made by the **Henry Heide Candy Company**, founded in 1869 by **Henry Heide**, who immigrated to New York from Germany. Heide Candy became known for Jujubes, Jujyfruits, jellybeans, Red Hot Dollars, Gummi Bears and Mexican Hats, which have been perennial favorites in movie theaters and five-and-dimes.
o   The business stayed in the Heide family through four generations and was sold to **Hershey Foods** in 1995. In 2002, **Farley's & Sathers Candy Co.** acquired the Heide brand products from Hershey. The current Brach's candy is made by **Ferrara Candy Company** in Chicago.
o   Although F&S owned Heide, they did not produce Heide's hearts.
o   Through the 2009 season, the hearts were distributed by **Mayfair Candy**, in Buffalo, New York. Over the years, I've encountered some really crappy hearts. Mayfair made the real thing. My dog loved them, too—but he never refused anything remotely edible.
o   Strangely, there were two (maybe more) kinds of JuJu Hearts distributed by Mayfair. The "original" version was sold by **Rite-Aid** (and possibly others). I discovered another inferior version for the first time in 2007, at **CVS**. The individual candy pieces were smaller

than the originals, and they had a second heart shape molded onto the front of each piece. They didn't taste nearly as good as the originals: they were too sweet and not as chewy. Strangely, the same packaging, with same ingredients and same stock number, was used for both.

- You can get JuJu Hearts online in-season at **Candy Favorites**. I have not tasted them. **Amazon** offers several varieties and still had them in stock as late as April in some years.

More of my gustatorial eccentricity:

- I detest dark chocolate, chocolates filled with gooey stuff, and candy bars.
- For dessert, I love cake, ice cream cake, ice cream, ices, gelato, and many fruits—but never Jello, berries, pies or yogurt.
- I recently started to reduce my salt intake.
- With fried seafood, I combine tartar sauce and cocktail sauce. My father taught me this.
- My wife puts all kinds of crap onto eggs and lox. I am relatively a purist.
- I like to creatively combine leftovers, like egg foo young and corned beef hash.
- In the fruit section of a supermarket, I'll gladly load my shopping cart with apples, pears, grapes, cherries, pineapple, watermelon, honeydew, cantaloupe, oranges, tangerines (large and firm only) and grapefruit—but not in the same shopping trip). I absolutely reject bananas, peaches, plums, nectarines, berries, kumquats and kiwis.
- I detest avocado in any form, including guacamole. I like "California Roll" sushi, but I use a chopstick to push out the dreaded avocado.
- The tomato is actually a *fruit*, but it's used as a *vegetable*. In 1893 the U.S. Supreme Court ruled that tomatoes should be classified as vegetables rather than fruits for tariffs, imports and customs. **Justice Horace Gray** delivered the opinion that the Tariff Act of 1883 used the ordinary meaning of "fruit" and "vegetable," instead of the technical botanical meaning.
- I like tomatoes in almost any form, but not tomato soup or juice. I only recently started eating burgers and fries with ketchup at **Mickey Dee's**.
- I always order pizza "heavy on the sauce, light on the mootz." Some people are pizza dough aficionados, but to me, *the essence of pizza is its sauce*. I'll even eat tomato sauce right from a jar with a spoon—or a finger. I never order "extra cheese" or eat "white pizza," but strangely I like both white *and* red clam sauce.
- My tastes have evolved over the years. As a young child in the Bronx, I loved salmon salad for breakfast but rejected tuna salad. When we moved to New Haven in 1952, I reversed my preference, but I don't know why.
- At one time I liked mushroom gravy—but not actual mushrooms. Now I like the 'shrooms.
- I like olive oil, but not actual olives.
- I like pickles and pickled tomatoes, but not cucumbers.
- If I order a gyro in a Greek restaurant, I always specify that I want it with tomato sauce (the way I first had it in Manhattan), but not with traditional tzatziki sauce.
- As a kid I loved to eat chocolate eclairs filled with whipped cream, but *not* with custard. In my early 70s I accidentally bought a custard-filled eclair, and—big surprise—I liked it a lot.
- I've long detested soft cheeses, particularly ricotta. At annual Christmas meals with my wife's Christian relatives, her brother made me a special lasagna, without the dreaded ricotta. I love

lasagna, and when served it in restaurants I used to laboriously scrape the ricotta off the noodles. I stopped scraping a few years ago. I don't actually like ricotta, but I can tolerate it.

o   In Italian restaurants I love tortoni for dessert, not spumoni. Sadly, tortoni has disappeared.
o   Other favorites have disappeared, too, including **ice cream cake roll**, **Uneeda Biscuits** and **Nabisco Zwieback toast**. Of course, Nabisco now uses the **Mondelez** label, and pancake mix formerly from **Aunt Jemima** is now branded as the **Pearl Milling Company**.

My mother was an excellent baker and "company cook," but routine family meals were nothing special. When I was in elementary school, my mother, like most of my classmates' mothers, did not have jobs outside the home. Even in terrible weather, kids would trudge home so mommies could serve us lunch.

Unlike most of my friends, I usually had two *meat meals* each day. Lunch might be a burger or broiled chicken, and supper could be broiled calves' liver or London broil. The side dishes could be potatoes, canned corn, creamed corn or the dreaded string beans, green peas or lima beans. If fried flounder fillet was the main course, the "vegetable" was delicious spaghetti, from a **Campbell's** can. Sometimes the side dish was barely edible heated-up frozen French fries.

As a kid I loved meat ravioli, sold in cans with the **Chef Boyardee** label. As an adult, it was hard to find meat ravioli in Italian restaurants, and I hated the ubiquitous cheese-filled pasta pods. My wife did not approve of my eating canned foods, and she frequently brought home various frozen meat ravioli for me to audition. They all failed my taste tests, and I've stuck with Chef Boyardee.

As kids, we seldom drank soda at home unless we had company or a cookout, because Pop regarded soda as an unnecessary extravagance. I remember our family going to a restaurant for lunch with relatives. I ordered a soda, assuming that my father would not want to appear cheap in public by canceling my drink. I was jealous of our next-door neighbors, the **Katzman** family. The father owned a grocery store and kept the house stocked with a variety of sodas, which the kids could slurp at will.

I gladly sip or slurp milk, water, tea (hot—not iced), hot chocolate, frozen chocolate from Dunkin', black cherry, diet cherry 7up, Coke, Pepsi, ginger ale, root beer, birch beer, pineapple juice, milk shakes, ice cream soda, root beer floats, egg creams, Slurpies, Frosties, Icees, Frozen Fanta and almost any cold beer. I've never tried Dr. Pepper, Mr. Pibb or Squirt. I'll drink almost any filtered or spring-sourced bottled water. I shun expensive imported water, and hate "yogi water" from Dannon.

From my *Fans of food, dubious and benign* Facebook group:

o   Bad food tastes good. In moderation it probably won't kill you.
o   The healthier the food, the worse it tastes.
o   Health is overrated.
o   Broccoli should be banned. Kale, too. And carrot juice.
o   Salsa *is* a vegetable.
o   A good pizza contains all of the vital food groups. So does a burrito.
o   You have to die from something, and it's much more fun to die from an overdose of KFC or Mickey Dee than a plane crash or ISIS attack.

My life-long love for brownies, and my beloved beverages

For as long as I can remember, I've loved to eat brownies. My favorite part of voting at schools used to be the bake sales conducted by PTAs to raise money. I'd try to be one of the first voters to arrive—and buy *every* brownie.

Sadly, in recent years the PTA ladies have sold friggin' Girl Scout cookies instead of their own creations. Future Girl Scouts could *be* Brownies, but not *sell* brownies. Without brownies, I may as well vote by mail.

Sometimes I bought giant trays of **Pillsbury** brownies at **Sam's Club**. I'd sneak them into my home and hide them from my wife. **Marilyn** used to work for the Girl Scouts and loved to eat brownies—but she tried to limit *my* consumption. At one time I expected to be killed by an overdose of brownies. I'm still here.

Marilyn and I sometimes baked brownies. But she was such an eager eater that she'd dig in while the brownies were still hot and damp. She'll also devour molten chocolate pudding!

My favorite brownies are the *corner pieces*, with two crisp and crunchy edges. I like them plain, or with nuts, but *not* with too-sweet icing.

A favorite dessert is a chocolate brownie sundae. I also love to munch frozen Devil Dogs, chocolate chip cookies, Mallomars (a bit too sweet, actually), a double-chocolate muffin from **Dunkin'**, a **Carvel** chocolate Flying Saucer, a chocolate éclair, chocolate cruller, chocolate Italian ices, chocolate pudding (especially the top "skin"), chocolate *gelato*, ordinary chocolate ice cream, chocolate-chip or fudge-ripple ice cream.

I'll gladly eat a chocolate Hershey bar, chocolate Hershey Kisses, a Tootsie Roll, chocolate taffy, some (not all) Lindor chocolate candy, chocolate M&Ms, chocolate Easter eggs and bunnies, Nestle's Crunch and Mr. Goodbar—but *not* chocolate candy bars like Snickers, BabyRuth or MilkyWay.

I find Oreos to be too sweet and chocolate licorice just uninteresting.

I love frozen chocolate at **Dunkin'**. I like the **Starbucks** cold chocolate drink with a name I never remember (but not their too-sweet hot chocolate), hot chocolate from **Dunkin'**, **Cumberland**, **Swiss Miss** or **Keurig**, or a chocolate egg cream.

I've never been to a **Shake Shack** but I love the robot-made **Freel** chocolate shakes at **Cumberland Farms** and man-made shakes at **Dairy Queen**, **Carvel** and **Mickey Dee's**. Some chocolate ice cream sodas are OK, but many are not.

[Cruller pic from randysdonuts.com, egg cream pic from Max Falkowitz. California roll pic by Tim Reckmann from Hamm, Deutschland. Thanks.]

Conversation in Walmart:

Me: "Where is the distilled water?"
▶ Him: "What flavor?"
Me: "Distilled water has no flavor."
▶ Him: "Why not?"
Me: "Because it's distilled."
▶ Him: "What flavor is distilled?"
Me: "It's not a flavor. It's a lack of flavor."
▶ Him: "All water has flavor."
Me: "Not distilled water."
▶ Him: "Why do you drink distilled water?"
Me: "I don't drink it. It's for medical equipment, science experiments, car radiators and batteries, steam engines, aquariums and beer brewing."
▶ Him: "How does it taste?"
Me: "I don't know, but where is it?"
▶ Him: "I'll ask the manager."

Chapter 62
Make words, not war

The Lehigh University campus and the rest of Bethlehem, Pennsylvania were solidly behind the American effort in Viet Nam. My "Make love, not war" bumper sticker was a frequent target for snowballs, rocks, feces, urine and other unpleasant substances.

A couple of students complained about ROTC and campus recruiting by napalm-maker **Dow Chemical**, but peace rallies seemed to attract more FBI photographers than protesters.

One year, Pentagon biggie **General Maxwell Taylor** was invited to speak on campus, and out of a university population of over 5,000, *only six people* marched on a picket line. Taylor thought that even six was too high a number and tried to have us removed. Free speech prevailed.

Taylor was annoyed the next morning when some protesters attended a press breakfast. We were on the student newspaper, wearing anti-war pins with our press badges.

We had been given a list of questions compiled by several journalism classes. One query referred to "covert" operations in Viet Nam, but, because of a typewriter problem, the letter "v" was missing. None of us bright college boys recognized the word, and we couldn't figure out the missing letter. One student reporter favored "comert," and another suggested "cosert."

I was unsure, and it was *my job* to ask the question; but I avoided the problem by pronouncing the word "co-ert." Taylor's brain filled in the missing "v," and he answered the question.

I was in and out of college for five and a half years and often just a few steps ahead of the draft board. They wanted me to report to Wilkes-Barre for a physical, but I kept postponing it.

One day, I was making a movie with some friends in a local park. I had to slide down a waterfall carrying my dog, "**Sniffer**," and then walk through a stream. I stepped on a concealed broken bottle, which nearly passed through my foot, and it took 54 stitches to close the wound.

As soon as I got home from the hospital, I contacted the Federal marshal and said I was ready for my physical, but unfortunately Uncle Sam didn't want me just then. I spent months using a wheelchair and crutches and swallowing Darvon painkiller capsules like popcorn.

I was scheduled for a pre-induction exam nearly six months later and I hoped the foot would not heal too quickly. By the time I had to report, I was in pretty good shape and walking unassisted—but I used crutches and limped and groaned and tried to look like I was in agony.

The Army's doctor was sharp. After looking up my asshole, he closely examined the scar on my foot and even checked my armpits for crutch calluses, but I did *successfully fail* my physical.

I also failed the mechanical aptitude test because I didn't know enough about carburetors, and I confessed to being a member of some international friendship league that labeled me as an Unwitting Dupe of the International Communist Conspiracy.

The final verdict was that if I *really* wanted to serve my country and had some political pull, I just might get an assignment as an orderly in a war zone hospital. I didn't pursue this option because I saw no reason to kill Viet Cong or haul bedpans for people who did. And, compared to Saigon, even Bethlehem looked good.

Chapter 63
Mamma Mia! Nobody alliterates like Italians

Alliterations are awfully appealing. They show a bit of creativity in a tiny space—like haiku and Tweeting. They can be memorable and effective book titles and names for people and products.

Even without an effort to be cute, a real name can be alliterative, like General William Westmoreland, publisher Doubleday, sing-alonger Mitch Miller and me—Michael Marcus.

My brother Marshall Marcus and sister Meryl Marcus Alpert are alliterative, too. So are Mommy Marcus and my father—Mister Marcus. Mom's father was Dr. Jay Jacobs. My cousins include Kenneth Kessner and Karen Kessner. One of my author buddies is Barbara Barth.

America's first lady list includes Abigail Adams and Barbara Bush. Alliterative presidents are Herbert Hoover, Calvin Coolidge and Ronald Reagan. Our Veep list includes Hannibal Hamlin, William Wheeler, Calvin Coolidge and Hubert Humphrey.

Some politicians have alliterative nicknames. Andrew Jackson was called "the people's president" and Zachary Taylor was labeled "Old Rough and Ready." President Lincoln was "Uncle Abe" and "Honest Abe." Andrew Johnson was the "Tennessee tailor." James Garfield was our Preacher President." Grover Cleveland was known as "Grover the Good." William McKinley was criticized as "Wobbling Willie." The first Roosevelt POTUS was called "Telescope Teddy." Huge William Howard Taft was derided as "Big Bill." Flip-flopping Warren G. Harding was nicknamed "Wobbly Warren." Calvin Coolidge was known as "Cool Cal" and "Cautious Cal." President Truman was "Haberdasher Harry." Lyndon Johnson was called "Landslide Lyndon." Bill Clinton was honored as "the Comeback Kid." Joe Biden was derided as "Beijing Biden" and "Genocide Joe." Critics of Donald Trump have used many adjectives beginning with "D" such a "Despicable," "Deluded," "Despotic," "Demented," "Destructive," "Dishonest" and "Disgraced" Donny.

This book, published by **Silver Sands Books,** is *filled* with alliteration. I consciously or unconsciously often insert alliterations in my prose. Alliterations don't have to use adjacent words, as long as they're nearby. I'm particularly proud (alliteration!) of this one, used elsewhere in the book: "imBedded in my Brain and Bonded to my Body."

The **United States** is responsible for Alcoholics Anonymous, Baa Baa Black Sheep, Baby Boomers (now becoming Senior Citizens), Ball Breaker, Band of Brothers, Basket Ball, Bat Boy, Beach Blanket Bingo, Bean Bag, Bed Bath & Beyond, Beef Burger, Best Buy, Big Balls, Big Bang, Big Boobs, Big Box retailer Circuit City, Big Burger, Biker Babes, Bats in Belfry, Bird Brain, Black and Beautiful, Blackberry, Black Bird, Blonde Bombshell, Blueberry, Bluebird, Blues Brothers, Bonus Baby, Boston Braves, Bra Burning, Brass Balls, Brew Burger, Bronx Bombers, Brutus "the Barber" Beefcake, Buckaroo Banzai, Bucky Beaver, Buffalo Bill, Bumblebee, Cap'n Crunch, Carole King, Chainsaw Charlie, Charlie Chan, Chevy Chase, Chinese Checkers, Chuck E. Cheese, Clark Kent, Clem Kadiddlehopper, Coca-Cola, Colby College, Cool as a Cucumber, Corn on the Cob, Creamed Corn, Crispy Critters, Crystal Clear, Daisy Duke,

Danny DeVito, Denizens of the Deep, Department of Defense, Derring-Do, Devil Dogs, Dipsy Doodle, Dirty Deed, Dodge Dart, Donald Duck, Double-Dare, Dragon's Den, Dynamic Duo, Edible Arrangements, Elephant Ears, Enormous Ego, Family aFfair, Family Feud, Family Physician, Fast Forward, Ferrari F-50, Feathered Friends, First Family, Fly Fishing, Ford Falcon, Ford Fiesta, Ford Fusion, Fortune Five hundred, Fox & Friends, Frankie Fontaine, Friendly Frost, GooGle, Gordon Gekko, Great Gatsby, Great Gildersleeve, Hamburger Helper, Hebrew hammer, Helen Hunt, High Heavens, Holly Hunter, Hudson Hornet, Ice Cream Cone, Intel Inside, Janet Jackson, Janis Joplin, Johnson and Johnson, Kentucky Colonel, Killer Kowalski, Krispy Kreme, Ku Klux Klan, Kurt Cobain, Lady Levi's, Lana Lang, Lois Lane, Lucky Lindy, Lucky Luciano, Mad Max, Mad Men, Magic Marker, Marilyn Monroe ("va-va-va-voom!"), Martin Mull, Marvelous Mrs. Maisel, Master Mechanic, Meow Mix, Mercury Marauder, Minute Maid, Minute Man, Mix Master, Moms Mabley, Motor Mouth, Mrs. Miniver, Mutated Monsters, Nightly News, Olds Omega, Palm Pilot, Party Pooper, PayPal, Pepe's Pizza, Pepperoni Pizza, Pickled Peppers, Pig Pen, Pink Panther, Pink Petunia, Piper Palin, Piss-Poor, Pittsburgh Pirates, Pizza Parlor, Porch Pirates, Porch Pirates, Road Rage, Road Rally, Road Rash, Rocky Road, Ronald Reagan, Roy Rogers—King of the Cowboys, Rudolph the Red-nosed Reindeer, Sailor Suit, Samantha Sterlyng, Savanna Samson and too many other porn stars to list here, Seven & Seven, Seven Sisters, Seventh Seal, Seventy-Seven Sunset Strip, Sex Star, Sid Caesar, Sin City, Social Security, Solar System, Son of Sam, Star-Studded, Sultan of Swat, Super-Sonic, SuperStar, Swan Song, Sweet Sixteen, Swinging Singles, Sylvia Sidney, Tea for Two, TexasToast, Tonka Truck, Tongue Twisters, Tony the Tiger, Tough Titty, Triple Treat, Turkish Taffy, Turkish Towel, Vivid Video, Wascally Wabbit, Way With Words, Weight Watchers, Wendell Wilkie, West Wing, the great White Way, Wild One, Wild Wild West, Wild Women, Wonderful World, World War, World Wildlife Foundation, World Wrestling Entertainment, Worldwide Web.

Alliterative Cartoon Characters include Beetle Baily, Betty Boop, Gerald McBoing-Boing, Bugs Bunny, Dudley Do-right, Daffy Duck, Daisy Duck, Fred Flintstone, Merry Melodies, Mickey Mouse, Minnie Mouse, Olive Oyl, Roger Rabbit, Sad Sack, Sufferin' Succotash, Woody Woodpecker.

The **United Kingdom** has given us Big Ben, Big Brother, Sunshine Superman, Tea for the Tillerman, Enery the Eighth, Herman's Hermits, Mannfred Mann, King Crimson, Merry Men, Peter Pan, Tetley Tea, Peter Piper's Pickled Peppers, MG Midget and the Vauxhall Victor.

The **Spanish** are responsible for con carne.

From **France**, we get cherchez la femme, Brigitte Bardot and the Michelin Man.

Sweden was the source of the Saab Sonnett.

Japan gets credit for Toyota Tundra, Mitsubishi Motors and Mitsubishi Montero.

Germany was the location of Checkpoint Charlie (but it was named by English-speakers) and gave us the Mercedes Maybach, Volkswagen Vanagon and Porsche Panamera.

But **Italian**—the most musical of languages—is *il campione del mondo* (the champion of the world) in alliteration. Here are my three favorites:

Mille Miglia (pronounced mee-luh meel-yuh) means "Thousand Miles," an open-road endurance race which took place in Italy from 1927 to 1957, with time out for Word War Two.

Cinecitta (pronounced cheena-cheeta) means "Cinema City," a huge movie studio in Rome founded by **Mussolini** in 1937 and used by **Federico Fellini** for *La Dolce Vita* and *Satyricon*. The studio was also used for "American" films including *Ben-Hur*, and *Gangs of New York*.

Cinquecento (pronounced cheenka-chento) means "500." It's FIAT's popular minicar, first made in 1936, and back in the USA in 2010.

From Dr. Bree Belford, a great alliterative name. "There are many medical alliterations: aortic aneurysm, sick sinus syndrome, homonymous hemianopsia, poor prognosis, pyrvinium panoate, staphlycoccal scalded skin syndrome and acute arterial occlusion. The winner is pneumonia, pneumothorax, pulmonary spasm (asthma)."

NOTE: Some alliterative sequences begin with similar sounds, but not identical letters.

Chapter 64
Things, like people, don't last forever

I'm usually fastidious about backing up computer files, especially for important documents like the books I write, passwords and tax info.

I recently could not access my "F-drive," an external box. I assumed it contains a solid-state drive.

It's made by **Orico**. I went to its website and was shocked to learn that the company had supplied me with an *EMPTY* housing with *NO* memory.

I slid off the cover and discovered a 250-gig hard drive, made by **Western Digital**, way back in 2008. I was disappointed, but probably had no right to assume a drive of that vintage would still work.

I did some clicking on my PC screen and found a **Microsoft** utility that could allegedly fix my ancient hard drive. The price was zero—my favorite price.

The process took about 20 minutes, and then PERFECTION.

I have no idea how much life this drive has (or how much life I have), so I stared copying files to another external drive.

You can find several online instructions for the disk repair.

So, backup frequently, in multiple places! And backup your backups.

Mechanical devices, and even solid-state devices, don't last forever.

- Phonograph records and 8-track tapes and cassettes start wearing out the first time you play them.
- There are cars on the road made a century ago. Modern cars could last longer, or not long at all.
- I still have cameras I received as bar mitzvah gifts in 1959. They still work, but I don't use them.
- I also have an amplifier I bought at **Radio Shack** that same year. It still works—with its original vacuum tubes.
- How long will my iPads and iPods work?

Who knows?

Chapter 65
This beard's for you

Our high school assistant principal was **George Kennedy**, a mean SOB with a short haircut that made him look like he had just recently left the Marines. "Granny" glasses made him seem very old-fashioned—the exact opposite of the image that **John Lennon** would give to the same eyeglass style a few years later.

He seemed to break balls just for the sheer joy of it.

Kennedy rode a bicycle to school each day and students dreamed of flattening his tires or shoving a stick between his spokes and knocking him off the bike and onto his ass.

During my junior year, one day I was at my friend, **Howie's**, house after school, and I left a little rubber alligator there. The next day, Howie brought it to school, and when he saw me in the hallway near my locker, he tossed it to me so I could put it away.

Some busybody teacher with too much time on her hands reported the episode to Kennedy and I was called down to his office to be prosecuted and sentenced.

Kennedy informed me that I had violated Board of Education Rule # 7,934,726,422,079, subsection B, revision 7.02, paragraph 9—that banned rubber alligators from school property without a permit, and he confiscated my artificial reptile.

The SOB kept the gator until the last day of school. He may have performed voodoo or satanic rituals with it.

In 1963, in the fall of my senior year, I was out of school with mononucleosis ("the kissing disease") for about six weeks. I didn't have much else to do, so I grew a beard. It was a little beard, but it was pretty good for a 17-year-old. Some other kids in my class didn't even shave yet.

On my first day back at school, another busybody teacher spotted my new growth and sent me to Kennedy for a chin and cheek check. (The picture was taken on 10/11/63 with my beginner's beard enhanced with Photoshop.) Kennedy was able to see the fuzz and he insisted that it was against the rules for students to have beards.

I asked him to show me the rule and he frowned. He flipped through the pages of several notebooks. He couldn't find the rule, but he came up with another solution. The evil prick said that if I didn't shave off the beard, he'd shave it off for me—but *without shaving cream*. I caved and I shaved.

I've had a beard since 1965. My wife has never seen my chin.

Around 1972, I happened to be in New Haven at the time of an important football game between my high school and its traditional rival. I stopped by the stadium to see who else might show up. I couldn't find any of my old classmates, but I did see George Kennedy, and I couldn't resist showing off my beard. This time he said it looked good, and he couldn't send me home to shave it.

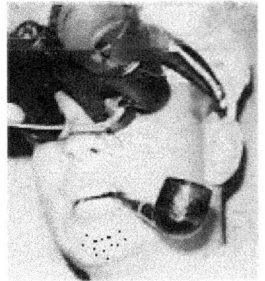

I think he was jealous. He probably couldn't grow one.

Chapter 66
How I accidentally got into the advertising business (Also: I had a beard and was a "beard")

Lying down with headphones on your head is like kissing a girl with braces on her teeth.

Hear Muffs

I got into the advertising business by accident. In 1971 and 1972, I was audio-video editor at *Rolling Stone* magazine and wrote reviews of lots of products. When I wrote good reviews, it was common for the manufacturers to ask permission to quote me in their ads. This was good for the manufacturers, good for *Rolling Stone* and very good for my ego.

I almost always agreed, but I insisted on the right to review the ads before publication to make sure I was being quoted correctly and not made to seem like a complete asshole.

At one point, I said something nice about a **BSR** turntable and I got a call from someone at **Kane Light Gladney,** the turntable manufacturer's ad agency. He explained that they had done an ad with a quote from my review and would buy me lunch if I'd come by and take a look at the ad. Their office was near mine and a free lunch was hard to turn down, so I agreed.

I met a couple of their guys at a restaurant, and then the three of us walked to their office, where a bunch of "rough" ad layouts were tacked to the walls in a conference room. I took a quick look and saw that, while the quotations were accurate, the ads absolutely sucked, and I did not want my name to be associated with them.

With permission, I yanked a couple of layouts off the wall and sat down at the conference table. Within minutes I was an unpaid copywriter. It was easy, I enjoyed it, and my hosts were impressed. They asked if I could come in on the following Saturday to do some writing for pay.

The Saturday freelancing went on for about a month, and then the agency boss, **Gerry Light**, asked me a powerful question: "How would you like us to triple your salary?"

He didn't realize it, but at the time I was only freelancing at *Rolling Stone* and making $75 for each column I wrote twice a month, so I didn't actually have a salary to triple.

The proposed advertising salary was MUCH more than I had been making, I had a new wife, and I could keep doing the freelancing at *Rolling Stone*, so I quickly accepted the offer.

It was a strange new environment, with a new set of policies and politics to get used to.

When I started work, there was a plaque on my new door that identified me as "Mr. Marcus." It was removed a few days later, and the next week a new plaque was attached to the door that said merely "Michael Marcus."

I found out later that the office manager got into trouble with one of the partners for labeling me a "Mr." before I had been on the job for a year. Office politics suck.

My impressive business card said, "Associate Creative Director." After a few months, I learned that the agency's one other copywriter had the *same damn title*. There was no Supreme Creative Director above the two of us. Perhaps our titles were intended to keep our egos in check or to give us something to strive for.

I guess we were expected to associate with each other.

Although my work was creative and not administrative, I also sometimes got to serve as the "account guy." Mainly, this meant that I got taken out to gaudy and expensive restaurants to hear sales pitches from extremely boring media salesmen that the agency partners or real account executives wanted to avoid dealing with.

I was often in an awkward position creatively.

My straitlaced bosses were frequently too timid to show our clients what I felt was my best work. They were constantly telling me to "tone it down," but I had an edgy style and was in my early 20s, writing for my contemporaries, as I had done when I was at *Rolling Stone*. We had several showdowns where I said, "You hired me because you like the way I write, so either show my work, or fire me." They almost always caved in.

Sometimes, I'd come up with far-out ad concepts and hold secret meetings with our clients and win them over. If the clients liked my stuff, my bosses had little choice but to go along.

There were other times I went to *another kind* of secret meeting.

In addition to our work turning out ads, press releases and sales promotion gimmicks, we also arranged dates for some of our clients, often with magazine models.

Jack, boss of one of our client companies, had a long-running affair with a *Penthouse* Pet and sometimes, when he was in town to be with her, I went along as the "beard." If any people saw the three of us, and they knew that Jack was married, they'd assume that I was with the Pet who had the cleavage deep enough to get lost in for several days.

I suppose I might have been flattered, but it was really a waste of my time, and all I got was food and incredibly boring conversation. After dinner in a hotel dining room, the three of us would go upstairs in an elevator, but I'd make a quick U-turn and go back down to the lobby and go home.

I learned a lot about the ad agency business at Kane Light Gladney, but it was not always a pleasant educational experience. There was a lot of conflict. They seemed to see me as a threat as well as an asset, and their threat assessments had major lapses in logic.

I had a freelance client that made a unique headphone design called the **HearMuff**—"the first headphones you wouldn't kick out of bed." It was never very successful, and I never made much money from my work. I did the work mostly for fun, and at the end of my assignment I got paid in HearMuffs. I still have a few.

The KLG partners tried to stop my HearMuff freelancing, based on the absurd argument that two of the agency's hi-fi clients—**AR** and **BSR**—*might* decide to make stereo headphones in the future and my work could become a conflict of interest.

What these blind assholes somehow missed was that both AR and BSR *already* made record turntables, a definite conflict of interest that didn't seem to bother either company. And I wrote the ads for *both* companies.

Then the partners started referring to me as a "profit center" and urged me to work faster. In April, my boss told me that I had accomplished so much that there was no need for any more ads to be done until September, and I was *out*.

There's absolutely no job security in advertising and an important rule that I was taught by several veterans was that "The day to start looking for a job is the day that you get a job."

Fortunately, I had good contacts from my days at *High Fidelity Trade News* and *Rolling Stone* and I quickly got a job writing at **Muller Jordan Herrick**. I then helped them to take the **Columbia** recording tape account away from the Kane Light Gladney guys, who had taught me the ad business *very well*.

Revenge is sweet—*very* sweet.

Muller Jordan Herrick wasn't perfect, but it was much bigger and better than KLG.

Our office was at 666 Fifth Avenue (now using the number 660), in the **Tishman Building**, opposite **St. Patrick's Cathedral**. The floor below us was larger than our floor and, on nice days, we'd open our big windows and move out our chairs, phones, tables and typewriters and use the roof of the lower floor as an outdoor office, dining room and tanning salon.

I won a big-deal award from the **Advertising Club of New York** while at Muller Jordan Herrick. We had mostly good clients with interesting products that I enjoyed writing about, and only one *absolutely idiotic* client.

That was **United Jersey Bank**, where marketing was controlled by castrated dullards in the legal department. (If anyone from that miserable bank is reading this, FUCK YOU! FUCK YOU! FUCK YOU! FUCK YOU! I still hate your guts.)

One time I had the brain-numbing assignment of writing a boring ad about savings account interest rates.

The head guy on the bank's team, a government-intimidated ball-less shyster, insisted that I write "*a minimum deposit of at least $500 or more.*" I tried explaining to this testosterone-depleted wuss that all this was repetitive and redundant and superfluous and unnecessary—and that we did not need to say all three!

The pathetic castrato would not give in—and neither would I. I told him to write his own fucking ad and I left the room. My only regret was that I didn't shut the light off and slam the door and leave the asshole sitting in the dark, crying and caressing his empty nut sack.

It would have been worth getting fired for.

My office had a weird phone with two number-seven buttons on it, but *no eight*, and a very nice couch, inherited from the previous inhabitant.

I liked to close my door at noon time for a siesta, but my boss, **Andy Weiss**, hated closed doors and he had a nasty habit of opening the door and interrupting my naps.

For some reason, Andy didn't mind if I took an hour to eat, but he didn't like the idea of my taking five minutes to eat and 55 minutes to sleep, even if it recharged my creative battery.

After a while, my couch mysteriously disappeared, and I slept at my desk for 55 minutes.

[Building photo from David Shankbone. Thanks.]

Chapter 67
What the blind man could see
(names have been changed)

Anton Bonn Inc. (the company deliberately left out the comma) was an advertising and public relations agency with two specialties: electronic equipment and what many on the staff cynically called "wetbacks." They were clients with limited command of the English language who were inadequately prepared for life or commerce in the United States.

Once or twice each year, company execs would fly to Europe in search of potential clients. The wetter their backs, the more likely they could be convinced that Anton Bonn Inc. would be their savior, their source of riches in the new world.

Anton, the company founder, was an immigrant from Eastern Europe. His twinkling blue eyes, ample charm and old-world courtliness appealed to many of the European manufacturers who yearned to make the transatlantic leap and emulate Anton's apparent success. He looked a bit like **Montgomery Burns** on *The Simpsons*.

Unfortunately, Anton's twinkling blue eyes were failing.

He sometimes wandered into the art department and critiqued advertising layouts that were lying on a counter with their bottoms at the top.

Ad designs were often drawn on thin, nearly transparent paper and, once, when a paper on a desk near an open window had flopped over, Anton offered his opinion of an ad design while looking at the *back* of the page.

There were some things that Anton could see *very well*, however. When he looked out a window from his office many floors above street level, he could easily determine which women crossing Fifth Avenue were braless.

Anton loved to look at—and to be seen with—beautiful, young women.

He had a perpetual help-wanted ad running in the *New York Times*, with slight variations in job description from time to time, including "secretary to poet" and "secretary to playwright." Despite ads aimed at presumed intellectuals, Anton evaluated job candidates as eye candy.

Secretaries seldom stayed on the job more than a month. Some were so frustrated that they lasted only a day, or half a day. Their main duties were to read Anton's mail to him, read employees' mail to him, slice his fruit and hold his hand and look beautiful as he wandered around trade shows.

Anton's second-in-command was hyperkinetic, abrasive, annoying, irritating, pretentious, egomaniacal, obnoxious, height-impaired and geeky **Gerard P. LeDoux**.

When the LeDoux family crossed the Atlantic, their last name was probably Ledewitz or Ledowsky. But just like my high school principal who morphed from Jewish Levine into fake French LeVine, the LeDoux clan seemingly preferred to mask its ethnic origins. But Gerard's wife shopped at a kosher meat market without hiding behind a mask.

When little Gerard LeDoux made a phone call, he identified himself as "Mister LeDoux." At least he didn't say "Monsieur LeDoux."

Behind his back, however, other employees referred to Gerard as "The Vontz"—the Jewish word for a hyperkinetic, abrasive, annoying, irritating BEDBUG.

In the 1983 movie *War Games*, the **Matthew Broderick** character consults a hyperkinetic geek named **Malvin** for advice on computer hacking. Malvin and Gerard are clones.

Bedbug Gerard was supposed to be the "rainmaker" for the agency, the guy who brings in the clients who spend the money to pay salaries and expenses and, with any luck, generate a profit. He would devise a list of potential naive ad candidates, and then lead Anton in his periodic conquests of Europe. Sometimes it seemed that Gerard picked companies based on getting product samples he wanted to play with.

I don't know if Anton was ever a creative genius, but both his writing ability and his knowledge of business and technology had faded before he hired me. When he tried to get involved in creative work, the results were disastrous, embarrassing and frequently funny.

He once failed to win the **NEC** computer account with a pun-based campaign that said, "If computers give you a pain in the neck, you need NEC." (The folks at NEC like their company name to be pronounced "any see," and never "neck.")

Another time, the Bonn agency won the advertising business for a manufacturer of computer-testing equipment, but Anton completely misunderstood the market.

He demanded that we produce ads that tried to sell the sophisticated test gear to computer *users*, rather than to computer *manufacturers* or service companies. It was like trying to sell wheel alignment apparatus and tire balancers to every person who drives a car.

Although some clients had stayed with the agency for many years, others left as quickly as Anton's secretaries. I remember seeing a telex come in from a new client, asking if we could recommend *another ad agency*.

Anton's son, **Martin**, supervised the creative side of the agency. He would never have gotten his job without nepotism, but he was a passable writer, and a convincing phony.

Along with his job, he had inherited blue eyes and some of his father's European ways, but his Continental aura was as temporary as a spray-on suntan. Martin Bonn normally identified himself as a vice president; but he morphed into a "managing director," to match the title of European executives he might have to deal with and to make him seem more like them. He even had a second set of business cards with the foreign-sounding "managing director" corporate title.

Even his voice changed if he perceived the potential benefit. When dealing with native-born Americans, Martin spoke perfect American English. But when he introduced himself to Europeans, he performed a retro-morph, to become "Martin Bunn," the new immigrant from Zee Continent who had trouble vid zee Americain pronunciation.

The Bonns did not like to spend money. When they moved into new offices in the mid-70s, they reused an ancient cord switchboard, instead of getting a more modern phone system. When we wanted to make a call, we had to "flash" the operator, and nasty **Gloria** made it obvious that she resented interrupting her nail polishing to put in a plug.

We were always busy, but we wasted a lot of time and money redoing bad ads, and the place may not have been profitable. It was tough to get a raise. Once, I was rewarded with a lousy FIFTEEN BUCK weekly raise for my efforts above and beyond the call of duty for coming in at 6 AM for nearly two months at a particularly busy time!

Then we underpaid serfs found a way to use Anton's well-known paranoia and sneakiness to our own financial advantage.

If someone wanted more money, he or she would arrange to have a friend at another company send a letter on that company's stationery offering a new job, knowing that Anton would open the mail and learn about the bogus opportunity.

We'd wait a few days and then pop the question. Anton would assume he was in a bidding war and would have to pay well to keep an important employee.

The agency had a public relations department, with some talented and hard-working recent graduates and old pros, and others who were not so talented or professional.

For a major trade show, the agency distributed press releases with "challanges," "emphasizeng," and "discoteque." They used commas to separate sentences and spelled one client's name *two different ways on the same page*. Maybe Anton did the proofreading.

I had worked at better ad agencies before Bonn, but this place was the equivalent of a "gut course" in college, where minimal work could earn an easy "A."

It seemed to be an ad agency where I could stay for years, quickly cranking out stuff that impressed the bosses and clients. Although it was below my traditional standards, it left me plenty of time for naps and freelancing.

One day, Anton approached me in the art department and asked if I knew what a "sinecure" was. I said that I didn't.

Anton explained that it was a position in a church given to a respected elderly priest, where he could live out his life while doing very little work.

Anton's eyes weren't very good, but he sure saw through me.

[Switchboard photo from Joseph A. Carr. Thanks.]

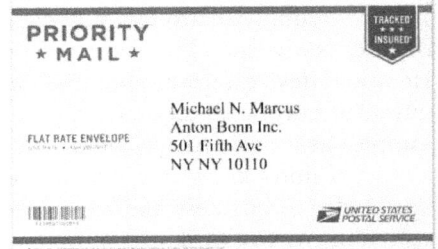

Chapter 68
Marcia, Bob the giant penguin, and Harry's exploding belly

Our Latin 2 teacher in high school was **Marcia Young**. She was a few years older than the kids in our class—but she looked like she was *younger*—and could best have been described as unsophisticated, sheltered and naïve. In short, she was no match for 30 wiseass suburban kids.

We definitely didn't dislike her, but Marcia was such an easy victim that she invited exploitation. I frequently "cooperated" on tests with **Patty**, who sat in front of me. At first, we passed notes back and forth. Later, I built an intercom system for low-volume verbal consultations.

Here are two of the Class of 64's Greatest Hits:

Bob was a big kid. One of the other kids (probably me) had a pair of swim fins in a gym bag, and we persuaded Big Bob to put them on while he sat in the back of the class. When Marcia called on him to go up to the blackboard to write something in Latin, Bob waddled to the front of the room like a *giant penguin*.

Bob kept a straight face.

Marcia was terrified.

The rest of us were hysterical.

YAY, BOB!

Our Latin class was interrupted by lunch period. One day, I happened to have an inflatable flotation vest in my gym bag. (I know it sounds weird, but I used the same bag for SCUBA diving classes after school.)

During lunch, **Harry** and I went to the boys' john and he put on the deflated vest *under his sweater*, and we went back to class.

We did our normal Latin work for a while, but then Harry started moaning, and he waved his hand frantically. Marcia asked what was wrong.

Harry stood up and slowly walked to the front of the room while hunched over and clutching his abdomen with both hands. He seemed to be shivering. Then he stood by Marcia's desk. Stammering, Harry said he thought he got food poisoning from the school cafeteria.

Harry's classmates and Marcia—who all ate the same food Harry ate—were horrified by Harry's condition and their own potential peril.

Harry told Marcia he had a terrible pain in his stomach. He said, "It keeps going up and down and up and down and..."

At that point, Harry sneakily put one of his hands inside his sweater and pulled on the ripcord which punctured the gas cartridge to inflate the life vest.

In less than two seconds, his torso seemed to *double in size*.

Marcia screamed.

So did we. **YAY, HARRY!**

Chapter 69
The right connections

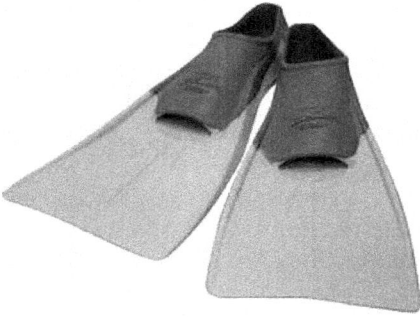

Our high school guidance counselors pointed out that we could enhance our chances of college acceptance by participation in community organizations, particularly if we held important offices in those organizations.

Not wanting to miss a chance, classmates **Howie, Barry** and I formed a SCUBA diving club called the **New Haven Finsters**. We had been diving together for years, so why not formalize it? For the cost of a sheet of paper, an envelope and a stamp, we got listed in *The International Roster of Diving Clubs*, and our scam became reality.

To further enhance our credentials and impress college admissions officers, we decided that each one of us would be president of our important community organization.

I think we had different guidance counselors in school, so no one noticed the duplication of titles. Internally, we had different titles. Barry was the "lowest lump of whale blubber on the bottom of the Mariana Trench." I've forgotten what Barry called Howie and me, but our nicknames were probably comparable. I remember a lot, but not everything.

Our esteemed organization was even listed in *Skin Diver* magazine, and we started getting mail from all over the world, including offers of bargains on lead weights. However, they were not such bargains if the shipping charge from Louisiana to Connecticut was included.

In retrospect, I really don't know if the Finster presidency enhanced our college acceptability. Howie went to Yale, but I'm sure he would have gotten in even if he hadn't been the leader of the Finsters.

On New Year's Day of 1964, we went *ice diving*.

It seems like a stupid thing to non-divers, but divers think it's a great adventure. You find a lake with sufficiently thick ice on top. You use a chain saw to cut a big hole in the ice and put a long ladder across the hole. A rope is tied to the ladder and the other end is tied to the divers.

On this particular day, it was *brutally cold* out, something like six degrees Fahrenheit at Bolton Lake in north-central Connecticut, with a wicked 50 MPH wind whipping across the ice.

The good news was that it was so fucking cold that there was little danger that the ice would melt, and we would get dumped into the lake. The bad news was that it was so fucking cold that we were freezing our asses off.

Actually, we couldn't really freeze our asses off, because major parts of those asses were safely behind two layers of quarter-inch-thick neoprene rubber that provided ample insulation.

However, the exposed parts of our faces were quickly covered with ice during the short walk from our car to the ice hole—and that's not healthy or pleasant. Also, the first stages of our *regulators*, the mechanical parts of our breathing apparatus mounted on the tops of our air tanks behind our heads, also froze up. We had to dip them below the surface of the lake to defrost them before making the dive. People thought we were nuts to dive under the ice.

In reality, we felt comfortable and safe, and it was really nice down there. It looked beautiful, with eerie light filtering through the ice and much better visibility than during the summer because there were no motorboats to stir up the mud and crud from the bottom.

The water temperature had to be above 32 degrees, and the "wetsuits" raised our temperatures another 30 degrees—so we were warm enough. It wasn't nuts to go *in* the water, but it *was* nuts to come out and get undressed in the six-degree temperature.

None of us wanted to strip down in the cold car so we decided to stay in our cozy rubber suits until we got home where it was warm and dry.

Unfortunately, when we reached New Haven, our car full of rubberized weirdos collided with another vehicle while crossing an intersection about a block from police headquarters, and the smash-up was, of course, witnessed by a cop.

He didn't want to write us up in the freezing weather, so he told everyone to follow him to the PD HQ.

It was a holiday, so we decided to have some fun.

Howie, Barry and I marched into the cop house, wearing our swim fins and masks, carrying our spear guns and boldly displaying long knives strapped to our legs.

We could have been locked up "for observation," but we had guessed right, and the cops were also in a holiday mood. They had a good laugh and didn't object to our awesome weapons.

After a few minutes of discussion, it turned out that *both* drivers had close relatives with important connections in City Hall. The official report of the incident stated that the traffic light was "simultaneously green in both directions."

None of the drivers got a ticket and we all got hot chocolate. One of the cops even tried my spear gun.

Chapter 70
They wanted my brain, but not my penis

Sometime in the 1980s, I was looking for work as a copywriter. Conveniently, at the same time, the **New York Telephone Company** was looking to hire a copywriter. I went for an interview high up in their new headquarters in Manhattan.

I was informed that I was the top candidate. No one else who had applied for the job could match my experience and writing ability, my broad knowledge of business and technology and my specific knowledge of telecommunications.

Unfortunately, this was during an affirmative-action drive, and they were trying hard to hire non-whites and non-males and people with disabilities and unconventional sexual orientations and sundry minority classifications.

The ideal candidate apparently would have been a 90-year-old, left-handed, one-legged, cross-eyed, red-haired, albino Wiccan Samoan lesbian cannibal with bad breath who had served in the Korean War and was deserted by her husband.

My interviewer apologized for the situation.

He admitted that the company, its customers and its stockholders would *suffer* by not hiring me, but they had to hire a woman to counteract past discrimination.

On the bottom of my employment application was a list of government agencies I could notify if I thought that the New York Telephone Company was *discriminating against me*.

HA!

Chapter 71
What's more important: your brain or your teeth?

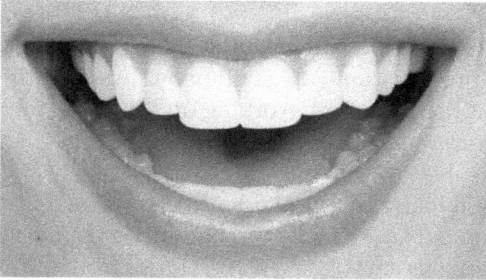

The best ad agency I ever worked at was **Scali, McCabe & Sloves**, under the creative supervision of legendary art director **Sam Scali** and writer **Ed McCabe**. **Marvin Sloves** was the businessman in the founding trio. **Bob Schmetterer** joined them as an account executive and eventually became president, although his name wasn't on the door.

I worked on prestigious accounts like Perdue chicken, Volvo cars, Pioneer stereo, TDK recording tape, Barney's, Castrol and others. However, I was not working in the prestigious part of the agency.

I was a copywriter on the lowest floor we had in the building, in the sales promotion department. We did some national ads, but our specialty was local advertising, radio scripts, packaging, contests and even promotional T-shirts.

I did a lot of T-shirts. Sometimes I still see people walking around, wearing shirts that I created over 40 years ago. It's a good feeling. A couple of times, I spoke to people wearing "my" shirts. One wanted me to autograph it. One thought I was nuts and ran away.

While at Scali, I was paired at different times with two very talented art directors, **Barbara Schubeck** and **Larry Lee**. They both had famous family connections. Barbara was the sister of TV newsman **John Schubeck**. Larry was the nephew of architect **I. M. Pei**, who designed the glass pyramid at the **Louvre Museum** in Paris.

The basic creative team that does the work in an ad agency consists of an art person and a word person. They respond to directions from the client, relayed through the account executive. Either the art director or the copywriter may come up with the concept for an ad or a sales promotion project, and then the two people work on it together.

While they have to work together, there is often a subconscious jealousy or rivalry because there's a big difference in titles and perks.

The person who draws is called a DIRECTOR, but the writer is just a writer.

The art director got to hire photographers and models and photo retouchers, and chose typesetters (back then), filming and photo locations and various suppliers. Art directors got to travel to exotic locations. They influenced spending tons of money each year and were rewarded with lavish gifts at Christmas time. Bottles of liquor or even cases of champagne were not unusual. The lowly copywriters—who were usually the source of the creative concepts that made the champagne possible—were lucky to get a $5 box of chocolates. Getting nothing was more common.

Most art/word teams fought constant battles, with the art directors wanting to chop words to make the ads look better and the copywriters insisting that every word was vital.

I was much more flexible than most of the other writers. Although I took great pride in every word I wrote, I had gone to art school as a child and had great respect for the visual images that accompanied my words.

I also knew that perhaps 90% of the people who saw an ad would see the picture and headline and they'd *never read another word*, no matter how hard I had worked to choose the perfect word and its perfect position.

At Scali, the upstairs art-and-copy teams made the big bucks and had more prestige than our lowly sales promo department. But we frequently functioned as a top-secret "skunk works" that management knew they could call upon to produce a last-minute miracle when the highly paid upstairs teams came up dry.

Several times, **Victor**, an account exec, came to us in the late morning, ashen faced, and explained that his clients were coming for a campaign presentation ("dog and pony show") at the end of the day and that the highly paid "national team" that had been working on the project for six months had turned out worthless crap and the agency was in deep shit.

This was our time to show off—and eat well.

In order to get in the proper creative mood, we'd insist on a *culinary bribe*.

At Victor's expense (or maybe at the client's expense), we'd order in a banquet of Japanese food from **Mr. Yakitori** for everyone in our department, plus a few favored secretaries from other departments and even the mailroom guys and assorted hungry hangers-on.

After a leisurely meal and postprandial cigars, we'd finally get to work around 2 PM and, by 5 PM we'd have fantastic stuff that wowed the clients and pissed off the jealous, overpaid, big-ego upstairs team that didn't get free cigars or the food from Mr. Yakitori.

Although Scali, McCabe & Sloves was a great place to create advertising, as in all ad agencies, politics took its toll. The problem was not internal office politics, but *client* politics.

Often, particularly with Japanese clients, it was just not possible to get a simple "yes" or "no" when we needed approval for one ad or an entire campaign.

Sometimes there would be six people from the client company in a conference room for a presentation. They'd all sit with blank faces, waiting for a smile or a frown from Big Boss-san and, if the inscrutable chief didn't show emotion, no one else did.

After meetings like that, I'd go back to my office and show *my* emotion. I'd kick a hole in the wall and label the hole with the name of the client and the date of the meeting. Every few months, I'd replace the Sheetrock and start kicking again.

While I worked at Scali, my wife hit the Big Four-Oh and was very depressed. Her last words at night and first words each morning were: "I'm so depressed."

I'd leave for work, have a little vacation during my half-hour subway commute, and then I'd face **Adele**, our department secretary, who'd greet me with an all-too familiar refrain: "I'm so depressed." It was very depressing.

When the agency chose a new health insurance company, the personnel department distributed a survey form to determine which optional coverages the staff wanted.

Psychiatry won over dental care, *six-to-one*.

At one time, the employees were summoned to gather on an unoccupied floor of our office building for drinks, snacks and an important announcement. One of the partners told us that the agency was being bought by international advertising giant **Ogilvy & Mather**.

He reassured us, saying that, although the partners were going to make a lot of money, the operation of the agency would stay pretty much the same.

"We're not selling out; we're just cashing in," he explained.

I thought it was a *great* headline.

Chapter 72
Even Connecticut has hillbillies

While I was in high school, I worked Saturdays and summers at a clothing store in a shopping center.

For a few days each summer, employees would haul out slow-selling items and specially purchased bargain merchandise and display it in front of the stores for a *sidewalk sale*.

We had a carnival environment—with balloons, music, clowns, costumes, cotton candy and silly announcements. It was very different from our usual way of doing business. Even the customers were different.

Instead of our usual upper-middle-class patrons, the sidewalk sale drew in low-income hicks. But they were *nice hicks*—and we *never* had any trouble.

The super-low prices attracted folks who would be more appropriate in a welfare office or on the *Jerry Springer Show* than in our classy store. Some apparently never went to a dentist and might attend family reunions to pick potential spouses. They'd buy slightly soiled underwear, shirts with missing buttons, a red sock paired with an orange sock or pants that had faded from being displayed in the window. They didn't mind the smell of mildew.

Some of these customers loved to bargain, and some of our salespeople were such skilled hagglers that we sold merchandise for *higher* prices than on normal days. Sometimes, we got out-haggled, but it was all fun.

Walter McAfee was a regular sidewalk sale customer who showed up every year with a sheet of wrapping paper bearing outlines of his six kids' feet. He'd expect me to suggest shoes to fit each absentee. I did OK and Walter came back year after year.

One year I just didn't have anything that would fit his oldest daughter without exceeding his budget. He liked one pair a lot, but it was obviously a bit too small. Ever the optimist, Walter said, "That's OK, I'll just tell Abilene to curl her toes up just a tad."

In England, one of the major prep schools is **Eton**. It's pronounced like *Beverly Hillbilly* **Jethro Bodine**'s "eatin'" and was founded in 1440 by King Henry VI. Starting in the 19th century, young boys were required to wear the "Eton suit" with huge, stiffly starched, white collars. The Eton suit was copied by other English schools and even crossed the Atlantic and became a style of dressy clothing for American boys in the 20th century.

However, if a salesperson in an American store suggested the garment and referred to it with a proper British pronunciation, a prospective customer might think the salesperson was a hillbilly and that the suit was suitable only for "eatin'" grits, chicken-fried steak, gizzards and ham hocks.

I sold boys' clothes in a store where the personnel were instructed to mispronounce the name of the school and the garment as "ee-tahn." Jethro would probably have been very confused.

Chapter 73
And so does Pennsylvania, but why is this town named after the capital of Libya?

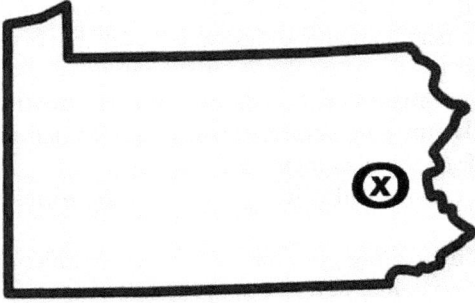

Pennsylvania is smaller than Texas, but it's still a BIG state. It has more than 12 million people, about 50,000 square miles and measures about 280 miles from west to east. Pennsylvania's southern border is the famous Mason-Dixon Line. States north of the line were "free states" during the Civil War. South of the border were the "slave states."

The western end of Pennsylvania is Midwestern, with steel mills, coal mines, oil wells, forests and deer hunters. It touches Great Lake Erie.

The east end comes close to the Atlantic Ocean. It has Philadelphia, with its Philadelphia lawyers, universities, hoagies, pretzels, cheese steaks, Rocky Balboa and the Liberty Bell. It's part of the Washington-to-Boston East Coast metroplex.

Within the state's borders are the usual mountains and rivers and turnpikes and tunnels, and even something known as the "Grand Canyon of Pennsylvania." PA's diverse populace includes Philly's cheese steak makers, Slippery Rock students, Pottsville brewers, Pittsburgh Steelers, Pocono honeymooners, Three Mile Islanders, Hershey chocolate makers and Intercourse Amish.

The most exotic Pennsylvanians I ever encountered were gathered one Sunday in the late 1960s at **Ontelaunee Park** in **New Tripoli.** They wouldn't have seemed exotic or out of place in rural Georgia, and some of these creepy country folks could have acted, quite naturally, in *Deliverance*. Ba-da-bing-bing-bing.

New Tripoli is in Lynn Township, in Lehigh County, between Allentown and Scranton, and it seemed like it had been transplanted from well below the Mason-Dixon Line.

Strangely, for a reason that's long forgotten, it is named after the capital of Libya, immortalized in the Marines Hymn ("From the halls of Montezuma, to the shores of Tripoli"). But it's pronounced differently: nu-tri-PO-lee.

The area was settled mostly by Pennsylvania Dutch (who were really German, not Dutch), who had farms and small businesses that supported the farms.

New Tripoli is known for farming, country music and crappie fishing. Apparently, the crappie fishing was not crappy. However, I think most country music *is* crappy and, had I known about the country music connection, I probably would never have gone to New Tripoli.

From 1929 to 1988, New Tripoli was the site of Ontelaunee Park, a woodsy recreation area with a carousel, miniature train, swimming pool, picnic tables and a stage that featured country music performers.

Over the years, the park showcased the talents of countless country performers whom I never heard of, like Shelby Nestler, Al Shade and Shorty Long; as well as Conway Twitty and Loretta Lynn. I did know of them.

Although I own CDs by Willie Nelson, Johnny Cash, K. D. Lang and the Dixie Chicks, I *hate* most country music.

When I was in college, I was a partner in a booking and management company that supplied bands for bars, discos and fraternity parties. Our bands performed Motown, classic rock, blues, psychedelic, oldies, hard rock and heavy metal—but *no country*.

We heard that a "battle of the bands" was planned for Ontelaunee. It would be an opportunity to showcase one of our groups and perhaps even win some money. Unfortunately, we had no idea that Ontelaunee was hillbilly territory and might not be the best place to exhibit **Oredad**.

Oredad (from "metal" and "father") was a high-wattage heavy-metal group, with lots of banging and clanging and long drum solos and minimal lyrics.

The Ontelaunee audience, on the other hand and unbeknownst to us, craved acoustic pickin' and pluckin' and twangin' and strummin'—and sad lyrics about adulterers and gamblers.

After a long and dusty ride (that sounds like a country lyric), we unloaded the U-Hauls near the stage and waited our turn for what we were told would be the "rock segment."

After endless hours listening to songs about wayward wives and worn-out mules (or maybe worn-out wives and wayward mules), we learned that Oredad *was* the rock segment. Apparently, other rock bands had the good sense to do some research, and they all stayed away.

At least we seemed to have a good chance of winning first prize in the rock category. Maybe all three prizes.

The musicians in Oredad were high school kids and did not have the freedom to shave heads, pierce chins, grow pink Mohawks or have tattoos like adult heavy-metal bands.

Their clothing was tamer, too, with no Kiss-like leather and spikes. They wore ratty jeans, scuffed work boots and faded T-shirts—like regular high school kids—which contrasted with the polished cowboy boots, fringed leathers, bandanas and ten-gallon hats worn by the other Ontelaunee performers. Oredad's appearance marked them as alien invaders the minute they took the stage, even before a string was stroked.

The emcee announced who they were, and the groupies and siblings and parents who had made the trip applauded.

The rest of the audience was cynically silent. We heard unpleasant murmurs and rustling as people noticed the band members had no fiddle, pedal-steel guitar, banjo or dulcimer.

Oredad's performance began with the lead guitarist, rhythm player and bass player silently facing the rear of the stage. The keyboard guy stared into space, above the audience, his fingers motionless. The drummer wailed with sticks and feet and began his trademark 15-minute drum solo.

Within seconds, the audience was in wide-eyed, shocked silence.

It was like in *Back to the Future* when **Marty McFly** leads the band in a noisy version of *Johnny B. Goode* and startles the kids and **Principal Strickland**, who put fingers in his ears.

The silence at Ontelaunee quickly turned into loud boos and catcalls. And then the audience started throwing food at Oredad. And then beer cans. And then sticks and stones.

Oredad was definitely *the best rock band* to perform that day at Ontelaunee Park in New Tripoli, Pennsylvania. But they took no trophy home.

Actually, they were lucky to leave alive.

Chapter 74
Lemme outa here!

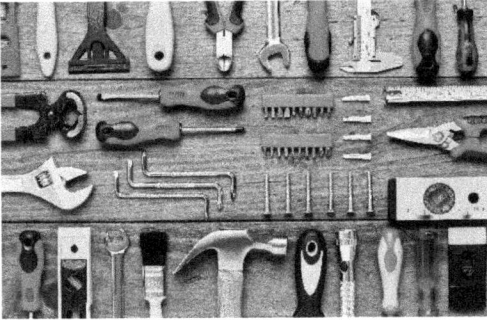

I was always good with hands and tools and was attracted to electronics quite early. When I was in first grade my father and I built a telegraph set. Later, with no parental assistance, I built a radio out of cardboard. (Well, at least it looked like a radio, and my first-grade teacher was very impressed).

I later went on to make fake walkie-talkies, fake telephones, fake robots, a fake car videophone, fake computers and eventually some real ones.

In ninth grade I won a prize for a computer I built that used a telephone dial to input numbers to be added and subtracted. It was based on the *Eccles-Jordan Bistable Multivibrator.* You can look it up.

I wrote a lot of letters to electronics manufacturers. They were impressed by the tech questions that my teachers could not answer, and I frequently was able to mooch freebie parts for projects. Sometimes, I even got invited to visit the factories. Unfortunately, some of the most interesting factories were 3,000 miles away and airfare was not included with the invitations.

Although I understood the science behind it, the telephone was always *magical* to me. I loved the notion of a voice going in one place and coming out somewhere else.

Whenever a telephone repairman was in the neighborhood, I'd beg for spare parts, old instruction manuals, surplus tools and bits of wire. I was a cute kid and usually got what I wanted.

CONFESSIONS:

o   Twice, when I desperately needed parts for an important project, I deliberately broke a telephone in our house so a repairman would come, and I could mooch supplies.

o   Once, when I was in fourth grade, I raided a repairman's truck when he was busy in our house. I took an old dial and a bunch of wire from his scrap bag. I doubt that it impacted the phone company's finances.

Starting at around age-12, I supplemented my pathetic allowance by installing intercoms and public address systems, and I was in the phone business long before it was legal to compete with Ma Bell. Years later, the U.S. Supreme Court decreed that it was OK to do it.

My high school guidance counselor strangely ignored the facts that my math College Board scores kept going down and my "verbal" scores kept going up. She decided that I should become an engineer. She knew I liked electronics. But the electronics that I liked was based on soldering irons and screwdrivers and she apparently didn't know what engineers did.

I went to Lehigh University and was quickly disappointed to learn that engineering was mostly math, and slide rules were not nearly as much fun as soldering irons. I wanted to build things myself, not to design things for other people to build.

As one of the few literate people in my engineer-filled freshman dormitory, I quickly built a lucrative business editing term papers.

It seemed to me that most of the engineering students were familiar with only the six of the 26 letters of the English alphabet (A, B, C, X, Y and Z) that were necessary for plugging into mathematical formulas, plus the few Greek letters that went into formulas or were needed for identifying fraternities. These guys were good customers for my editing.

In those days, for a college known for training future engineers, Lehigh had some peculiar anti-technology rules. Personal computers were not prohibited because they did not yet exist, but students could not have televisions in their dorm rooms. The rule seemed illogical because it did not stop kids from watching TV. There was a TV in the lounge of our dorm and there were others around the campus. The prohibition did not seem based on power consumption either, because we could have stereo systems in our dorm rooms with no limitation on wattage, and music could certainly be as distracting as television.

We were also not allowed to have telephones in our rooms, and there was just one public pay phone near the front door that the kids were constantly trying to hack into for free phone calls.

One kid's girlfriend lived less than 20 miles away, but a phone conversation with her was considered a long-distance call. He frequently tried "modifying" the phone to make free calls, and the phone company threatened to take it out if he didn't stop.

This guy was a sadist as well as an experimenter, and sometimes forced other freshmen to swallow chewing tobacco.

When he needed extra money, he had an elaborate sucker bet to extract money from his classmates. He would carefully open a pack of cigarettes and remove one cigarette. Then he'd meticulously close the pack, so it looked absolutely virginal. Next, he would choose a victim and engage in some small talk about the accuracy of modern packaging machinery and how no cigarette pack ever leaves the factory with just 19 cigarettes.

It didn't take much effort to get the sucker—confident in technology—to bet $20 that there were indeed 20 cigarettes in the apparently randomly selected package. The victim looked over the pack, opened it up, counted the contents and paid up!

I got into deep shit for installing an intercom system between my room and a friend's room two floors below. There was no specific prohibition against intercoms, but perhaps I antagonized some higher power because "our" red phones were labeled BELL SYSTEM PROPERTY. I also had trouble explaining the presence of a pay telephone in my suitcase in the storage room.

One Lehigh administrator, **Clarence "Clarabell" Campbell**, had a really dumb title: "Dean of Residence" (Dean of all people who live anywhere?)

Apparently, **Joe**, my super-straight dorm counselor, found out about the hotline phones installed between my room and **Jim VanderKloot's** room on the first floor. Joe didn't have to be much of a detective. It wasn't hard to miss the wire hanging out my window and heading down to Jim's room.

Super-straight Joe ratted me out to Clarabell, who searched my room and luggage and found my illicit payphone. I had "liberated" it from a Connecticut beach club during the off season. Clarabell called his contacts in the Pennsylvania Bell Telephone Company Gestapo, who alerted their contacts in the Southern New England Telephone Company Gestapo, who called my old man.

The phone company was mostly concerned that I had ripped off a big bunch of their dimes. I couldn't care less about the money, and the coin box was empty when I pried the phone off the wall. I just thought it was cool to have a pay phone. I later had 14 pay phones and two phone booths—all bought legally.

My father, a pillar of the community, rolled over. He turned over my illicit phone collection and even got rid of some of my favorite traffic signs.

A while later, at about 4 AM while studying for a calculus exam, a mighty voice from an invisible source said to me, "Michael, are you sure you want to do this for the rest of your life?"

I said, "No."

Then the powerful voice said, "Michael, do you want to do this for four years?"

I said, "No," again.

And then I heard from the mystery inquisitor one last time: "Do you want to do this for the rest of the semester?"

I shouted, "HELL, NO!"

The next morning, I switched from engineering to journalism.

I've been writing ever since—and I still play around with phones.

This rare photograph shows the author in around 1965 working on the *Brown & White* student newspaper at Lehigh University. I had temporarily shaved off my beard so I could get a job between semesters working in a clothing store that regarded facial hair as sinister.

The machine in front of me is called a "type-writer"—a primitive word-processing device that worked without electricity, had just one typeface and no display or memory. A human-powered return lever was activated after entering each line of text, and the machine made a cool "ding" sound when I reached the end of a line

In the photo, I was clutching my chest because I was about to puke after reading something I had typed. My cheeks were puffed up because of retained vomit, not nuts stored for the winter.

Note the fashionable "sawed-off" White Levis, sweater with amputated sleeves and anti-Vietnam war pin. The clothing and protest pin were typical of the period. I can't imagine what caused me to wear that femme ID bracelet.

I vaguely remember having hair like that. I do not remember having a nose like that. The big nose is an optical illusion caused by primitive photographic equipment of that era.

Chapter 75
Boys are dumb

The Great Jockstrap Debate:

At our first gym class in seventh grade in junior high school, we were given a list of supplies we would need: sneakers, thick white socks, white T-shirt, white gym shorts, a combination lock for our clothing basket and something few of us were familiar with: an athletic supporter (more commonly known as a *jockstrap)* to protect our precious and fragile genitalia.

A week later, we reported to class with bags of new or hand-me-down supplies and, as we waited on the benches for our teacher to appear, the jockstrap became the subject of a heated debate.

The 12-year-olds were evenly divided as to whether the strange garments were to be worn *under* our underpants or *over* our underpants.

We were completely unprepared for the shocking truth that was revealed when the teacher finally showed up and gave us instructions for "suiting up."

Jockstraps are worn *instead* of underpants. Ooh.

Where do babies come from?

When I was at the **Quinnipiac Day Camp** in the summer between fourth and fifth grades, **Alfie** told me that babies came out of an opening in a woman's upper leg called the *magenta*.

Sal, a year older, insisted that they came out of the belly button.

Who does the chores?

In around third grade, our Cub Scout troop had a fund-raising project. Three of us went door-to-door to earn money by performing odd jobs. At one home, Larry asked a housewife, "Do you have any chores to do?"—not "Are there any chores that *we can do*?" Larry made it seem like he was conducting a survey, not trying to raise money, and we were not hired. At the next house, Billy made the proper sales pitch, and we earned ten bucks.

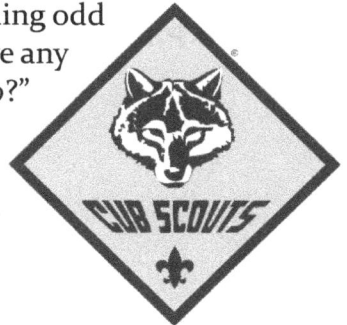

Chapter 76
Smart, sarcastic & canine

Hunter J. Marcus (2001-2017) was officially a golden retriever, but I regarded him as "my four-legged son." He could be willful, affectionate, athletic, curious, ravenous, thirsty, stubborn, smart and sarcastic.

Hunter usually slept in the bedroom with wife **Marilyn** and me. My office was close to our bedroom, and I often went to my desk between 3 and 4 AM.

At around 7 AM, Hunter would usually wander into my office, give me a greeting, let me know that I should take him downstairs and let him go out to pee. He'd start walking toward the back stairs, which (please take note) were carpeted.

To save a few seconds one day in June of 2011, I told him to follow me in the *other direction*, so we could go down the front stairs, which are *not* carpeted.

I was wearing socks, which provided *no traction* on the bare wood. I slipped, and slid on my ass, bumpety-bumpety-bump, all the way to the bottom.

When I got to the bottom, I sat, trembled, and assessed the damage.

Then, my sweet, smart, sarcastic Hunter brought me *a pair of sneakers*, as if to say, "You need traction, you idiot."

I developed a big, painful, purple-and-green hematoma (blood clot). A surgeon made three new holes in my ass to suck out about four ounces of blood with a huge syringe.

Lesson: Pay attention to your dog.

Chapter 77
The sex chapter: my first dry hump, and more
Maybe, because of Betty Friedan and Anthony Quinn, 1965 was much sexier than 1964.

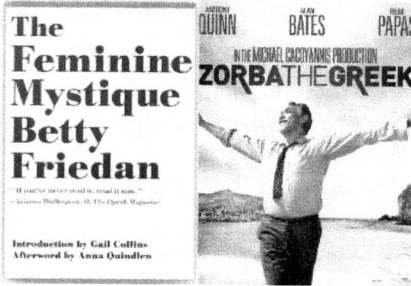

The attitude about sex for most baby-boomer boys who became teenagers in the late 1950s and early 60s was not much different from the attitude in previous decades and centuries, dictated and reinforced by religion and parents.

Boys wanted to do "it," but nice girls didn't do it.

Therefore, the girls who did it were *not nice*.

A man would choose one woman for love and another for sex, but none for both.

Before the feminist revolution, the girls who did "it" were frequently perceived to be whores or sluts, or were physically undesirable They provided sexual favors to attract and keep a boyfriend—unlike the more desirable girls who could remain virgins until their wedding night.

Before the feminist revolution, sex was assumed to be pleasurable for most men but not for most women.

Women were advised to look at the ceiling during sex and think about something else. On the wedding night, and through decades of marriage, women often endured sex because it was considered a *marital duty*, necessary to keep the husband from straying and to perpetuate the species. I heard women, born in the beginning of the 20th century, speak of being "bothered for sex" by their husbands.

The human female is among the few creatures that engage in sex during non-fertile periods, and this facet of evolution may have developed to keep the man around to protect and provide for the family. This leads some feminists to insist that marriage is long-term, legalized prostitution.

There's a lot of sex in the Bible, and most sex was performed by men *on* women. Jacob asked Laban for his daughter Rachel so he could "go in unto her." Moses ordered the men of Israel to "come not at your wives" before he went up Mount Sinai.

Although they are in the minority, there are several sexually assertive women in the Bible. Ruth sought the advice from her mother-in-law, Naomi, for seducing husband, Boaz. Naomi told Ruth to wait until Boaz was drunk and sleepy and "go in and uncover his feet (meaning genitals) and lay thee down."

For many wives, sexual pleasure was accidental, unthinkable, infrequent or impossible.

Betty Friedan's *The Feminine Mystique* and other books that followed helped establish women's right not just to equal pay for equal work but also to equal pleasure from sex.

For a teen boy in the early 60s, there were big questions about "what to try" and "what I can get away with." Some boys were slapped for kissing a cheek or touching a breast. Others—so I heard—received look-but-don't-touch stripteases or hand jobs while still in junior high.

It seems quaint in the 21st century when ten-year-olds have oral sex and junior high school girls email nude photos, and there is endless talk about hooking up, friends with benefits, sexting, fuck buddies and booty calls; but back then it took *guts* to kiss a girl on a first date.

Thoughts of progressing from "first base" to a "home run" were more likely to result in wet dreams than in real sex.

The assumption was that, since sex wasn't fun for females, they didn't want to have sex, and must be seduced, coerced, forced, persuaded, bribed, paid, drugged or gotten drunk.

The vocabulary reflected this. Males "got something off her" or screwed, hammered, drilled, boffed, banged, bonked, boinked, porked, poked, schtupped, shagged, slammed or knocked up.

Until recently, "fucking" was mostly done by males to females, but both genders can "get laid." Men are more likely than women to "get lucky." Women like to "make love."

"Fuck" is a transitive verb for a male, as in "Steve fucked Jane." But, for a woman, at one time it was mostly intransitive and a description of a loose woman, as in "Yeah, Jane fucks." It was different in 2009 when **Sarah Silverman** proudly sang, "I'm fucking **Matt Damon**" to **Jimmy Kimmel**.

Females lack an equally assertive or aggressive term to match "screw" or "bang." It may be that the physical essence of the genital apparatus leads to the imbalance. A hard penis just looks more aggressive than a soft vagina, and penetration is more assertive than being penetrated.

In *Moving Beyond Words*, feminist author **Gloria Steinem** considered this language deficiency, and the most forceful verb she could think of for the female function was "envelop." That doesn't seem very assertive.

My wife Marilyn and I spent our first few years in a Bronx apartment, and were often so horny that, instead of rushing to the subway in the mornings, we stayed in bed—and were late for work. Years later we had a huge house in Connecticut. We referred to a spare bedroom as our "nookatorium," and escaped to that room for intimacy without our dog's growling, sniffing and humping.

At my advanced age, I suppose it's normal to look back and ponder missed opportunities for premarital ecstasy.

- o I dated a pretty girl in 1962-63, my junior year in high school. I had the normal desires for **Lynn**, and the normal inhibitions to keep me from acting on them. We held hands and eventually got to goodnight kisses, but nothing more. Physically, she seemed much colder than previous girls I had dated and had made out with. The gossip at school was that she was "frigid." I asked my mother about it. She said, "There's no such thing as a frigid woman, only clumsy men." My mother did not suggest the possibility that this young lady might be a latent lesbian, and thus not receptive to any male.

- o In my senior year of high school, I dated several other girls. I liked one of them enough to think about marrying her. On the Freud scale (he wrote of *The Madonna-Whore Complex*), I considered **Maria** to be much more of a Madonna than a whore. We never went beyond kissing, and my balls frequently ached. Years later she described me as a "horn dog." I've been meaning to ask her how she knew, because I always suppressed my lust for her. Maria grew up faster than I did. She once told me a joke: "What if someone hosted an orgy, but no one came?" I laughed, but I didn't really understand it until a few months later. That may be the first time someone faked laughing about an orgasm.

- o **Barbara** was a dear friend, (my "platonic girlfriend") when I was in college, and we're still quite close. She attended my 75th birthday party via Zoom. We had so much to say to each other that I'm afraid we monopolized the event. At one point I asked her if she would have gone to bed with me back then. Barbara replied, "Well, it was the sixties..." Hmm.

The next section is *not* about a missed opportunity.

Anita was physically different from most other girls I was attracted to. My standard set of fetishes included dark hair and deep cleavage. Anita was one of very few blondes I dated and had what she described as *French tits* ("just big enough to fill a champagne glass").

She was a very smart, sexy, precocious and pretty girl whom I probably should not have gotten involved with. But I lacked the information that would've kept me away.

When we met, she told me she was a "sophomore at Moravian." I assumed she meant that she attended nearby Moravian College, which would have made her probably 19 years old, a year younger than I was at the time. Boy, was I wrong!

It was only after several months—several months of frequent and recklessly unprotected sex—that I found out that Anita was a *sophomore at Moravian Preparatory Academy* (a high school) and was only 15 years old!

For some unknown reason, Anita had trouble losing her virginity both with previous boyfriends and with me. She had remained a "technical virgin" with an intact hymen much longer than she wanted to.

One time, the two of us were in my bedroom during a whole-house party and we were trying unsuccessfully to break down the barrier. We were humping so hard that I—not Anita—started bleeding. I got a nosebleed for my efforts to break her hymen. I guess the blood pressure was very high throughout my entire circulatory system.

That night, Anita really wanted to show her best friend that she finally "became a woman" so she faked the evidence. She used some blood from my nose to redden the sheet to show off.

A few days later, after she got advice from her older sister, we tried a new position and 15-year-old Anita became a woman, though still not an adult.

She had a key to my apartment, and often stopped by to provide me with an oral awakening on her way to school.

Sex was almost a toy for Anita, and we tried it in strange places, including the garden just below her parents' bedroom window and in the deep end of the pool while treading water. (It doesn't work. The motions that keep you from drowning are not the motions you want to make.)

We once followed the **Beatles**' suggestion, "Why don't we do it in the road?" and were chased away by the farmer who owned the road.

If you want to do it in the woods, make sure there are no park rangers, bears, hikers or hunters in the area. Air mattresses floating in the pool flex too much, and it's easy to fall off. Water beds don't provide enough support and the sloshing is distracting. Don't have sex in a room with a dog, because the pooch may want to sniff or hump. Cars are cramped. Vans are fine. Couches and big chairs work well. All in all, a conventional bed is probably best, but a deserted beach can be nice, especially at a freshwater lake where you can rinse off the sand.

And some others:

- **Joanie** (known as "Jo-Fuck") was a lusty young lady and a frequent attendee at our parties in Bethlehem. One night she got so plastered that she passed out in my bed, next to me. The next day she reported to a friend that I "was not very sexy." I suppose I shouldn't have disappointed her, but the idea of having sex with a drunk was just not appealing.

- After college I moved to New York City and had a number of media jobs and a number of female friends. As mentioned elsewhere, a young lady whose name I've forgotten lived in Brooklyn and had a southern accent. She got pregnant by someone else and had a painful abortion. She recuperated in my bed. I was a very good friend, but we never went beyond kissing.
- **Sandy** was a year older than I was. She had worked at a magazine in Manhattan, and then moved back to her parents' home in Bethlehem. We dated, but not exclusively. Her mother made the best non-Jewish chicken soup I'd ever tasted, and Sandy had the best smile I'd ever seen. We made out, even in bed, but never went "all the way." Eventually we drifted apart. I don't remember why.
- I met **Virginia** in an elevator when we both worked in the same building in Manhattan. We dated for about a year, but not exclusively. One evening we were in her office, and she stripped down to her bra and panties. She wanted me to use a Magic Marker to draw a plant growing up a leg, bypassing her panties, and then continuing upward to sprout a flower around her navel. I long wondered how she would have reacted if I pulled down her panties to eliminate the gap in my artwork—but I never found out. Damn!
- My first Bronx apartment was no palace, but it was affordable ($66.21 per month, thanks to New York's weird rent-control laws), convenient and good enough. It was considered to be a "professional apartment," the type of dwelling often rented by a doctor, on ground-level with its own private entrance. My front hallway turned out to be the perfect place to park my Vespa motor scooter. The law required landlords to paint apartments for each new tenant, but my landlord refused and wasn't worried about prosecution. He was, however, willing to give me a free month's rent and six gallons of white paint and some brushes, rollers, trays and drop cloths if I agreed to take care of the painting. I had recently met a beautiful, smart and very funny girl named **Laurel** at a mutual friend's party. It was a terrific party. One of the guests had a copy of a studio master tape of what would turn out to be **Elton John's** *11-17-70* album. Laurel, too, had recently moved to New York and she offered to help me paint. I liked her a lot and hoped for a weekend of painting plus passion. After we painted and had sandwiches and beer, I embraced her and kissed her romantically. She kissed me back *sisterly*. Then she told me she was a lesbian.

In the fall of '64, I went away to college and became aware of changes in sexuality. Male attitudes had shifted from "getting something" to "giving pleasure." Female attitudes had shifted from "letting him do it" to "wanting him to do it."

In *Zorba the Greek*, **Anthony Quinn**'s character advised his younger companion, **Basil**, played by **Alan Bates**, "God has a very big heart but there is one sin he will not forgive: if a woman calls a man to her bed and he will not go." This movie scene was my first "official" notice that females might actually like sex. Alas, I can't remember which girl I saw the movie with or what we did after it.

I saw *Zorba* in late 1964. In early '65, there was a dance in our freshman dorm at Lehigh, and my blind date from **Cedar Crest College** turned me on during a slow, close dance. I made no effort to hide my erection. Not outraged, my date seemed to be complimented. She did not slap me or move away. We danced closer and she did a grind against me. It was my first dry hump, and wet ones soon followed.

So, thanks, Zorba, for explaining the facts of life and changing my life. I just wish you'd done it a year earlier.

Chapter 78
Playing the numbers

Numbers are usually useful, often interesting, sometimes dangerous, sometimes funny—or even perverse.

Before I get to the serious stuff, here's something funny from my funny father: He showed me how the digits in the nine-times table always add up to nine. Nine times three is 27. The two plus the seven equals nine. Nine times five is 45. The four plus the five equals nine. It's not very useful, but it's definitely amusing.

And now, some horrors and giggles:

I lived in Westchester County, New York in the 1980s. I got TV service from **Cablevision**. Service was usually fine, and I paid my bills on time.

There were ten TVs in my house. (Don't ask why.) Five of the sets were connected to cable boxes, for which I paid monthly rental fees. The five less-important sets had no boxes because we seldom used them and didn't need lots of channels.

The FCC decreed that the nation's cable companies were responsible for minimizing "*ingress and egress*" (interference from and to other customers' televisions). To monitor my system, which included segments of cable that I had personally installed when the house was being built, and for which I paid no monthly fees, Cablevision established a list of the freebie teevees. (I like that phrase.)

Because Cablevision's accounting system could not produce monthly statements with more than six devices, they established a *second account* for me, listing the unbillable chunks of cable within my walls. Each month the company paid a few cents to generate and mail an invoice, showing a balance of *zero dollars and zero cents*. That seemed silly but was apparently harmless.

However, Cablevision's mighty computer eventually noticed that I was not paying the silly zero bills. I got increasingly threatening collection letters from the company and one of its attorneys. Naturally, I called to complain. And, naturally, my calls accomplished nothing.

Eventually, out of desperation and because I'm a wiseass, I went to the nearby office and presented a check for the amount of *zero dollars and zero cents*. The cable cashier smiled, laughed, looked at my bill and used her computer to enter my payment of zero dollars and zero cents.

I felt relieved, but the relief was just temporary. I was planning to move across a state line, to Milford, Connecticut, which was also in Cablevision territory. When I called to arrange for moving my TV service, my request was denied because of my outstanding balance of (you guessed it) *zero dollars and zero cents*!

○ While doing a math problem on the blackboard in my senior year of high school, my teacher pointed out that I wrote the number **5** *backwards*, as I had done since first grade.
○ At one time I had cellphone service from **AT&T**. For some unknown reason I slightly overpaid my monthly bill, and an AT&T computer generated and mailed me a check for

15 cents. It must've cost a few bucks to make the silly payment, which I was not expecting. I was still a customer, and the money could've been credited to my next month's bill. But that would have required uncommon common sense. Out of spite, I never cashed or deposited the check.

o   For my bar mitzvah in 1959, I received shares in two mutual funds. I received small dividends each year. In around 1985, a law changed to allow the dividends to be re-invested rather than distributed. I contacted the funds' banks to make the changes. Both banks insisted that I provide a letter from a parent stating that I was over the age of 21 and could make this decision. None of the financial geniuses was able to calculate that in the 26 years between 1959 and 1985, I passed the age of majority.

o   Some years ago, my house was burglarized, and among the purloined property was a toolbox, filled with my nice **Craftsman** tools. Our home was insured by **Allstate**. Allstate, like Craftsman, was part of **Sears**. After I submitted my claim, the Allstate adjuster applied a depreciation deduction formula for the stolen tools, based on their age and presumed decrepitude. I responded that Craftsman tools are sold with a Lifetime Warranty, so there *can't be any depreciation*. I told him that I could take a bent, dull, rusted, 30-year-old Craftsman tool into any Sears store and it would be immediately replaced with a bright and shiny new model. The adjuster responded that "everything depreciates except land," and he gleefully pointed out that "a brand-new Cadillac drops 20% in value when it leaves the dealer's lot." I told Mr. Allstate that I would rather drive a Craftsman than a Cadillac and I was not giving up and he'd better check with corporate headquarters. Apparently, there soon was a battle for supremacy in the Sears Tower in Chicago and it was ultimately decided that the image of Craftsman was more important than the profitability of Allstate. I got every penny I wanted.

o   On one day in the early 70s, I received mail *rejecting* me for a gasoline credit card and *accepting* me for a house mortgage.

o   On another day, I received acceptance and rejection credit card letters *from the same company*. Aaaaarrrrggghhh.

o   In 1963 my parents paid $150 to buy me a top-of-the-line ten-speed Raleigh "racing bike." While pedaling around New Haven I spotted a new Corvette "split-window" Sting Ray at a local Chevy dealer. I parked my bike and went in to drool. A salesman detected my obvious lust and offered me an amazing deal: $1,000 trade-in for my $150 two-wheeler. The deal was very tempting, but I did not buy the car for two reasons: (1) I would not be able to afford the monthly payments, and (2) I did not have a driver's license. Oh, well.

[Corvette photo from MercurySable99. Thanks.]

Chapter 79
Gunning & dying

A highly inept and inarticulate teacher (discussed elsewhere) told our class that "Death kills instantly."

o   In recent years about 50,000 people died from gun-related injuries in the United States. This figure includes both murders and suicides, along with other less common types of gun-related deaths. In 2021, 54% of these deaths were suicides (26,328), while 43% were murders (20,958).

o   About 81% of U.S. murders in 2021 involved a firearm, marking the highest percentage since at least 1968.

o   Over 55% of suicides in that year also involved a gun. This translates to *approximately 132 people dying from a firearm-related injury each day*. Acts of violence committed with the use of firearms have become an everyday phenomenon.

o   The United States is the only high-income country to report such a high death toll from gun violence.

o   Firearms are by far the most used murder weapon in the nation.

o   The number of mass shootings and school shootings has been increasing over the last few years, with younger Americans emphasizing the reduction of gun violence and mass shootings as one of the most important issues to their generation.

o   Despite rising rates of gun violence, however, many Americans remain fiercely protective of their constitutional right to bear arms.

o   According to a survey conducted in the United States in 2022, white respondents were more likely to either personally own a gun or live in a gun owning household than their non-white counterparts. During the survey, 36 percent of white Americans reported that they personally owned a firearm, compared to 27 percent of non-white respondents. (These statistics come from *Statista.com*.)

o   *Time* said that "Every year, more than 3,500 children and teens—defined as infants through age 19—are shot and killed in the U.S., and another 15,000 are wounded in shootings..."

o   *KFF* reported that "The United States has by far the highest rate of child and teen firearm mortality among peer nations. In no other similarly large, wealthy country are firearms in the top four causes of death for children and teens, let alone the number one cause. U.S. states with the most gun laws have lower rates of child and teen firearm deaths than states with few gun laws. But, even states with the lowest child and teen firearm deaths have rates much higher than what peer countries experience."

o   The number of children and teens killed by gunfire in the United States increased 50% between 2019 and 2021, according to *Pew Research Center*.

o   Gun deaths of Black kids are *more than five times* the figure for other racial and ethnic groups. Among African American children, the rate of gun deaths per 100,000 people was

11.8. For white children and Hispanics, the figure was 2.3 per 100,000, and for Asian children, it was even lower, at 0.9.

o Not only do kids get killed with guns, many kids—as young as two years old—have accidentally shot others.

o *NBC* reported that "At least 157 people were killed and 270 were injured last year in unintentional shootings by children ... The children who pulled the trigger were most often teenagers from 14 to 17 or children aged 5 and under ... Roughly half of the incidents involved children who shot themselves. In the other half, someone else was shot—usually a child."

o "The victim is often a sibling, a cousin or a friend," said **Sarah Burd-Sharps,** senior director of research at *Everytown*. "It leaves multiple families facing grief and regret. Nearly once every day, a child gets their hand on a loaded gun and shoots themselves or someone else," Burd-Sharps said. "It's so preventable." Those who died include a 2-year-old girl in Indiana who shot herself with a gun she found in her home and an 8-year-old boy in Alabama who was shot with a firearm that had been removed from his mother's car. In Florida, a 12-year-old boy died and a 15-year-old was injured by a 14-year-old who was playing with a gun that he thought was unloaded."

o While I was finishing this book, a 14-year-old boy confessed to fatally shooting two teachers and two students at his Georgia high school. His father was charged with two counts of second-degree murder, four counts of involuntary manslaughter and eight counts of cruelty to children.

I hate guns. I've never owned or even touched a *real* gun, but I had toy guns as a child. This strange photo shows me "packing heat" while visiting Santa Claus. I don't know why I was armed.

The Second Amendment is dangerous, obsolete and should be canceled. Guns are OK for cops, military and guards ONLY. Americans don't need to hunt for food. People who have an urge to shoot at targets can use arrows, paint balls or laser beams. We no longer need a militia. The Redcoats were defeated long ago and went back to England.

Chapter 80
Universal emotions

Some human feelings are so wide-spread that clichés exist in multiple languages, and span time from antiquity to today.

o   Some unknown ancient Roman declared in Latin that "*De gustibus non est disputandum*," meaning "In matters of taste, there can be no disputes." The implication is that personal preferences can't be either right or wrong and should never be argued over, as if the opinion differences could be settled by reason or with evidence.

o   In Italian, the sentiment is "*Non dovrebbe esserci discussione sui gusti.*"

o   In English, we have "there's no accounting for taste," "to each his own," "do your own thing," "whatever turns you on, "whatever floats your boat," "do what you like," "your mileage may vary, "one man's meat is another man's poison," "That's why they make chocolate and vanilla." And, of course "opinions are like assholes. Everybody has one." There are probably more.

o   In France, the sentiment is rendered as "*À chacun son goût*" or "*Chacun son goût.*" It's pronounced [ah shah koo (n) so (n) goo]. It translates into English as "(to) each one his taste."

o   A Spanish version is "*no hay que tener en cuenta los gustos.*" CONFESSION: I got this from Google translator, and I have no idea if Latinos really say it. There are probably other versions in other languages, maybe even Vulcan and Klingon. I did say "universal."

o   In Hebrew a phrase roughly translates as "On taste and smell there is no point in arguing."

- o And, speaking of Hebrew, an old Yiddish proverb is *"Mann Tracht, Un Gott Lacht."* It means, "man plans, and God laughs."
- o My online multilingual buddy **Karen Albert** provided this Spanish version: *"El hombre propone. Dios dispone."*
- o American poet **Ralph Waldo Emerson** (1803-1882 CE) was optimistic. He wrote that "Once you make a decision, the universe conspires to make it happen."

Mark Twain wrote: "It were not best that we should all think alike; it is difference of opinion that makes horse races."

The **Jefferson Airplane** sang: "It doesn't mean shit to a tree."

Chapter 81
The last girl on Earth (and hiding hard-ons)

Cindy was a petite seventh-grader with an enormous ego, better suited to someone with greater beauty, brains and talent. So great was her opinion of herself, and so low the opinion that others had of her, that there seemed to be permanent graffiti in the street in front of her house proclaiming, "CINDY IS CONCEITED."

She and I attended **Cotillion**, a ballroom dancing school that also attempted to teach the social graces to young teenagers on Friday nights. One Friday night was also Halloween night, and Cotillion management wisely realized that the only way they could get 12-year-olds to forsake trick-or-treating for dancing school was to have a costume party.

For me, this was the second-best reason to go to Cotillion. The *best* reason was to dance with the 18-year-old female dance instructors who had breasts and hips.

Halloween was my favorite holiday back then. I started preparing costumes in mid-summer and consistently won prizes for my efforts.

I don't remember what I wore that year, but as I expected, I won "Best Boy," and my peers applauded. My prize, unexpectedly, was not a trophy or even a big bag of candy.

I got to choose to dance with any girl I wanted to. Conceited Cindy assumed she was the leading candidate and, aware of my rock-bottom social status, she tried to hide behind some taller friends. She wasn't completely hidden, however. I moved close to the microphone, looked at her and announced in a deep voice, "Don't worry, Cindy, I wouldn't pick you if you were the last girl on earth!" There was thunderous applause, especially from other girls.

Then, instead of skinny, conceited Cindy, I picked **Gloria**, one of the 18-year-old dance instructors who had breasts and hips.

Gloria was much nicer than Cindy and gave me a kiss on the lips to congratulate me, and then we did a slow Foxtrot in the spotlight. We danced much closer than normal for 12-year-olds, but probably normal for 18-year-olds.

I can still remember the Foxtrot steps from over 60 years ago: Forward. Sidestep. Back. Feet together. Slow. Cross that foot.

Gloria did a grind against me and gave me a woody.

It lasted for a long time and fortunately I didn't dance close with the next girl, or I might have been banished from Cotillion for being a pervert.

In seventh and eighth grade, as our female classmates were starting to "develop" and male hormones were also raging. Schoolboys often had wet dreams in bed at night and inflated pants in school during the day.

One time I was called to the blackboard in Spanish class while aroused. I walked bent-over at the waist to avoid revealing my erection and then practically buried my penis in the wall at the front of the classroom. I suppose in the 21st century, teenage boys are proud to wave their flagpoles in public, but back then we were advised to wear jockstraps every day, to take a lot of cold showers and to stop thinking about breasts. It's *impossible* for heterosexual teenage boys not to think about breasts.

Summer times were great for breast watching. At our beach club, the 14-year-old boys in *Titty Club* would float in the deep end of the pool with diving masks and snorkels, facing the diving board, ogling females who'd dive off the board. When they'd plunge down to the bottom of the pool and quickly reverse direction to swim up to the surface, sometimes their bathing suit tops would pull back and we'd actually spot a breast.

A few times we got really lucky. Some girls had not tied their bikini tops tight enough before diving and they lost them in the water, and we got to see TWO COMPLETE BREASTS.

For a change of pace, the horny young divers would head for the shower shows.

There were undetectable peepholes under the benches in the individual shower rooms. Whenever a hot female went into a shower room, one of us would go into the adjacent room. Sometimes our view was blocked by a towel, but we saw a lot.

WRONG "PLAY" Before I was old enough to have a real job, I worked Saturdays in the toy department of my father's store. Once, I was telling an attractive woman about a toy and could not avoid noticing her breasts. I said that the toy was made by "**Playtex**" (the bra brand) instead of "**Playskool**" (the toy brand).

ADOLESCENT MALE SECRET REVEALED Elvis Presley and my friends and I had nicknames for our penises. The King called his "Little Elvis." Ours were called Rover, Fido, Schnickenflritzer, Joe, Max and Axolotl. We even had a song about them. Sadly, I no longer remember my dick's name. We don't talk much anymore.

Chapter 82
They don't need a telephone man.
They need a psychiatrist.

After years of writing magazine articles and advertising during the day, and installing phones at night, I reversed my schedule in around 1980 and became a full-time phone guy. I installed phones and phone systems for businesses and homes. I worked for ordinary people and famous people, very rich and not-so-rich, normal and nutso.

I learned that certain stereotypes apply about 85% of the time.

o   Doctors were the cheapest.
o   Lawyers were the most crooked.
o   Interior decorators were the nuttiest.
o   People with old money tended to be looser with their money than people who had just recently struck it rich.

Superstars and billionaires defied stereotyping. They could be the nicest people in the world, or bitches and bastards and raving lunatics. Some rich people felt they had plenty and had no objection to others' making money. Others felt that any dollar that someone else had, was one less dollar available for them to have.

It's hard for me to think of my worst customer. There's probably a three-way tie. Actually, if I keep thinking, maybe it's a ten-way tie.

I said that the decorators were the nuttiest and the lawyers were the crookedest. **Mrs. Statler** was a decorator, married to a lawyer, and together they *drove me nuts*. I had installed a phone system in their house, but this esteemed "officer of the court" wanted the bill made out to his business so he could claim it as a tax deduction, and he offered to pay me in cash so he could avoid paying sales tax.

Mrs. Statler insisted that I remove all of the light bulbs from their phones because they were "too businesslike." But then both Statlers complained because they were constantly interrupting each other's calls and disconnecting held calls.

One time, Mrs. Statler summoned me to her house, complaining that the phone in her bedroom sounded like crap and asked why it couldn't sound as good as the phone in the den.

I checked the bedroom phone, and of course it was fine. I then went into the den and encountered **Mr. Statler**. He said, "I'm glad you're here. This phone is a piece of shit. Get rid of it and get me a good one, like the phone in the bedroom."

One valuable lesson in business that businesspeople seldom learn early enough is that *sometimes it's better to turn down business*.

Once, when I was young, foolish and hungry, I ignored a warning from a friendly competitor, and I agreed to work for a customer who was an absolute lunatic.

I was in **Mandy's** house for three long days, installing a state-of-the-art phone system, and during that time, the tip of her nose was seldom more than an inch away from my screwdriver's tip.

I don't know if she didn't trust me, was in love with me or was trying to learn the business. She was a real pain in my ass, but that initial pain was just the beginning of the torture.

The real agony began *after* I thought my work was finished. For two days, this maniac escorted me from room to room so I could fine-tune her telephones. She had me open up each telephone handset and adjust the volume of the transmitter and receiver by inserting varying thicknesses of different textiles.

She had me experiment with diapers, napkins, felt, nylon stockings, perforated rubber—an endless parade of both natural and synthetic materials. And when Mandy was finally satisfied, she asked her husband and daughter for their opinions, and we started the agony *all over again*.

I lived through the ordeal, and I got paid and the check cleared. The phone system seemed stable—a lot more stable than Mandy—and I prayed that I'd never hear from her again.

But I was not to be that lucky.

She called from a neighbor's house to complain that none of her phones were working. Reluctantly, I honored my obligation, and I went right over. I found that the main "brain" of the phone system was blackened and smelled like smoke. I asked what happened. Mandy said her daughter's boyfriend had used the system for a school science experiment.

I told her that the warranty was void and I quickly opened the front door. Then I gleefully skipped to my car, invoked the spirit of **Dr. Martin Luther King, Jr.** and loudly proclaimed to Mandy and her neighbors: "Free at last! Free at last! Thank God almighty, I am free at last!"

There is not enough money on Planet Earth to pay me to go back there again.

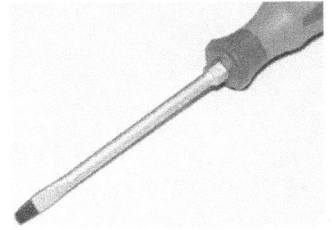

Chapter 83
Clams and Klingons

Yucky or yummy?

It's been said that the bravest man in the history of the world was the first guy who ate a raw clam. Or maybe it was really a raw oyster. Or a lobster. It doesn't matter much. The principle is the same. Some delicacies are best devoured in the dark, at least for the first time.

As a kid I loved fried clam strips.

I naively thought that frying was the only way that clams could be prepared for eating. (I now know better, and I even operated a website called *WeLoveClams.com* devoted to the many ways of preparing and eating the beloved bivalve.)

One time I was waiting for a bus to take me back to college from the Port Authority terminal on Eighth Avenue in Manhattan. I was hungry and nearly broke and went across the street to a sleazy neighborhood dive for a cheap meal.

I was relieved to see clams on the menu at an affordable price, so I placed my order.

I expected a plate with familiar, crunchy, golden-brown, fried clam strips on a roll with tartar sauce, like I got at **Howard Johnson's**.

But I was presented with a dozen squiggly, slimy, quivering, wet iridescent gray and purple things on the half shell.

They reminded me of a picture I had seen when a friend and I sneaked a look at his mother's obstetrical nursing textbook.

Or maybe the inside of a cow's eye that we dissected in biology class.

I was also presented with a bottle of Frank's Louisiana Hot Sauce and two previously used pieces of lemon on a faded and scratched plate.

I was staring at the scariest food I had ever seen. This was before live Klingon food was shown on *Star Trek*.

Joe's Bar was not a place where a suburban college kid could survive sending a meal back to the kitchen. Besides, I was hungry and now broke.

Somehow, I got up the courage to stab and swallow one of the disgusting gray slime balls, and I liked it.

I still do. (I once ate 144 clams at one sitting, my "personal best.")

Hunger and poverty can cause human beings to discover unknown courage.

Chapter 84
The lasagna chapter

Cat lasagna

One Saturday while we were in junior high school, best buddy **Howie** and I went to **Pepe's**, a neighborhood Italian restaurant, for lunch. It was not glamorous. It was a dingy, long and narrow place with tables against two walls, and a center aisle that ran from the front door to the counter and kitchen in the back.

Instead of our usual pizza, we both ordered lasagna, and we waited. We waited for a very long time. Periodically, our waitress apologized for the delay, refilled our water glasses and promised that our meals would be out "soon."

At some point, a bedraggled alley cat came in through the open front doorway, and quickly walked down the center aisle, made a quick jog around the counter and went into the kitchen.

A moment later, we heard a clatter and squealing that sounded like an episode of Itchy and Scratchy on *The Simpsons*. Or maybe the velociraptors in the *Jurassic Park* kitchen.

After a little while, the waitress brought out two plates of lasagna.

Howie and I turned pale, got up and walked out without eating or paying.

Too-famous lasagna

Another time, **Howie** and I were wandering around Greenwich Village in Manhattan. We were hungry and almost out of money and were looking for an inexpensive way to fill our bellies.

We were both relieved and pleased to find a crappy-looking restaurant with grease-encrusted windows, a door with cracked glass, tufts of litter swirling near that door, a drunk sleeping under the torn awning and a suitably unimpressive name.

"**Joe's Italian**" seemed to be a likely source of cheap, two-buck lasagna.

When we went inside and sat down and started looking around, we sensed that we might be wrong. This Joe was not merely an anonymous Joe. He was **Giuseppe Marcello Bacciagaluppe**, an award-winning chef who apparently had no need to pay anything to enhance the exterior décor of his famous establishment.

Photographs on the wall showed Joe with **Frank Sinatra**, **Dean Martin**, **Tony Bennett**, **Perry Como**, **Annette Funicello**, **Connie Francis**, a pope, two mayors, a governor, two presidents and a *capo de tutti capi* from the Mafia.

Joe's lasagna would have cost $14.95 each (very expensive in the sixties).

We quickly sneaked out before the waiter put water on the table and we found a **Sabrett's** hotdog cart that better suited our budget.

The Sabrett's cart had a picture of just one president, and **Jack Kennedy** was not shown shaking the hand of the Greek hotdog man.

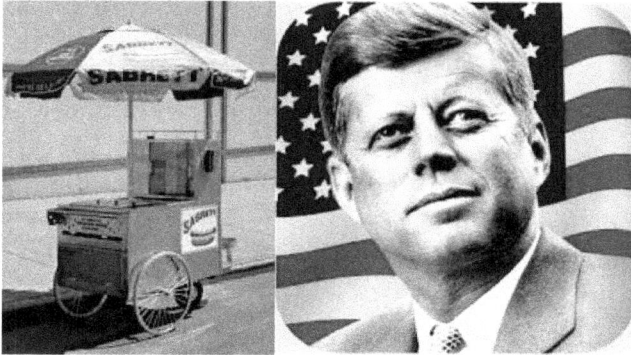

Chapter 85
Sautéed piscatorial penises

Steve was hired to teach biology, but he wasn't much of a teacher. He read each textbook chapter just before the students did, misassembled a human skeleton and had trouble pronouncing words—even one-syllable words.

Steve's first love was music, and hardly a day went by without his demonstrating some newly discovered sound that would emanate from one of the major orifices of the ventral or dorsal surfaces of his body.

But even if he had insufficient gas to belch or fart, the show would go on.

Steve would treat our class to a mangled recitation of the cafeteria menu. He loved to announce *"fried fish dicks"* instead of fish sticks.

[Photo from displayfakefoods.com. Cartoon from Tharakorn. Thanks.]

Chapter 86
Electrocution experimentation

Although practices vary around the world, and even within individual countries, in those places where the electric chair is used to carry out the death sentence, 2,000 volts seems to be the right number.

When I was in the eighth grade, we were assigned to do "research" for **Anthony Accurso's** science class, and I was curious to see if I could build up immunity to electric shocks. I had no expectation of being tried for murder and facing two kilovolts in the chair in the Big House, but I wanted to see how much "juice" I could take.

I knew that even the puny 90 volts that ring a phone could provide a nasty jolt. On the other hand, I knew that the 12 volts that powered a doorbell were not even noticeable. I figured my limit was somewhere between 12 and 90; but perhaps, with training, I might be able to go higher. Like a golfer, I hoped to break 100, but in the opposite direction.

I had heard that if you put a live frog in a pot of cool water on the stove, and then turn on the burner, the water would heat so gradually that the frog would just cook, rather than notice a sudden high heat and try to jump away. But this story is not about heating or eating frogs.

I was curious to see if I, acting as a somewhat larger and perhaps smarter frog, could apply a gradually increasing voltage to electrodes on my forehead—and remain comfortable and alive.

I attached a couple of screws with washers and nuts to a headband and used wires to connect the screws to a variable transformer with a voltmeter that showed how much juice it was putting out. I wet my forehead where the screws would touch me to decrease resistance and improve the connection, put a chart on my clipboard and went to work. I did not tell my parents or write a will. I did not have an ambulance standing by.

I started rotating the knob and was surprised that I felt nothing as I passed through the 20s, 30s, 40s, 50s and even the 60s. But, at around 70 volts, something strange happened. I still didn't feel a shock. At most, it was a tingle. But the tingle was accompanied by a *sizzle*.

The water that I had put on my forehead to improve electrical conductivity, mixed with my perspiration from nervous anticipation, was starting to boil and bubble.

HOLY SHIT! I was cooking myself!

I remembered the dead frog story and quickly unplugged the transformer. After I cooled down and wiped off, I thought up a new experiment that could use the same equipment. I removed the wires from the headband and attached them to two nails that I hammered through a pine board.

Instead of cooking me, I then stuck a Hebrew National hotdog onto the nails, cranked up the transformer to 250 volts, and in about a minute it was *chow time*.

I submitted a beautiful graph to Mr. Accurso showing Heeb-Nat cooking time versus voltage. I got an "A" for my experiment, and a nice snack! Apparently, I have had no lasting damage from either eating the electrocuted hotdogs or zapping my head.

But, on the other hand, maybe people with brain damage just can't tell if they have brain damage damage damage damage.

Chapter 87
How a radio station lost business
from the gay matzo maker

One of Kane Light Gladney's advertising clients was a major manufacturer of Jewish foods. While the company made a variety of products that were sold year-round, the bulk of their business, and the bulk of our advertising efforts for them, were focused on the eight-day Passover holiday in the spring. That's when Jewish people eat special foods, most notably *matzo*, a large, thin, flat and crunchy bread substitute.

One February, representatives from the company met with several of us at the ad agency to discuss the upcoming advertising plans. We went over new products, the advertising budget, promotional themes and media selection—both national and in the New York City metropolitan area.

One of the agency guys suggested advertising on the highly rated, but controversial, **Bob Grant** radio show. One of the client execs quickly put up his hand like a cop indicating STOP and told everyone in the conference room that Grant was an antisemite. The subject was quickly dropped, and the money was scheduled to be spent elsewhere.

I was the only other person in the room who had ever listened to the Bob Grant show. While I hated his right-wing politics, I knew he was *no* antisemite. In fact, although he was not Jewish, Grant was extremely pro-Jewish.

However, Grant was very much anti-gay, and this matzo maker had just stepped out of the closet.

Chapter 88
My Bermuda Triangle was on a sailboat

Wikipedia says, "The Bermuda Triangle, also known as the Devil's Triangle, is an urban legend focused on a loosely defined region in the western part of the North Atlantic Ocean where a number of aircraft and ships are said to have disappeared under mysterious circumstances. The idea of the area as uniquely prone to disappearances arose in the mid-20th century, but most reputable sources dismiss the idea that there is any mystery."

I nearly got killed by a Bermuda Triangle. It was the shape of the sail on a tiny sailboat.

In the early 1970s, while I was an advertising copywriter, the ad agency I worked for sent me to Bermuda. It wasn't truly a vacation because I had to attend meetings with clients of the agency, but the trip didn't cost me a penny and I had ample spare time to explore, swim and sail.

Our hotel had free boats for guests. They weren't big or complicated. They were **Sunfish**, weighing about 150 pounds and measuring about 14 feet long. They were intended to be sailed by just one person, and all that the single sailor had to handle were a few ropes and the rudder.

Designed in 1951, the Sunfish is both simple and durable, basically a **VW Beetle** that moves on a liquid highway, with a sail instead of an engine. It's said to be "the most popular boat ever produced!"

The guy who was in charge of the hotel's fleet asked me if I had sailed before, and I quickly answered, "Yes, Admiral!" and gave him a fake Navy salute. He said the Sunfish was "a cute little boat and shouldn't give you any trouble at all."

Fortunately, the admiral of the fleet did not ask me for details and there was no written application, test or oath. I did not have to supply dates, diploma or references.

I did not lie when I said I had sailed, but most of my sailing was in motorized vessels that had no sails. I also rowed some rowboats and paddled some canoes, and I had once been a passenger on a 24-foot sailboat. When asked or commanded by the real sailor, I willingly moved from port to starboard or from starboard to port. I also coiled up some ropes and hung bumpers over the side when we neared the pier.

My major achievements were staying out of the way, not falling overboard and getting a good tan. I knew that the bow was up front, the stern in the back, a john is a head, a rope is a line and food is in the galley. I know a bit about halyards and clevis pins and cleats and I even know that "forecastle" is pronounced "foc's'le." I also like to swim in and drink water, and if drafted to serve my country—Aye, Aye Sir!—I'd choose the Navy or Coast Guard.

Despite my only partially impressive résumé, I felt up to the task. A Sunfish is an itty-bitty boat—not much bigger than a canoe—and I was sure I could handle it. Sunfish advertising talks about simplicity, stability and a "forgiving feel" that's "suitable for beginners."

That's my kind of boat.

And since my mother didn't have any stupid kids, I was sure I could teach myself to sail in Bermuda's beautiful, protected harbor, where Spanish sailor **Juan de Bermudez** arrived in 1503 CE. Bermuda was named after him.

I quickly figured out how to get the mast vertical and unfurl the sail. A convenient puff of air took me gently away from the pier, and I felt ready to skip right from raw recruit to admiral.

Had I attended Annapolis like an actual admiral, or even read the *Boy Scout Manual* chapter on water safety, I would have known to check the weather forecast before venturing out. It turned out that the little puff of air that kindly and conveniently propelled me away from shore was actually an advance sign of THE BIGGEST FUCKING WINDSTORM TO HIT BERMUDA IN 68 YEARS.

That initial puff was very quickly followed by a breeze, and then a wind and then a squall. The wind speed hit 52 MPH—the fastest non-hurricane wind on record.

According to an excellent article in *The Smithsonian* magazine, ▶ Jagged reefs reaching far into the ocean easily punctured wooden hulls, a threat made more menacing by the unpredictable weather. Sir Walter Raleigh warned that Bermuda was surrounded by **"a hellish sea for thunder, lightning and storms."** English captain Francis Wyatt wrote that **"all seafaring men"— whether English, French or Portuguese—agreed "that hell is no hell in comparison to" Bermuda's fierce weather.** They avoided the islands "as they would shun the devil himself," another Englishman, Silvester Jourdain, wrote. Not all succeeded. One of many ships that sank offshore was a Portuguese vessel; a casualty of the wreck survived long enough to carve "1543" into an island rock. This fearsome reputation extended to the land itself. The eerie calls of the cahow were ascribed to demons. One European wrote that Bermuda was **"an enchanted den of furies and devils, the most dangerous, unfortunate and forlorn place in the world."** While Europeans scrambled to grab New World territory, the archipelago was considered out of bounds. ... When Shakespeare heard the stories, he wrote a play about a magical spirit-filled island, referred to at one point as the "Bermoothes." The King's Men thespians first performed ***The Tempest*** for James I and the royal court on November 1, 1611." ◀

I was never so busy in my life. I was simultaneously trying to learn how to sail, keep the boat upright, keep it from taking me into the Atlantic Ocean, and trying to avoid being decapitated by the boom that kept swinging from port to starboard to port to starboard.

I longed for an outboard motor, or even a simple rowboat, and gained new appreciation for the HMS Bounty mutineers.

I was wrestling with the Sunfish, and it was both wrestling and boxing with me, and karate-chopping, too.

The "cute little boat" was *beating the crap out of me*.

Every time I got up, I got knocked down or knocked overboard. My arms and legs were abraded raw and red from the sandpaper-like surface of the deck.

I was clearly no match for the Sunfish or the squall.

I suddenly realized that my worst prospect for the formerly sunny day had progressed from merely having a lousy time to actually *dying* of a concussion from a swinging boom or drowning or being lost at sea and becoming fish food.

There was no way I could control the "cute little boat."

Applying some very basic nautical analysis, I realized that the wind—normally a source of cooling and propulsion—might actually *kill* me.

The only way to minimize the effect of the wind was to minimize the size of the wind catcher—my triangular sail. I had hoped to lower the sail and just use the Sunfish as a giant surfboard or kickboard and slowly move it back to the beach. Unfortunately, the ropes were so snarled that there was no way to lower the sail.

Reluctant to abandon ship, I wrestled with the mast and tipped the boat over. With mast submerged and keel facing the sky, I was able to both kick and paddle it back toward shore. After a while I noticed that the mast, boom and sail had become detached from the hull socket, but they were still tethered to the Sunfish by rope and were following me to the distant shore.

Despite the much smaller profile without the sail, I still had to fight the wind, and the waves were *growing*. It seemed to take forever to reach land. When I got close, I saw an ambulance with flashing lights on the beach, and two men wearing white shirts with red crosses and white Bermuda shorts and knee-high socks were running toward where they thought I'd come ashore.

As soon as the boat stopped moving, I crawled away from it through the shallow water and onto the sand. I collapsed and tried to spit out the water, seaweed and sand in my mouth. The medics kneeled in the sand next to me and seemed to be examining me. They spoke, but their words didn't register.

I either rolled over on my back or was rolled over by them, and eventually I sat up with their support. I felt like I was still bouncing on the waves. One of them opened a medical kit and took out bandages. Then the two of them started swabbing me, and I saw that the bandages were quickly turning from white to red. There were even red spots on their white Bermuda shorts.

When my head stopped spinning and my breathing returned to normal, they helped me to stand up slowly. They supported me under each of my arms. I looked down and saw that I was covered with blood from shoulders to fingers and toes. My nose was bleeding. I was told I had a black eye and that I should be X-rayed. My sunglasses were gone. My diver's watch was gone. So were my waterproof camera and most of my bathing suit. Every part of me that had feeling felt *really bad*.

One of the medics asked me if I had been attacked by just one shark or by several, and if I had lost a passenger. I said that I was sailing alone, but it took a while before I could admit that I had been attacked by a cute little Sunfish.

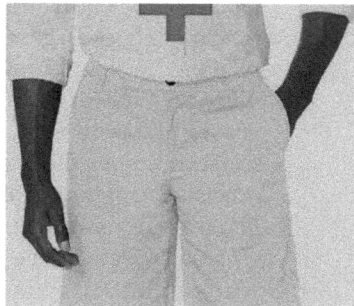

[Boat photo from Sunfishdirect.com. Thanks.]

Chapter 89
Religious observances

○   In some ancient Eastern Christian traditions, Hell and Heaven are distinguished not spatially, but by the relation of a person to God's love.—*Wikipedia*

○   "Jews, atheists, agnostics and evangelical Protestants, as well as highly educated people and those who have religiously diverse social networks, show higher levels of religious knowledge, while young adults and racial and ethnic minorities tend to know somewhat less about religion than the average respondent does. Jews are top performers on questions about other world religions, getting 7.7 questions right, on average, out of 13 questions about Judaism, Islam, Buddhism, Hinduism, Sikhism and global religious demography. In terms of the survey overall, Jews get 18.7 questions right, on average. One possible explanation for why Jews, atheists and agnostics score among the highest is that all three of the groups are highly educated, on average. Jews, atheists and agnostics display greater religious knowledge than other groups even after controlling for education and other demographic characteristics associated with knowing more about religion."—**Pew Survey**

○   Jennie. Groff, 42, grew up just outside Lancaster, Pennsylvania, in a Mennonite family that regularly helped to resettle refugees. "To love your neighbor is a really big, foundational part of what we believe," she said. "It is what people once did for us, so it's seeped into the cores of who we are as a community."—*New York Times*

○   "Jesus, forgive me for ever being a Republican."—**Joe Scarborough** (host of *Morning Joe* on MSNBC and former four-term Florida Republican congressman)

○   "When I was in 5th, 6th and 7th grade I attended a secular summer camp. One of the three owners was Jewish. We started each day by reciting *The Lord's Prayer*. I didn't know it was a Christian prayer until years later."—**The Author**

○   "It is inconceivable that a rabbi would deliver a sermon on salvation through faith, a most common subject in Christian sermons."—**Rabbi Joseph Telushkin** & **Dennis Prager**, *The Nine Questions People Ask about Judaism*

○   "My mother was a conservative Jew who eloped with a French-Canadian Mohawk. My stepfather was a Scotch-Irish convert. We were raised Reform, and I was Bat Mitzvah. My husband is a very lapsed Catholic Arab. Our daughters celebrated the holidays with us but had no formal Jewish education because I could never afford to join a temple. They consider themselves Jewish, but secular. My oldest granddaughter also had virtually no religious education, but wears a *chai* [Jewish charm necklace] and considers herself a Jew. I wrote earlier that Jews are not an ethnicity since we come from every country. Jews are not just followers of a religion since there are so many secular Jews. My educated conclusion is that we are members of a bronze-age tribe that survived to modern times. We are born into the tribe and encouraged to marry within the tribe. But I was told that religion is all that matters, and you have to follow the Jewish religion to be a real Jew. So, am I Jewish since I no longer practice? Are my kids and grandkids? Is a JuBu Jewish? What is a Jew?"—A Jewish group on *Facebook*

o "Invoking God and calling for prayer should never seem obscene. But it is always obscene to use the Almighty to escape our own responsibility. "God bless the people of El Paso Texas. God bless the people of Dayton, Ohio," President Trump said in a Sunday morning tweet from his New Jersey golf club. Yes, may God bless them. But may God also judge Trump for a political strategy whose success depends on sowing racism, reaction and division. May God judge him for stoking false and incendiary fears about an immigrant 'invasion,' the very word echoed by the manifesto that police suspect was the El Paso shooter's. May God judge the president for cutting programs to fight white extremism at the very moment when the FBI is telling us that we are more at risk from white-nationalist terrorists than Islamist terrorists."—**E. J. Dionne Jr**., *Washington Post*

o "When I say I don't believe in God, I don't mean that that is written on my pillow, and that's the first thing I say when I look in the mirror in the morning. I mean that you can't prove a negative like that. I never go around and do debates with people about the existence of God, because it's stupid! You can't prove that there is no God. I just say that for all of the evidence I've seen, my conclusion is that God does not exist." —**Susan Jacoby**, *Religion News Service*

o "How much history lies behind the story of Genesis? Because the action of the primeval story is not represented as taking place on the plane of ordinary human history and has so many affinities with ancient mythology, it is very far-fetched to speak of its narratives as historical at all."—**Jon Levenson** (Harvard professor of Jewish Studies)

o "If the Jew did not exist, the antisemite would invent him."—**Jean-Paul Sartre** (philosopher, playwright, novelist, screenwriter, political activist, biographer and literary critic)

o "Christianity is the religious form of the formation, development, and advancement of Western Civilization; i.e.; the engine of bringing prosperity and equality to all of humanity. The Straight Pride Coalition recognizes that these foundational principles and values of life are under a massive, coordinated attack. The 'enemies of the cross' (Phil. 3:18), for the purpose of establishing their own replacement belief system of Satanic Humanism as the dominant cultural and societal paradigm of an enslaved humanity, desire the total destruction of Christianity. Specifically, the destruction of the cultural and social institutions founded upon it including the natural nuclear family, the sovereign nation state; the inherent recognition of Christian value, wonder, and awesomeness of human life, and the most fundamental concepts of human identity including masculinity and femininity. The Straight Pride Coalition hence declares our unequivocal and total allegiance to Christ … and our equivalent opposition to Satanic Humanism and its anti-humanity principles. With a firm recognition of our inadequacies, we appeal to God, our Creator and Redeemer, to counsel, equip, and guide us to victory in the societal, cultural, and national War in which we are engaged. May future generations celebrate our actions that protected these foundational pillars of culture, society, and nation as the standards upon which civilization is founded. We hence seek God for all of our needs in this great endeavor, invite all people of good will to join

us in the defense of our current and future generations in The War which is upon us."
—**Straight Pride Coalition**

o "Religion is for the brain, not for the belly."—**The author's non-kosher mother**

o "Hath not a Jew chicken soup"—**The author's funny father**

o (Q) Why do nuns wear crosses? (A) So nobody will think they're Jewish. —**The author's funny father**

o "Rabbis never agree. They're Jewish."—The author's bro-in-law **Rabbi Alan Alpert**

o "A Jew is twenty-eight percent fear, two percent sugar, and seventy percent chutzpah (audacity)."—Unknown

o "We returned to Judaism recently and part of me struggles with the God thing. It's not that I deny the possibility. Rather I am mentally and spiritually exhausted trying to comprehend what I believe. I believe that it's up to me to make things in life better. No God snapped his fingers and fixed my problems. I disagree with my AA group because of magical thinking. It's almost meaningless to debate theology because nobody can agree on what God is. I am currently a Reform Jew but wonder if we had them here that I would want to consider Reconstructionist or Humanistic."—*Facebook* commenter

o "Over decades of polling, a majority of Americans have consistently indicated a negative opinion of atheists and nonbelievers. Even in this enlightened twenty-first century, where we've proved ourselves ready for a black president and welcomed elected officials representing every group, approximately half of all Americans say they would refuse to vote for a well-qualified atheist candidate for public office. In other words, one out of every two Americans admits to being prejudiced against fellow citizens who don't believe in God. No other minority group in this country is rejected by such large numbers. This prejudice ought to concern us all. Because prejudice anywhere endangers not only its targets, but all who believe that we should be judged not by the color of our skin, or our gender, or sexuality, or by our religious preference or lack thereof, but by the content of our character. If we can convince ourselves today that one entire group comprising millions of people might be incapable of goodness, might be "no good," then we harbor inside us the ability to turn against and hate any other group as well, and no one should feel safe. It is not easy to live a good life or be a good person—with or without a god. The fact is that life is hard. Living well and being a good person are difficult to do. But that doesn't mean we should give ourselves permission to judge an entire group of people as incapable of goodness unless they're being good the majority's way."—**Greg Epstein**, *Good Without God*

o "Evangelical Christians have long supported Zionism not because they have affection for Judaism and its adherents but because of their powerful belief in biblical prophecy that declares the Messiah's second coming will and must be preceded by God's gathering and resettling of the Jewish people in a homeland. For decades, support for Israel has been a key component of political platform of the evangelical right, as is evident in the words of prominent spokespeople such as Pat Robertson. The Christian narrative of the Messiah's return cannot be fulfilled without the existence of Israel."—**Tim Libretti**, *PoliticusUSA*

o "Mormon Church members who followed the [health] code had a life expectancy 8 to 11 years longer than the general white population of the United States."—**Mormon website**

o "People who may not have been that close to Jewishness, they feel suddenly like it's very important to express who they are as Jews in the context of their activism and in the context of their collective memory."—**Arielle Angel**, *Jewish Currents*

o "I would never dare challenge my grandfather. He believed that all of the answers to any of life's problems could be found in the Torah. He had his own synagogue, and the family lived upstairs. I lived with my grandparents (in the synagogue) when I went to Yeshivah of Flatbush high school. It was very structured. That's probably why I rebelled. My grandfather never let me or my female cousins talk at the dinner table because he considered anything a girl said to be nonsense, so I became a trial lawyer and essentially get paid to talk."—**Joyce David**, *Facebook*

o "I'm either a Buddhist or a Catholic."—**Steven Colbert** (comic genius)

o "No, I am not a human being, I am a soul created by God indwelled in the flesh that is called a human being."—**Lee Gipson**, *Facebook*

o "A man once told me to walk with the Lord. I'd rather walk with the bases loaded." —**Ken Singleton** (ball player)

o "About 26 percent of Americans 65 and older identify as white evangelical Protestants. Among those ages 18 to 29, the figure is 8 percent. Why this demographic abyss does not cause greater panic—panic concerning the existence of evangelicalism as a major force in the United States—is a mystery and a scandal. With their focus on repeal of the Johnson Amendment and the right to say, "Merry Christmas," some evangelical leaders are tidying up the kitchen while the house burns down around them. ... Since 2000, according to Gallup, the percentage of Americans with no religious affiliation has more than doubled, from 8 percent to 19 percent. The percentage of millennials with no religion has averaged 33 percent in recent surveys."—**Michael Gerson**, *Washington Post*

o Nearly four in ten young adults ages 18 to 29 are religiously unaffiliated and are four times more likely as young adults a generation ago to identify this way, according to a study by the Public Religion Research Institute. Among college students surveyed by Trinity College, 32% identified their worldview as religious; 32% as spiritual; and 28% as secular.—*Religion News Service*

o All religions change and develop. If they do not, they will become obsolete."—**Karen Armstrong**, *A History of God*

o "The source of love is God himself: the source of all of our lives."—**Episcopal Bishop Michael Curry**

o Greater acceptance of Jews into mainstream American society in recent decades means Jews are now welcome in all kinds of neighborhoods, universities, and workplaces, and most Jews no longer live in tight-knit Jewish communities that enforce the norms and practices of traditional Jewish life. We also live at a time when many of us view religion as something we can choose from: a marketplace of ideas rather than an inherited obligation we must unquestioningly fulfill. Today, we're all welcome to check out the offerings at the local Unitarian church or Buddhist sangha; or we can grab some crystals or hallucinogenic drugs; or we can do nothing religious or spiritual at all. The term "Jews by choice" is often used to refer to those who convert to Judaism. But these days, all American Jews are Jews by choice—and many of us are choosing to opt out."—**Sarah Hurwitz**, *Here All Along*

o "The Jew may love God, or he may fight with God, but he may not ignore God."—**Elie Wiesel** (writer, professor, political activist, Nobel winner, Holocaust survivor)

o Observant Presbyterians are always part of gatherings at **Rutgers Presbyterian Church**. But much of the time, so are Roman Catholics and Jews, as well as a smattering of people who consider themselves vaguely spiritual. **Valerie Oltarsh-McCarthy**, who sat among the congregation listening to a Sunday sermon on the perils of genetically modified vegetables, is, in fact, an atheist. It's something I never thought would happen,' she said of the bond she has forged with the church's community, if not the tenets of its faith. She was drawn to the church, she said, by 'something in the spirit of Rutgers and something in the spirit of the outside world.' **Katharine Butler**, an artist, was lured into Rutgers when she walked by a sandwich board on the street advertising its environmental activism. Soon, she was involved in more traditional aspects of the church, too. I can't believe I'm doing this, singing away and all the Jesus-y stuff,' she said. 'It was wonderful to find a place larger than me, that's involved in that and in the community and being of service. It's nice to find a real community like that.'" —**Rick Rojas**, *New York Times*

o Secular Jews, like all people, are believers, as one cannot be a member of any human society or culture without espousing some form of creed. One that has pervaded secular Jewish culture since Spinoza is the belief in the veracity of our scientific knowledge of the universe, the processes of which are self-regulating, in accordance with fixed laws pertaining to the "natural" order of creation. In such a universe, there is no place for a God who governs the world according to his personal will and performs miracles contrary to the laws of nature, or imposes religious precepts that bind only members of the Jewish people. This approach to knowledge of the universe is reflected in the essential Judaic belief in the sovereignty of the human being—the responsibility we bear as individuals, free to choose our paths in life, limited only by physical, social, and cultural constraints."—**Yaakov Malkin**, *Secular Jewish Culture*

o The percentage of Americans who belong to a church, mosque or synagogue has declined in the past 20 years, forcing some congregations to sell their houses of worship. More than 6,800 religious buildings have sold in the past five years and more than 1,400 are currently for sale, according to a real estate database. While some will become home to new worshippers, others are being converted into bed-and-breakfasts, apartments, coffee shops and more."—**Shahla Farzan**, NPR

o "True Judaism is in the heart, not in a building."—**Rabbi Phillip Sher** (after fire destroyed his synagogue)

o "Given the growth of the [Catholic] faith in Africa, it seems reasonable to expect that an African may be in [Pope] Francis's seat before another two generations pass, and perhaps much sooner. It is hard to see how European dominance of the College of Cardinals can persist indefinitely, given the demographics of the church. African leadership could take the church in a more progressive direction in some ways, but it might do quite the opposite in others. The only certainty is that while all roads still lead to Rome for now, the historic seat of the church is increasingly on the remote periphery of a new Catholic empire of the global south."—**Elizabeth A. Foster**, *Washington Post*

Chapter 90
To Hell with you, or Heaven, or nowhere

What's after life?
Beliefs & disbelief

Like other religions, **Judaism** offers multiple views on Heaven and Hell, including some similarity to Christian ideology. In ancient times, Jewish people frequently discussed the afterlife—but many modern Jews avoid the topic, preferring to focus on Earthly life.

Death is treated inconsistently in the *Torah* (the five books of the Jewish Bible, often called the "Old Testament" by non-Jews). Most often, the Torah suggests that physical death is the end of life. This is *my* belief, and the case with such major Biblical figures as **Abraham**, **Moses** and **Miriam**.

There are, however, several "Old Testament" references to **Sheol**. It's described as a region that's "dark and deep," "the pit," and "the land of forgetfulness"—where human beings descend after death. In Sheol, the deceased, although isolated from God and humans, *live on* in a shadowy state of existence.

While this vision of Sheol is bleak (setting precedents for later Jewish and Christian ideas of Hell) there is generally no judgment or reward and punishment. In fact, the more pessimistic books of the Bible, such as *Ecclesiastes* and *Job*, insist that all of the dead go down to Sheol, whether good or evil, rich or poor, slave or free.

The concept of life after death relates to the development of *eschatology* (speculation about the "end of days") in Judaism. Following the destruction of the First Temple in Jerusalem (586 BCE), Israelite prophets **Amos**, **Hosea** and **Isaiah** began forecasting a better future.

However, with repeated military defeats and exiles culminating in the destruction of the Second Temple in 70 CE, many Jews began to lose hope for an immediate change. Instead, they considered a messianic future and life after death. This was combined with the introduction of Greek concepts of the division of the material, perishable body and the spiritual, eternal soul.

The catastrophe of 70 CE caused a theological crisis. How could the God of Israel permit his temple to be destroyed and his people to be vanquished by the Romans? While rabbis often claimed that it was the Israelites' sinfulness that led God to allow them to be defeated "because of our sins," it was more difficult to explain why good and decent Jews were made to suffer. This dilemma also surfaced during and after the Holocaust.

This led to the development of another theological claim. **Rabbi Ya'akov** taught: "This world is compared to an antechamber that leads to *Olam Ha–Ba*, (the world to come)." Some rabbis claim that the righteous suffer in this world so their future reward will be much greater.

The nature of the next world is far from clear. Rabbis use the term Olam Ha-Ba to refer to a heaven-like afterlife as well as to the messianic era or the age of resurrection, and it is often difficult to know which one is being referred to. When the **Talmud** (the set of teachings and commentaries on the Torah that form the basis for Jewish law) speaks of Olam Ha-Ba in connection to the afterlife, it often uses it interchangeably with the term *Gan Eden* ("Garden of Eden"), referring to a heavenly realm where souls reside after physical death.

The use of the term Gan Eden to describe Heaven suggests that rabbis conceived of the afterlife as a return to the blissful existence of **Adam** and **Eve** before the "fall."

In the kabbalistic (Jewish mystical) tradition, there is much discussion about the voyages of the human soul to the Garden of Eden and other heavenly realms during life on earth.

Only righteous souls ascend directly to the Garden of Eden, say the sages. The average person descends to a place of punishment and/or purification, generally referred to as **Gehinnom**.

The name is taken from a valley (*Gei Hinnom*) just south of Jerusalem, once used for child sacrifice by the pagan nations of Canaan. Some view Gehinnom as a place of torture and punishment, fire and brimstone. Others imagine it less harshly, as a place where one reviews the actions of life and repents for past misdeeds.

Only the utterly wicked do not ascend to the Garden of Eden. Sources differ on what happens to these souls at the end of their initial time of purgation. Some say that the wicked are utterly destroyed and cease to exist, while others believe in eternal damnation.

[The section above is adapted from MyJewishLearning.com. Thanks.]

Mainstream **Christians** believe in the **Nicene Creed**, which includes the phrase: "We look for the resurrection of the dead, and the life of the world to come."

When questioned by the Sadducees about the resurrection of the dead (relating to who one's spouse would be if one had been married several times), Jesus said that marriage will be irrelevant after the resurrection because the resurrected will be like angels in Heaven.

Jesus also maintained that the dead would hear the voice of the Son of God, and all who were in the tombs would come out.

The *Book of Enoch* describes Sheol as having sections for several types of the dead: (1) the faithful saints who await resurrection in Paradise, (2) the merely virtuous who await their reward, (3) the wicked who await punishment, and (4) the wicked who have already been punished and will not be resurrected on Judgment Day. [The Book of Enoch is considered apocryphal by most branches of Christianity and Judaism.]

The author of the *Book of Luke* recounts the story of **Lazarus** and the rich man, which shows people in Hades awaiting the resurrection either in comfort or torment.

The author of the *Book of Revelation* wrote about God and the angels versus Satan and demons in an epic battle at the end of times when all souls are judged.

The apocryphal *Acts of Paul and Thecla* speak of the efficacy of prayer for the dead so that they might be "translated to a state of happiness."

Hippolytus of Rome pictures the underworld as where the righteous dead, awaiting resurrection, rejoice at their future prospect, while the unrighteous are tormented at the sight of the "lake of unquenchable fire" into which they are destined to be cast.

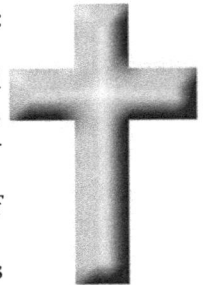

During the Age of Enlightenment, theologians and philosophers presented various philosophies and beliefs. **Emanuel Swedenborg** wrote 18 works which describe the afterlife according to his claimed experiences. He covers many topics, such as marriage in Heaven (all angels are married), children in Heaven (they are raised by angel parents), time and space in Heaven (none), the after-death awakening process in the World of Spirits (a place halfway between Heaven and Hell and where people first wake up after death), free-will choice between Heaven or Hell (not being sent to either one by God), the eternity of Hell (one could leave but would never want to), and that all angels or devils were once people on earth.

The **Catholic** conception of the afterlife teaches that after the body dies, the soul is judged, the righteous and sin-free enter Heaven. However, those who die in unrepented mortal sin go to Hell. In the 1990s, the *Catechism* of the Catholic Church defined Hell not as punishment imposed on the sinner but rather as the sinner's self-exclusion from God. Unlike other Christian groups, the Catholic Church teaches that those who die in a state of grace, but still carry venial sin, go to **Purgatory** for purification to enter Heaven.

Despite popular opinion, **Limbo**, which was elaborated upon by theologians since the Middle Ages, was never recognized as Catholic dogma. Yet, at times, it has been a very popular theological theory. Limbo is a concept that unbaptized but innocent souls, such as those of infants, virtuous individuals who lived before Jesus was born, or those that die before baptism, exist in neither Heaven nor Hell. They exist in a state of natural, but not supernatural, happiness, until the end of time.

Methodism founder **John Wesley** believed in an intermediate state between death and resurrection and in the possibility of "continuing to grow in holiness there." Methodism does not officially affirm this belief and denies the possibility of prayer helping anyone who may be in that state.

The **Orthodox Church** acknowledges the mystery of things that have not yet occurred. Beyond the second coming of Jesus, bodily resurrection, and final judgment, Orthodoxy does not teach much definitively. Unlike Western Christianity, Orthodoxy does not say that there are two separate locations of Heaven and Hell, but instead acknowledges that the location of one's final destiny as being figurative.

Orthodoxy teaches that final judgment is an encounter with divine love and mercy but experienced depending on the extent to which one was transformed, partaken of divinity, and is therefore compatible or incompatible with God.

Orthodoxy uses the description of Jesus's judgment as their model: "And this is the judgment: the light has come into the world, and people loved the darkness rather than the light because their works were evil. For everyone who does wicked things hates the light and does not come to the light, lest his works should be exposed. But whoever does what is true comes to the light, so that it may be clearly seen that his works have been carried out in God."

Jehovah's Witnesses occasionally use "afterlife" to refer to any hope for the dead, but they preclude belief in an immortal soul. Individuals judged by God to be wicked, are given no hope of an afterlife. However, Witnesses believe that after Armageddon there will be a bodily resurrection of "both righteous and unrighteous" dead (but not the "wicked"). Survivors of Armageddon and those who are resurrected are then to gradually restore Earth to a paradise. After Armageddon, unrepentant sinners are punished with non-existence.

The **Seventh-day Adventist Church's** beliefs regarding the afterlife differ from other Christian churches. Rather than ascend to Heaven or descend to Hell, Adventists believe the dead "remain unconscious until the return of Christ in judgement." Death is an unconscious state (sleep). At death, all consciousness ends. The dead person does not know anything and does not do anything. Adventists believe that death is an undoing of what was created. "When a person dies, the body turns to dust again, and the spirit goes back to God, who gave it." The spirit of every person who dies—whether saved or unsaved—returns to God at death.

The *Quran* (the **Islam** holy book) emphasizes the insignificance of worldly life compared to the hereafter. A central doctrine is the Judgment Day when the world will end and God will raise all mankind from the dead and evaluate their worldly actions. The resurrected will be judged according to their deeds, records of which are kept in two books compiled for every human being—one for their good deeds and one for their evil deeds.

Having been judged, the resurrected will cross the bridge of *As-Sirāt* over the pit of Hell. The condemned will fall off into hellfire below, while the righteous will continue on to Heaven.

Afterlife in Islam actually begins before the Last Day. After death, humans will be questioned about their faith by two angels, **Munkar** and **Nakīr**. Those who die as martyrs go immediately to paradise. Others who have died and been buried will receive a taste of their eternal reward from the grave. Those bound for Hell will suffer "Punishment of the Grave," while those bound for Heaven will find the grave "peaceful and blessed."

Islamic scripture gives vivid descriptions of the pleasures of paradise (*Jannah*) and sufferings of Hell (*Jahannam*). The gardens of Jannah have cool shade, adorned couches and cushions, rich carpets, cups of wine and every meat and fruit. Men will be provided with perpetually youthful, beautiful *ḥūr*, "untouched beforehand by man or jinn," with large, beautiful eyes.

In contrast, those in Jahannam will dwell in a land infested with serpents and scorpions; be burnt by scorching fire and when "their skins are roasted through, we shall change them for fresh skins" to repeat the process forever; they will have nothing to drink but "boiling water and running sores; their cries of remorse and pleading for forgiveness will be in vain."

Nonbelief in Allah, crimes and sins are grounds for going to Hell, such as the murder of a believer, usury, devouring the property of an orphan, and slander, particularly of a chaste woman. However, it is a common belief that whatever crimes or sins Muslims committed, their punishment in Hell will be temporary. Only unbelievers reside in Hell permanently. Thus, Jahannam combines both the concept of an eternal Hell (for unbelievers), and Catholic purgatory (for believers eventually destined for Heaven after punishment). The common belief holds that Jahannam coexists with the temporal world. Mainstream Islam teaches the continued existence of the soul and a transformed physical existence after death.

The **Bahá'í Faith** states that the afterlife is beyond the understanding of those living, just as an unborn fetus cannot understand the nature of the world outside the womb. Bahá'í writings say that the soul is immortal and after death will continue to progress until it finally attains God's presence. In Bahá'í belief, souls in the afterlife retain individuality and consciousness, and will be able to recognize and communicate spiritually with other souls with whom they have deep profound friendships, such as spouses.

Bahá'í scriptures also state there are distinctions between souls in the afterlife, and that souls will recognize the worth of their own deeds and understand the consequences of their actions. It is explained that those souls that have turned toward God will experience gladness, while those who have lived in error will become aware of the opportunities they have lost. Also, souls will be able to recognize the accomplishments of the souls that have reached the same level as themselves, but not those that have achieved a higher rank.

Early **Indian religions** were characterized by belief in an afterlife, Ancestor worship, and related rites. These concepts started to change after the period of the *Upanishads* (major Hindu religious texts dating to about 600 BCE).

There are two major views of afterlife in **Hinduism**: mythical and philosophical. The philosophies of Hinduism consider each individual consists of three bodies: physical body compose of water and bio-matter (*sthūla śarīra*), an energetic/psychic/mental/subtle body (*sūkṣma-śarīra*) and a causal body (*kāraṇa śarīra*) comprising subliminal entities, i.e. mental impressions etc.

A person is a stream of consciousness (*Ātman*), which flows through all the physical changes of the body and at the death of the physical body, flows on into another physical body. The two components that transmigrate are the subtle body and the causal body. The thought that occupies a mind at death determines the quality of our rebirth (*antim smaraṇa*), hence Hinduism advises to be mindful of one's thoughts and cultivate positive wholesome thoughts—mantra chanting (japa) is commonly practiced for this.

Afterlife in **Buddhism** is a spirit realm beyond spatial existence, which includes the six realms of existence, the 31 planes of existence, *Naraka*, *Tengoku* and the pure land after achieving enlightenment. Ancestor worship, and links to ancestors, were an important component of early Buddhism, but became less relevant. The concepts and importance of afterlife vary among modern Buddhists.

Buddhists maintain that rebirth takes place without an unchanging self or soul passing from one form to another. The type of rebirth will be conditioned by the moral tone of the person's actions (*kamma* or *karma*). A person who committed harmful actions by body, speech and mind based on greed, hate and delusion, would have rebirth in a lower realm. But someone who showed generosity, loving-kindness (*metta*), compassion and wisdom, will have rebirth in a happy (human) realm.

The most important activity that determines where a person is reborn into is the last thought. If none of this happened, residual kamma from previous actions can take over. According to **Theravada Buddhism**, there are 31 realms of existence that one can be reborn into: 20 existences of supreme deities (*Brahmas*), 6 existences of deities (*Devas*), the human existence (*Manussa*), and, 4 existences of deprivation or unhappiness (Apaya).

The *Tibetan Book of the Dead* explains the intermediate state of humans between death and reincarnation. The deceased will find the bright light of wisdom, which shows a straightforward path to move upward and leave the cycle of reincarnation. There are various reasons why the deceased do not follow that light. Some had no knowledge of the intermediate state in the former life. Others only follow basic instincts like animals. And some have fear which results from foul deeds in the former life or from haughtiness.

In the intermediate state it is important to be virtuous, adopt a positive attitude, and avoid negative ideas. No one can hurt them, because they have no material body. The deceased get help from different Buddhas who show them the path to the bright light. The ones who do not follow the path get hints for a better reincarnation. They have to release the things and beings they keep from the life before. It is recommended to choose a family where parents trust the Dharma and to reincarnate with the will to care for the welfare of all beings.

Jains believe that the soul takes on a body form based on previous karmas or actions performed by that soul through eternity. The soul is eternal and freedom from the cycle of reincarnation is the means to attain eternal bliss.

The essential doctrine of **Sikhism** is to experience the divine through simple living, meditation, and contemplation while being alive. Sikhs also believe in being in union with God while living. Accounts of afterlife are considered to be aimed at the popular prevailing views of the time so as to provide a referential framework without necessarily establishing a belief in the afterlife. Sikhism can be considered agnostic about afterlife. Some scholars also interpret the mention of reincarnation to be naturalistic, akin to chemical cycles.

Confucius did not directly discuss the afterlife. Nonetheless, Chinese folk religion has had a strong influence on **Confucianism**, so adherents believe that dead ancestors become deified spirits. Ancestor veneration is widespread in China.

In **Gnostic** teachings, humans contain a divine spark said to have been trapped in their bodies by the creator known as the Demiurge. It was believed that this spark could be released from the material world and enter into the heavenly spiritual world beyond it if special knowledge or *gnosis* is attained. The Cathars, for example, viewed reincarnation as a trap made by Satan, who tricked angels into entering the physical bodies of humans. They viewed the purpose of life as a way to escape the constant cycle of spiritual incarnations by letting go of worldly attachments.

It is common for **Shinto** families to participate in ceremonies for children at a Shinto shrine, yet have a Buddhist funeral. In old Japanese legends, it is claimed that the dead go to a place called *yomi*, a gloomy underground realm with a river separating the living from the dead. This yomi very closely resembles the Greek Hades; however, later myths include notions of resurrection and even Elysium-like descriptions. Shinto tends to hold negative views on death and corpses as a source of pollution called *kegare*. However, death is also viewed as a path towards glorification such as Emperor **Ōjin**, who became the God of War after his death.

Taoism views life as an illusion and death as a transformation into immortality. Taoists believe that immortality of the soul can be achieved by living a virtuous life in harmony with the Tao. They are taught not to fear death, as it is simply part of nature.

Traditional African religions are diverse in their beliefs in an afterlife. Hunter-gatherer societies such as the **Hadza** have no particular belief in an afterlife, and the death of an individual is a straightforward end to their existence. Ancestor cults are found throughout Sub-Saharan Africa, including cultures like the **Yombe**, **Beng**, **Yoruba** and **Ewe**. The belief that the dead come back into life and are reborn into their families is given concrete expression in the personal names that are given to children.

The Yoruba, **Dogon** and **LoDagoa** have eschatological ideas similar to Abrahamic religions, "but in most African societies, there is a marked absence of such clear-cut notions of Heaven and Hell, although there are notions of God judging the soul after death." In some societies like the **Mende**, multiple beliefs coexist. The Mende believe that people die twice: once during the process of joining the secret society, and again during biological death after which they become ancestors. Some Mende also believe that after people are created by God they live ten consecutive lives, each in progressively descending worlds. One cross-cultural theme is that the ancestors are part of the world of the living, interacting with it regularly.

Some **Unitarian Universalists** believe that all souls will ultimately be saved and that there are no torments of Hell. Unitarian Universalists differ widely in their theology, so there is no precise policy on the issue. Although Unitarians historically believed in a literal Hell, and Universalists historically believed that everyone goes to Heaven, modern Unitarian Universalists can be categorized into those believing in a Heaven, reincarnation and oblivion. Most Unitarian Universalists believe that Heaven and Hell are symbolic places of consciousness, and the faith is largely focused on worldly life rather than possible afterlife.

The **Wiccan** afterlife is most commonly described as *The Summerland*. Here, souls rest, recuperate from life, and reflect on the experiences they had during their lives. After a period of rest, the souls are reincarnated, and the memory of their previous lives is erased. Many Wiccans see Summerland as a place to reflect on their life actions. It is not a place of reward, but rather the end of a life journey at an end point of incarnations.

Zoroastrianism states that the *urvan*, the disembodied spirit, lingers on earth for three days before departing downward to the kingdom of the dead that is ruled by **Yima**. For the three days that it rests on Earth, righteous souls sit at the head of their body, chanting the *Ustavaiti Gathas* with joy, while a wicked person sits at the feet of the corpse, wails and recites the *Yasna*. Zoroastrianism states that for the righteous souls, a beautiful maiden, which is the personification of the soul's good thoughts, words and deeds,

appears. For a wicked person, a very old, ugly, naked hag appears. After three nights, the soul of the wicked is taken by the demon **Vizaresa**, to *Chinvat* bridge, and is made to go to Hell.

Yima is believed to have been the first king on Earth as well as the first man to die. Inside of Yima's realm, the spirits live a shadowy existence and are dependent on their own descendants who are still living on Earth. Their descendants are to satisfy their hunger and clothe them, through rituals done on Earth.

Rituals on the first three days are vital and important, as they protect the soul from evil powers and give it strength to reach the underworld. After three days, the soul crosses Chinvat bridge which is the Final Judgment of the soul. **Rashnu** and **Sraosha** are present at the final judgment. The list is sometimes expanded to include **Vahman** and **Ormazd**. Rashnu is the *yazata* who holds the scales of justice. If the good deeds of the person outweigh the bad, the soul is worthy of paradise. If the bad deeds outweigh the good, the bridge narrows down to the width of a blade-edge, and a horrid hag pulls the soul in her arms and takes it down to Hell with her.

According to alleged clairvoyant **Edgar Cayce**, afterlife consists of nine realms associated with the nine planets. The first, symbolized by Saturn, was a level for the purification of the souls. The second, Mercury's realm, gives us the ability to consider problems as a whole. The third realm is ruled by Earth and is associated with Earthly pleasures. The fourth realm is where we find out about love and is ruled by Venus. The fifth realm is where we meet our limitations and is ruled by Mars. The sixth realm is ruled by Neptune and is where we begin to use our creative powers and free ourselves from the material world. The seventh realm is symbolized by Jupiter, which strengthens the soul's ability to depict situations, to analyze people and places, things, and conditions. The eighth realm is ruled by Uranus and develops psychic ability. The ninth realm deals with the unconscious and is symbolized by Pluto. This afterlife realm is a transient place where souls can choose to travel to other realms or other solar systems, it is the soul's liberation into eternity and opens the doorway from our solar system into the cosmos.

A 1901 study by **Dr. Duncan MacDougall** sought to measure the weight lost by a human when the soul "departed the body" upon death. MacDougall weighed dying patients in an attempt to prove that the soul was material, tangible and thus measurable. Although MacDougall's results varied considerably from 21 grams. The title of the 2003 movie *21 Grams* is a reference to MacDougall's findings. His results have never been reproduced and are generally regarded either as meaningless or considered to have had little if any scientific merit.

[The section above is adapted from Wikipedia.com. Thanks.]

Chapter 91
Eating animals, being buried

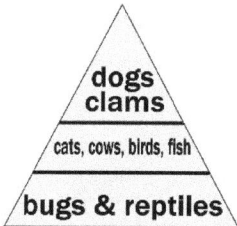

First-time visitors to our previous home may have thought that it was strange for a 75-lb. furry critter to be standing or lounging on the kitchen table. In some parts of the world a dog would be on the table not because he liked it there but because he was a *meal*. Yes, in parts of Asia, people eat dogs—and monkeys and other mammals regarded as near-humans elsewhere.

I would never eat a dog or a monkey, but I have no problem eating pieces of cows, pigs, chickens, flounders or lobsters. *What's the difference?* Should there be a difference? The difference is cultural and moral. I used to think it was cultural and health-related.

The Jewish *kashrut* rules for eating are commonly thought of as a means to avoid illness (e.g., un-refrigerated pork in an ancient desert could cause trichinosis, or pigs and shellfish are "dirty")—but there is a strong moral aspect about what makes food kosher or not.

According to **Dennis Prager** and **Joseph Telushkin**: "The Jewish ideal is that we not kill for food. Its compromise, known as kashrut, places a strict limit on the number of animal species which Jews may kill to eat, and legislates a uniquely humanely manner in which to kill the permitted animals." ... "The Torah, therefore, prohibited the Jews from consuming animals that eat other animals so that we do not ingest a killer instinct. [This seems like voodoo or witchcraft!] It is not a coincidence that every kosher animal is herbivorous, and that every carnivorous animal is nonkosher." ... "Judaism is uniquely preoccupied with life." ... "Judaism asks us to separate meat (death) from life (milk). One proof of this explanation is that only milk-producing animals may not be eaten with milk. We are allowed to eat fish and milk together because fish do not produce milk. Milk does not represent life with regard to fish, as it does with regard to mammals."

Vegans and vegetarians (I can never remember the distinction) pride themselves in not consuming other life forms, or only some other life forms. In India, emaciated cows roam streets.

Well, folks, we all consume other life forms—constantly. Even if you shun beef, poultry and sea creatures, and eat nothing but kale and radishes raised in your own garden, you are still killing things. (Experiments, particularly in Russia, have shown that plants can experience pain.)

And every time you inhale air, you inhale, kill and incorporate within your own body, the bodies of countless mini-size munchies you neither see nor taste. When you walk, you probably step on bugs. When you drive, your windshield shows the splattered evidence of countless insects violently executed by your vehicle—and you never get to eat them.

All life forms cause deaths of other life forms, often accidentally, and often deliberately.

In *Genesis*, very early in the Bible, God allegedly said about the new human creations, "let them have dominion over the fish of the sea and over the birds of the heavens and over the livestock and over all the earth and over every creeping thing that creeps on the earth." Also: "Behold, I have given you every plant yielding seed that is on the face of all the earth, and every tree with seed in its fruit. You shall have them for food. And to every beast of the earth and to every bird of the heavens and to everything that creeps on the earth, everything that has the breath of life, I have given every green plant for food." That sounds like animals are supposed to eat just green plants, but maybe not. Like much of the Bible, this is ambiguous.

We homo sapiens may think we are "top dogs," but we are merely part of the food chain, and if attacked by hungry dogs, maybe not the top. Clearly, we are not supposed to starve to death. But if we eat, we stop other creations from living. That's just the way it is.

The **U.S. Department of Agriculture** has published various "food pyramids" over the years that show "goals for both nutrient adequacy and moderation."

I think there is a parallel to the traditional pyramid of recommended nutrients. I rank potential animal-based foods based on how important it is to let the animals live.

Near the top we encounter creatures with admirable intelligence and utility, particularly pets (I hate that word) and working or entertaining animals. In western cultures, most of them don't get eaten by human beings.

In the middle are mammals bred to be food, plus birds and wet creatures that swim, crawl on the bottom or burrow in the mud. Clams, however, rank in the top row. A dolphin is more 'worthy' than a snail. I won't complain if you eat predatory alligators, especially if you eat one that tried to eat you.

On the very bottom are annoying bugs like house flies and mosquitoes that may be necessary in the overall ecosystem, but few humans would miss (or eat). Worms, snakes, gators and crocs go down there, too. You can make your own personal pyramid.

I've never been a farmer, but I've observed farm life and culture. I'll never understand how farm kids can lovingly raise chickens, ducks, pigs, lambs and cattle from birth to maturity—and willingly allow them to be slaughtered. As the **Supremes** sang in 1964, *"Where Did Our Love Go?"*

As I said, I believe that we are all part of the food chain. I don't preach that we should strip naked and go for a swim in a shark-infested sea or a gator-filled river, but we can become food when we no longer need our bodies. Any organs or tissue that can be used to extend the lives of others, or educate future doctors, should be promptly divested.

I used to believe and proclaim that unneeded body parts *should not be cremated*.

I deduced that cremation *cheats the system* and avoids paying the debt incurred by eating. It is our duty to decompose. By becoming worm food, we fertilize the plants that feed animals that feed other animals, and maybe even feed people. It's only fair. (Also: Cremation is opposed by many Jewish people, particularly those who are aware of the Nazis' cremation of Jews—both dead and alive.)

Luther Turmelle, in the *New Haven Register*, said: "according to the Wisconsin-based National Funeral Directors Association, burials represented 53.3% of all disposals of remains in the United States in 2010. This year [2019], the burial rate in this country is expected to drop to 39%, according to the NFDA. By 2040, cremation is expected to account for 78.7%."

According to **Nicole Wetsman** in *Popular Science*, "The practice of filling bodies with chemicals to preserve them dates back to ancient Egypt, but it caught on stateside in the mid-1800s as a way to transport fallen Civil War soldiers. Today, U.S. morticians embalm roughly 1 million people every year. It takes between 3 and 4 gallons of chemicals to preserve the average body. That's a lot of carcinogens to leave floating around for the sake of the dead.

The ripple effects are numerous and nasty. Conserved corpses can go on display in caskets that, collectively, use tons of wood and steel, which we then bury in concrete containers. Instead of returning bodily nutrients, like potassium and calcium, to the ground, we slowly molder while shielded from the dirt. Lack of oxygen causes wasting flesh to release methane, a greenhouse gas more potent than the carbon dioxide we'd produce in open air."

Chapter 92
Where'd I get my sense of humor?

As parts of this book demonstrate, I can be very serious when necessary, but I'm often a funny guy—in print and in-person. I admire **Groucho Marx** (pictured), but am a Marcus Brother, not a Marx Brother.

My sense of humor might be genetic. Although my mother said, "I'm not the funny parent," my father and his brother could be *very* funny. And my grandfathers, **Walter Marcus** and **Dr. Jay N. Jacobs**, were like **George Burns** and **Jack Benny**. Grandpa Jay could even juggle while telling jokes.

There was a lot of laughter in my house even before we got a television, and we were one of the first families to get a television. Pop introduced me to *MAD* magazine and **Allan Sherman's** funny records.

My wife often complains that I have a reckless sense of humor and I "go too far." She's afraid that I'm going to get into trouble like **Lenny Bruce** and **George Carlin**. I think artistic expression outranks domestic tranquility. In my domicile, we have much more expression than tranquility.

Like **Penn and Teller**, **Bart Simpson** and the folks on *Jackass*, I'll do almost anything for a joke. I don't mind being laughed at. Heck, I once needed firemen to pick me up from the toilet. I'm sorry there was no video for *YouTube*.

Other people occasionally describe my humor as sick, tasteless or black humor. That's because I can find humor in almost any situation—and that can make some people uncomfortable. I designed and wore the shirt shown when I went to a hospital to be treated for a kidney stone. Some people who saw me cringed or turned away, but *most* people laughed and some asked where to buy a shirt like it. **Laughter is the best medicine. Most people are too serious most of the time. Fuck 'em if they can't take a joke.**

I'm frequently able to find humor where others can't, like that pee-pee shirt.

I used to run a company that sold phone equipment. Competitors described the colors of a certain kind of wire simply as "blue and white." I decided to use flavors instead of colors and call it "blueberry-vanilla." Even the straitlaced Pentagon procurement officers ordered many thousands of feet of our flavorful blueberry-vanilla wire. And strawberry-clam.

It's good for bureaucrats to lighten up. One of my basic rules is, "If it's not fun, don't do it," and I'm often able to make dull things amusing. More people should try it.

General William Tecumseh Sherman said, "War is hell," but *Hogan's Heroes*, *McHale's Navy* and *MASH* made war funny. Someday the war in Iraq will seem funny.

I enjoy bloopers, errors and inconsistencies. In movies, I look for cavemen with wristwatches and shoes. I love typos on book covers, in ads and on big signs that were checked dozens of times.

Even menus make me laugh. In a typical diner, the price of a slice of ordinary cheese can range from a dime to a dollar or more, depending on what it's attached to. In a Chinese restaurant, you can pay $3.95 for a small order of fried rice, or $2.95 for four chicken wings *with the same rice*.

Most recent TV sitcoms do nothing for me. I watched exactly one episode of *Seinfeld* and hated it. I never watched *Cheers*. Nothing done in recent decades seems to equal *Lucy* or the *Honeymooners* or *Bilko* or *The Beverly Hillbillies*. Among latter-day sitcoms, my favorite is *Married, With Children*. I miss early *SNL* and *Johnny Carson*, but I enjoyed *Leno*, *Letterman* and *30 Rock*.

Boston Legal and *The Sopranos* can be hilarious, but they're not full-time comedies. *The Simpsons* is. And so are *South Park* and *Family Guy*. I wish I had time to watch every episode. Like most males and unlike most females, I like the *Three Stooges* and **Howard Stern**. I loved Jay Leno's *Jay Walking* segments and when **Dave Letterman** dropped stuff off the roof to smash in the street, and **Jimmy Kimmel's** on-the-street bits. I think this picture is funny. You first notice her hair and the hand on his mouth—but *count the hands*.

I don't like it when comedians pick on nice people, but I do like taking funny pictures of friends and relatives. (Those are my sister's kids.)

I also like elaborate pranks, spoofs and put-ons. I'm very good at manipulating the media and circulating believable phony news—a talent I inherited from my very funny father.

I try to make enforcers realize the absurdity of the rules they are enforcing. **Logic is good. Illogic is funny.**

I sometimes obey the letter of the law but not the spirit. In high school we had to wear ties, but there was no rule against wearing extremely ugly ties.

I like deflating pompous people and institutions.

When I was an editor at *Rolling Stone*, I often went to press conferences at the fancy-shmancy **21 Club** in Manhattan with friends from other magazines. The 21's dress code required that men wear jackets and ties, but three of us were noticeably informal. Our corporate hosts had paid big bucks for 21 to feed us, so, despite our scruffy appearance, we were too important to be rejected by the stuffy maître d' in the tuxedo.

Other customers wore $200 "power ties," but we had *real* power and dined *sans cravate*. The restaurant was lucky we didn't decide to dine *sans pantalons*.

Chapter 93
Creation recreation

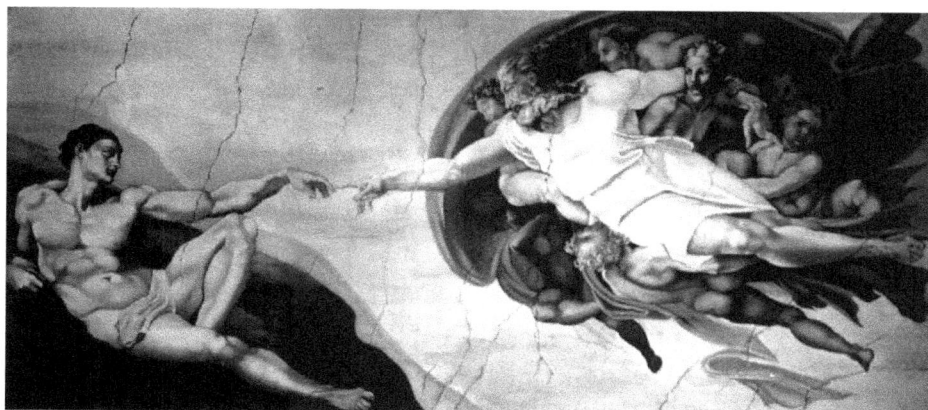

The Lutheran Church's Missouri Synod passed a resolution at their convention in 2019 affirming the belief that God created the Earth "**in six natural days**."

Resolution 5-09A, titled "To Confess the Biblical Six-Day Creation" states: "We confess that the duration of those natural days is proclaimed in God's Word: 'there was evening and there was morning, the first day.'"

The resolution also declared that the creation of **Adam** as the first human being was a "historical event" and rejected the claims of the theory of evolution.

Resolution 5-09A also called on pastors to equip congregations with resources on faith and science and drew from previous resolutions on the origins debate, including one adopted in 1932: "We teach that God has created Heaven and Earth, and that in the manner and in the space of time recorded in the Holy Scriptures, especially Gen. 1 and 2, namely, by His almighty creative word, and in six days. We reject every doctrine which denies or limits the work of creation as taught in Scripture."

Pastors are split on the age of the Earth. A 2011 *LifeWay Research* survey showed that 46 percent agree that the Earth is 6,000 years old while 43 percent disagree. Those with graduate degrees are less likely to support Young Earth creationism.

Young Earth creationists arrive at 6,000 years (for both the Earth and the universe) by adding five days of creation (since Adam was said to have been created on the sixth day in the Bible), around 2,000 years between Adam and Abraham, and around 4,000 years between Abraham and the present (scholars say Abraham lived in about 2,000 BCE).

A film titled *Is Genesis History?* was released in 2017 to support the Young Earth view and debunk the notion that those who hold such a position are "unscientific" or "stupid."

Creationist **Ken Ham** says there's a civil war happening in America against young Earth creationism and that an atheistic view of evolution is permeating the world. The film makes the case for creation in six literal days and presents evidence to support the accounts in Genesis.

Ham argued that despite what current popular science promotes, the Bible is a record of history that God revealed, and says all are sinners who rebelled against God and need salvation.

Chabad **Rabbi Schneuer Wilhelm** told me that there is scientific proof that creation took a *literal* six days, fewer than 6,000 years ago, and that Adam was created as an adult. I respect and like this rabbi a lot, but I believe that the planet took a loooong time to come together, is ancient, that we homo sapiens evolved from simpler creatures, and that the first one was *not* named "Adam."

In 2019 researchers at the Universities of Utrecht, Oslo and Zürich announced an ancient continent, now buried under the Mediterranean and called "Greater Adria." They analyzed the region as far back as the Triassic period, approximately 240 million years ago.

In *rabbiwithanswers.com*, **Rabbi Tully Bryks** responded to the question, "Was the world really created in just six days or are scientists correct that it took 13.8 billion years?" [Slightly edited, with my comments within brackets.]

"Since G-d is the one who created the world, a world which contains all the laws of science and nature, there can never be a conflict between science and the Torah. If there appears to be a conflict, it means that we either need to get a better understanding of the Torah, a better understanding of the science, or perhaps we need a better understanding of both. Biblical commentators disagree as to whether the first six days of creation were literally 24 hours each or if they were actually much longer than 24 hours. With regard to the seventh day of creation (the Sabbath), the general consensus [BY WHOM?] is that time functioned normally once Adam was created on the sixth day, which would make the world 5773 years old [when this was written], plus six "days."

Here are some of the many possibilities:

- o Since the sun wasn't created until the fourth day, it would make sense that at least the first 3-4 days were not 24-hour days. Days 5-7 could still be 24-hour days, but the first four days could represent billions of years.
- o Each "day" of creation could really represent an equal number of thousands, millions or billions of years. So, if the world is 13.8 billion years old, each "day" would really be 2.3 billion years.
- o According to scientists, most of the 13.8 billion years since the "Big Bang" involve development well before the existence of Earth, part of a relatively young solar system. Assuming that G-d's "clock" co-existed and tracked the mass/energy that would eventually form our planet, and since time passes more slowly when moving more quickly, then when his "clock" was surrounded by mostly energy in the earlier stages, time would have passed more slowly. Going with the literal approach, in which each of the seven days were 24-hour days as we know them, it could be that some of the miraculous events since the beginning of creation, such as the intense water pressure during the flood of **Noah** or the intense heat during the fiery destruction of Sodom, could have somehow corrupted our scientific methods for dating things. According to this approach, the entire universe is really under 6,000 years old. [*Hard to Believe*]
- o Another literal approach maintains that our world was preceded by other worlds. As such, all of the billions of years' worth of history, possibly even including dinosaurs, can be accounted for in these previous worlds. [No Evidence]
- o Another approach is that G-d created the world in six days, but did billions of years' worth of work each day. The Garden of Eden was created with lots of vegetation, including fully-grown trees, which would have been seen as hundreds of years old. Adam and Eve were created as fully grown adults.

Unlike the Torah, which we believe to be absolute, scientific knowledge is a fluid process. Scientific "facts" change multiple times, as new discoveries yield new and changing theories and "facts." One great example of what was once accepted as a scientific fact was the universal belief that the earth is flat. [Few people believe that now.]

The year number on the Jewish calendar represents the number of years since creation, calculated by adding up the ages of people in the Bible, back to the beginning. This does not necessarily mean that the universe has existed for fewer than 6,000 years of about 365 days each. Even many religious people readily acknowledge that the first six "days" of creation are not necessarily 24-hour days. A 24-hour day would be meaningless until the creation of the sun on the fourth 'day'."

HUMOR BREAK: The Jewish calendar started at creation and the new year 5785 begins in the fall of 2024 CE, as I was writing this book. But, according to the Chinese calendar, the year is 4722 (maybe). So, what did Jewish people eat for the first 1063 years until the appearance of Chinese restaurants?

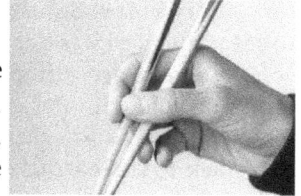

Human civilization has many creation stories, myths, legends and theories. Obviously, no human being witnessed creation. We're not even sure when the universe was created (14 billion years or six thousand years or another number) and what existed before the universe.

Just as young children ask their parents where they came from, and ultimately reject the explanation that they were found under a toadstool or delivered by a stork, many adult humans reject the creation stories. Ahead are a few, in no particular order, for your consideration (with BIG thanks to the *Wikipedia* god) NOTE: the symbol shown before each section ahead is *Aleph*, the first letter in the Hebrew alphabet. I think it's appropriate for beginnings.

The ancient **Egyptians** had multiple creation legends. In all of these myths, the world was said to have emerged from an infinite, lifeless sea when the sun rose for the first time, in a distant period sometimes transcribed as Zep Tepi, "the first occasion." Different myths attributed the creation to different gods: the set of eight primordial deities called the *Ogdoad*, the self-engendered god **Atum** and his offspring, the contemplative deity **Ptah**, and the mysterious, transcendent god **Amun**. While these differing legends competed to some extent, in other ways they were complementary. They all held that the world had arisen out of the lifeless waters of chaos, called *Nu*. They also included a pyramid-shaped mound, called the *benben*, which was the first thing to emerge from the waters.

These elements were likely inspired by the flooding of the Nile River each year; the receding floodwaters left fertile soil in their wake, and the Egyptians may have equated this with the emergence of life from the primeval chaos. The imagery of the pyramidal mound derived from the highest mounds of earth emerging as the river receded.

The sun was also closely associated with creation, and it was said to have first risen from the mound, as the general sun-god **Ra** or as the god **Khepri**, who represented the newly-risen sun. There were many versions of the sun's emergence, and it was said to have emerged directly from the mound or from a lotus flower that grew from the mound, in the form of a heron, falcon, scarab beetle or human child. The different creation accounts were each associated with the cult of a particular god in a major city: Hermopolis, Heliopolis, Memphis and Thebes.

א The **Cherokee** creation belief describes the Earth as a great floating island surrounded by seawater, hanging from the sky by cords attached at the four cardinal points. The story tells that the first Earth came to be when **Dâyuni'sï**, the little Water Beetle, came from Gälûñ'lätï, the sky realm. The Water Beetle was not affected by the natural laws of cause and effect and went to see what was below the water. He found no solid place to rest and dove to the bottom of the water and brought up soft mud. This mud expanded in every direction and became the Earth.

The other animals in Gälûñ'lätï were eager to come to the new Earth, and birds were sent to see if the mud was dry. A buzzard was sent first to prepare for the others, but the Earth was still soft. When he grew tired, his wings dipped very low and brushed the soft mud, gouging mountains and valleys in the smooth surface, and the animals were forced to wait again.

When it was finally dry, they all came down. It was dark, so they took the sun and set it in a track to run east to west, at first setting it too low and the red crawfish was scorched. They elevated the sun several times reduce its heat. The story also tells that plants and animals were told to stay awake for seven nights, but only a few animals, such as owl and panther, succeeded and they were given the power to see and prey upon the others at night.

The first people were a brother and sister. Once the brother hit his sister with a fish and told her to multiply. Following this, she gave birth to a child every seven days and soon there were too many people, so women were forced to have just one child every year.

א There are many **Mongol** creation myths. In the most ancient one, at the start of time there was only water. A *lama* came down from Heaven, holding an iron rod to stir the water. The stirring brought wind and fire which thickened the center of the waters to form the Earth.

Another narrative also attributes the creation of Heaven and Earth to a lama called **Udan**. Udan began by separating earth from heaven, and then divided them into nine stories, and creating nine rivers. After the creation of the Earth itself, the first male and female couple were created out of clay, and they became progenitors of all humans.

In another example, the world began as an agitating gas which grew increasingly warm and damp, precipitating heavy rain that created the oceans. Dust and sand emerged to the surface and became Earth.

Yet another account tells of the **Buddha Sakyamuni** searching the surface of the sea for a means to create the Earth and he spotted a golden frog. From its east side, Buddha pierced the frog, causing it to spin and face north. From its mouth burst fire and from its rump streamed water. Buddha tossed golden sand on his back which became land. And this was the origin of the five earthly elements, wood and metal from the arrow, and fire, water and sand.

א For ancient **Greeks** an account of the beginning is reported by **Hesiod** in his *Theogony*. He begins with Chaos, a yawning nothingness. Out of the void emerged Gaia (the Earth) and other Divine beings: Eros (Love), Abyss (the Tartarus), and Erebus. Without male assistance, **Gaia** gave birth to Uranus (the Sky) who then fertilized her. From that union were born first the Titans—six males and six females. After **Cronus** was born, **Gaia** and **Uranus** decreed no more

Titans were to be born. They were followed by the one-eyed **Cyclopses** and the **Hecatonchires** or Hundred-Handed Ones, who were both thrown into Tartarus by Uranus. This made Gaia furious. Cronus was convinced by Gaia to castrate his father and became ruler of the Titans with his sister-wife **Rhea** as his consort, and the other Titans became his court.

A motif of father-against-son conflict was repeated when Cronus was confronted by his son, **Zeus**. Because Cronus had betrayed his father, he feared that his offspring would do the same, and so each time Rhea gave birth, he snatched up the child and ate it. Rhea hated this and tricked him by hiding Zeus and wrapping a stone in a baby's blanket, which Cronus ate. When Zeus was full grown, he fed Cronus a drugged drink which caused him to vomit, throwing up Rhea's other children and the stone, which had been sitting in Cronus's stomach all this time. Zeus then challenged Cronus to war for the kingship of the gods. At last, with the help of the Cyclopses (whom Zeus freed from Tartarus), Zeus and his siblings were victorious, while Cronus and the Titans were hurled down to imprisonment in Tartarus.

After a prophecy that the offspring of Zeus's first wife, **Metis**, would give birth to a god "greater than he," Zeus swallowed her. She was already pregnant with **Athena**, however, and she burst forth from his head—fully-grown and dressed for war.

א The **Yoruba** regard **Olodumare** as the principal agent of creation. During a stage in this process, the "truth" was sent to confirm the habitability of the newly formed planets. The Earth was one of these, but deemed too wet for conventional life.

After a period of time, a number of divinities led by **Obatala** were sent to help Earth develop its crust. On one of their visits, the arch-divinity Obatala was equipped with a mollusk that concealed some soil, winged beasts and cloth. The contents were emptied onto what soon became a large mound on the surface of the water and soon after, the winged beasts began to scatter it until it gradually made a large patch of dry land; the indentations they created became hills and valleys.

Obatala leaped onto a high ground and named the place *Ife*. The land became fertile and plant life began to flourish. From handfuls of dirt, he began to mold figurines. Meanwhile, as this was happening on Earth, Olodumare gathered the gases from space and sparked an explosion that became a fireball. He subsequently sent it to Ife, where it dried much of the land and baked the motionless figurines. Next, Olodumare released the "breath of life" to blow across the land, and the figurines slowly came into being as the first people of Ife.

א In the pre-**Inca** and Inca mythology of South America, **Viracocha** is the great creator deity. Its full name (and some spelling alternatives) are **Wiracocha**, **Apu Qun Tiqsi Wiraqutra**, and **Kon-Tiki**—the source of the name of **Thor Heyerdahl's** raft.

Viracocha was one of the most important deities and seen as the creator of all things, or the substance from which all things are created, and associated with the sea. **Viracocha** created the universe, sun, moon, stars, time (by commanding the sun to move over the sky) and civilization itself. Viracocha was worshipped as god of the sun and of storms. He was shown wearing the sun for a crown, with thunderbolts in his hands, and tears descending from his eyes as rain.

Viracocha rose from Lake Titicaca (or sometimes the cave of Paqariq Tampu) during the time of darkness to bring forth light. He made the sun, moon, and the stars. He made mankind by breathing into stones. His first creations were brainless giants that displeased him, so he destroyed them with a flood and made new, better ones from smaller stones. Viracocha eventually disappeared across the Pacific Ocean (by walking on the water), and never returned.

He wandered the Earth disguised as a beggar, teaching his new creations the basics of civilization, as well as working miracles. He wept when he saw the plight of the creatures he had created. It was thought that Viracocha would reappear in times of trouble.

In one legend, he had one son, **Inti**, and two daughters, **Mama Killa** and **Pachamama**. In this legend, he destroyed the people around Lake Titicaca with a Great Flood called Unu Pachakuti lasting 60 days and nights, saving two to bring civilization to the rest of the world, these two are **Manco Cápac**, the son of Inti (sometimes taken as the son of Viracocha), a name meaning "splendid foundation," and **Mama Uqllu**, which means "mother fertility."

Scandanavian creation stories (and even news reports) are often difficult for Americans to follow because of the unfamiliar spellings, like "Häagen-Dazs." *Völuspá* is a poem that tells the story of the creation of the world and its coming end, related to the audience by a "völva" (not Volvo) seeress addressing the Norse god **Odin**.

The poem starts with the völva requesting silence from "the sons of Heimdallr" (human beings) and asking Odin whether he wants her to recite ancient lore. She says she remembers ancient giants who reared her.

She then relates a creation myth and mentions Ymir (a primeval being born from venom that dripped from the icy Élivágar rivers and lived in the grassless void of Ginnungagap. Ymir birthed a male and female from his armpits, and his legs begat a six-headed being).

The world was empty until the sons of Burr lifted the Earth out of the sea. The Æsir then established order in the cosmos by finding places for the sun, the moon and the stars, thereby starting the cycle of day and night. A golden age ensued where the Æsir had plenty of gold and happily constructed temples and made tools. But then three mighty giant maidens came from Jötunheimr and the golden age came to an end. The Æsir then created the dwarves, of whom Mótsognir and Durinn are the mightiest.

The seeress then reveals to Odin that she knows some of his secrets, and that he sacrificed an eye in pursuit of knowledge. She tells him she knows where his eye is hidden and how he gave it up in exchange for knowledge. She asks if he understands, or if he would like to hear more.

Thor, the god of thunder and sworn protector of the earth, faces Jörmungandr, the world serpent, and wins, but Thor is only able to take nine steps afterward before collapsing from serpent's venom. Víðarr faces Fenrir and kicks his jaw open before stabbing the wolf in the heart. The god Freyr fights the giant Surtr, who wields a fiery sword, and Freyr falls.

Finally a beautiful reborn world will rise from the ashes of death and destruction where Baldr and Höðr will live again in a new world where the Earth sprouts abundance without sowing seed. The surviving Æsir reunite with Hœnir and meet together at the field of Iðavöllr, discussing Jörmungandr, great events of the past, and the runic alphabet. A final stanza describes the sudden appearance of Nidhogg the dragon, bearing corpses in his wings, before the seeress emerges from her trance.

𐤀Genesis is the creation myth of both **Judaism** and **Christianity** and has similarities to the **Muslim** belief. The narrative is made up of two stories. In the first, **Elohim** (the Hebrew word for God or Gods) creates the Heavens and the Earth in six days, then rests on and sanctifies the seventh. In the second story, God, now referred to by the personal name **Yahweh**, creates **Adam**, the first man, from dust and places him in the Garden of Eden, where he is given dominion over the animals. **Eve**, the first woman, is created from Adam as his companion.

Borrowing themes from Mesopotamian myths, but adapting them to the Israelite belief in one God, the first major comprehensive draft of the *Pentateuch* (the five books which begins with Genesis and ends with Deuteronomy) was composed in the late 7th or the 6th century BCE. It was later expanded into a work very much like the one we have today.

How much history lies behind the story of Genesis? It is far-fetched to speak of it as historical. There is much debate, even among believers, about the actual timing of creation: Did the process take six days of 24 hours each, or millions or billions of years?

𐤀The **Muslim** *Quran* states that "the heavens and the earth were of one piece" before being parted. God then created the landscape of the Earth, placed sky above it as a roof, and created the day and night cycles by arranging an orbit for the sun and moon. Some modern Muslims interpret the Quran's story of creation in the context of science and believe that the scientific theory of an expanding universe is described in the Quran.

Sūrat al-Aʿrāf states that the "heavens and the earth" were created in the equivalent of six **yawm**. The Arabic word yawm (there's a nearly identical Hebrew word) means "day," and so some Muslims believe the universe was created in six days, akin to the story of creation in the Genesis. However, other scholars interpret the term yawm to mean a unit of time much longer than a day, as the Quran states that in the afterlife, one day is equivalent to 50,000 or 1,000 years.

Sunni theologian **Said Nursî** stated that the Earth was already inhabited by intelligent species before humankind. He believed the *Jinn* lived here before but were almost wiped out by fire. A few Muslims believe that even before Jinn, other creatures like *Hinn* lived on the Earth.

Adam and his wife (called **Ḥawwāh**) appear in the Quran as the first man and woman, created from clay and brought to life by the breath of God. Most Islamic scholars believe that Adam and Eve were supernaturally created through a miracle by God, though some modern scholars have instead asserted that they evolved naturally from a common ancestor.

𐤀Thousands of years ago a hollow meteorite carrying humanoids from a distant planet ("Mahubaca") crashed onto the island of Gibraltar, off the coast of what is now Spain.

One humanoid was a pregnant female, who came to be known as Tia Maria ("Aunt Mary"). She gave birth to the first Earthlings, Adam and Eve. They were Christians, and founded the sect called Meteorites.

A small remnant of Meteorites still lives on Gibraltar and in nearby Cadiz in Spain.

Deceased Meteorite people are "buried at sea" and await miraculous transport to and resurrection on Mahubaca, where they live forever but don't reproduce. [Confession: I created this.]

Chapter 94
Animal magnetism

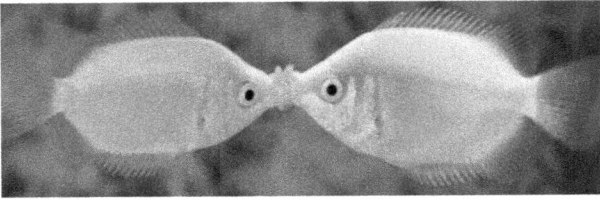

I've always loved animals. I've lived with dogs, cats, turtles, birds and fish. I lived with tropical fish from infancy through adulthood. I found them soothing, and often more interesting to watch than television. Although I had many varieties over the years, my favorite breeds were probably the Kissing Gourami, Tiger Oscar and Egyptian Mouthbreeder.

The **Gouramis** didn't do much, other than "kiss" the glass, rocks and other Gouramis. But they were pretty, and one of them, "**Carl**," grew huge and lived for six years. When he died, I froze his corpse, planning to defrost hm if a cure was devised.

Tiger Oscars were playful and willful and almost dog-like. Some fish can be *real pets*. They can be responsive, interactive and even trained—and don't have to be walked. I had Oscars who would wiggle their tails when I entered the room and even take food from my fingers.

I once had a big artificial plant in the center of a fish tank. An Oscar dug out the gravel from beneath it and knocked it down, horizontally, onto the bottom of the tank. I fixed it, and he knocked it over again. I fixed it again and he knocked it over again. Ultimately, I surrendered. I figured the tank was *his* home and *he* had the right to decorate it the way he wanted.

Despite their big size, Oscars were fragile beasts, subject to puffy fungus growths on their eyes, which I treated with tetracycline, an antibiotic also used on humans.

That was not my only fish-doctoring. One time an Oscar tried to eat a catfish—but he could not swallow it. The potential food was wedged in the Oscar's mouth, and he could not spit it out and eat his real food. I couldn't take him to a vet, so I became one. I removed him from the tank and lovingly wrapped him in a damp towel to help me grip him. I got an "alligator clip" and used it to grab and extract the catfish, and I had a happy Oscar once again.

The weirdest breed I ever lived with is the **Egyptian Mouth Breeder** ("Haplochromis Strigigena," if I remember correctly). After the female's eggs are fertilized by her mate, the tiny tykes hatch and immediately start swimming. If the babies were in danger of becoming fish food, mom would open her mouth and the little ones would stream in, like New Yorkers entering a subway station at rush hour. Mom would protect her offspring, not swallow them, and release them when the coast was clear. As with many species, male Egyptians are more colorful than the females. When my female died, her male morphed, taking on her pale coloration. Very sentimental, I thought.

I once had a "**spitting fish**" but I don't recall its real name. It could take a gulp of water, swim to the surface, stick its face above the water and SPRAY. I thought it would be fun to breed a spitter with a flying fish. I imagined that if I had a smoker visiting, the amazing fish would fly out of the tank, go to the visitor and extinguish the cigarette.

WARNINGS:

- Fish tanks are usually made of glass and can be fragile. When I lived in the Bronx, I had a huge tank built into a wall. When it was time to move to a new apartment, I arranged to use a big Checker taxicab that could fit the tank across the back seat. A friend met me at my new place, and we carefully removed the tank from the cab, took it into the building, put it in the elevator and went up to the fifth floor. As we left the elevator, the door whacked the tank and destroyed it. Fortunately, I had carried the fish separately and they got a new tank in my new home.
- Fish (and turtles) need more than water. They need food, filtration, maybe heat, and maybe medical care. It's very important not to overfeed.
- A fish tank will leak at the worst possible time. I once had a 55-gallon tank that sprung a leak when I was away for a few days. The dirty, smelly water leaked down through two levels of my house. My insurance company sent a crew to dry and deodorize the carpeting. Unfortunately, the sweet smell of the chemical drew a horde of ants!

When I was a young teenager, we had a **parakeet**. It never spoke or sang and didn't do much at all. The most interesting thing it ever did was to escape from its cage and fly around the kitchen. I don't remember how we got it back into its cage.

It can be fun to have a bird flying around your house. It's also potentially messy (feathers and feces) and it may be hard to get the bird back in its cage. If a bird goes out a door or window, buy a new bird and be more careful.

Canine vs. Feline Comparison:

- A dog will love you, but the most you can expect from a cat is toleration. Cats are much pickier eaters than dogs. If you die at home with a dog, it will lick you. If you die at home with a cat, it will eat you (said on *The Simpsons* and reported by cynical observers). Dogs have lived with humans for at least 30,000 years, providing service and companionship. Dogs are often called "man's best friend" and can be found everywhere in the world where there are people. One Russian dog—**Laika**—even went into space before any human made the trip.
- So, what makes dogs so attractive to people? The list could be very long, and different canine aspects appeal to different people. A few suggestions: • They're furry (most breeds, anyway). • They're cute (most breeds, anyway). • They're affectionate (most breeds, anyway). • They're cuddly (most breeds, anyway). • They're energetic (most breeds, anyway). • They're amusing (most breeds, anyway). • They're responsive (most breeds, anyway). • They're useful (some breeds). • It's fun to observe a non-human acting in near-human ways. • They don't object to doing tasks that people shun. • They might keep you warm on a cold night ("Three Dog Night"). • They're loyal and protective. • A dog will follow instructions from a child or an adult with a handicap, who mostly *takes* orders.

In 2002, neighbors announced that they were divorcing and moving away. The wife was getting custody of the kids—and we could have the dog.

My own wife had never lived with a dog, but had gotten to like theirs and was willing to go along with the deal—if I agreed to clean up the crap.

My first dog was named **Rusty** because he was the color of rust. He joined my family when I was two or three years old, and we lived in an apartment in the Bronx. I was a smart kid, but I don't know if I was perceptive enough to come up with his name. Maybe one of my parents named him. Actually, I don't know if Rusty was a "him." Rusty was a *stuffed* dog and probably was not anatomically accurate.

Rusty was followed by "**Sniffer**." I named him that because he sniffed a lot. He also peed a lot in our apartment, and we did not keep him for long. He was followed by a succession of other dogs with the same name when we lived in suburban houses in Connecticut. One was a combo cocker spaniel and golden retriever. He was a very good friend.

"**Sniffy**" (his nickname) was highly intelligent, observant and highly anthropomorphic. He copied human activities and may have even thought he was human. Sniffy had learned to slap when play-fighting with human beings. When he got into a fight with another dog his initial impulse was to slap with his 'hands.' It was unproductive. Then he'd recognize the presence of his opponent's tail, four legs and sharp teeth and re-evaluate his strategy. He'd withdraw and assume a traditional canine battle stance—growling and biting.

In the morning Sniffy'd go outside, cross the street and knock on the front door of the Cohens' house. When **Poochie Cohen** came out, Sniffy and Poochie would go down the block and knock on the Gordons' door so **Buttons Gordon** would come out and play. The dogs were mimicking the behavior of the human children in the neighborhood. But no one had taught them or bribed them to do it.

Sniffy was a car nut, a *four-legged, furry automotive aficionado*. He loved to ride in cars. He understood "go to the Plymouth: (Mom's car) and "go to the Chrysler" (the paternal vehicle). At night, he'd often fall asleep in our den while my siblings and mother and I watched TV and my father worked late. At around 9:30 PM, Sniffy would suddenly stand up, shake himself and run to the front door. Even while apparently asleep, he heard and recognized the sound of my father's car, from about a quarter-mile away, and wanted to be the first to greet him.

Although he liked being a passenger, he was an *amazing* runner and often preferred to *run* alongside the family's cars instead of riding inside. He often followed my mother from our home in the Westville section of New Haven to her teaching job in Shelton, a distance of about ten miles. When they got to school, he stayed there for the day, playing with and entertaining the children. Sometimes he ran alongside my father's car—on the Wilbur Cross Parkway and through the West Rock Tunnel, to his office in Hamden (about six miles away). When they arrived, my father would somehow lure him back into his station wagon, drive him home and lock him inside.

My parents became both amused and annoyed by these adventures but were not cruel. While Sniffy was on the road, my folks would periodically stop so our peripatetic perambulating pooch could pee and rest for a few moments. At these stops they tried to get Sniffy inside their vehicles, but he preferred to complete his journeys on his legs. At least once, he had a broken leg, in a cast. That injury was not a handicap, however. Athletic **Sniffer John Marcus** (his full name, per my brother Marshall) became a Paralympian. He folded up the dysfunctional limb and eagerly ran on three legs!

Once he ran as I drove a few miles to nearby Woodbridge. I heard a siren, saw flashing lights in my rearview mirror and stopped the car. A police officer had observed Sniffy and me. He was understandably upset and warned me that I could be fined $100 for *animal cruelty*.

I explained Sniffy's traveling preference to the officer and said, "I'll gladly pay the hundred bucks if you can get him into the car." He tried, but Sniffy remained obstinate, and the dog-loving officer smiled and wished us well. When I reached my destination, I bought Sniffy a treat, lured him into my car and drove him home.

One time, my mother drove to **Luigi's**, our favorite pizzeria, to pick up a pizza, lasagna and a couple of hero sandwiches.

When she got home, she realized that one of the heroes was missing. She left the food on the kitchen table and drove back to Luigi's to get the rest of our supper.

When Mom came home for the second time, there was nothing on the table.

In the corner of the kitchen floor was the open and empty pizza box. Sniffy was sitting in the box, smiling and burping.

Buon appetito, mio piccolo cane.

As much as he liked to ride and to run, Sniffy also liked to walk around the neighborhood on his leash. The family had to speak cautiously. If one of us casually mentioned the word "leash," smart Sniffy would run to the door and start wagging his tail.

After a while we started substituting a code word, "Archibald" (named for poet **Archibald MacLeish**.) It didn't take long for Sniffy to decode the subterfuge. He'd react as if we had simply said "leash."

>>While a dog may love you and comfort you, DO NOT assume it will protect you or your home. If a burglar comes in, equipped with a steak bone or some cookies, your pooch will likely kiss the marauder and then settle down to chew while your home is ransacked.

Sniffy, however, was my mother's *personal protector*. Years ago, she and my father employed a male dancing instructor to prepare them for a major social event. Whenever the instructor tried to dance with my mother, Sniffy growled and tried to get between them. Apparently, he thought that Mom needed protection.

As I mentioned, Sniffy was half golden and half cocker spaniel. Perhaps the cocker half was the protective half.

Sniffy once stayed with me in Bethlehem, Pennsylvania while my parents ("*our* parents"?) were on vacation. One day, I was making a movie with friends in a local park. I had to slide down a waterfall carrying Sniffy, and then walk through a stream. I stepped on a concealed broken bottle, which nearly passed through my foot. It took 54 stitches to close the painful wound, but it kept me out of the army. Thank you, Sniffy.

Sadly, there are more canine and human children than families who want them. If you'd like to add a dog to your family, please check with shelters and rescue organizations. The photo shows **Hunter**, an adoptee from Connecticut, and his greyhound cousin **Mitzi**. She traveled from Puerto Rico to Massachusetts to join her adoptive family. The man is Mitzi's human father, my bro-in-law **Alan Alpert**.

Hunter was a "rescue dog," but not in the normal sense. He originally belonged to a man and woman who had been high school sweethearts. She got pregnant. They got married. It was a bad marriage, so they had a second kid to make it better. It got worse. They bought a dog to make it better. It got worse again. Ultimately the marriage fell apart. The wife got the kids. We got Hunter. Hunter was a *golden retriever*—probably the most common breed in TV commercials and very popular with people.

Retrievers are very gregarious and need interaction with other intelligent life forms. Sadly, the other family kept him in a cage in their basement—a miserable existence for any dog—especially a retriever. (Golden retrievers and Labrador retrievers have similar personalities and both love being cold and wet. Goldens have longer fur.)

I worked from home at the time (early 2002) and started borrowing Hunter for longer and longer periods each day. My office contained the head of a swordfish caught by my father and a stuffed dog. Initially Hunter got along well with them, but after a few days he dismembered poor "**Stuffy**."

My wife approved the "rescue," if I'd scoop the poop. Someone suggested feeding condoms to dogs in the hope that turds would come out pre-wrapped for easy disposal.

I had always liked dogs, and since the places where Marilyn and I had lived previously were not dog-friendly, I never seriously considered getting one. Hunter was my dream-come-true. I don't often dwell on my lack of human children. Marilyn and I tried to reproduce, but we didn't; and adopting seemed like too much of a gamble. Hunter, however, was adopted, and he was just fine. If I had to be a dog, I'd like to be like him. But I'd want parents like us, to spoil me.

Hunter had proper AKC papers. The neighbors had paid $1,000 for him, but he'd be ours for just the price of food and a few toys and the annual shots.

HAH!

It didn't take us long to realize that Hunter wasn't happy going for morning and evening walks and spending most of the day in the house. We spent $100 for a gate on our rear deck, and then $3,000 for a custom awning over the deck to keep him cool when it was sunny.

As he grew bigger, Hunter needed more room to roam than the rear deck provided, and he wasn't happy being tied up in the backyard, so we decided to have a fence put around the yard. A three-foot-high fence would be tall enough to keep him in and would cost $5,000.

The very helpful salesman pointed out that if we spent just $2,000 more, we could have a fence that was five feet tall—tall enough to protect a pool, "just in case."

How can a free dog cost $100,000?

"Just in case" came the next year and cost us about $75,000. We didn't buy the pool just for Hunter, but we probably would not have gotten it if we didn't already have the dog fence. Hunter used the pool much more than people did.

Hunter ate dog food, but only for snacks. Breakfast was a can of **Costco** chicken breast meat, costing over $2. Supper was roasted chicken breast from **ShopRite**, costing about $6. When he was thirsty, he drank **Poland Spring** water.

We took him on vacations to dog-friendly hotels, and he was never left in a kennel. Our kitchen table had a stainless-steel top. It was one of his favorite places to nap and lounge with **Copper**, his Chihuahua-Beagle girlfriend.

Before we bought Hunter his pool, we got him a swing set—with *no swings*. When it was delivered, the truck driver apologized to us. He thought that the order was not processed properly because there were no swings. I explained that the set was for dogs, not humans. Hunter loved to climb, hang out and slide, but did not swing. If he could swing, we would have bought him swings. Nothing was too good for our furry four-legged son. Hunter's tower was a great place for him to spot invaders approaching from the distance.

Unlike a Belgian Malinois, German Shepard or Husky, Hunter had flaps over his ears. However, his hearing was extremely good. Even from upstairs to downstairs he was able to hear the sound of foil, paper or cellophane being unwrapped and he'd quickly appear to share whatever was wrapped inside. A few times he found and ate Hershey's Kisses and pooped out the foil.

If Hunter was in the back yard and we wanted him to come in, we'd yell "chicken" or "cookies." It was much more effective than "come in now!" He escaped from our yard a few times but never roamed far because he knew how good he had it at home. We usually found him across the street at the front door of the house where his best friends **Copper**, **Cheech** and **Buddy** lived.

Hunter traveled wherever 'mommy and daddy' went, and usually sat in the right-front seat of the car or van. I usually drove and Marilyn sat in the rear—because she was a good mommy and would do anything for our furry four-legged son. People thought it was strange. We thought it was normal.

Hunter had no passport for international travel, but did have a castration certificate. Unlike a passport, it does not have to be renewed.

Although he lived to be an 'old dog,' Hunter did learn new tricks and loved to perform. He understood about 30-40 human words (maybe more that he chose to ignore) and was quite able to make his wishes known by barking, whistling, whining, tapping, posturing and pointing. I learned to understand "doggish" and sometimes we'd sing together. (Actually, we howled.)

Until his hips became weak when he was 14 years old, Hunter started each morning with "tripod." He raised his right-rear leg in front of me and stood on the other three legs so he could get scratched under the raised leg. People thought it was strange. We thought it was normal. Ironically, when Hunter did tripod with my brother **Marshall**, Hunter raised his left-rear leg—not the right one.

Hunter J. Marcus never won a trophy for Best-of-Show or set records for speed or strength. He never achieved the worldwide acclaim of Snoopy, Bullet, Lassie or even Yutz-the Wonder Dog.

Nevertheless, thanks to his master media manipulator father (this book's author) Hunter *did get known.* • He has had a *Facebook* page since 2012. • His picture was in a dog calendar. • He was on the cover of several books. • He was Executive Vice President for Canine Affairs at AbleComm, Inc. • He was honored by the Continental Broadcasting Network. • His photo is inside several books • He's had nearly 1,700 Google links.

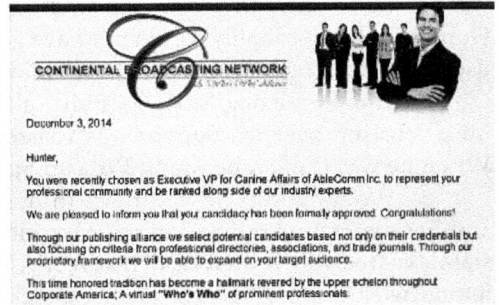

CONTINENTAL BROADCASTING NETWORK

December 3, 2014

Hunter,

You were recently chosen as Executive VP for Canine Affairs of AbleComm Inc. to represent your professional community and be ranked along side of our industry experts.

We are pleased to inform you that your candidacy has been formally approved. Congratulations!

Through our publishing alliance we select potential candidates based not only on their credentials but also focusing on criteria from professional directories, associations, and trade journals. Through our proprietary framework we will be able to expand on your target audience.

This time honored tradition has become a hallmark revered by the upper echelon throughout Corporate America; A virtual "Who's Who" of prominent professionals.

o Hunter's athleticism—like most of his activities—was often motivated by food. He'd gladly jump up and take a cookie from my mouth ("Cookie Kiss"). Dog lovers think it's cool. Other people think it's disgusting.

o We had several silly rituals that were fun for all: In "Cookie March," I'd hold a cookie in each hand near my hips and start plodding round the house, repeatedly saying "We're doing the cookie march. We're doing the cookie march." Hunter would follow close behind me and press his nose against my hands to try to get me to release a cookie. Ultimately, we'd go into the living room, and he'd jump up onto the couch. I'd sit with him and then say "Kiss One" and he'd give me a kiss. After we concluded "Kiss Five," I'd put my closed fists in front of him and he'd try to guess which one contained a cookie. He always guessed correctly because each fist contained a cookie.

o Sometimes when we were in bed, I'd roll him on his back and give him a thorough inspection. I'd start at the tip of his tail and examine (tickle, actually) every part of him as I worked my way up to his forehead. I'd criticize him for his shortage of fingers and toes but complimented him on his tail. I'd look into his ears to make sure no light was coming in from the other side and I'd make sure the ears were pink and did not stink. At the end I proclaimed him fit to be my son, and I renewed his contract for another week. I helped him clap hands to celebrate passing the exam.

o If Hunter was lying on his belly I'd start "crawling" up his back using two fingers as legs. I'd say "I'm coming to get the woofy. I'm coming to get the woofy." The point of the game was for me to get up to his nose without getting bitten. I usually got bitten, but they were *love bites* and no blood flowed.

o If I made a fist, put it near Hunter's face and said, "nose wrinkle," he'd wrinkle his nose, bare his teeth and make believe he's a ferocious animal instead of a cuddly animated pillow. Strangely, he would *never* perform this trick when outsiders were present. It was as if he was very conscious of his image and did not want to be seen as a vicious beast.

o Sometimes I'd put a towel or blanket over Hunter's head and say "Where's the doggie?" He'd growl and start snapping through the fabric and I'd let him clamp his jaws on my hand. Again, no blood flowed.

o Television's **Lassie**, and **Einstein** from *"Back to the Future"* were great actors—but other dogs can learn the difference between fake and real. Hunter definitely understood acting. He and I engaged in mock combat every morning. We started with an energetic tug-of-war and then we wrestled. He would clamp his jaws on me. But, as in *"The A-Team,"* there was never any blood. A casual observer might think he wanted to maim me. He would growl, breathe heavily and bite my arm, hand or fingers. But Hunter knew exactly how much pressure to apply to make the fight seem realistic without doing real damage. If he accidentally chomped too hard and I complained, he'd instantly change from biting to kissing. He understood guilt—and knew how to apologize.

- o When we were ready to leave the house, I'd tell Hunter to "walk the doggie" and he'd pick up the end of his own leash and walk to the door.
- o At hotels, we'd go to the lobby, and he'd stand up and put his paws on the counter as if he was going to sign the guest register.
- o Hunter visited many hotels up and down the east coast and was usually a very welcome guest. Human guests were eager to play with him and take selfies with him. Both guests and staff often gave him food. The chef at one hotel cooked him a plate of steak and scrambled eggs for breakfast.
- o When we stayed at hotels, Hunter liked to get up in the middle of the night to explore and socialize, even if he did not have to pee. We frequently stayed at a Sheraton on Long Island. He knew to go behind the front desk where the dog treats were kept. One time a tipsy guest walked up to the desk and Hunter stood up behind the desk as if he was a hotel employee—eager to help.
- o Another night we were at the hotel when a wedding celebration was going on. At around 2 AM the bride, groom and parents left the reception and sat down in the lobby. The new wife (slightly drunk) saw Hunter, got off her couch to greet him and fell on the floor. Hunter licked her face, she kissed him back, and soon the bride and Hunter were making out on the lobby floor—while the groom and parents scowled.

It took a lot to upset Hunter. Loud noises went unnoticed. He liked almost all people but got upset when a lawnmower was used nearby or when a strange car passed our house. He used to hate vacuum cleaners but later adjusted. Hunter had a few dog friends he liked to play with, but he generally didn't play well with strange dogs. However, he seemed to recognize other goldens and labs as cousins and was instantly eager to play with them.

Although Hunter was sort-of trained (he always knew what he was supposed to do, and sometimes he was willing to do it), he trained Marilyn and me very well. We kept a water bowl in our bedroom, about five feet from the bed. At night, Hunter knew that if he started panting, one of us would fetch the bowl and put it in front of him on the bed. We seemed to exist to serve him.

Hunter was extremely strong, able to pull an adult on a sled or in a wagon. He could be tough to control on a leash when he wanted to go off-course to smell something disgusting, but was very gentle with small children.

Petco says it's "where the pets go." Hunter did "go" on the floor of Petco four times. Fortunately, the store has clean-up supplies.

Hunter and I often bathed together in our Jacuzzi-like tub. The first time we did this I washed his right side and then said, "turn around." He immediately turned around so I could clean his left side—even though I had no reason to expect him to know what "turn around" meant.

When Hunter was young, we often took a morning walk of nearly a mile. One day when we had gone about a quarter of the way, it started raining. The sky quickly darkened, and I saw lightning and heard thunder. I said to Hunter something like "we'd better go back now." I had never before tried to teach him how to respond to "go back" but he instantly made a U-turn and headed for home. Just as parrots may unexpectedly talk dirty—saying words they heard but were not taught—a dog may surprise you by mimicking you. Be careful to set a good example.

I've often said that every human being is born with a unique set of abilities, and it is our obligation to find a market for those abilities. Similarly, canines and young Homo Sapiens have amazing capabilities that adult humans may not give them credit for. I believe in setting a "high bar" to encourage striving and achieving (with love and rewards, of course). I almost always use adult English—not baby talk—when speaking to a human baby or a non-human of any age. I've never said, "me go bye-bye" and hope I never will.

In a way, it seems strange to refer to Hunter as *my dog*, as if I owned him—like my iPad. Hunter was a live being, capable of independent thought (sometimes much too independent)—and not my possession. However, since I speak of "my wife" or "my friend," Hunter was "my dog."

Just as I don't believe in racism, sexism or ageism, I don't believe in speciesism. All mammals have full rights and privileges in our home. If Hunter wanted to nap on a couch or on the kitchen table or eat or sleep in our bed—that was his right, and we never complained. Hunter got away with a lot.

Wife Marilyn and I rewarded bad behavior because Hunter was a perpetual puppy, and we considered that *everything he did was cute*. We have no human kids, so Hunter got—and returned—a lot of love.

Hunter was the ultimate SBD (silent-but-deadly) farter. His farts smelled as bad as his poop, but I never heard him fart—even once. His butt was a stealth weapon, striking with no warning.

Despite the occasional stink bomb, dogs have advantages over human kids. No bad report cards. No bar/bat mitzvahs, college or weddings to pay for. I just picked up poop. I also paid for Hunter's castration—not necessary for human sons.

For humans a blizzard is often misery. For goldens, it's *ecstasy*. Hunter loved to lie or sit in the snow to chill his belly or behind.

We had a front-door intercom speaker connected to our phone system. When someone pressed the intercom button, our phones rang in bursts of three rings, a different cadence but with the same sound as when a phone call comes in. Hunter was able to *count the rings*. When our phones rang "normally," Hunter ignored the sound. When the phones did a ring-ring-ring, Hunter barked and went to the front door to greet the visitor. We didn't teach him this (and I don't know if we could). He just figured it out. Dogs are surprisingly smart.

If I squirted water onto the sidewalk from a hose, Hunter tried to drink it from the sidewalk, as if the sidewalk—not the hose—was the source of the water. Smart dogs do stupid things.

While animals can be taught many useful and amusing things, they also learn through observation. Be careful of what you let your pet see you do. Even after canine vision is diminished, the senses of hearing and smell will probably be much better than what any Homo Sapiens has.

Dogs and cats use their feet as both feet and hands, and their mouths as hands. Elephants use their trunks as hands. Porpoises use their mouths as hands. Monkeys use their feet and tails as hands. My father showed my brother and me that we could pick things up with our feet. Mom thought this use of *prehensile toes* was disgusting. I sometimes use my teeth as tools or fingers.

There's an animated movie called *All Dogs Go to Heaven*. I warned Hunter not to die, because Heaven wouldn't be nearly as good as what he had here and now.

Sadly, Hunter did die, in 2017, at the "ripe old age" of 16. He lived longer than most goldens, because he gave and got *lots of love*.

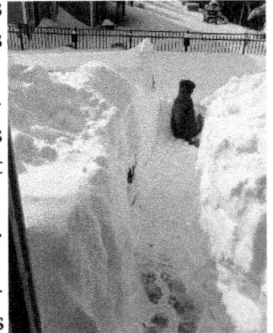

> **"A human child may talk back and rebel, but dogs follow you like you are the center of the universe."— Kim Su-hyeon in the *New York Times*, 2024**

Hunter couldn't wait for "his" pool to be filled before getting wet. Girlfriend Copper preferred to be dry.

As soon as the pool cover came off in the spring, Hunter was wet.

The cover had perforations to allow rain and melted snow to drip into the pool. Genius Hunter discovered that if he lied down on the perforations, water would rise up and create a frigid lake for him. Friend Rocky was not impressed.

Important Questions

Q: Why do dogs lick themselves? A: Because they can.
Q: Why can't dogs dance well? A: Because they have two left feet.
Q: How do you catch a runaway dog? A: Make a noise like a cookie.
Q: What breed of dog does Dracula have? A: A bloodhound
Q: What goes tick-tock, bow-wow, tick-tock, bow-wow? A: A watch dog
Q: Why does a dog wag its tail? A: Because no one else will wag it.
Q: Why did the dog cross the road twice? A: He was trying to fetch a boomerang.

In my sophomore year at Lehigh, I rented the master bedroom and adjacent john in a private house. **"Poppy George" Webster** started working at **Bethlehem Steel** (called "The Steel") at age-15 and he was close to retirement when I moved into his home. It was a suburban split-level, several miles northeast of the steel mill's noise, flames and filth.

Mrs. Webster ("Annie-Love") slept in one of the children's bedrooms, and George slept downstairs in the family room. He said that this was because he was Catholic and she was Episcopalian. They did have a child, so I assume they were once in the same bedroom for a few minutes.

The son, **Wayne Webster,** was 21 years old and could have been mistaken for **Jethro Bodine** on TV's *Beverly Hillbillies*—but Jethro was smarter. A neighbor told me that the family had paid bills for a few of Wayne's teachers to get him promoted, but he was forced to leave junior high school on his 18th birthday.

Wayne volunteered for military service during the war in Viet Nam and was trained to drive a truck, but he confused oil and gasoline and couldn't shoot straight. Despite the Army's need for large numbers of warm bodies, Wayne was not permitted to re-enlist.

Wayne was working in a fabric store when I moved in with the family, but was soon fired because he confused inches and yards and couldn't cut straight. He spent a few weeks in a junkyard, and then found his true calling as a cab driver.

He awoke each morning at a little after four, ate breakfast and was behind the wheel of a taxi from six to six. He then came home, had supper, watched TV, and nodded off before nine. The schedule never varied except for one weekend each month when he had a free Sunday. That meant that he could stay up late the night before, and he often went to the burlesque (pronounced with three syllables) in neighboring Allentown to "look at the naked ladies."

Wayne loved his job and urged me to leave college and drive a cab because of all the ladies I'd get to meet.

Wayne never had a date or went to a disco or dance while I lived with the family, but he kept porn magazines under his bed. And whenever the Websters' dog, **Flower**, was in heat, she seemed particularly attentive to Wayne. Flower would often raise her tail and wiggle her rear end in his direction, and she spent an awful lot of time in his bedroom.

Mrs. Webster awoke early each morning so the dog could watch the chickens on the farm report. The family's favorite program was *My Mother the Car*. Years later, *TV Guide* decided it was the second-worst television show of all time, just behind *The Jerry Springer Show*.

The family felt that any color program was better than any black-and-white program. Mrs. Webster said, "I don't understand why you go out on Saturday nights when you could stay home with us and watch all the pretty colors on *Lawrence Welk*."

For my third year in Bethlehem, I rented the top-floor apartment in a dilapidated-but-convenient house. It was an old, three-story, peak-roofed place on the south side, one block from the movie theater, next door to a newsstand with pinball machines and across the street from a pizza joint that sold joints. The house was one block downhill from the campus and split down the middle, with different people owning each half. One half was owned by a dentist, "**Dr. Steve**," who once lived in the building, but had moved to a nicer part of town.

He kept his office on the first floor and rented the rest of the building to students. He charged very little, just about enough to cover costs so the building would always be occupied, and his office would be watched.

Dr. Steve was a good man and a nice guy. He seemed to get vicarious fun from his attachment to student life and never bothered his tenants, even if rent was months overdue. Sometimes, he provided us with discount-priced dental care, or even freebies. Dr. Steve really cared about us.

For some unknown reason, the building had traditionally housed students from India. They'd move in, stay for a year or two to earn a graduate degree and then pass the rooms on to their countrymen. **Dave** was the only non-Indian who lived in the building. I had met him in my freshman year, and although we were not particularly friendly, he introduced me to Dr. Steve and got me a place to live on very short notice.

The building was not divided into formal apartments, but had a setup resembling suites, each with one or two bedrooms and one or no bathroom. There was one kitchen, in the rear of the first floor, which was shared by the three-to-five students who lived in the building at any given time.

The third floor, which was really an attic and had been unoccupied for several years, became my home for just $35 per month. It had two bedrooms, a living room, and a bathroom. There was no kitchen, but the bathroom measured about 8' by 16'. I put up a partition between the sink half and the toilet-and-tub half, built a counter, found a cabinet, bought a fridge and settled in.

I cooked whatever could be made with a hot plate, toaster, electric broiler and electric skillet. I blew a lot of fuses, and washed dishes in the bathtub. We were less than immaculate; I once slipped on a ravioli pod while getting into the tub to take a bath.

I went to the supermarket by motor scooter, and often towed a shopping cart home.

We'd use the empty carts to hold empty beer cans, and more than one of them went down a flight of stairs like us, fully loaded.

The apartment came unfurnished, but it was equipped with an all-black cat named **Burger**. Its history was a mystery. But to get the apartment, I had to agree to care for the cat as long as I lived there, and then pass her along to the next student tenant.

I had always liked dogs and fish, but never knew cats. Burger was a *terrible* roommate. If she was canine or human rather than feline, I'd call her a "bitch." She was noisy, unaffectionate, unresponsive, annoying and destructive. I would have gladly paid more for the apartment it if was cat-less. Allegedly, black cats bring bad luck. Burger sure did.

In those days I had many hundreds of record albums lined up on a living room shelf. Bitchy Burger would often use her claws to slash the exposed edges of the albums! I once tried to bathe her, and she used those claws on *me*. When I had to drive her to a vet, she shit on the seat of my car.

At some point my parents were going on vacation and I was asked to dog-sit for Sniffy. So, Burger and I drove to New Haven. I tried to sneak her into the house but apparently Sniffy sniffed her and was not happy about the intrusion. They got along like, well, "cats and dogs."

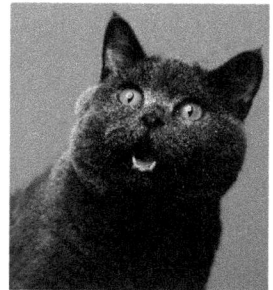

Chapter 95
We need smarter computers, or programmers

Many of today's techie gadgets seem fine for smart nine-year-olds. (I used to be one.)

But they can create *big problems* for senior citizens like the current me. It often seems like modern technology is smarter than the people who need to use it—but *it's often not smart enough.*

- My phones have a feature called **Talking Caller ID**, with a robot who reads me information about the callers without my having to look at the screen. The robot should know that "NJ" is the abbreviation for New Jersey, and not announce "NJ" as "oonj."
- The telecom robot often mispronounces names, like making "Raul" rhyme with "Paul."
- It's common for business websites to provide **driving directions**, distances and travel times to the nearest locations. However, many companies, even tech companies, don't realize that most potential visitors to their 'nearby' stores or offices are not prepared to fly or swim or sail to them. I live in Southern Connecticut. South of me is a body of water called Long Island Sound. South of the Sound is Long Island, where many businesses are located. The website for **Best Buy** (home of the mighty **Geek Squad**) tells me that the Best Buy in Riverhead, Long Island is a mere 35.1 miles away. That's the mileage as the crow flies, the flounder swims or the crab crawls. But, if I'm driving my car, and it's not on the ferry ($152 to $214 roundtrip), I must go *around the Sound*—not over or through it, and the distance is *141 friggin' miles*. Stoopid **MapQuest** and **Google Maps** make the same annoying error as Best Buy. These companies need *better geeks*!

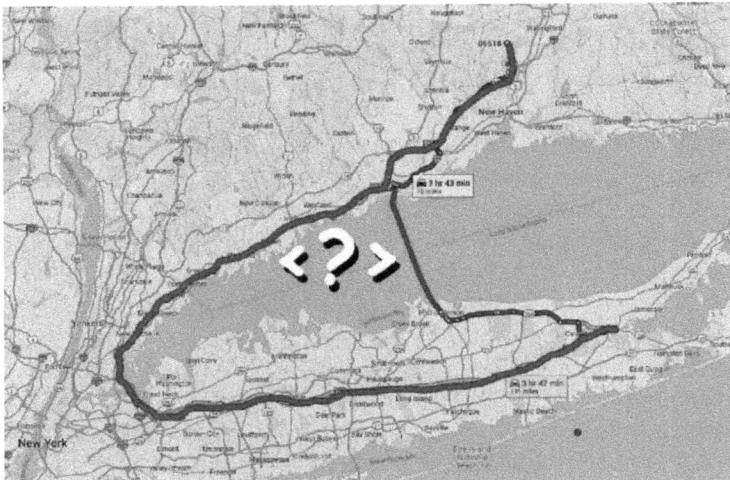

Chapter 96
My sporting life

I didn't understand baseball until I was 55 years old.

I was born in the Bronx in 1946 and spent the first six years of my life just a few miles north of **Yankee Stadium**. Despite this proximity, I never became a baseball fan—probably because I never received a proper explanation of the sport.

When kids asked me who my favorite player was, I'd quickly say **Mickey Mantle**. It was an easy answer—because Mick and I shared initials, and nobody would disagree.

In college in the late 1960s, I was briefly in an intramural softball program. A bunch of hippies and assorted misfits thought it might be fun to form a team to play stoned, with absolutely no intention of winning. We'd get to smoke some weed, enjoy the great outdoors, work on our tans and get free T-shirts. It sounded like a good plan.

But, what I didn't plan on was being a "power hitter," a "homerun king," just like Mickey Mantle. I found no joy in running around the bases, or catching balls hit by opposing teams, but I *loved* to whack those balls as far as I could.

My teammates thought I was a traitor to the cause. The team fell apart, and it was many years before I picked up a bat or saw another ball game.

In 2001 a nephew and nieces begged me to take them to a game at Yankee Stadium. I packed a radio with a headset, and a book. I set the radio to WCBS, allegedly an all-news station, and I was shocked to encounter a play-by-play analysis of the game in front of me. Soon I began to understand "the national pastime."

In baseball, it had always seemed to me that it was the *hitters* who were the *heroes*. People like Mantle hit the balls that drove up the scores that won games and the World Series. But what I learned from the radio was that it was the *pitchers and catchers*—not the hitters—who were really in control. Balls—not bats—made the big difference.

Throwing was more important than hitting, and it was the silent, stealthy, sneaky catchers squatting behind home plate who signaled instructions to pitchers who caused hitters to strike out. Because of good pitchers, even good hitters seldom got good hits. And, if they did, the balls were usually caught by good fielders. I actually *enjoyed* baseball that day.

My late understanding of baseball made me appreciate the sport, but too late to make me a fan. Similarly, I had my first coffee on my 70th birthday. I liked it, but never became a fan.

In my first semester as a journalism major at Lehigh, our class was assigned to write a large variety of news items. One assignment was to write about an intramural baseball game. I hated baseball and resented the assignment. I knew nothing about the game and felt absolutely feeble. My vocabulary had none of the appropriate idioms for "hit a home run." I read a published report on the game and unconsciously absorbed a phrase. My hawkeyed professor noticed it and he *flunked me for plagiarism*! It was a valuable lesson.

Years later, nephew Joe (a major baseball fan) begged me to take him to the **Baseball Hall of Fame** in the end of the world (Cooperstown, New York). Joe hated it, because he hated museums. I loved it, because I love museums—regardless of specialty.

[Yankee Stadium photo from By BuickCenturyDriver at English Wikipedia. Thanks.]

Chapter 97
Not strictly kosher (a love story)

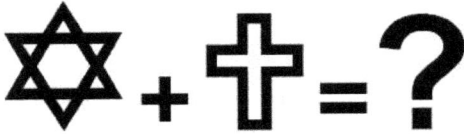

When I was in fifth grade, our synagogue distributed a survey with questions about parental attitudes on interfaith dating.

At the age of 11, I had little chance of being a traitor to the Chosen People and dating a pretty blonde gentile girl (a "shiksa"). But my politically liberal mother—probably without much thought about the future consequences—indicated on the survey form that she and my father would allow me to date a girl who was not Jewish.

Fast-forward from age-11 to age-17.

In my senior year of high school, I worked part-time in one of my father's clothing stores. So was **Maria.** She was not a blonde, but a dark-haired Italian-American who was a senior at Mary Immaculate Academy—unknown territory to someone who had studied religion at B'nai Jacob.

It was easy to be attracted to Maria. She was gorgeous, smart, played the guitar and seemed to like me.

We engaged in some mild flirting. I made frequent visits to her cash register to get change for big bills. Once, I even asked her to give me "three threes for a nine." She laughed. It was a good sign. The flirting was a little awkward at first, partly because I was the boss's son. If this happened today, I could be accused of sexual harassment.

Red Skelton, a popular TV comedian at the time, had done an episode about an alien landing on Earth and needing change for the parking meter near his flying saucer. Red played the saucer pilot who asked a friendly Earthling something like, "May I have three hizzins for a hern?" I printed up a piece of hern currency in the store's sign shop and I asked Maria for change. She laughed at that, too.

My attraction to her was pretty obvious, and some employees encouraged me.

Mickey, who was the buyer for teenage girls' clothing, even revealed Maria's impressive bra size and urged me to ask her out. **Eddie,** an Italian-American who worked with me in the men's department, cautioned me to stay away. He said, "Don't shit where you eat." I wondered if he was trying to give me useful advice or just wanted to protect a member of his ethnic tribe from an alien marauder.

Eventually, the hormone pressure was impossible to resist. After years of dating girls with last names like Cohen, Kaplan and Berkowitz, it was time to try a name that ended with a vowel.

In 2024, the notion seems quaint; but, in 1963, I asked my parents. I don't remember the dialog other than that there was a negative reaction. But, when I reminded Mom about the form she had filled out years earlier, she gave me the keys to her Plymouth.

Maria and I dated on and off, even after I went away to college. It was a time of transition for both of us. I let my hair grow longer, grew a beard and discovered sex (but not with Maria). She dated some older Yalies. We hung out at the **Exit** coffee house in New Haven and drove to Greenwich Village.

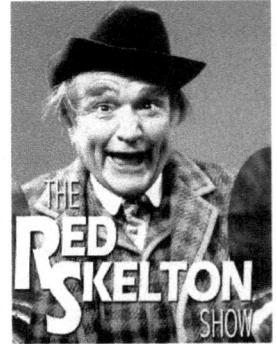

Our families tolerated the relationship. Her mother was a great cook, and I loved Italian food. I was terribly disappointed to learn that Italian mothers never cooked lasagna in the summer because it made the kitchens too hot.

Maria also crossed over the ethnic food line and liked to eat Jewish kosher deli foods. She even introduced me to Peking duck and Chinese rice chips.

Late one night, when we were a year or two under 21, we were in a car in a country club parking lot, drinking beer and eating corned beef sandwiches.

Suddenly, we saw the flashing lights of a police car approaching. When the cop got out of his car and aimed a flashlight into our car, Maria was frantically stashing our Heinekens under the front seat.

The cop caught Maria with her hands under the seat, but he couldn't see the beer. He asked what Maria what was doing, and she quickly said, "Oh, I'm just looking for some salt for the corned beef." Fortunately, the officer of the law didn't know enough about kosher cold cuts to realize that no one puts salt on corned beef; and Maria and I were not arrested for underage drinking. I assume that, after 60-plus years, this confession can't cause trouble.

Although I liked her a lot (and maybe I loved her—whatever love is for a teenager) and thought about marrying her, I called Maria, "Maria" only one time. It just sounded *too Catholic* to me. Every other time, I used her nickname, "**Marty.**" I also was not prepared to have a crucifix or a Jesus picture on the wall of my home. Religion ruins a lot of good things.

So does bad communication. In 2009 I learned that Maria considered me to be her boyfriend back in 1963 and '64. It made me feel good, even though she was now a grandmother. Back then, we both dated others, and I didn't realize I was that significant to her.

Revisionist History: in 2009 I also learned that Maria had become disenchanted with Catholicism back in high school. Had I known in 1964 what I learned 45 years later, I might not have thought our relationship was doomed and I could have tried harder to keep her as my girlfriend and maybe even make her my wife (but not at age-18).

Despite her physical beauty and a relationship that lasted over a year, we never got beyond holding hands, hugging and kissing. One time, we were at a beach, and she asked me to rub suntan lotion on her. I was tempted to do some additional rubbing, but I restrained myself. I don't know now if I was shy, stupid, scared, over-indoctrinated into being a "gentleman," afraid of getting slapped and losing her, or a victim of the Madonna/Whore Syndrome. Maybe it was all of the above.

Sigmund Freud apparently invented the term "Madonna/Whore Syndrome," where males divide females into two types. There are the nice girls ("Madonnas," like the Virgin Mary) and the overtly erotic, uninhibited and available "whores." A man would choose one woman for love and another for sex, but none for both.

Some males, at least at some time in their lives, assume that females must fall into one of the two categories, but never both; i.e., nice girls can't be sexy and sexy girls can't be nice girls. I *now* know differently.

Just as **Groucho Marx** said that "I don't want to belong to any club that will accept me as a member," many young men wanted to have sex with "whores," but preferred to marry "Madonnas." The beautiful girl with the Catholic name from the Mary Immaculate Academy was appropriately—but unfortunately—a Madonna to me.

In later years, I wondered if Maria was insulted or disappointed that I didn't "try something" at the beach or another place. Maybe I just didn't turn her on or maybe she just wasn't ready.

Was the request to apply lotion a hint to do more? Maybe it's better if I don't know. As time went on, I cared less about the answer. Years later she described me as a "horn dog." I've been meaning to ask her how she knew, because I always suppressed my lust for her.

How would I have reacted if she was sexually aggressive? I'm not sure. In later years, I was with sexually aggressive women who said, "I need to get laid"—just as a man might. I liked that just fine. But, back in 1964, aggressiveness might have moved the needle on the Madonna/Whore scale away from Madonna and I might not have liked it.

Allegedly "men think with their dicks," but sometimes there can be a battle for control between the penis and the brain. If the brain wins, the result can be erectile dysfunction or the avoidance of sexually stimulating encounters. Small-brained animals don't have this problem.

Toward the end of my relationship with Maria, I began dating **Donna**. She was Jewish and my soul mate. We were two halves of one whole. In the 1965 movie *A Thousand Clowns,* we *both* identified with eccentric **Uncle Murray**. She was the first woman I definitely wanted to marry. We seemed to like and dislike all of the same things, but we were so much alike that it might not have been a good marriage. It's probably better to have debates and second opinions.

Donna referred to Maria as *"Lubavitcher."* I'm not sure if it was because she couldn't remember the Italian name, or a sarcastic disapproval of my dating a gentile. It could have been both. The **Lubavitcher Rebbe** was the leader of a group of Hasidic, ultra-Orthodox Jews, based in the Crown Heights neighborhood of Brooklyn.

I was a year ahead of Donna in high school. I no longer remember if we knew each other then, or even when and how we met. The peak of our relationship was 1966-67.

That was supposed to be my junior year at Lehigh, but I had screwed up and was back in New Haven. I had enrolled in the **University of New Haven**, but seldom went to class. I worked part-time, but don't remember much about the rest of the time, except for my time with Donna.

Although she went to college out of town, we spent a lot of time together. I sometimes visited her at college, and sometimes she came "home" to see me. We wrote a lot and were together many days in the summer.

Once I joined her family at another relative's beach cottage. Donna didn't feel well and did not want to go in the water, so her 15-year-old sister and I swam out to an island. When we got there, the sister relaxed on her back to collect some sunbeams. She had an adult's body and was wearing a small bikini. I positioned myself to look into her cleavage and watched her breasts move as she breathed. I was soon having "Should I?" and "What if?" thoughts.

Eventually, common sense prevailed, and I went into the dark, cool water to hide the evidence of my excitement. I had to wait about two years before I had sex with a 15-year-old girl.

The guest room in the basement of my family's house became my bedroom when I was 12. By age-19 it morphed into a "bachelor's pad" with a bar and a condom collection. I had my own door from the street, and young ladies could enter and leave without encountering my parents.

Donna was very affectionate—sometimes too affectionate. When we were out on the street, her PDAs (Public Displays of Affection) embarrassed me and I sometimes asked her to cool it, at least until we got back to my place. We never went "all the way" but we were "on the way." Several times I had worn Levi jeans when we went to a movie, but I changed into thinner and looser chinos for "improved tactile sensation" in make out sessions in my room later on. She stripped down to her underwear. I feel a tingle just writing about it.

After one particularly stimulating session, we talked about getting married. I gave her a college pin from Lehigh, and she decided to call herself my "pindel." I remember going to work the next day in a haze and telling some of the other employees that "I think I'm engaged, but I'm not sure."

One time, when I visited Donna at her college, we decided to check into a motel, presumably to consummate our relationship. Donna and I had a debate about whether I should register as just "Michael Marcus" or "Mr. & Mrs. Michael Marcus." In retrospect, I doubt that **Mr. Patel** at the front desk would've cared if I signed in as "**John Smith**," "**John F. Kennedy**" or "**Pope John**."

There was no consummation that night. Donna spent most of the time crying. This was the beginning of years of unhappiness and depression for her.

At one point, Donna's doctor decided that I was the cause of her problems (including attempted suicide!), and we were forbidden to see each other. We had a last goodbye in the summer of 1967. It was the last time I saw the woman I once thought I'd spend the rest of my life with. I cried. Donna did not cry. She could not cry. Therapy had robbed her of emotion. She was like a zombie, and nothing like the funny and affectionate girl I had fallen in love with.

Over 40 years later I was relieved to learn that Donna was still alive, apparently happy and healthy, and her troubles were caused by her mother; and I was *officially non-toxic*.

Later I married **Marilyn Cafarelli**. Marilyn's father, **Joe**, was a non-church-going Catholic Italian. Her mother **Sally** was Jewish. That makes a good combination, even if it's not strictly kosher.

Sally's culinary repertoire was multi-ethnic. She served luscious lasagna, perfect pasta "fazool" and spaghetti sauce with sausage and pork chops in it; as well as magnificent chopped liver, chicken soup, potato pancakes and stuffed cabbage—but not at the same meal.

Sally's kitchen was a wonderful place for a gourmand like me, and her cooking probably helped Marilyn induce me to pop the question.

In August, 1971 we were introduced by **Jill,** who worked with Marilyn in New York and who used to live across the street from me in New Haven. Marilyn was tired from unpacking after moving from the Bronx to Manhattan and fell asleep the first time we met—not a strong testimony to my conversational abilities—but I was strongly attracted even before I had tasted Sally's food.

Marilyn resembled both Maria and Donna. My fetishes seldom varied. My standard package: five feet tall, dark hair, large breasts. Hmm! That describes my mother, too.

Marilyn and I were both dating a few others at the time. My social calendar was full, and I waited about a month before calling her, but I passed the word via Jill that I was interested, and I eventually called her. She thought her falling asleep had turned me off, but I'm a napper, too, and it didn't bother me. We started dating regularly, and, by October or November, we planned a quick marriage in December. It seems ridiculous now. It probably was ridiculous then.

If we had known each other longer, we probably would not have gotten married. We argued a lot (and we still do). At one time, we considered canceling the wedding, but one of us said (and I don't remember who said it), "What the hell, the invitations have gone out, so let's do it."

I no longer remember why it was planned so soon, but I'll state here for the record that she wasn't pregnant. I do know that we got a good deal from a caterer who had a cancellation on the date we picked, so maybe that was an influence. We probably also saved on taxes by marrying by the end of the year. Maybe we were just extremely in love and wanted to get married ASAP. That's a good reason.

Marilyn's cousin **Manny** was a printer, and he gave us free wedding invitations as a gift. Unfortunately, they were printed with my father's given name—that few people would recognize—instead of his well-known nickname. When Manny reprinted them, he got Pop's name right, but he printed the *wrong year*.

We didn't want to ask Manny for a third freebie or insult him by taking our business elsewhere. (He kept a gun strapped to his ankle and I used to refer to him as **Mafia Manny** although I had no real knowledge that he was in the mob.) The wedding date was rapidly approaching, so my future mother-in-law used a pen to correct the year on each invitation. It wasn't elegant—in fact, it looked like **shit**—but it was definitely a rare collector's item.

Unfortunately, the printing was just the first in a series of nuptial fuckups.

Depending on whom you ask, the wedding was either very nice, OK or terrible. The photographer was a tyrant and made Marilyn cry while posing for pictures. And while he had us posing for pictures, we missed what were said to be the best latkes (potato pancakes) in the world—even better than Sally's homemade latkes.

Marilyn's **Aunt Hilda** (Mafia Manny's mother-in law) complained because there were no cigarettes on the dining tables, fomenting loud disagreement over whether it was the responsibility of the bride's family or the groom's family to finance the wedding guests' lung cancer.

Marilyn had designed her own wedding gown, and, on the day of the wedding, she realized that it was not the right decision to have a vertical seam down the center. It was too late to change.

When we went to cut the cake, the two of us applied all of our power to the ceremonial knife. We tried slicing, sawing, stabbing, pressing and poking, but we just could not penetrate the icing on the beautiful triple-decker. We wondered if the cake was frozen or if we were victims of a joke.

After what seemed like hours of snickering from the guests, the catering manager came out of the kitchen and whispered a little secret to us.

Apparently, someone had neglected to tell us that this gorgeous cake was a wood and plaster *fake* and we were supposed to just make believe to cut it while everyone sings "The bride cuts the cake, the groom cuts the cake..." The servers had a sheet cake in the kitchen already cut and ready to roll out and serve to the guests.

About a month after the ceremony, the photo studio delivered the wedding album with Marilyn's name spelled wrong on the cover. They eventually provided a corrected replacement, but in over 52 years we have not been motivated to switch the covers. I'm not sure if we're too busy, too lazy or just sentimental. More likely, we just don't care anymore.

We got some really nice wedding gifts, but the one I liked best was a bunch of **McDonald's** gift certificates that **Ken Irsay** gave us. It's easy to spend money. It's harder to make me smile. Jill, the woman who introduced us, stiffed us. Maybe she felt that introducing us was a sufficient gift. Maybe so, but a toaster would have been useful, too.

Marilyn did not approve of my eating habits. She promised to make me homemade soup every day of my married life if I'd give up eating canned Campbell's soup.

We got married on December 12, 1971, and she's already made enough homemade soup to take us through January 8, 1972. That's lunchtime, not supper.

Marilyn is an excellent cook who hates to cook. I would be less frustrated if she was a lousy cook. She does a great job microwaving the contents of doggy bags and ordering meals to be delivered, but there's no one in the world who can make a better roast chicken or turkey. Not only do they taste delicious, but they look good enough to be on the cover of *Good Housekeeping*.

Marilyn can't resist a bargain at the supermarket and our freezers periodically filled up with large, plastic-wrapped carcasses, bigger than bowling balls. Unfortunately, she seemed to give away more frozen poultry than she defrosted, cooked and fed to me.

Despite abundant and consistent negative reviews, Marilyn insisted on buying a particular $7,000 pro-style stove because of the way it looked. On a good day, we were lucky if two of its six burners worked. I would have been happier if she hung up a pretty picture of the $7,000 failure and bought a bunch of $1.59 cans of **Sterno** that could be reliably ignited with a match.

Marilyn has trouble deciding anything and is constantly re-playing decisions made years and even decades ago. Her most common phrase is, "Maybe I shoulda got." Marilyn is always looking back, but I never look back, except when I'm driving.

Our first house could have been carpeted with the little carpet samples she collected. Our second house had wooden floors because Marilyn couldn't pick carpet for it.

Big decisions, like picking a house or a car or a husband, come much easier than the little ones, like picking carpet color or deciding on coleslaw versus string beans.

If Marilyn asks for help making a decision, I give her a very quick answer, knowing that it doesn't matter what I say because she'll soon change her mind anyway.

Our "regular" waiters learned to wait a few minutes before telling the chef what to prepare for her because there's a good chance that Marilyn will soon run into the restaurant kitchen to change her order—maybe even twice.

Her difficulty in deciding and her extreme cautiousness and paranoia can be very frustrating and terribly time-wasting. I grew up in a family where, if you weren't ten minutes early, you were *late*.

I know that she really meant the best for us and I love her for it—and in spite of it. She's kept me out of trouble many times. Marilyn is my second-guesser, my censor and my conscience.

Marilyn sometimes says she wishes she could be fearless like me, but it's probably better that she's not like me. Opposites attract. But two of me could be in jail—or maybe dead.

Our friends who seemed to get along perfectly well got divorced long, long ago. Apparently, they just didn't care enough to fight.

☺ ADVICE FOR A LESS-UNHAPPY MARRIAGE

Michael's Alternate Victory Plan

Forget about compromise decisions. If one of you wants black walls in a room and one of you wants white walls, and you get gray walls, neither of you will have what you want. You'll both be pissed off when you enter the room.

Try alternate victories. Let your mate make some unilateral decisions, and try to ignore the car, paint, carpet, vacation destination and furniture that you hate. Then *you* make some unilateral decisions, and you'll get to enjoy your personal victories.

Overall, life together will be a compromise, and that's nice.

Warning: My alternate victory plan doesn't apply to everything. It's probably best that you agree on the city and the house you live in and on kids' names. My father let my mother pick my middle name. I hated the name for many years, and I wish he didn't give in.

Chapter 98
Nicer names for medical maladies

I've had pink eye and blue balls—but so far no yellow jaundice, red death, black plague, black lungs, scarlet fever, green thumbs or purple haze.

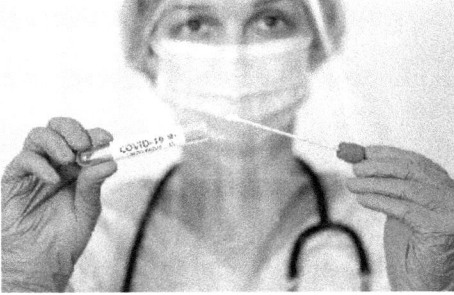

"Kissing Disease" sounds like much more fun than "mononucleosis."

"Pink eye" is much cuter than "conjunctivitis."

"Dead butt" seems funnier than "gluteal amnesia."

"Sinister" sounds much worse than "left-handed."

"Myopia" sounds much worse than "nearsighted."

"Edema" sounds more frightening than "swelling."

"Depression" seems much sadder than "sadness."

A "weak weenie" sounds cute compared to "erectile dysfunction" or "impotence."

"Bellyache" sounds much less drastic than "gastroenteritis."

"Mad cow disease" is the common name of "Bovine spongiform encephalopathy." Which would you rather have?

"Orchitis" sounds like a food or flower. Actually, it's swollen balls.

"Drippy shit" is funnier than "diarrhea."

"Halitosis" sounds deadly, but it's merely unpleasant ("bad breath").

"Blue balls" sounds comedic, but it's extremely painful and its official name is "epididymal hypertension." It occurs after an erection without an orgasm.

A few years ago, my cardiologist told me I had "congestive heart failure." That sounded *really scary*, like I could be dead the next day. Actually, it's usually not immediately fatal. A simple term like "a bum ticker," would be easier to take, or something simple and inoffensive like "farina," "bongurgy" or "corbo."

Even body parts have both technical and more friendly, easier-to-understand labels. A "clavicle" is not a musical instrument or a kid's toy. It's a collar bone. A "digit" is a "finger."

Chapter 99
Carvel and me

When I was a kid in New Haven, our phone number was one digit different from the number for a nearby **Carvel** ice cream store. We got lots of wrong-number calls for Carvel, which put me in the mood to go there.

I used to pass Carvel on one of the two routes I took home from junior high school, and I frequently stopped there.

I invented a special treat.

If there were no other people to witness it, owner **Bill** would make a large cone with half vanilla and half chocolate ice cream and dip the combo in chocolate syrup to make the glorious hard crust.

This "Marcus Special" cost the same 25 cents as a single-flavor large Brown Bonnet cone. Years later, Bill made the Marcus Special for my brother **Marshall**.

Not all Carvel treats have had the longevity as the Marcus Special, Brown Bonnet, Flying Saucer and Fudgie the Whale. When I was a kid, I could buy a Lollapalooza, which was a tubular ice cream pop dipped in sprinkles. There was also a Papapalooza, but I don't remember what it was.

I lived in Westchester County, New York from around 1977 to 2001. Our house was conveniently located about halfway between the first Carvel store and Carvel University. The "university" was a motel where new franchisees stayed to learn the business.

In addition to classrooms, the facility included a large Carvel store, where students practiced making delicious treats. Some of them turned out less-than-pretty, but they tasted fine and were sold at half price.

Tom Carvel (1906—1990) was born **Athanasios Karvelas** in Greece and emigrated to the USA. He's known for inventing and promoting soft-serve ice cream in the northeastern United States.

Tom entered the delicious business with a truck in Hartsdale, New York in 1929. On Memorial Day weekend in 1934, his truck had a flat tire, so he pulled into a store's parking lot and began selling his melting ice

cream to people who were driving by. Surprisingly, people liked the soft ice cream, which led to Carvel's iconic dessert.

Initially, Carvel stores described their product as "frozen custard"—a popular dessert in the first half of the 20th century; but later the stores sold "ice cream."

Gradually the product line expanded, as the number of franchised stores also grew. Today, Carvel's innovative treats and classic ice cream cakes are enjoyed at celebrations, and are a standard munchie found in many home freezers. They are available at over 300 Carvel stores and at many supermarkets. My four previous "adult" homes were near Carvel stores. Alas, there are none in Hamden, Connecticut where I now live, but my nearby Shoprite supermarket can supply me just fine.

Tom Carvel was a test driver for Studebaker cars in the mid-1920s, when he produced the first machine to turn out soft ice cream. This invention was the first of his many patents, copyrights and trademarks.

He first sold the machines to store owners, who had so much trouble operating them that many owners defaulted on loans provided for the purchase. Tom decided instead to start people in business, teach them to use the machine and charge them a royalty on sales. The Carvel Corporation took root, pioneering multi-flavored soft ice cream.

By 1955, when Tom put his own voice on television and radio as spokesman for the company, he had gained a reputation as a tough businessman who rode herd on his franchisees, refusing to let them start dealer organizations and forcing them to buy supplies from Carvel at prices they considered inflated.

A group of franchise holders sued the company on the ground that it was illegally restricting their products, prices and sources of supply. But Carvel beat the franchisees in court and won a $10.5 million judgment against plaintiffs' lawyers for provoking litigation.

"Sure, they call me strict when I try to control them," Tom said of the franchisees years later. "But poison one child and 50 years of business goes down the drain."

In October 2009, Tom's niece **Pamela Carvel** sued to have Tom's body exhumed for an autopsy because she suspected he was drugged or suffocated by employees. Her petition was denied, and she later became a fugitive from justice in a personal bankruptcy case. She had been vying for control of his $67-million estate.

Carvel Rebellion: One time a nephew and two nieces were visiting and wanted ice cream. I started driving to a nearby **Baskin & Robbins**. The kids became furious and loudly chanted, "WE WANT CARVEL. BASKIN AND ROBBNS SUCKS!"

We went to Carvel.

Chapter 100
Tips from the Marcus kitchen

I've never been trained to be a professional chef, but I am an enthusiastic eater, a *gourmand* rather than a *gourmet*. My mother once asked me, "Do you eat to live, or live to eat?" My answer was "both."

I generally don't like fancy foods, but I like some weird foods.

Here's some of what I've learned about food and drink:

o   When ordering a meal in a restaurant, if you want a beverage other than water, and you want to start your meal with soup, ask to have the drink delivery delayed. Beer doesn't go with clam chowder, and if a cold beverage arrives early, it will no longer be cold when you drink it. • In a cafeteria where you fill your own soda glass, fill it with soda but no ice, and put ice in a separate glass. When you get to your table, pour some soda into the glass with ice. Don't pay the same price for ice as for soda. • In an "Asian buffet" tip a buck to the guy at the grill or the sushi counter. Make eye contact when you put the money into the tip container, smile and say, "thank you." Maybe you'll be remembered the next time you want some special treatment. • Unless it's busy all day, don't go to a buffet restaurant at off-peak hours. Food will be less fresh and there will be less food than when there are many customers eating.

o   The test of good pizza is whether it tastes good cold.

o   **Devil Dogs** taste better frozen than at room temp.

o   Amazon.com is a great source of all kinds of food items—especially with free shipping.

o   Staples and other office-supply dealers are good sources of bargain-priced snack foods.

o   You can have a free lunch—one bite at a time—by eating samples at warehouse clubs.

o   You don't have to drink a lot to have a free or inexpensive supper at a happy hour.

o   A clam is like sex. When it's good, it's terrific. When it's bad, it's awful.

o   Nothing tastes worse than a bad pistachio nut. But, by the time you realize it's bad, it will be impossible to get the terrible taste out of your mouth.

o   Fish is generally less forgiving than meat. Don't undercook or overcook. Experiment before you cook for others.

o   When you're cooking meat, put some salt and pepper on it, and maybe onion powder and garlic powder.

o   But, be careful with seasoning. I once made spaghetti sauce for a girlfriend's family and poured in salt instead of garlic powder!

o   When you're eating, don't add salt or pepper before tasting it unless it's a dish you are very familiar with.

- Expiration dates on food packages are guidelines, not real limits of safety.
- From my father: don't go to a restaurant until it's been open for at least 30 days, even if you have previous experience with the owner. Let the crew make mistakes with someone else's stomach.
- Margarine is nice for spreading because there is no need to wait for it to soften, but butter tastes better. Competitive health advantages are indecisive.
- Unless you are kosher, try melting some butter onto steak while it broils. My father learned this in France.
- When cooking almost anything, remove it from the flame or microwave oven a little bit before it's supposed to be done. It will continue to cook with its own internal absorbed heat. You can always heat it a bit more—but you can't do anything to make it rarer.
- It is sometimes OK to use a higher heat to cook something faster—but only sometimes.
- Pizza at restaurants like **Hometown Buffet** can be improved by adding spaghetti sauce.
- At home or work, frozen pizza can be improved by adding extra sauce and toppings.
- You can "go shopping" in your own refrigerator and pantry. You may be surprised at what you find and have already paid for.
- Throw out food that has gone bad. There's no point in refrigerating garbage.
- If you dislike a dish at a particular restaurant, analyze why. I had long disliked the pasta at a particular Italian restaurant that my wife likes, and assumed the sauce was at fault. I eventually realized that the sauce was fine, but the pasta tasted dry because there was not enough sauce. Now I ask for extra sauce and all is well.
- Microwaved popcorn never tastes as good as real popcorn. However, **Jolly Time's** "**Homemade Classic Stovetop Flavor**" is excellent—and much better than any **Orville Redenbacher** popcorn I've tried.
- In a restaurant, don't accept food or drinks that are too sweet, too salty, too spicy, too rare or too well-done. Hot food should not be cold. Cold drinks should not be warm. Carbonated beverages should not be flat.
- If you're served a meal in someone's house and you don't like it, eat a little and invent an excuse for not finishing it.
- If you get sick after a restaurant meal, call the restaurant and the Board of Health. Wife Marilyn and I once got food poisoning from stuffed lobster and our prompt calls probably stopped others from being poisoned.
- If two of you are not very hungry, don't be embarrassed to share a meal. Maybe buy an extra soup or dessert.
- As you get older, you'll probably require less food. It's OK to skip meals or have a piece of fruit and a cheese chunk.
- If you like "Jewish style" chopped liver, (a) don't order it in hot weather, and (b) don't order it in any restaurant that does not have Jewish or Greek owners.
- Traditional ideas of what gets eaten at what time of the day are guidelines, not commandments. I often have cold pizza for breakfast, or soup, or microwaved Chinese food.
- Hot chocolate from a **Keurig** machine will taste better if you add some milk or **Cremora**.
- Don't be reluctant to ask for a doggie bag. *You* paid for the food, and *you* get to decide where and when you'll eat it. Label the package with date and contents. Don't lose it or forget about it. Again, don't refrigerate garbage.
- Be creative with doggie bags. I enjoyed a breakfast blend of leftover egg-foo-young and corned beef hash.

- Managers of movie theaters will not be happy if you bring in food and drinks from the outside. Theaters don't make much money by selling movie tickets and are dependent on revenue from expensive snacks to stay in business. However, theaters always provide free drinking water from water fountains. It's unlikely that you'll be stopped from bringing in an empty bottle, filling it at the fountain and drinking the free water at your seat.
- Don't be afraid to ask for substitutions and upgrades. You can probably get a second salad instead of a vegetable or pay 50 cents more for a bowl of soup instead of a cup. Greek-owned diners are often very flexible in giving customers exactly what they want—not just what's on the menu. I love *gyros* but not the white *tzatziki* sauce that is normally applied to the grilled meat in Greek restaurants. I always ask for a "red gyro," with tomato sauce.
- In some restaurants—but not in any Greek-owned restaurant I ever visited—a cup and a bowl of soup contain the same amount of soup. Be careful, and don't be afraid to ask.
- At home, try modifying prepared soups. Add chunks of chicken to chicken-noodle or chicken-rice soup. Add crushed tomatoes to Manhattan clam chowder. Add chopped clams to any clam chowder.
- In a buffet restaurant, you can get creative with soups, too. Add cheese and croutons to French onion soup. Combine wonton soup and egg drop soup. Put some rice and/or shrimp or chicken in egg drop soup.
- Even in a very cold refrigerator, meat sauce doesn't last for a month. It starts to stink and it sprouts disgusting fuzzy stuff.
- If you can't find dishes, glasses, forks, etc., look in the dishwasher. Maybe you were more organized than you thought.
- Prepared foods can save time but may taste crappy or be too sweet, too salty, etc. Ask for a sample before buying.
- The thing in the dishwasher that looks like a basket with a handle may actually *be* a basket with a handle. It's much easier to lift the basket out and put it on the counter for unloading silverware rather than constantly bending over.
- If you buy a large loaf of bread, divide it into thirds. Put one third in the fridge and the other two thirds in the freezer.
- If someone else usually dispenses your medications, make a chart so you can check off the drugs as you take them. I also use my chart to record my glucose levels and blood pressure. I may spot a problem, or provide info for a doc.
- If you find some food in the supermarket that seems interesting, buy a small portion so you can test it. One of my traditional rules has been "never buy less than a pound of anything." That rule was suspended while wife Marilyn was in a hospital. It's no good to eat one ounce and throw away 15 ounces.

Marilyn & Michael's Famous Clam Sauce (with steamed clams bonus):

1. Get two dozen fresh littleneck clams, (roughly 2.5—3 inches in diameter). You can keep them in the fridge for a couple of days before use.
2. Put a big pot in your sink. Start filling it with cold water, and put the clams in the pot, one by one. If any clam has opened, tap lightly on the shell. If the clam doesn't close, throw it out.

3. Every 10-15 minutes, dump the water out, and fill again. Continue this rinse cycle for an hour or more. The more you rinse, the less sand in the clams.
4. Take out enough clams to fill a microwavable bowl. Hold each clam under running water and rub off any clinging dirt. Put the clams in the bowl, without any clam on top of another clam.
5. Heat the clams in your microwave oven until all of the shells have opened. Save the juice. You can freeze it if you're not making the sauce right away. You can eat the clams now or save them to put into the sauce.
6. Chop up a huge onion, and two big garlics.
7. Pour extra virgin olive oil into a large skillet (one of those things that used to be called a frying pan). Let it get about a half-inch deep.
8. When the oil is hot, carefully dump in the chopped onions and garlic, and spread it around. Add about a half-stick of butter, maybe three tablespoons of oregano, and, if you feel like it, red or white pepper and maybe some parsley.
9. Stir every few minutes, for about ten minutes.
10. When the onions have gotten a little bit browned, carefully dump in the clams (BUT NOT THE JUICE) from four cans of chopped clams, or a quart of fresh chopped clams if you can get them.
11. Add the juice from the clams you cooked in the microwave.
12. Add 4-6 ounces of dry white wine.
13. Stir every few minutes as the mixture simmers.
14. Cook your linguine and pour on the sauce. Add the steamed clams if you like, in or out of the shells.
15. *MANGIA!* (Eat!)
16. Any sauce left in your plate should be sopped up with Italian bread (stale is OK) or added to clam chowder.

Make a high-speed nuclear hotdog

If you have an urge for a hotdog/frankfurter/wiener and don't want to ignite the grill or use the stove or broiler, you can use your microwave. Here's how:

1. Put a hotdog in a hotdog roll.
2. Wrap it in one thickness of a paper towel.
3. Heat it in your microwave oven. (You may have to experiment to determine the proper time. I set my nuker for 45 seconds.)
4. Remove, unwrap, apply desired condiments.
5. Enjoy.

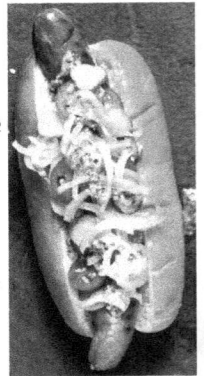

Sink spaghetti

Before I was allowed to use the stove, I tried to cook spaghetti by putting it in the bathroom sink and running hot water over it for about 15 minutes. After it softened up, I dumped in a jar of sauce and stirred the glop. It was terrible, but I ate some of it. I didn't realize that boiling was a critical part of the pasta- preparation process. I also failed in my effort to store ice cream sandwiches in my toy chest by loading up the big maple box with ice cubes. I'm sorry about the mess on the floor, Mom.

Barbecued spaghetti

Many years later, while waiting for the kitchen to be completed in my new house, we did most of our cooking on a barbecue grill on our rear deck. We even tried to make spaghetti. The water almost boiled. That mushy meal tasted almost as bad as sink spaghetti.

Michael's improved homemade egg cream

The egg cream is nothing like a crème egg and contains neither eggs nor cream and is like an ice cream soda made with milk instead of ice cream. It has been a basic part of the New York City diet for over a hundred years.

It apparently was invented in a Brooklyn "candy store" (like a rural general store moved to the city—plus a soda fountain) and gradually became common at other candy stores. The egg cream was copied by soda jerks in drug stores and ice cream parlors throughout New York City (but maybe not Staten Island—which is more like Kansas than New York).

The drink then followed New Yorkers to Long Island, Connecticut, New Jersey, Florida, Las Vegas and California.

In an episode of *Law & Order: SVU*, a little girl told a detective that her kidnapper made her a *chocolate fizzy*. It was an egg cream.

I enjoyed my first egg creams at **Morty & Etta's** candy store on East 205th Street near the Grand Concourse in The Bronx. When my family moved from The Bronx to New Haven in 1952, my father taught multiple soda jerks how to make egg creams. I later taught the owner of a diner in Milford, Connecticut how to make them.

The origin of the name is open to debate, as are the techniques for making the drink. Writing in *The New Yorker* magazine, **Eric Lach** declared that "egg cream" is a misnomer. I am willing to recognize that publication as an authority on the egg cream.

My wife and I have been making egg creams at home for many years. Hers are too foamy and sweet for me, and my own had too little foam and too little flavor—and were never cold enough. I have a 1970s- or 80s-vintage Pepsi glass with a bulbous top that has become my official egg cream glass because it enables me to judge the mix pretty well, and the large top surface provides plenty of room for the foam.

Traditionally, there are only three ingredients. 1. COLD Milk (whole is best, but you can use less-fatty types.) 2. Chocolate syrup (Fox's U-Bet is the traditional syrup but Hershey's is fine.) 3. COLD Seltzer (best from a real seltzer bottle, but you can use club soda) I recently started adding a fourth ingredient—some crushed ice—and the result is heavenly. For me, there is no such thing as a drink that's too cold. I love beer in frosted mugs. I'd probably love an egg cream in a frosted mug.

There is great controversy about the proportions and the sequence for blending the ingredients, and I recommend that you experiment. Here's what I do:

1. Fill about 15% of the glass volume with crushed ice.
2. Fill about 10% with chocolate syrup. (You can also use other syrup flavors including vanilla, cherry and coffee.)
3. Fill about 25% with milk.
4. Stir with a long "iced tea spoon."
5. Fill the rest with seltzer. I pour the seltzer into the spoon and let it overflow into the glass.
6. Stir until you get a thick white frothy head on top of light brown.
7. If you want to get artsy-fartsy, drizzle some chocolate syrup onto the foam.
8. Drink with or without a straw. Without a straw you'll get a telltale egg cream mustache—nice for people and dogs who kiss you.
9. Drink quickly (with a salty pretzel rod, if available) before the bubbles dissipate and the ice melts. You have only about two minutes of ecstasy.

[Egg cream photo from Max Falkowitz. Thanks!]

What language do they speak at Mickey Dee's?

The Inn of the Golden Arches (Mickey Dee's/McDonald's) featured a "Grilled Onion Cheddar Burger." It sounded really good because I like grilled onions, cheddar and burgers. However, since I didn't like the pickles, mustard or ketchup often plopped onto McBurgers, I asked a simple question: "what comes on the Grilled Onion Cheddar Burger?"

The cashier looked at me with puzzlement. I repeated my question. She shrugged her shoulders but said *absolutely nothing*.

And at Chipotle?

Wife Marilyn and I were at Chipotle for lunch. When I reached the checkout, I made what I assumed was a simple request.

I asked the cashier for a tray so I could carry our meals to a table. She looked puzzled, muttered something undecipherable, and called a co-worker for help.

He explained that the cashier understood Spanish but very little English.

OK, I recognize that it can be hard to learn a second language. But shouldn't a restaurant cashier be taught such a basic word as "tray"?

And in Quebec?

A few years ago, I was at a wonderful produce market/self-service restaurant in Quebec, Canada. When I got to the cash register, the pleasant cashier said "bonjour" and "merci" to customers—many of whom were apparently Americans like me.

When it was my turn to pay, I saw a big kettle of soup with a ladle and a stack of bowls.

I assumed the soup was self-service and started to scoop some soup into a bowl.

The cashier glared at me, and asked in perfect American English, "what the fuck do you think you're doing?" Apparently, the soup was not self-service. I replaced the ladle and muttered "excusez-moi."

Chapter 101
Health can be sickening

In the early 1960s, **Patrick J. Leone** taught health and science at the **Dr. Susan S. Sheridan Junior High School** in New Haven, Connecticut.

Leone preferred that his name be pronounced as a two-syllable anglicized "Lee-On," and he was obviously shaken if anyone acknowledged his Italian ancestry and pronounced the final vowel.

This seemed strange, because New Haven was a very Italian city with many Italian-American teachers and students in the schools. Another Italian-American teacher would deliberately piss him off by calling him "Pasquale" or "Patsy Lay-o-nay."

Leone would squirm and blush.

Unfortunately, Leone had lower standards for his own verbalizations than for others, pronouncing health as "helt" and science as "sines."

His speech defect was complemented by a persistent memory problem. Every time my class entered his room—three times a week for ten months—he'd look at us plaintively and ask, "Division Eight, helt or sines?" He didn't know which subject he was supposed to teach us; and even when we confirmed that we were in his classroom to learn about helt, he sometimes tried to teach us sines.

Leone knew a lot about sines. He once told a class that "Det (death) kills instantly."

Unlike our friends who had other teachers for helt, or health, we had *no* textbooks. Leone blamed the problem on the "Board of Ett," and for months he assured us that the texts would be arriving soon.

Leone gave no lectures. There were no discussions and few quizzes. Most of our classtime consisted of laboriously copying into our notebooks the words that he had laboriously written onto the blackboard.

Sometimes one of us would notice an error on the board, such as a "to" that should have been a "too." Usually Leone would blame "juvenile delinquents" who'd sneak into his room during lunch period and change his words. Other times he'd try to justify his writing and deliver a long dissertation on grammar with parts of speech we never heard of in our English classes ("subdulated abominative"). A few times he blamed defective chalk that twisted in his hand.

Leone was a wannabe performer/producer/director. Parents' visiting day was SHOWTIME. Our folks would be welcomed by the class singing the *Brusha Brusha Brusha* song from the **Ipana** toothpaste commercial (starring **Bucky Beaver**), and then Leone sailed an embalmed bat around the room like a balsawood model airplane. For his grand finale, he squirted the children with water from a hypodermic syringe.

I was not the only Michael in our class. The other Michael, whose last name Leone always mispronounced, got sick early in the school year and was out for several months. Leone confused the two Michaels, and frequently reported me for skipping class.

Throughout the school year, there was a mysterious stack of cardboard boxes gathering dust in a corner of the classroom.

In June, with summer approaching, the kids were feeling frisky, and one of them dared to sneak into the unoccupied classroom during lunch period. He cut open the cartons and found our *missing textbooks,* which had been in the room since September and had not been delayed by the inefficient bureaucrats downtown.

The burglar noticed that one carton had been opened previously. And after flipping through some pages, the familiar words soon made it obvious that Leone had removed one of our books for personal use.

Each week, he secretly copied a chapter onto the blackboard, and then we'd spend three days copying those same words from the blackboard into our notebooks.

The kids in our class had assumed that Leone, and not some wise medical authority hired by **Houghton Mifflin** or **Prentice Hall**, was the author of those words we were ordered to copy each day, while Leone sat and stared out the window and hummed for 45 minutes.

We were never allowed to see "our" books because Patsy Leone found it much easier to copy and have us copy, than to learn and to teach.

He was not a helty man.

I've lived many years longer than I expected to, thanks to skilled doctors, good insurance and effective medications. However, there are occasional lapses—some serious and some simply silly.

What they don't teach at medical school

In the 1980s I had a severe pain in a foot. I no longer remember which foot it was or what caused the pain, but it hurt so bad that I went to a hospital.

I was interviewed, tested and X-rayed, and given a bill to sign. I was also given one crutch that was adjusted to the right length for my height, and a prescription for a few weeks of painkillers. The crutch is a simple device. It comes without a user's manual, and it wasn't hard to figure out how to use it. I raised my bad foot off the ground, let the tip of the crutch serve as a substitute foot, and headed for the exit.

The orthopedic surgeon who had examined me yelled at me to STOP and come back. He explained to me that the crutch is "supposed to be used on the good side, not the bad side." That didn't make much sense, but I'm not a doctor.

Then the orthopedic nurse who had assisted the orthopedic surgeon, yelled at him. She said that the crutch is "supposed to be used on the bad side, not the good side." That *did* make sense, but I'm not a doctor. The two medical experts then started a lengthy and spirited debate, each citing appropriate arguments for their divergent opinions. I stood around for a while, and then I plopped into a chair. The audience grew, with supporters for each side cheering and kibitzing.

After ten minutes it became apparent that neither one was going to surrender, and that no higher authority was likely to intervene. My wife was waiting in the parking lot and I had to get out of there, so I came up with a solution. I grabbed a second crutch off a rack, grasped it with my other hand, raised my bad foot off the ground, and hopped out of there without looking back.

What they should teach at medical school

In 1999, to help a busy storekeeper, I went behind the front counter to answer his phone.

I looked ahead toward the phone and didn't notice a step. I fell forward. Reflexively, I put both hands out to break my fall.

My left hand impacted the sharp edge of a metal electrical box. A long flap of skin peeled away from my left thumb, and I was quickly bleeding like the proverbial stuck pig. An ambulance rushed me to the hospital and a hand surgeon was summoned from the golf course and the ugly gash was stitched up.

I still have a faded U-shaped scar and limited motion in that thumb. The precisely calculated permanent disability paid me not nearly enough money to retire to Monaco. I was instructed to see my own doctor in a week to have the dressing changed.

When I did, I mentioned that my right hand—not the one with the cut—was swollen and hurt a lot, and I was X-rayed. The film revealed that I broke the *fifth metacarpal bone*, a bone in the midsection of the hand that connects to the pinky. A week earlier, when I was in the emergency room, I had complained about pain in both hands and the E. R. staff knew I had landed on both hands, and my right hand was obviously red and swollen. But all they cared about was the hand that was gushing blood all over their nice clean floor.

I think it would have been logical to examine *both* hands, but I didn't go to medical school.

What doctors don't tell patients

The pinky is a small and not particularly useful finger, but an orthopedic technician constructed a monstrous cast to contain, protect and immobilize it.

My pinky and fourth finger of my right hand were wrapped in gauze and encased in plaster and frozen in a curl, pointed at my palm. The cast covered all of my hand except for three fingers and extended beyond my wrist to just below my elbow.

You might think that having three functioning fingers meant life was OK, but life actually sucked. I'm right-handed and the cast weighed so much and restricted me so much that I could hardly use the hand. I couldn't even dress myself. It took so long to unzip my fly that I often peed in my pants. I saved a Post-it note I wrote a few words on at that time. It's hard to read.

Using a computer keyboard and mouse was extremely difficult. I ultimately hung a wire from the ceiling over my desk with a loop that could support my arm while I tried to type. My typing was a little bit neater than my handwriting.

When I got the cast, I was told to come back in eight weeks to have it removed.

It was a miserable eight weeks. I gained new sympathy for amputees. I couldn't drive, and I had to learn how to urinate lefty if I had the need to pee while out of the house.

At home, it was easier to just "drop trou" and then pee hands-free in the shower. (I hope my wife isn't reading this.) Wiping my ass was difficult, uncomfortable and unsanitary.

I'll spare you the gruesome details and just say the cast got dirty.

Eating was sloppy, too, and sleeping was never restful. I went in the swimming pool with plastic bags over both arms, as instructed. I perspired inside the bags, so the cast and bandages got wet anyway. I had created my own, personal, enclosed weather system—and there was a danger of softening the plaster, so I gave up on water sports for a while.

When I had a mid-arm itch, I shoved a chopstick into the cast to scratch it. Lovemaking was possible, but dangerous, and required caution. Casts are great for S&M fans. Life goes on.

When the eagerly anticipated date finally arrived, I went back to the orthopedic surgeon's office, expecting but not receiving quick relief. A nurse X-rayed me and looked at my cast and told me that I was doing fine and should come back in a month. I protested, saying that I had been told that the cast would be removed after two months, and my time was *up*.

She smiled and said, "I know. We *lied* to you. We always lie about the time casts stay on. If we told patients the truth, they'd get depressed and cut the casts off."

Who decides who decides?

On a Saturday morning some years ago, my wife Marilyn's eyes were burning, possibly because makeup got under her contact lenses. She called her ophthalmologist, and he told her to immediately go to **White Plains Hospital**, about ten minutes from our home.

Marilyn was promptly examined and fixed up, and the hospital submitted a bill to **Empire Blue Cross/Blue Shield**, that provided our medical insurance.

A few weeks later we received a notice that the claim was denied. This didn't seem right so I called customer service (more like dis-service). A clerk, probably making minimum wage and lacking any medical training, said that Marilyn *should not have gone to the hospital.*

I pointed out that my wife's doctor, who had decades of experience and was familiar with my wife's eyes, told her to go to the damn hospital! The clerk stood her ground, and I appealed up the chain of command. Ultimately, I got an apology and the hospital got its money, but the ordeal should not have been necessary.

When should you seek care?

Years ago, we were on vacation in Orlando, Florida, and my foot felt like it was on fire. I figured the pain would go away by itself, and we drove south to visit my parents in Delray Beach. The foot still hurt, and I went to the emergency department in a local hospital. I forgot what the diagnosis was. Maybe it was gout. But they prescribed medication, and I soon felt fine.

I called my insurance company to find out the proper procedure for submitting a claim. The customer service rep started filling out a form while I was on the phone. She asked me when the pain started and when I went to the hospital. I didn't realize it, but they were *trick questions*.

The claim was denied because more than 48 hours had elapsed between the onset of the pain and my arrival at the hospital. If the time was over 48 hours, my problem was *not* considered an emergency. I should *not* have gone to the emergency department and the insurer would *not* pay the bill! **I learned an important lesson. If something hurts, and even if you think the pain will go away if you do nothing, go to a hospital right away!**

Medical problems can be fads, and money-makers.

- In the early 1980s, many dentists suddenly diagnosed patients as having "**TMJ**" (temporomandibular joint) disorder, which limits jaw movement, often causing pain.
- A few years later, orthopedists discovered the profitability in diagnosing and treating "**CTS**" (Carpal Tunnel Syndrome), a condition with excessive pressure on a wrist nerve. Symptoms can include numbness, tingling, and weakness in the hand and arm.
- Now, in the early 21st century, it seems that most human beings are "**pre-diabetic**." I had a spot on my face that was declared to be "pre-cancer." Aren't we all pre-something? Isn't birth pre-death?
- Treatments can be silly, useless fads, too: LEDs to cure neuropathy, safflower oil for weight loss, coffee enemas, juice cleanses, supplements, probiotics and prebiotics, corn flakes, exercises to cure too-frequent urination, sexual abstinence, crude oil bathing, anal contraction.

Chapter 102
The obligatory pizza section
(plus disgusting foods I like)

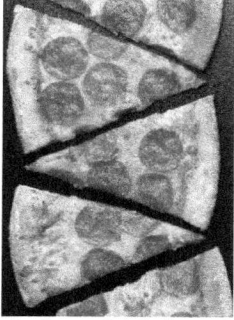

I live and write in Hamden, Connecticut. Hamden is in New Haven County, an area known for—and proud of—excellent Neapolitan pizza. (Many of our traditional pizzerias spell pizza as "apizza" and pronounce the beloved word as *ah-beetz*). "New Haven" is often pronounced *N'haven*.

Besides our ah-beetz, you'll also encounter *tomato pies* in this city.

According to *USA Today* three of the nation's best pizza joints are located on one street (Wooster Street) in New Haven's "Little Italy."

Some of our local pizzerias have been owned by the same families for two or three generations, and new pizzerias seem to open every few weeks. Because of the loyalty of the locals, it has been hard for the national chains, which have been so successful elsewhere, to build businesses here.

Everyone in this part of Connecticut has one or two favorite pizzerias (I have four faves). We are experts, fans, aficionados and *snobs*. People here are less likely to switch pizza sources than to switch cola, perfume or jeans brands.

By Mafia decree (or maybe simple collusion) most local pizzerias are closed on Mondays so pizza makers can spend time with their families.

Apparently, **Pizza Hut** and **Domino's** have dispensations from the Pope or from *il Capo di Tutti Capi* ("the boss of all bosses") in the Mafia, and are open seven days a week. This means that locals who must have something vaguely pizza-like on the first workday of the week, will go to the Hut or Dom's on that day—but probably not on other days.

On all days, the pizza chains serve customers who have recently immigrated from places like Kentucky or Utah and don't know what *real* pizza is supposed to look and taste like. New Haven pies traditionally have charred crusts. Newbies complain that they are "burnt."

Pizza can be baked (or charred) with heat from gas, electricity, wood, charcoal, coal, oil or maybe other sources. I know a woman who converted her Bronx home's furnace from coal to gas. She donated the coal to a pizzeria in exchange for a lifetime supply of pizza.

- "In any given day, more than 40 million Americans will eat pizza," according to BBC.
- On TV's *The Food That Built America*, we are told that pizza is the most popular food in the world!
- *Britannica* says: "Americans love pizza so much that they eat 100 acres of pizza a day. If you don't measure your pizza consumption in acres, that's about 350 slices of pizza per second!"
- According to *Statista*, "Pizza is probably American's number-one dinner choice. It is estimated that more than 200 million Americans eat frozen pizza, well over half the total U.S. population."

Some of the original Wooster Street pizzerias are expanding nationally, both to nearby cities and states, and as far away as Florida. In some places, local pizzerias use "New Haven" or "Wooster Street" in their names or on their menus and websites.

- **Pete's New Haven Style Apizza** is in Washington, DC
- **Fantini's Italian Restaurant** in Stuart, Florida is proud of its "New Haven Style Apizza." Owner Jimmy Fantini worked at **Pepe's** as a teenager. According to the *New York Times*, "he has filled his pizzeria with New Haven paraphernalia—old pictures of New Haven, a Yale banner, even an 'apizza' definition. But even he says nothing can beat a real New Haven slice, made in New Haven, eaten in New Haven. Is anything ever going to be better than the original? As far as I know, no."
- **Jet's** in New Haven (!), Michigan is near Deroit. Naturally it serves Detroit-style pizza, but it also serves pizzas inspired by New York and New Haven pizzerias.
- **Papa's Pizza** has two delicious restaurants in Milford, Connecticut, near my former home and a few miles from New Haven. Its menu proclaims, "New Haven Style Pizza."
- Also in Milford is **New Haven Pizza Place**, appropriately on New Haven Avenue.
- **Eli's Brick Oven Pizza and Market** is near my current home in Hamden, Connecticut. It promotes both "brick oven pizza" and "New Haven style pizza." It's convenient and popular, but I don't like its pizza. Others disagree, of course. *De gustibus non est disputandum* (Latin for "In matters of taste, there can be no disputes."
- A bit north of New Haven is **Randy's Wooster St. Pizza**, in Manchester, Connecticut.

According to *Foodrepublic.com*, "Distinguished by a delightfully crispy yet chewy crust that is expertly charred, as well as a distinct lack of mozzarella cheese, the foundation of a New Haven pizza is close in style to traditional Neapolitan pizzas. The difference is that New Haven pies use sturdier bread flour in order to keep the slices from collapsing, and the pies are cooked lower and slower. While Neapolitan pizza is famously baked in ovens that reach over 1,000 degrees Fahrenheit, so the pizza can be cooked in as short as one minute, New Haven pizza is baked in the same type of oven, but farther away from the heat source. The pies cook at around 600 to 650 degrees Fahrenheit for roughly five to 12 minutes.

The classic toppings for apizza are crushed Italian tomatoes, Pecorino Romano cheese and olive oil, but you can also get your pizza with other toppings like sausage, clams with bacon (which is a local specialty), and vegetables. The name "apizza" is a nod to the dialect of early Italian immigrants who settled in New Haven."

As a young child, I once visited my paternal grandparents in Brooklyn, and we went to a local pizzeria. I was shocked that the place did not offer meatball as a topping, which was common in New Haven. The cook made me a meatball-topped pie as a special favor for Grampa Walter, and it was later added to the menu.

(Shown) Vaguely round, sloppy and delicious traditional New Haven ah-beetz from **Sally's**, as opposed to the perfectly round and bland pizza from a national chain's factory.

My cousin **Dave Marcus** is a pizza *maven* (enthusiastic expert) with very high standards—but he will sometimes tolerate

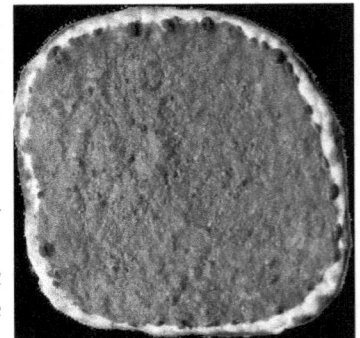

chain pizza. Rather than dismiss Pizza Hut's mass-produced products as substandard pizza, Dave says, "It's not pizza. It's pizza HUT."

(from *Wikpedia*] Henry Winkler, Lyle Lovett, Chris Murphy and Michael Bolton discuss the history of New Haven Pizza in Gorman Bechard's documentary *Pizza: A Love Story*. In the film the black char imparted from the ovens is described as adding a smoky barbeque flavor not found elsewhere. A recurring phrase spoken by several in the movie is, "It's not burnt, it's charred."

Ken Morico wrote, "When I was a kid, I loved pizza. Growing up in New Haven, Connecticut, there were so many great pizza restaurants around. At the time, I didn't realize how special they really were, and how difficult it is to create a great pizza. The secret, I found out, is in the rich tomato flavor with flavorful San Marzano tomatoes, spicy oregano, and thin, crispy & charred crust. New Haven pizza requires more time and expensive ingredients in my opinion. For instance, you can taste the sauce and actually SEE it in the pizza. In fact, the sauce is often so good that a popular New Haven Pizza is plain—no toppings—just the sauce.

In cheap pizzas you'll often see just gobs of low-quality cheese covering a little bit of sauce. Maybe New Yorkers care more about speed and money... for me, I'll take a New Haven pizza. New Haven pizza also often has a little bit of charring... the coal-fired ovens make it delicious. For the home baker, it probably won't be possible to achieve the charring because home ovens don't get very hot, but we can get a little close."

Eater.com says, "There is pizza, and then there is *apizza*. New Haven-style pizza is the latter; a hotter, crispier, and dirtier descendant of Neapolitan style pie. What ribs are to Kansas City, cheesesteak to Philadelphia, and crabcakes to Baltimore, pizza is to New Haven. If you grew up in or around the "Elm City," your pizza parlor allegiance can be fierce. So how did Connecticut's second largest city become ground zero for some of the best pizza in the United States? Just what is New Haven-style pizza?

First, a bit of history. At the turn of the twentieth century, New Haven became a popular town for Italian families who settled in the United States during the country's diaspora. Neighborhoods such as Wooster Square became home to many displaced southern Italian families primed with palates that appreciated the thin-crusted Neapolitan style pizza of their homeland."

In *Forbes*, **Scott Wiener**, founder of New York's **Scott's Pizza Tours**, said, "It's a real gritty style of pizza. You're even going to get oddly cut slices. I love that about New Haven." **Frank Pepe's** nephew **Salvatore Consiglio** started **Sally's Apizza** in 1938, on Wooster Street near his uncle's place. **Modern Apizza** also opened during the 1930s. With Pepe's, these pizzerias make up the trinity of New Haven pizzerias, according to **Colin Caplan**, a pizza tour guide in New Haven.

Caplan added that **Frank Sinatra** and **John F. Kennedy** favored Sally's. And Pepe's has attracted a long list of celebrity pizza aficionados, including Yale Law graduate **Bill Clinton**.

If you're new to New Haven, according to Caplan, a "plain" pizza from Pepe's, Sally's or Modern will strike you with its flavorful simplicity. It will feature that famous New Haven thin crust, a light sauce of gently crushed tomatoes, Romano cheese and a lashing of olive oil.

While I was happy to eat at any of Wooster Street's famed pizzerias, I most often went to **Abate's**. It did not have long lines of tourists and Yalies, had easy parking, and was next door to **Libby's**, which sold delicious Italian pastries, gelato and ices.

Sally's — For PIZZA

Phone 624-5271

S. A. CONSIGLIO, Mgr. — 237 Wooster Street — New Haven, Conn.

		Small	Med.	Large
Mozzarella	If Mozzarella is requested on any Pizza there is an extra charge of:	1.45	2.90	4.35
Anchovies		1.45	2.90	4.35
Bacon		1.75	3.50	5.25
Sausage		1.90	3.80	5.60
Tuna Fish	.25 (Small)	1.90	3.80	5.60
Onion	.50 (Med.)	1.45	2.90	4.35
Mushroom	.75 (Large)	1.90	3.80	5.60
Peppers		1.45	2.90	4.35
Clams		1.90	3.80	5.60
Plain		1.20	2.40	3.60
Pepperoni		2.00	4.00	5.90

All Special Combinations, Extra Charge

Rheingold   Schaefer   Miller

Soda   -   Coffee   -   Hot Chocolate

Friday, Open 12:00 Noon to 12:00 P.M.

Sadly, Abate's was badly damaged by a fire in 2023, but reopened in North Haven, which is closer to where I now live. Abate's is connected to a major ah-beetz dynasty in the New Haven area, with several branches. As a kid I often went to Abate-owned **Luigi's** in the Westville section of New Haven. Back then a small pie cost just 65 cents.

As with most things, pizza prices have increased dramatically over the years. The ancient menu from Sally's shows prices starting at a lowly $1.45.

I've never been to the raved-about **Bar, Zeneli Pizzeria & Cucina Napoletana** or **Zuppardi's** in nearby West Haven. My only experience with the popular **Modern** was disappointing. It was takeout, and cold.

I lived in Milford, Connecticut before moving to Hamden and was a regular at **Papa's Pizza**. Its pies were as delicious as those in New Haven, and as with Abate's, there were no long lines of tourists and Yalies.

I always order pizza "heavy on the sauce, light on the mootz." Some people are pizza *dough* aficionados, but to me, *the essence of pizza is its sauce*. I'll even eat tomato sauce right from a jar with a spoon—or a finger. I never order "extra cheese" or eat "white pizza."

Frank Pepe Pizzeria Napoletana (usually called "Pepe's") in New Haven is famous for, and allegedly the originator of, *white clam pizza*. It's very popular, but to me, there is a special relationship between tomatoes and shellfish, so I *shunned it*. I once ordered a red clam pizza at **Papa's** in Milford. Someone in the kitchen assumed the order was an error and made it *white*. I rejected it and it was replaced.

One day, pizza-loving **Harry Tramontanis** and I decided to do a definitive comparative taste test (what *Car & Driver* magazine calls a "comparo"). We went to the original Pepe's on Wooster Street and ordered both red and white pies. (Part of the test is on *YouTube*.) The test results shocked us both. The white pie was surprisingly good. The red, which we assumed would be superior, was disappointing—probably because it didn't have enough sauce. Nevertheless, I've never eaten a white pie since that test.

Some of the best pizza I ever had was not lunch or supper in a pizzeria, but breakfast on a beach. **Big Green Truck Pizza** was founded by New Havener **Doug Coffin**. The company operates five trucks that travel through Connecticut doing over 50 parties a week during the height of their season.

The trucks are ancient International Harvesters. Each truck is restored and customized with a wood-fired oven, refrigerator, espresso machine, sink, storage space and more. The sides on the bed of the truck come off and function as the prep and serving tables, so no space is wasted. Pies from the hot wood fire come out FAST, and many types are available

There has long been a powerful affinity between Jewish people and Italian people, and there are some culinary similarities. I can't think of any Jews who don't like Italian food. My wife's father was Italian-American and her mother was Jewish. She made great meals of both types.

o   I used to know a teenage boy who was the grandson and nephew of kosher rabbis. He introduced me to the joys of "double-pork pizza"—with bacon *and* pepperoni.

- Scott **Wiener** conducts pizza tours in New York City.
- Colin **Caplan** is a pizza tour guide in New Haven.
- Dave **Portnoy** founded Barstool Sports. His *One Bite Pizza Reviews* is an internet show with reviews of pizza from restaurants around the world, ranking them from zero to ten.
- I assume that Wiener, Caplan and Portnoy are members of my Tribe (i.e. Jewish). If I'm wrong, it's an understandable error.

Every culture and ethnic group has disgusting foods.

Judaism has some that are so disgusting that I refuse to eat them, and others that are disgusting to some but and quite loveable to me.

- To me, *gefilte fish* looks like frog larvae (potential tadpoles), and I always avoid it.
- *Cholent* is a stew. I don't like stews and have never tasted cholent. *Wikipedia* tells us [edited] that "Shabbat stews were developed to conform with Jewish laws that prohibit cooking on the Sabbath. The pot is brought to a boil on Friday before the Sabbath begins and warmed until the following day. It originated as barley porridge in ancient Judea. Over the centuries Jews created variations based on local foods and neighborhood influence."
- *Gribenes* (three syllables) consists of pieces of crisp chicken or goose skin and onions, fried in poultry fat. It's delicious, addictive, and fatal in large quantities. I seldom eat it—but I love it. It's one of those "to die from" dishes. *Wikipedia* tells us that "gribenes can be eaten as a snack on rye or pumpernickel bread with salt, or used in recipes such as chopped liver, or all of the above. It is often served as a side dish with pastrami on rye or hot dogs. The dish is eaten as a midnight snack or appetizer. In Louisiana, Jews add gribenes to jambalaya in place of *treyf* (non-kosher) shrimp. It was served to children on *challah* bread as a treat. It can also be served in a **GLT**, a modified version of a BLT sandwich that replaces bacon with gribenes."
- Some people reject a *tongue sandwich*, merely because of its name. I *love* tongue, no matter what it's called, from the Katz's Deli in Manhattan (shown) or the one in Woodbridge, Connecticut. They share a name but are not related.
- Some people say that *Gehakte Leber* (chopped chicken liver) looks like dog crap. I don't like canine feces, but I *love* liver. At family Passover meals (*seders*), I usually traded my gefilte for another relative's gehakte.
- Early in our marriage, new wife Marilyn hosted parts of both families for a meal in our Bronx home. We bought chopped liver at a local Jewish deli. Marilyn's cousin Barbara (a Jew married to a Catholic) advised Marilyn to add some chopped onions to the liver, to con my parents into believing it was homemade.

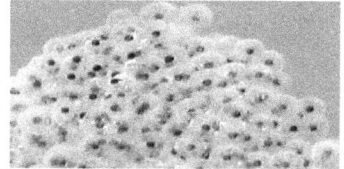

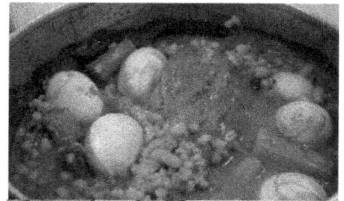

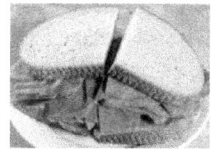

I love many Asian dishes, but have never tasted *fugu*, the sometimes-fatal Japanese blowfish. My reluctance may have kept me alive. According to *Wikipedia*, the inhabitants of Japan have eaten fugu for centuries. However, Fugu has lethal amounts of the poison tetrodotoxin.

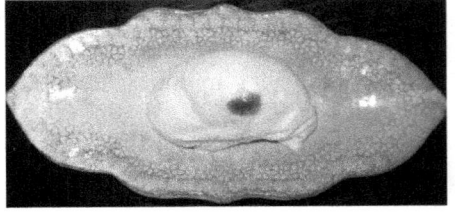

The poison paralyzes muscles while the victim stays fully conscious. The poisoned victim is unable to breathe and eventually dies from asphyxiation. There is no known antidote for fugu poison. The standard treatment is to support the respiratory and circulatory systems until the poison is metabolized and excreted by the victim's body.

Because of the potentially fatal poison, governments in Japan, Korea and some other countries require meticulous preparation to eliminate poisonous components and prevent the fish meat from being contaminated. Only chefs who have qualified after three or more years of rigorous training are allowed to prepare the fish. Preparation at home occasionally leads to accidental death.

No thanks! I'll stick to sushi, sashimi, miso, gyoza and teriyaki.

YUCKY or YUMMY?

It's been said that the bravest man in the history of the world was the first guy who ate a raw clam. Or maybe it was really a raw oyster. Or a lobster. It doesn't matter much. The principle is the same. Some delicacies are best devoured in the dark, at least for the first time.

Most lobsters are dark colored, usually greenish to blend in with the ocean floor, but they can be found in many colors and turn orange or red when cooked. Lobsters with unusual coloring—even blue or white—are very rare, and are usually not eaten, but are released back into the water or donated to aquariums. Lobsters live up to an estimated 45 to 50 years in the wild, but much less in restaurants' tanks.

There are more than 50 varieties of lobster. In another book, I described the tiny crayfish (or crawfish) as "a cockroach wearing a lobster costume."

Most lobsters served in restaurants weigh about 20 ounces, but according to *Guinness World Records*, the largest lobster ever caught was in Canada, weighing over 44 pounds. In general, lobsters are 10 to 20 inches long. They move by slowly walking on the sea floor but can swim *backward*. A speed of 11 miles per hour was recorded.

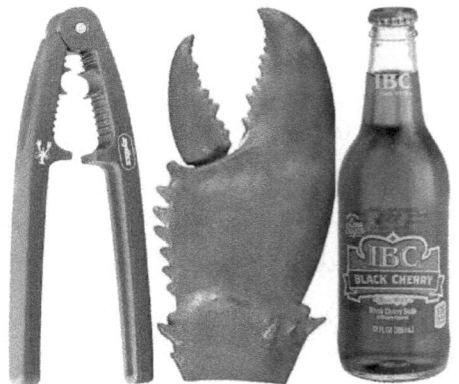

Lobsters, like snails and spiders, have blue blood—unlike humans and many other red-blooded animals. Lobsters possess a green *hepatopancreas*, called the *tomalley*, which functions as both lobster liver and pancreas.

One of my kitchen drawers contains a lobster shell cracking tool. Sadly, it's more often used to open soda bottles than lobster claws.

Despite their scary appearance, I *love* to eat lobster. The super-spicy Italian *lobster fra diavalo* is one of my favorite dishes. I also love lobster rolls (either hot as served in southern New England or the cold ones sold up north), grilled or steamed or baked or roasted or broiled or boiled lobster, cold lobster, stuffed lobster, lobster tails and claws, lobster chowder, lobster bisque, lobster sauce (Chinese and Italian), lobster salad and probably more. However, I've never tried lobster Thermidor, lobster Newburg, lobster scampi, lobster ravioli or curried lobster. Some may go onto my gustatory bucket list.

When I eat a lobster, nothing goes to waste. All I leave are shells, antennae and eyes. I even suck the meat and juice from the feelers. Other messy foods are usually eaten without chest protection, but the "lobster bib" is an important invention. There are many choices: basic, beautiful or funny, sized for adults and kids. Most are disposable, others are meant to be saved for reuse.

The lobster has permeated modern life. Many homes have lobster forks, picks and shell crackers. You can find clothing and wallpaper adorned with lobster images, and even dance to *Rock Lobster*. It's a song from the **B-52's**, first released in 1978. It was Number 147 on the *Rolling Stone* "500 Greatest Songs of All Time" list in 2004. The song inspired the name of Georgia's ice hockey team, the **Rock Lobsters**.

While today's lobsters can be expensive delicacies, supposedly native Americans chopped them up to use as crop fertilizer. Wow. What a waste.

Despite its popularity, lobster is forbidden by the dietary laws of Judaism and some branches of Islam. I must note, however, that I was once served lobster in a *Rosh Hashanah* (Jewish New Year) meal served by the former wife of a rabbi!

"Lobbies" or "lobstuhs" are weird. I read a book called *The Secret Life of Lobsters: How Fishermen and Scientists Are Unraveling the Mysteries of Our Favorite Crustacean*. Author **Trevor Corson** informs readers that when a male lobster is horny, he tries to seduce a mate by *squirting her with urine*. Kinky!

Lobsters reproduce sexually when a male deposits a packet of sperm into the female's sperm pouch. The lady lobbie carries the sperm, joins it to her eggs, and carries the eggs until they hatch. Lobsters mate after the females *molt* (lose their shells). Females breed about every two years, and lobster mating occurs in summer when water temperatures reach about 55°F.

In addition to cooking lobsters, eating lobsters and reading about lobsters, I also caught one, while SCUBA diving as a teenager.

They are tough to catch because they can move quickly into hiding places. However, I was once able to grab a big slowpoke. I put it into a nylon mesh bag hanging from my weight belt. He was not a happy prisoner and used one of his mighty claws to chomp through the nylon and *three layers* of my neoprene rubber wetsuit, to give me a painful pinch. I had the final victory, however. I cooked it and ate it and it was delicious.

Since lobsters are hard to catch by hand, most commercial lobster men and lobster ladies use lobster traps ("lobster pots") which lure and confine the hungry crustaceans on the ocean floor.

I've eaten luscious lobsters up and down the east coast, from Canada to Florida. I don't have one favorite lobster provider, but there are several.

I GOT INTO HOT WATER AT
Cindy's
FISH · CHIPS
US Route 1 Freeport, Me.

Presented to
THE PLACE
Guilford, CT
In recognition of
many years of
cooking and serving
THE BEST NON-FRIED CLAMS ON EARTH
United Clam Lovers of America
April 2004
www.WeLoveClams.com

I miss the fabulous **Cindy's**, formerly in Freeport, Maine (photo at left). I've been happily eating at **The Place** in Guilford, Connecticut since 1963. I've had very happy meals at the **Seashore** on City Island in the Bronx, and at several **Red Lobsters**. In some summers, even **Mickey Dee's** sold lobster rolls.

When I was a kid, I could get a superb warm lobster roll at **Jimmie's** in Connecticut's Savin Rock. Back then the price was just 65 cents. Now you may need a mortgage to pay for one.

I first learned about **Cousins Maine Lobster** when the company was seeking an investor on the *Shark Tank* TV show. They now have roving lobster trucks, and one visits my neighborhood about once a month.

Years ago, a hotel in Stamford, Connecticut (probably the Marriott) promoted a bargain-priced all-you-can-eat deal on lobster "culls"—with one missing or undersized claw. They looked weird but tasted just perfect. **Marshall,** my eager-eating kid brother, once joined me to eat a bunch of sad specimens; and shortly thereafter the bargain deal was discontinued. This reminds me of a famous line: "**No buffet made money feeding a Marcus.**"

This photo shows Michael and Marilyn, with rumps on stumps, at **The Place** in Guilford, Connecticut

Here's what was left after a feast at **The Place**.

In some summers, **Mickey Dee's** offered bargain-priced lobster rolls.

[Sally's and Pepe's photos from Mike Urban. Gribines photo from Zserghe. Cholent photo from Gilabrand. Fugu photo from Qwert1234. Thanks!]

Chapter 103
Bullshit moments can be real

Sometimes, while in a movie theater, on-screen images (such as **The Joker** shooting down the Batplane with one bullet from his gun, or amazing leaps onto speeding cars, helicopters or boats) were so unbelievable that I reflexively yelled, "BULLSHIT."

Some audience members were annoyed, but some fellow cynics applauded or repeated the epithet.

Off-screen, in real life, I've experienced notable bullshit moments.

One time, I was in the backyard of girlfriend Alicia's house with her father, talking about cars. His new Cadillac was nearby in the driveway. I mentioned that I had read that, despite all the many millions of cars that General Motors produced, they had only 1,000 different key patterns.

I said that I happened to have the key for the Chevy Greenbrier van that my father's store used for deliveries, and that it was possible that the Chevy key would open and start his Caddie.

He laughed, of course. I tried it, of course. It worked, of course. I swear it really happened; but if I saw the scene in a movie, I'd yell, "**BULLSHIT!**"

Years ago, a friend and I pedaled our bikes from New Haven to Hartford, a distance of about 40 miles. I don't remember why we went there, but I do remember getting caught in a terrible downpour as we pedaled homeward on the Berlin Turnpike. We were wet, cold, tired, achy and miserable.

Suddenly, I heard a horn honking. I turned my head and saw a familiar vehicle with flashing headlights. The driver was my father, traveling in our station wagon after visiting one of his northern stores. Pop stopped, we loaded our bikes, and had a dry and safe ride home.

I swear it really happened; but if I saw the scene in a movie, I'd yell, "**BULLSHIT!**"

During lunch hour one day in 1971, my buddy **Ken Irsay** and I were wandering around the upper east side of Manhattan, trying to find a BMW dealer. I don't remember which one of us was shopping for a car and which one was just looking, but the dealership wasn't where we thought it would be.

There were no cellphones in those days, and even a pay phone wouldn't help because we didn't know the actual name of the place. We needed a Yellow Pages phone book, where we could go through the classified listing of car dealers until we recognized the right one.

You might think it would be easy to find a phone book in Manhattan, but on that day it wasn't. Every phone booth we found was barren of books. Bodegas, bars and newsstands had White Pages but no Yellow Pages. A restaurant owner said their phone books were for patrons only. A kindly dry cleaner offered his directory, but vital pages had been ripped out.

Disappointed and dejected, and with the end of our lunch hours approaching, we decided to give up and go back to our offices in midtown.

As we walked, a big delivery truck pulled up to the curb ahead of us. A driver and two helpers got out of the cab and opened the side door of the cargo area and set up a ramp to the sidewalk. They went up the ramp into the truck, and then they rolled out three handtrucks, loaded with *five-foot-tall stacks of the Yellow Pages*. We each got a book.

I swear it really happened; but if I saw the scene in a movie, I'd yell, "**BULLSHIT!**"

When I was in the third grade, I dropped my eyeglasses and could not find them. Maybe if I was wearing my glasses, I could find my glasses.

The next day a neighbor found my missing glasses.

They had spent about 30 hours in the *middle of the street*. Strangely, they did not get run over by a vehicle or chewed by a dog. Except for some dust, they were in *perfect* condition.

I swear it really happened; but if I saw the scene in a movie, I'd yell, "**BULLSHIT!**"

[BMW photo by Mic from Reading-Berkshire, United Kingdom. Thanks.]

Michael's Doppelgangers
(with Austin Powers, poet Allen Ginsberg, Ming the Merciless— emperor of the planet Mongo)

Chapter 104
Massive & minor media malfunctions
(I can't avoid addictive alliterations.)

The End.

I'm not perfect in writing or in anything else. There are errors in this book, maybe even on this page. But I *try* to do the right thing. I can't stand people who *don't* try to do the right thing, or don't care, or won't correct errors, or have low standards.

I am frequently amazed at mistakes I find in books, maps, websites, newspapers and magazines that could have and should have been easily avoided or corrected later.

I used to send letters about mistakes, but I stopped.

An employee at a map publisher that showed non-existent streets through many annual editions, told me that they'd sell just as many inaccurate maps as accurate ones, so there's no reason to improve. That's pathetic!

A lot of the errors I've found are esoteric or technical in nature, and I have the feeling that editors assumed that the author was an authority who should be trusted. That's often not the case.

When I read books, I often mark errors I find, and I record the page numbers in the back of the book. I never had a plan to do anything with my evidence of incompetence, but now I have a place to put it—in this chapter. I hope readers will notice *my* errors and tell me about them. Unlike the map maker, I *will* fix them. Thanks.

In the 6/22/08 issue of the *New York Times*, there's an article about the *Mad Men* TV series. Writer **Alex Witchel** says that **Matthew Weiner**, the show's creator, producer and writer "approves every actor, costume, hairstyle and prop." *Entertainment Weekly* said there's "a team of researchers who ensure period accuracy on all fronts."

Weiner goofed on one prop. The suburban New York bedroom of the main character **Don Draper** has a GTE Starlite phone in a color chosen to go with the green velvet headboard. Unfortunately, in the 1960s, that headboard would have been located in AT&T territory, not GTE territory. And since this was before a Supreme Court ruling that allowed freedom of phone use, it would have been illegal to use that phone.

The February 2009 issue of *Automobile* magazine said that **Thomas Edison** was the source of "Mr. Watson, come here." Actually, Edison was the guy with the light bulb, moving pictures, phonograph and concrete houses. **Alex G. Bell** was the one who spoke to Watson on the telephone.

Outskirts Press publishes books for writers who can't or don't want to be published by traditional publishing companies. Its publishing packages include editing services, but the company's own publications can use better editing. On the second page of the foreword to *Self Publishing Simplified*, Outskirts Press boss **Brent Sampson** refers to "off-set" printing, with a hyphen between the "off" and the "set." The term also appears on four other pages in the book.

Thats a really stupid error, especially for a book publisher.

The correct term is "offset," and it's been that way for over 100 years since offset printing was invented by **Ira Rubel** in Nutley, New Jersey.

On his company's website, Sampson urged writers to use an editor and he says, "Errors in your writing cause readers to question your credibility." I question his.

The back-of-book bio says Sampson is an "accomplished artist and writer." His personal website has a stupid flub: "earn up to tens-of-thousands a dollars." So far, I'm not impressed with his writing accomplishments.

The book has a foreword written by Sampson—which goes against the book publishing rules I've learned. Forewords are not supposed to be written by the author. Sampson should have called it a preface or an introduction or hired someone else to write the foreword.

According to Sampson, "**Peter Mark** first published the *Thesaurus* in 1852," strangely ignoring the much more famous **Peter Roget** who published his Thesaurus in the same year. Actually, Mark was the middle name of **Peter Mark Roget**, so Sampson was two-thirds right.

A special **Lifetime Achievement Award** must go to my nearby *New Haven Register*. It's hard to find an issue without a blooper, including misspelled words in giant headlines. One of my all-time favorite issues had two different dates printed on two pages. Another issue dealt with a Civil War veteran who died in the 1700s.

Another Lifetime award goes to a whole class of people, all those writers and editors who misspell the name of an audio equipment company as **Harman-Kardan**. It's Kard**O**n. This has been going on for 40 years or more and will probably never stop.

And, as long as I'm talking about advertising, here's a loud BOO to **Danbury Porsche-Audi**'s radio commercials that mispronounced "Porsche." Unlike English, in German, the final "e" *is* pronounced. It's "por-sha," not "porsh." When a reader of *Popular Mechanix* magazine asked how to pronounce "Porsche," Tom McCahill answered, "Portia." Some of us understood.

Another car commercial BOO goes to **Jaguar**, recently sold by **Ford** to **Tata Motors** of India. There are different ways of pronouncing the name of the car, on each side of the Atlantic; but the pronunciation should at least be consistent *within* a commercial. I heard one that spoke of both "jag-you-were" and "jag-waah." A friend of mine had a gorgeous Jag XKE. Its license plates said, "JAGWAH."

Every November, at least one talking head on TV will refer to the Macy's Day Parade. The name of the holiday is Thanksgivings Day, and the event in Manhattan is the **Macy's Thanksgiving Day Parade**, you idiots!

Another common New York broadcast blooper, at least for beginners, is **Port of Authority**. The real name of the organization is the **Port Authority of New York and New Jersey**.

For some unknown reason, *Newsweek* seems to be much sloppier than *Time* magazine. Many issues of *Newsweek* included a correction paragraph in the letters section with a "*Newsweek* regrets the error" statement. However, *Time* once identified *MAD*'s Alfred E. Neuman as "Newman."

Orange County Choppers: The Tale of the Teutuls by **Keith & Kent Zimmerman** has silly geography errors. It's disturbing that three Teutuls plus two Zimmermans plus fact checkers and editors at Warner Books let obvious errors get printed. On page 11, **Paul "Senior"** talks about his parents charging people to park in their driveway on Cooper Street in Yonkers, to watch horse races in Yonkers Raceway or baseball games in Yankee stadium, which were within "walking distance."

While the track is just a few blocks away, the stadium is about 8.5 miles south. The 17-mile round trip is not "walking distance" for most people. I hope Paul calculates more precisely while building bikes. Twice on page 15, He mentions his house in "Muncie", New York. Muncie is in Indiana. The Teutuls lived in MONSEY (which is pronounced like Muncie).

In *Against the Odds. Inter-Tel: the First 30 Years,* author **Jeffrey L. Rodengen** claims that in the early 1970s, "there were no domestic phone system manufacturers except AT&T."

He inexplicably ignores GTE (with roots going back to 1892), Stromberg-Carlson (1894), ITT (1897), Northern Telecom (founded in 1895 in Canada and operating a US factory since 1972), and Rolm (1969). Jeff also misspells company names and seems to confuse intercom systems with phone systems.

In *Desperate Networks* by **Bill Carter**, an otherwise excellent book, there is this strange sentence on page 366: "What do expect for this?" What the heck does that mean?

In *So You Wanna Be a Rock & Roll Star* by **Jacob Slichter**, another book I liked very much, there's also some silly stuff. On page 237 it says, "...and did whatever the man in the headsets shouted at them to do." I used and sold headsets for years. I've even designed a few. But in all my experience, I've never seen a man who wore more than one headset at a time. Most men have two ears, and one headset will take care of both them just fine. However, it's OK for one person to wear "headphones."

Steve Vogel's *The Pentagon, a History* is an extremely good book and I recommend it highly. Alas, it, too, seems to have some imperfections. On page 302 Vogel describes a 1,000-foot-long vehicular tunnel illuminated by rows of neon lights. Neon lights are used for signs. I'd bet $20 that the tunnel was really illuminated by fluorescent lights. On page 276 Vogel says the original Pentagon phone system had "68,600 miles of trunk lines." I'd bet $100 that's not true.

Joshua Levine's *The Rise and Fall of the House of Barneys* is a very interesting retail history that details the destruction of a once-powerful institution by the dysfunctional family members that followed its founder. (At least it's very interesting to me, and I read a lot of retail histories.)

On page 147 we are told that "inventory shortage is the term applied to discrepancies between the inventory recorded as sold and the actual depletion of stock on hand." The proper term is "shrinkage," not "shortage." Retailers know this, and so should writers and editors doing a book about retailing.

On page 186, Levine mentions "people called factors," who advance payments to stores based on accounts receivable. It's possible that hundreds of years ago factors were individual people, but during the Barneys era, factors were companies.

On page 244, Levine tells us that Fred Pressman "didn't have the kichas for it... a Yiddish expression for intestinal fortitude." The proper term is *kishkes*. This error is unforgiveable for a writer with a name like "Joshua Levine." The word originally meant "intestines," and is now slang for "guts."

In a *Wall Street Journal* article published on April 2, 2008, **Amy Schatz** wrote, "The Carterfone rule required traditional wireline phone companies such as AT&T to allow consumers to use any phone they wanted in their homes, instead of renting or buying a phone from their local carrier."

The Carterfone decision was in 1968, but at that time the phone companies were renting, not selling phones to their customers. Sales did not come until much later, as a defensive reaction to retailers who were selling phones that could now be legally plugged in. (Disclaimer: some smaller phone companies may have sold some equipment earlier, but not the Bell System.)

Actually, the Carterfone decision did not permit massive private phone ownership. That was enabled by a Supreme Court decision in 1977. And even then, people could not "use any phone they wanted." Phones had to meet FCC standards (basically dictated by AT&T), or else they had to be connected behind a protective coupler device.

On December 12, 1988, the *New York Times* published an article by **Calvin Sims** about the aftermath of the 1984 Bell System breakup. Sims wrote, "consumers have to decide whether to buy their telephones or rent them in a market where dozens of telephone manufacturers offer equipment of varying quality." While that statement was true, it had absolutely nothing to do with the demise of the Bell System. As I stated above, freedom of choice goes back to 1977.

Sims also wrote, "Consumers must choose among the nation's three long-distance carriers—American Telephone and Telegraph, MCI Communications, and U S Sprint." While those three companies had captured the majority of the long-distance calling business, there were dozens of other regional, national, and international competitors, including ITT, Metromedia, RCI, TDX and Allnet. And if consumers did not want to make a choice, a long-distance carrier could be assigned arbitrarily by the local phone company. Also, long distance competition existed as far back as 1970, long before the Bell breakup.

Sometimes reporters and editors get into trouble when they think they understand what someone said, but they really didn't understand. Years ago, the *New York Daily News* reported on a teenage fashion trend: "wearing pumice." In reality, high school kids were not wearing lumps of volcanic rock that are normally used as an abrasive to remove calluses from feet. They were wearing *Pumas*, a brand of sneakers.

Pumice   **Pumas**

The *Essential Guide to Telecommunications* by **Annabel Z. Dodd** does a pretty good job covering the subject, but has some silly errors. On page 40 she says, "Rotary telephones, called 500 sets, were introduced in 1896." Actually the 500 model designation was not used until after World War II. Before that were the 300, 200 and others.

Because the letters on Linotype keyboards used for printing presses were arranged by letter frequency, ETAOIN SHRDLU were the first two vertical columns on the left side. Linotype operators who made a typing error had to finish the line before they could re-key a new one. Since the line with the error would be

> Nova Scotia's men's basketball team downed Alberta, 79-68, but the Alberta women reversed the result, winning 65-34.
> m e etaoin shrdlu cmfwyp

discarded and its contents didn't matter, the quickest way to enter enough letters to finish it was to run a finger down the keys, creating a nonsense phrase. Sometimes, the phrase would get printed erroneously, as in the example above from the *New York Times* of 15 February 1967. (from *Wikipedia*)

One of my first assignments at my first post-college job was to write an introduction for a trade-in guide that helped hi-fi dealers decide how much to allow on traded-in equipment.

I wrote something about how trading in old models for new has been an American tradition since someone turned in an aging model A Ford for a new model T, and submitted my manuscript to my boss, Jerry, the editor.

Jerry didn't say anything to me about the article, but the publisher showed me a note Jerry had attached to it and given to the publisher. Jerry implied that I was an ignoramus for writing that the Model A came out *after* the Model T. Jerry insisted that I should have written about trading a T for an A, not an A for a T.

I was not ignorant, but Jerry sure was. I knew T and A better than he did. (You're supposed to chuckle, or at least smile, after reading that line.)

What I knew, and what Jerry didn't know, was that there were *two* Model A Ford cars. One was first built in 1903, before the Model T, which was produced from 1908 through 1927. Another Model A was first built in 1927, after the Model T was discontinued.

On November 9, 1965, there was a major failure of the electricity supply affecting 11 states and Ontario, Canada. Over 30 million people and 80,000 square miles were without electricity for up to 13 hours. The cause of the failure was a protective device near Niagara Falls.

I heard a government official on WOR radio. He discussed the failure of the "power grid," and said that as soon as the grid was replaced, power would be restored. He apparently thought that the grid was an electrical part that could be purchased at a nearby RadioShack. In reality, "grid" was a term for the huge, interconnected network of power cables. This before people spoke of living "off the grid."

An article in the August 2024 issue of *Tech Briefs* magazine dealt with research by a professor named either **Giannis Mpoumpakis**, or **Giannis Mpourmpakis**. I'm not sure which spelling is correct—or how to pronounce his family name.

After a brutal murder in Brooklyn in the 2024-'25 season opener of *FBI Most Wanted*, agent **Remy Scott** (played by **Dylan McDermott**) said "let me see if I can find an onion bagel, also known as a bialy." A bagel is NOT a bialy, and the error is unforgiveable in Brooklyn!

Hyp-hen Hil-a-ri-ty: I enjoy discovering stupid hyphenations. **Microsoft Word** gives us *bin-aural*, instead of *bi-naural*. The *New York Daily News* printed *iP-hone* and *Fa-cebook*. Ebooks produce gems. *The Brothers Emanuel* presented *swit-ching*. Is it related to the *I Ching*? I've also seen *booksto-re*, *disappoin-ting*, *depen-ding* and *increa-sing*—in one book.

Usually the first fragment of a hyphenated word provides a hint of what's on the next line, but not always. I found *min-dreading* in the excellent bio of **Walt Disney** by **Neal Gabler**.

Hyphenation can be debatable. Microsoft Word and Dictionary.com accept *eve-ryone*. Merriam-Webster does not. Neither do I. My rule is that the first part of a hyphenated word should not be pronounced differently by itself than when it's part of a larger word. I think most people expect "eve" to be pronounced "eev"—not "ev" or "ev-uh." The "eve" in "evening" is not pronounced like the "eve" in "everyone." Word sometimes makes bad guesses and you'll have to overrule its decisions. Proofread very carefully and never have complete faith in robots.

"The-rapist" is my favorite abomination sanctioned by Microsoft. I also really like "of-fline" "who-lesaler," "books-tore," "upl-oad," "wastel-and," "proo-freading," "apo-strophe," "li-mited," "identic-al," "firs-thand,'""fi-ne," "fru-strating," "whe-never," "foo-ter," "miles-tone," "grays-cale," "distri-bute," "percen-tage," "prin-ter," "fami-liarity," "misunders-tanding," "mi-nimize," "sa-les," "me-thod," "libra-rian," "mi-spronounced," "alt-hough" and "bet-ween."

Word often assumes that the letter "e" indicates the end of a syllable as in "be-come" and causes errors like "Ste-ve," "the-se," "cre-dit" and "se-tup."

Word recognizes that "par" is a common syllable, which leads to "par-chment."

You may want to override Word's hyphenation decision with heteronyms—words that are spelled the same way but have two meanings and are pronounced in two ways. Word gives you "min-ute" when you want "mi-nute" and rec-ord even if you want "re-cord." The automatic hyphenation "inva-lid" makes it seem like you are writing about someone who is ailing, not an "in-valid" contract. Word 2007, 2010 and 2021 won't hyphenate either "Po-lish" or "pol-ish."

Word's automatic hyphenation can give weird results with proper names, such as "Fe-dex," "Publi-shAmerica" and "Pa-nasonic."

"Writer" software from **Open Office** has problems, too. It produced "unders-tanding."

A book advised, "If you do not use a professional your manuscript will not be perfect. Do not proofread it yourself and declare it perfect." The book approved "loo-ked," "winso-me" and "proo-freader." Ouch.

Chapter 105
Universal time

I'm sorry to tell you this, but there is *no such thing* as 12 AM during the day; and the nighttime 12 could be considered to be *either* AM or PM.

It's better to say, "12 noon" or "12 midnight." The "m" stands for "*meridiem*," the Latin word for the day's halfway point. The "a" is from the Latin word "*ante*," meaning "before," and the "p" is from "post," meaning "after."

From *Wikipedia*: Since the word *meridies* means noon or midday, it is, strictly speaking, illogical to refer to noon as either "12 AM" (12 ante meridiem, 12 hours before noon) or as "12 PM" (12 post meridiem, 12 hours after noon. On the other hand, midnight could logically be called either "12 PM" (12 post meridiem, 12 hours after the previous noon) or "12 AM" (12 ante meridiem, 12 hours before the following noon). In the United States, largely because of the preponderance of digital clocks and computers, which change from AM to PM (and vice versa) when changing the hour from 11 to 12, noon is often called "12:00 PM" and midnight "12:00 AM", as at the beginning of a day."

Strangely, this common usage is contrary to the *U.S. Government Printing Office Style Manual*, which recommends the opposite: "12 PM" for midnight and "12 AM" for noon. It would be much easier if we all used 24-hour "military time."

Sadly, clocks often disagree. My home is filled with digital time displays. They often show the same digits, and often they do not.

The disagreement is not just in homes. When I worked in Manhattan in the early 1970s, if I stood in one spot on Madison Avenue and pivoted around, I could view giant clocks on the buildings housing both *Newsweek* magazine (444 Madison) and IBM (590 Madison).

The digital displays provided by renowned information authorities often disagreed by more than a minute! Which one should people trust? Could they both be wrong?

Of course, analog clocks also abound. Some are indoors, some are outdoors, some are up high, some at street-level, some are ordinary, and some are iconic like those in Grand Central Terminal, and in front of Trump Tower, and London's Big Ben.

Chronological cliches are common (another automatic alliteration). Some are classic, like "time flies," "take your time," "time out," "time in," "time to go," "lunch time," "time for a break," "time is money," "time study," "it's time to shit or get off the pot" (another chapter in this book), and "time for a change."

Some are commercial like "It's Howdy Doody time" and "it's time for a bagel."

Time is the subject of a great many song and album titles, particularly *Time Has Come Today* by the Chambers Brothers, *Time is On My Side* by the Rolling Stones, *Yesterday* by the Beatles, *Some Enchanted Evening* by Rodgers & Hammerstein, and *Time Out* by Dave Brubeck.

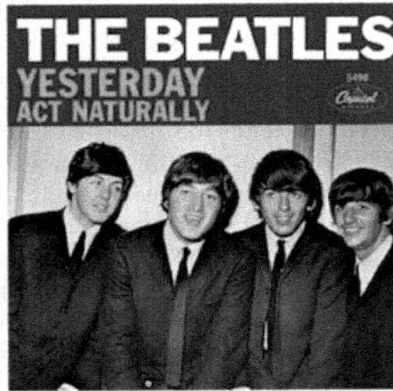

And of course, we have *Time* magazine, the *New York Times,* the *Los Angeles Times* and many other time-related printed, broadcast and online media titles and slogans.

Seasons are timely, too: *I Love Paris in the Springtime, Summer in the City, Autumn in New York, Springtime for Hitler, Younger Than Springtime* and *Winter Wonderland.*

There are also poems and movies about time, such as Emily Dickinson's *A Clock Stopped,* Joyce Kilmer's *Alarm Clocks,* Maya Angelou's *Passing Time,* the *Back to the Future* films, plus *Groundhog Day, Time Lapse, Time Trap, A Clockwork Orange, Time Bandits, Time Cop* and the classic *The Time Machine.*

Time is probably not on my side.
"Tempus fugit," as an ancient Roman said.
"Optima dies...prima fugit," as another one said.

Chapter 106
Is it time to shit or get off the pot?

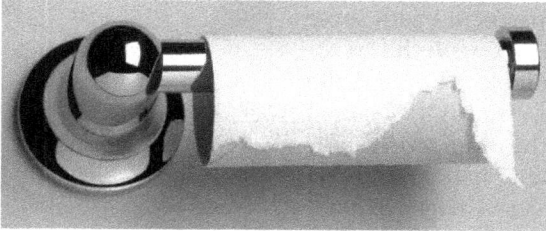

The chapter title above refers to an often-used cliché, directed at people who are uncooperative, unmotivated, indecisive or simply slow.

Many writers suffer from "**writer's block**." It's a condition where they freeze up before they can write the first word. The blockage can last for minutes, hours, days or longer.

- **Harold Brodkey** wrote short stories for *The New Yorker* magazine. He spent three decades struggling to finish a book.
- **Henry Roth**'s *Call it Sleep* has been called "a classic of 20th-century immigrant fiction," published in 1934. It didn't attract much attention until it was republished in 1964. During the intervening 30 years, Roth published *nothing*, crippled by one of literature's most famous cases of writer's block. Critic **Jonathan Rosen** wrote that "the reasons for Roth's monumental block—which include but are not limited to Communism, Jewish self-loathing, incest, and depression—are ultimately as mysterious as the reasons for his art and are in some ways inseparable from them."
- **Ralph Ellison** had a long blockage, from the publication of *Invisible Man* in 1952 until his death in 1994. Ellison reportedly wrote about 2,000 pages of notes for his second novel. In the 42 years after *Invisible Man*'s publication, he claimed that the new book was "nearly completed."

I sometimes had the *opposite* problem. I had no trouble starting to write, but it could be tough for me to *finish* a project. Delayed completion can be even more deadly and disappointing than not starting. Not finishing is no good when writing for a publication or doing advertising copywriting. Deadlines were usually important, and missed deadlines could cost money, be embarrassing and piss people off.

I majored in journalism at Lehigh University in the late 1960s and worked on the *Bown & White*, our student newspaper.

After a few unpleasant episodes where the copyeditor butchered my prose and hurt my pride, I *became the copyeditor*, and also got a part-time job proofreading at our printer. I then had complete control of my work, all the way from my brain to the printed pages. I loved having control, but, of course, I couldn't blame anyone else if my articles turned out to be substandard when published.

I was fired from my first post-college job as assistant editor of a magazine because I took much too long to complete writing an important article. I was a perfectionist and wanted my work to be as perfect as possible. My boss didn't care much about literary quality, but he very much cared about speed. He often told me that "good enough is good enough."

When I was writing for *Rolling Stone* in the early 1970s, I was always rewriting until the last possible minute. This was in the pre-fax, pre-email era, and I'd drive to the airport and pay to have my column air-freighted from NY to CA. There wasn't much profit left.

Words are almost toys for me, like a child's building blocks, Lincoln Logs, Legos or an Erector Set. I love to *play* with words, to rearrange them and try alternatives. Rewriting sentences and changing page formatting—especially now with a computer—is *fun*. The danger is that a perfectionist never finishes.

After *Rolling Stone* I became an "award-winning Madison Avenue copywriter" at several advertising agencies. I partnered with some fine art directors. Most teams fought constant battles, with the art directors wanting to chop words to make the ads look better and the copywriters insisting that every word was vital.

I was much more flexible than most of the other writers. Although I took great pride in every word I wrote, I had gone to art school as a child and had great respect for the visual images that accompanied my words.

I also knew that perhaps 90% of the people who saw an ad, would see the picture and headline and they'd *never read another word*, no matter how hard I had worked to choose the perfect word and its perfect position.

When I was working as an advertising copywriter, I was notorious for not "releasing" an ad until the last possible moment. When agency execs nagged me to "hurry up" and "shit or get off the pot," I remembered what my first boss had told me: sometimes "good enough is good enough" and I learned to let go.

Now, as the owner of a small publishing company, I have to be a businessman as well as an artist. I realize that no money will come in if I don't approve a proof and let a book start selling.

However, I seldom stop editing. I even re-do old blog entries.

The New Yorker magazine published an excellent article about **Steve Jobs**, which said that his real genius was tweaking—not inventing.

I'm a tweaker, too, but being a tweaker can be dangerous because nothing is ever really finished. (When I was in college, I was still building bookshelves a week before I was due to move out of my apartment.)

Printing on demand and ebooks make it easy to keep tweaking. Maybe too easy.

With POD and e I can make improvements to my books whenever I want to.

Unfortunately, sometimes when I should be working on new books, I instead work on old ones. (And vice versa.)

Most of my books go through hundreds of revisions but the first one to be published is good enough to not embarrass me. A person who buys version 2.13 gets a better book than the person who bought 1.28, but I know that each version was "good enough" at a particular moment.

One time I decided to delay a book by a week so I could change a comma to a period and uppercase the next letter. I doubt that anyone else would have noticed the perceived imperfection, but I could not let it be.

Steve Jobs may have been more of a perfectionist than I am, the ultimate tweaker; and my iPad is better because of his obsession. I hope my books are perceived as better because of my obsession. One of my books is nearly three years behind schedule.

It's getting better and better.

Chapter 107
Con artistry

I'm not Bernie Madoff, but...

Like my funny father, I've enjoyed and created hoaxes and pranks.

When there was a bad snowstorm in Connecticut, Pop would call a local radio station to have it announce a cancellation of the **Fafnir Society** meeting at New Haven's **Hotel Taft**. There was *no such organization.* Fafnir was the name of his partner's dog.

Once Pop was in a Gimbel's store in Manhattan and convinced employees to move pocketbooks from one counter to another.

It wasn't his store, and he wasn't their boss.

This taught me valuable lessons: If you act like you have authority, you *have* authority. And most people would rather accept authority than challenge it.

I once needed a smock to protect my clothes while painting. I noticed that cashiers in a nearby **Bradlees** store wore the perfect garments. I told a cashier to see the manager and give me her smock so I could take over her checkout lane. She gave me the smock. I could've emptied the cash register, but I didn't. (A few days later I returned the cleaned smock.)

My favorite holiday is April Fools' Day (I was born in April). I probably surpassed my father's pranking, because I may have bigger balls, majored in journalism, was employed to write articles, ads and press releases—and became a **Master Media Manipulator**. I could write *very convincing bullshit*, that circulated far and wide.

Below are 'news stories' about Dr. Wendy Kopfschmerzen that were published on dozens of websites around the world.

They're *false*. Dr. Kopfschmerzen's last name is the German word for "headache." The non-existent doctor received emails and phone calls, and the producer of a TV show wanted to interview her.

New HeadsetHouse "Therapist" Answers Online Shoppers' Questions

19 March 2007 -- Dr. Wendy Kopfschmerzen has joined HeadsetHouse.com, the online headset venue of telecom supplier AbleComm, Inc., to provide advice and answer questions from prospective purchasers.

According to company president Michael N. Marcus, "while telephone headset use is growing, most people—even those who spend many hours on the phone—don't use headsets and miss their benefits of comfort and efficiency. Part of the problem is the overwhelming choice of products. There are literally hundreds of telephone headsets available, and we want it to be easier for people to pick the right product."

Marcus continued, "We are extremely pleased to be able to offer to the public, the experience and knowledge of Dr. Kopfschmerzen, who has degrees in acoustics, audiology and anatomy, and has used headsets herself for many years. We have given Dr. Kopfschmerzen the title, "Headset Therapist," to imply knowledge, understanding and patience."

Before joining HeadsetHouse, Dr. Kopfschmerzen worked as an engineer for TransducerLogik GmbH in Germany; Audiktia, a Danish maker of hearing aids; and for Hegeman Laboratories, a speaker manufacturer based in New Jersey. She maintains dual US-German citizenship and was educated in both countries. Dr. Kopfschmerzen answers email, and both emails and general advice are published on the HeadsetHouse.com website for everyone's benefit.

500th "Patient" Wins Free Headset from Online "Therapist"

Milford, CT, April 07, 2007 -- On March 1, HeadsetHouse.com began offering online advice about telephone headsets; and the 500th person to seek advice has been awarded a free Plantronics CS55H wireless headset system, worth $280.

The winner is Miranda Wright of Enid, Oklahoma. Ms. Wright is a freelance illustrator who works for book publishers and advertising agencies; and a work-at-home mother of three. She sent an Email to HeadsetHouse.com about buying a wireless headset, and ironically she got one for free.

Questions about headset purchasing and use are answered by "headset therapist" Dr. Wendy Kopfschmerzen, who has degrees in acoustics, audiology and anatomy. In late February, Dr. Kophschmerzen joined HeadsetHouse.com after working as an engineer for TransducerLogik GmbH in Germany and Audiktia, a Danish maker of hearing aids.

When notified of her good luck, Ms. Wright said, "This is amazing. I've been entering contests and buying lottery tickets for years, but until now the most I've ever won was extra cheese on a pizza. This time I didn't buy a ticket or send in a coupon. In fact, I didn't even know there was a contest; and now I'm getting a headset that is better than the one I was planning to buy. It will make it a lot easier for me to handle business calls at home, while watching my kids or doing household chores, or working at my computer."

Bike Tires Cause Cancer

This was probably my first printed prank. In the early 1970s, I was an editor at *Rolling Stone* magazine. This was a time when bicycle riding had become quite popular for healthful exercise, so it was natural for me to invent something *terrible* that could be caused by bicycle riding.

I invented a mythical scientist at **Johns Hopkins School of Medicine** who found a problem with the high-pressure tires commonly used on ten-speed "racing" bikes. He discovered that with each revolution of the tire, many minute rubber particles were abraded by the road surface.

The rubber particles became airborne, and some were inhaled by the bike rider, particularly if she or he was riding bent-over and face-down to minimize wind resistance and increase speed.

The phony scientist, whose phony name I've long forgotten, found that people who rode often developed lung cancer and black lung disease, like coal miners.

Westchester Citizens for Recreation On Water

For 24 years, until 2001, I lived in Westchester County in New York, very close to the beautiful **Sprain Lake Reservoir**. It was built in the late 1800s and was part of the Yonkers municipal water supply system until 1981 when the city tapped into the New York City water system.

From 1981 on, the lake just existed, looked beautiful, and did not much besides entrapping golf balls from the adjacent golf course, breeding frogs and turtles, and attracting illegal fishermen.

I thought it would be a great place to go canoeing. I suggested it to the various departments that governed the water and was either turned down or ignored. In early 1995 I invented an organization called *Westchester Citizens for Recreation On Water* ("ROW"), designed a letterhead, and sent out a press release to a local newspaper that outlined the reservoir history, my suggestion, and my frustration with local government.

I got a quick response and made arrangements to meet a reporter and photographer on the snowy banks of the lake. I bought a canoe paddle to use as a photo prop, and the paper ran a nice story about my "group" with a picture of me standing in the snow, toting the paddle.

I'm not sure if the law changed. I moved to Connecticut, where I lived just minutes from the beach, and I had a pool in my back yard where I could paddle a rubber boat.

Pranking Panasonic

My day job was being boss of AbleComm, Inc.—a company specializing in Panasonic phone systems. I also owned some Panasonic stock, and I reviewed Panasonic electronic products.

Starting in the mid-1990s, I distributed an April Fools' 'news report' about a mythical press conference that took place at a non-existent hotel, where fake people announced fake corporate policy changes and fake new products. It became an eagerly awaited annual tradition in the telecom business. Lots of people loved it, but believers, of course, didn't.

In 2007 I produced a masterpiece about Panasonic owning the "VoIP" trademark (*Voice of International Panasonic*) and seeking royalty payments, or injunctions against such companies as AT&T, Microsoft and Cisco for using the term without Panasonic's permission. They, and most of the world, used "VoIP" to mean "Voice over Internet Protocol," a system for using the Internet for phone calls. The spoof got some media coverage, but its circulation was limited by the telltale 4/1 date.

It could be real someday.

For 2008, I decided to celebrate the holiday a couple of days late to improve my chances of success. Early on Thursday April 3, 2008, I launched a 90%-false press release. The press release contained several revelations, but the most important was that Panasonic would be manufacturing cellphones with plasma video displays. Back in January, Panasonic had demonstrated the world's largest plasma TV, so now I thought they should also have the smallest.

Through very lucky timing, a few days before my news went out, AT&T had announced their Mobile TV service for watching shows and sports on cellphones, which added usefulness and legitimacy to my fictitious device.

Within a few hours, the story was picked up and published by websites around the world. Many news writers added original material to demonstrate their extensive knowledge of the subject; but only one of them called me to check on the story, and I told him that it was a spoof.

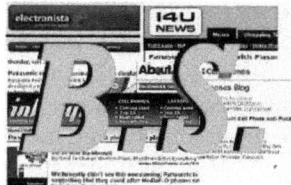

Mobileburn.com was particularly fanciful in enhancing the fake news (but I'm not sure if they were being playful or stupid). They said, "Panasonic took the stage at CTIA 2008 this week with partner AbleComm to announce that it has been working with AT&T to develop plasma displays for mobile phones, for use with the carrier's new Mobile TV service."

There was absolutely nothing in my news about an appearance at the CTIA event or Panasonic "working with AT&T." The closest I came was saying that the new plasma displays were "for cellphones to use with" AT&T's service.

Crunchgear.com had a headline that read, "AT&T wants Panasonic to develop plasma screens for cellphones." I never said that, and I doubt that AT&T did.

Several websites, such as *Mobilemag.com* stated that Panasonic "will be offering cell phones for the AT&T service."

AT&T had previously announced that their service would use cellphones made by Samsung and LG. If someone read carefully, he or she might conclude that Panasonic would be supplying displays to either or both companies, or for another company. But few people read carefully.

My news release said that Panasonic had licensed technology from AbleComm. Some websites twisted this and reported that AbleComm would be making plasma display screens for Panasonic. I never said that AbleComm makes anything.

As a clue to its falsehood (which is part of April Foolery tradition), my press release said that a key event took place on Tuesday. Some experienced writers recognized the day as April first, and knew the news was not to be believed. Many others got caught. Some laughed. Some didn't.

As in the past, reaction within Panasonic was mixed. There was some laughter, some grumbling, and some snarling. One outraged exec sent an email saying that I caused "people to loose (sic) thousands of productive working hours." Maybe he needs a new calculator.

Perhaps Panasonic was talking to its lawyers, but a lawsuit would only mean more fun for me—and bad publicity for them. I assumed that common sense would prevent them from taking me to court. After all, I said only *good things* about the company, and it would be hard for them to prove a loss. Even more importantly, they'd certainly lose in the "court of public opinion."

A few hours after the news went out, I authorized a retraction through the service that sent out the original press release, but the original news continued to circulate and expand. Some websites that received the retraction accused me of forgetting what day it was. One critic said it was a "late, poorly executed April Fools joke," and another called me an "April Idiot." Actually, it was not late, and it was extremely well executed, and my mother didn't have any idiotic kids.

There's certainly no rule that limits hoaxing to one day per year. No one who was filmed for TV's *Candid Camera* on 3/20 or 10/15 objected because it wasn't 4/1. Similarly, the celebrities who were victims on the MTV show *Punk'd* may have grumbled, but not because they were not punked on the first day of the fourth month. And the subjects of "Stuttering John" interviews on *The Howard Stern Show* didn't check the date before deciding to participate.

Although I was born in April, I'm not a fool or idiot. I was smart enough to write the phony news in a certain way, and send it on a day, that increased the likelihood of its publication. I am not the idiot. I wasn't punked. I didn't publish a phony news story on *my* website.

Some victims were at least partially complimentary.

Dailytech.com said "Yesterday AbleComm sent out a press release that was all very believable talking about how Panasonic was going to be using small plasma displays in a mobile phone designed to be used on the new AT&T Mobile TV service launching in

May. The release was professional, interesting and all very plausible, replete with quotes form Panasonic and all. It didn't take long before the story was all around the internet with posts on *Engadget*, *Slashphone* and more. As a freelance guy I posted the story myself at other publications."

Some websites were suspicious of the retraction. *Phonemag.com* said it "Looks like someone let the plasma cat out of the proverbial bag too soon, and is now desperately backtracking to try to salvage a business relationship. It's unclear whether this was a deliberate or accidental occurrence, though the release was sizable and contained multiple quotes from all the parties involved which lends weight to the idea that it was an authentic document prematurely distributed." **GOTCHA!**

Many of the websites that ran the news of the retraction, but had not run the original fake news, ran it *with* the retraction, thus increasing the circulation and readership of the spoof. **GOTCHA again.**

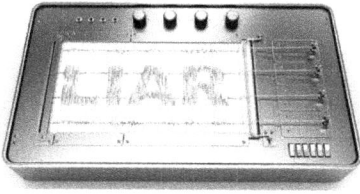

We all know that "truth can be stranger than fiction," and eventually some of my April fictions turned out to be true. A few days after I announced the fictional Panasonic plasma-screen cellphone, I learned that Panasonic had a REAL cellphone in Japan with enhanced viewing of mobile TV. However, its screen was an LCD, not plasma, but that's OK.

Am I a Polish Joke?

As mentioned elsewhere, our family name has been Marcus only since the early 20th century. The last name of my father's father **Walter Marcus** originally started with "Dzm" and ended with "ski"—and had many more consonants than vowels.

He came from *Sopotskin*. The town's location changed a lot, although it didn't move.

When Walter's family left town in 1906, Sopotskin was in Poland.

Since 1991, it's been in Belarus, near Poland and Lithuania. It's also been part of Lithuania, the Belarusian People's Republic, White Russia, the Byelorussian Soviet Socialist Republic, the Lithuanian-Byelorussian Soviet Socialist Republic and the Union of Soviet Socialist Republics.

It depended on who had the most powerful army and made the map.

My maternal **Grandma "Del"** viewed herself as an inheritor of high-class Viennese culture and initially dismissed my father-to-be as a "Polish peasant." Pop did some historical research and determined that her forbears were just as Polish as his were.

In the 1970s, I was a member of **PRDA (Polish Racing Drivers of America)**, a just-for-fun group sponsored by **Auto World,** a seller of car parts and accessories and sponsor of race cars.

As I recall, there were several classes of membership:
(a) Polish racing drivers
(b) Non-Polish racing drivers
(c) Polish non-racing drivers
(d) Non-Polish non-racing drivers
(e) Non-drivers

Chapter 108
Save some words

Since the end of the last century, many words have been written and said about minimizing the use of vehicles, fuel, heat, power, water, food, packaging, building materials and more. We are supposed to SAVE vital resources.

I think it's time to say a few words about using *fewer words*.

If the sign shown on the right did not say "NOW CARRY-ING," would you be less likely to enter the store to buy frozen food?

The archaic phrase "Inquire Within" has pissed me off since I was a teenager. The sign shown did not display a phone number or a web address. If the sign did not say "Inquire Within," and you wanted to get hired, exactly what the hell would you do but open the door, walk in and inquire?

I bought gas from a pump that said, "Product Contains Up to 15% Ethanol." If the first two words were deleted from the sign, would the message be less clear?

If the "No entry without..." door sign did not say "being accompanied by," would the warning be less impactful?

The same principle applies to writing. Almost any page can easily shed a word or ten—and be improved by pruning.

I am often pedantic (a trait from my father). I naturally give lots of examples to prove a point. I recently self-imposed a rule to limit examples to THREE—and my arguments are no less forceful.

Print-on-demand and ebooks are certainly efficient. But if every writer would eliminate two, three or ten pages out of every hundred pages, book printers would use less paper, ink, toner, glue, energy and time; and trucks that move books would save fuel, and the UPS drivers might last longer.

AND... the books would probably be better if they were briefer. I originally planned for this book to have fewer than 200 pages. Then 220 seemed fine. Then the book somehow ballooned to 363 pages, as if it had ingested the literary equivalent of growth hormone. I started chopping.

In an electronic medium like a blog or ebook, writers have unlimited space to spew all of the words they want to—and the lack of limits encourages sloppiness.

Advertising is very different.

If a copywriter writes too many words to fit in a one-page ad, she shouldn't use tiny type or assume that the client will pay $30,000 extra to run a two-page ad. If she writes too many words to fit into a 30-second commercial, she can't decree that the actors must speak faster, or that the client must pay for more airtime.

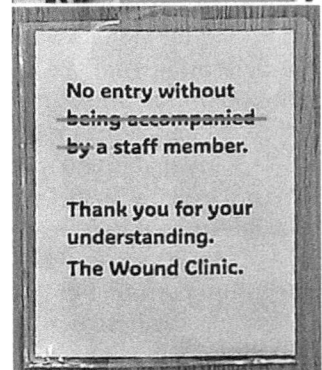

Impose limits on yourself. It won't hurt and will probably help. People are busy and don't have endless time to read. When you think you've finished, try to chop 10%. Briefer is often better.

Don't say anything extra in court.

I was once on the Board of Managers in my condominium. An annoying, unhappy resident sued the Board, for a reason I've long forgotten. It was a *nuisance suit*, and the Board's president wanted to punish the plaintiff and discourage future frivolous suits.

I had to testify in court. Our attorney advised us to answer the plaintiff's attorney *precisely*, with minimal information—to waste time and increase the plaintiff's legal expense.

I was initially asked, "Can you tell me your name?" I responded, "Yes."

I was then asked, "Will you tell me your name?" Again, I responded, "Yes."

When I was finally asked what my name is, I gave the desired answer.

The silly scenario continued with "Can you tell me your address?", "Can you tell me your age?" and "Can you tell me how long you've been on the Board?".

The plaintiff's attorney seethed. The Board's attorney smiled. The case was dismissed.

Help Wanted photo from *www.newstimes.com*. I forgot where the gas pump photo came from.]

An 86-year-old man goes for a physical. All of his test results come back normal.

The doctor says, "George. everything looks great. How are you doing mentally and emotionally? Are you at peace with God?"

George replies, "God and I are tight. He knows I have poor eyesight, so he's fixed it so when I get up in the middle of the night to go to the bathroom, POOF—the light goes on. When I'm done, POOF—the light goes off."

"Wow, that's great," the doctor says.

A little later in the day, the doctor calls George's wife. "Marianne," he says, "George is doing fine but I had to call you because I'm in awe of his relationship with God. Is it true that he gets up during the night and POOF—the light goes on in the bathroom, and when he's done, POOF—the light goes off?"

"OH NO!" Marianne exclaims. "He's peeing in the refrigerator again!!!!"

[From **Harry Newton**, slightly modified].

Chapter 109
Aging (& t-shirts)

I saw a preview for an HBO special with **Carl Reiner**, **Mel Brooks**, **Dick Van Dyke** and others praising the joys of being 90 or older. I recently passed my 78th birthday and I spend a lot of time contemplating being old. But I'm still middle-aged, of course. "Old" doesn't start until people begin shoveling dirt on top of you.

Young people eagerly contemplate becoming 5, 10, 13, 16, 18, 21 and—if they have presidential pretensions—35. The next decades don't mean much until age-65 for Medicare and 62 to 70 for Social Security. Social Security works like putting quarters into a slot machine for five decades and then—KA-CHING—coins start flowing out.

I had foolishly and eagerly thought that SocSec would buy me a second home and worldwide travel. Sadly, it's needed for such frivolities as food, medicine and taxes.

After finance, physical and mental health are the big issues for senior citizens. Lots of body parts no longer work as well or as often as they used to—or at all. Every year I add more *'ologists* to my list of medical specialists.

I'm a wreck, physically. (Mentally, not yet so bad.) Some people deal with pain and dysfunction with increasing amounts of drugs, or acupuncture, spirituality and other conventional or exotic remedies.

So far, I've been able to deal with my failing body by combining conventional medicine with disobedience, egomania and self-deprecating humor.

In my world, *everything* is a proper subject for laughter, and I have no secrets.

I recently told the world (at least the *Facebook* world), that I had peed in my pants while rushing to the men's room in a supermarket. I was amazed by the number of men and women who confessed to the same malfunction.

Someone said that "the eyes are the window to the soul." I think that T-shirts do the job quite well. A few years ago, I expected to have surgery for kidney stones. I ordered and wore a shirt that proclaimed "CAUTION! Do Not Bump. I Have A Pee-Pee Bag." It turned out that I did not need the bag, but I wore the shirt to the hospital and to other places since then. People's reactions vary. Some gasp. Some giggle. Some turn away. Some ask where they can buy the shirt.

In 2016 I had diplopia ("double-vision") for several months. I wore an eye patch to compensate by blocking one eye. I also often wore a pirate T-shirt and sometimes put a fake parrot on my shoulder. When kids asked me if I was a real pirate, of course I responded, "aaaarrrggghh."

Back in the 70s I was an advertising copywriter. One of my favorite mediums (not "media" in this usage) was the T-shirt. The objective was to turn millions of human bodies into mobile billboards. To get those millions to carry our messages, each wearer of the shirt had to become part of the message, maybe part of a joke.

At that time **Castrol** introduced a new motor oil designed to stand up to the high temperatures of small, high-RPM car engines. I devised a slogan and shirt that proclaimed, "I don't stop when I get hot." The oil and sexy shirt were very successful, and I saw some of the shirts being worn even 30 years later.

Back to health: I've been able to deal with incontinence, diabetes, neuropathy, skin pre-cancer, arthritis, sleep apnea, hand pain, Parkinson's, kidney trouble, enlarged prostate, too-frequent urination, missing teeth, fading memory, trouble typing and other issues. (However, I did eliminate nosebleeds, outgrew migraines, never had a venereal disease and I outgrew childhood allergies.)

I can accept the loss of hairs, but what scares the shit out of me is the loss of my mind!

Is trouble thinking of a word—or typing a wrong word—no big deal?

Or is it the onset of dementia that reduced my parents from near-genius to near-vegetable in a few years?

In his last year, my father simply ran out of things to do. He *decided to die,* and he stopped wearing his eyeglasses and hearing aids. Sometimes I saw him in his bed in the nursing home, apparently asleep. Suddenly a big grin would spread across his face, and then a big stink would spread across the room.

In *Love Story*, we learned that "Love means never having to say you're sorry." Maybe being 87 means you can fart without having to say you're sorry.

I designed t-shirts to publicize some of my websites, books and events.

Chapter 110
Hairs

Human hair has always interested me, sometimes fascinated me, sometimes attracted me, sometimes repulsed me—and sometimes *pissed me off!*

The following verses occupy valuable parts of my brain, and I can't delete them:

o "But Jacob said to Rebekah his mother, 'Behold, my brother Esau is a hairy man, and I am a smooth man.'" (*Torah*)

o "Gimme head with hair. Long beautiful hair. Shining, gleaming, Streaming, flaxen, waxen. Give me down to there hair. Shoulder length or longer. ... Flow it, show it. Long as God can grow it. My hair." (*Hair*, by James Rado & Gerome Ragni)

Hair has symbolized female beauty, female monstrosity, and male virility.

o The Biblical *Song of Solomon* says, "Behold, you are beautiful, my love, behold, you are beautiful! Your eyes are doves behind your veil. Your hair is like a flock of goats leaping down the slopes of Gilead." (I never said that to a woman.)

o In Greek mythology, **Medusa** was one of the three monstrous **Gorgons**. She had *live snakes* in place of hair, and her appearance was so hideous that anyone who looked at her was turned into stone.

o In the *Torah*, ultra-strong judge **Samson** fell in love with **Delilah,** a Philistine, and she tricked him into revealing that the source of his strength was his hair. As he slept, Philistines cut his hair, blinded and enslaved him. However, his hair quickly grew back, and his strength was restored. In vengeance, Samson destroyed a Philistine temple, killing thousands of enemies, and himself, in the process.

o The *lack* of male hair can also imply virility, as exemplified by the shaved heads of countless wrestlers (**Dwayne Johnson**), athletes (**Kobe Bryant**), actors (**Yul Brynner**) and both real and fictional bad guys (**Charles Manson**, **Lex Luthor**). And even politicians like **Cory Booker** and **John Fetterman**. The last bald American president was **Dwight Eisenhower**.

o **Mr. Clean** is fictional, powerful and bald.

o Not macho, but many Buddhists and Vaisnavas, especially Hare Krishnas, shave their heads. Some Hindu and most Buddhist monks and nuns shave their heads upon entering their order, and Buddhist monks and nuns in Korea have their heads shaved every 15 days. Muslim men have the choice of shaving their heads after performing the Umrah and Hajj, following the tradition of committing to Allah, but are not required to keep it permanently shaved. [from *Wikipedia*]

- Cartoon character **Shrek** is bald. So are **Homer Simpson**, **Popeye**, **Elmer Fudd** and **Charlie Brown**.
- *Bald* is a movie, and *Bald Headed Woman* is a song.
- According to *Men's Health,* "the hottest men's hairstyle is not having one;" and **Power Bald** "is a surging movement of men who've shaved off their insecurities about being bald. While baldness has always existed, a recent cultural shift both on screen and off has shown the strength in grooming to a simple, sleek appearance. One that allows worth and beauty to be defined by principles other than the lusciousness of one's mane or the uniformity of their crew cuts."

I've always been amazed that some hairs seem *smarter* than other hairs.
- Head and beard hair would reach the ground if never trimmed.
- In contrast, hair on limbs and in eyebrows, eyelashes, armpits and crotches somehow know when to stop growing.
- Head hairs can be manipulated and *trained*. **Donald Trump** is famous for his strange hairstyle, enforced by lavish doses of hairspray. My Bronx-born mother dictated that I have a *pompadour*, trained with vile hair tonic in the 1950s). It took me years to untrain my hair, to get a more natural look.

When I was a kid, my father insisted that I go to **Charlie's Barber Shop** every ten days—not as long as every two weeks. In college, I let my hair reach my shoulders. Pop also said, "I don't understand why so many beautiful blonde women dye their hair roots black."

Bald women can be beautiful, as exemplified by **Persis Khambatta.** She was an Indian actress, model and beauty pageant winner best known as **Lieutenant Ilia** in *Star Trek: The Motion Picture.*

I had my head shaved for my 70th birthday. I liked the look, but it was a lot of work, and I regrew my modest mane after about two years.

It's been said that "that the higher the hair the closer to God." I like to think that my super-powerful brain destroyed my hair follicles.

I recently found an old photo that showed my hairy chest, arms and legs. My limbs are now nearly bald. In my freshman year in college, some of my classmates and I pondered over the loss of our leg hair. One kid suggested that the depletion was due to sex-depressing hormones in the dining room food. A doc in the medical center suggested that it was probably caused by the abrasive denim fabric in the jeans we now wore daily. But, who knows?

Although I stopped shaving my head, I can't regrow my youthful hair. I have sometimes *bought* hair for Halloween or dyed my hair green or orange.

Chapter 111
Food frustrations

In the 1960s, I was a student at Lehigh University in Bethlehem, Pennsylvania. The city's cuisine was a massive culture shock. It borrowed a bit from Philadelphia and a bit from Lancaster and had touches of Atlantic City and Germany—but there was very little to make the saliva flow in the mouth of someone born in New York City.

Cream soda was red instead of brown. Root beer was clear instead of brown. Corned beef was gray with iridescent green edges and came pre-sliced and laminated to a piece of cardboard that hung on a Pegboard hook between the olive loaf and the head cheese. You couldn't find imported beer, and most domestic brews had names ending in "itz," "atz," or "utz." The big cheese store had 200 varieties, but no **Munchee** for me. Hotdogs were seldom all-beef. Despite the city's pervasive Germanic heritage, sauerkraut was unavailable.

One translation of the biblical name "Bethlehem" is "house of bread." To me, that means a *bakery*. But when I lived in Bethlehem I couldn't buy a fresh rye bread or even a frozen bagel. Bethlehem's restaurants offered four ethnic foods: pizza, tacos, kielbasa and pierogies. The nearest Chinese food was in Allentown or across the New Jersey state line in Phillipsburg; and the city's one kosher delicatessen was replaced by a parking lot during the summer between my freshman and sophomore years.

Lehigh's University Center snack bar specialized in the "California hamburger" (a normal burger with lettuce and tomato) and Coca-Cola mixed with any flavor syrup you dared to order—even chocolate.

A lot of local people seemed to get their total daily nutrition from **Rolling Rock Beer** and the juice of chewing tobacco, but Bethlehem's favorite "real" foods were hotdogs and scrapple (a dry, off-white granular sausage loaf, made from skin, snouts and other pig parts that were normally thrown out, plus cornmeal, flour and seasonings).

If you're thinking about trying scrapple, this description from *Wikipedia* may change your mind: "Scrapple is typically made of hog offal, such as the head, heart, liver, and other scraps, which are boiled with any bones attached (often the entire head), to make a broth. Once cooked, bones and fat are discarded, the meat is reserved, and cornmeal is boiled in the broth to make a mush. The meat, finely minced, is returned, and seasonings are added. The mush is cast into loaves and allowed to cool thoroughly until gelled. Scrapple is typically cut into quarter-inch to three-quarter-inch slices, and pan-fried until browned to form a crust. It is sometimes first coated with flour. It may be fried in butter or oil and is sometimes deep-fried." Sometimes it's fried in lard, to provide even more of the authentic pig taste.

In the 21st Century, Rolling Rock beer has achieved almost cult status and, as part of the **Anheuser Busch** empire, is available in most parts of the country. Back when it was independent and bottled in Pennsylvania, it was merely *cheap beer*. Some students called it "Rolling Piss," rating it just slightly above urine. We bought it only if we couldn't afford **Bud** or **Colt 45**, or as an end-of-binge beer to chug or swig after many bottles of better brews had been consumed and our taste buds were numb.

The major hotdog brand was **Yocco's**, a simplified spelling of the family name of **Lee Iacocca**. He was an Allentown boy who shared my alma mater and helped develop the **Mustang**, save **Chrysler** and refurbish the **Statue of Liberty.**

Hotdogs were normally served with mustard or a red chili-and-onion mixture (no sauerkraut, sadly) and washed down with some **A-Treat** soda in whatever color was then in fashion. (Local folks ordered soda by color; visitors from outside picked actual flavors.)

When parents visited campus, it was traditional to get dressed up and go to the **Hotel Bethlehem** on the north side of town for the "Famous Sunday Roast Beef Buffet." Some of the students, particularly country hicks, thought it was a big deal, but two of Yocco's tube steaks tasted better to me, and could be eaten without a necktie.

If I had some serious money to spend (over four bucks), my favorite restaurants were the **Grotto** and the **Tally Ho**. The Grotto had great Italian food in a not-quite-Little-Italy atmosphere ("Jo-eeeey, I need two annie-passed-uhs!"). It was fun to rearrange or swipe the beer tap handles when the bartender wasn't looking. I still have some of them!

The "Ho" was a traditional campus saloon with initials carved in the tables and four varieties of condoms in the men's room vending machine. Since contraception was opposed by the Catholic Church and no one challenged a church in a city named Bethlehem, rubbers were "Sold Only for Prevention of Disease" before anyone heard of AIDS.

The Tally Ho was a great place to go with friends or professors. You could sit forever, devouring steamed clams, grilled ham-and-cheese sandwiches and juicy Ho-burgers with crisp raw onion slices.

Both draft beer and talk flowed endlessly. My friend **Vicky** and I once sat down around 11 in the morning and didn't leave until they locked up at 3 AM the next day!

For low-budget meals, students visited **Pete-the-Greek** or **Louie-the-Greek**. Pete's place was known for hotdogs. Louie's **Blue Anchor Steak Shop** had the best cheese steak sandwiches, and Louie let me run up tabs between checks from home.

Louie worried a lot about Greek and American politics. He was a kind man, with compassion for everyone but the dreaded communists. Louie complained about an old guy who'd spend all morning lingering over the same cup of coffee—but Louie delayed increasing the price from 10 to 15 cents a cup until he really had no choice. He regarded his customers as family and some of us felt the same way about him. I tutored his son and tended his fish tank. I got paid for the tutoring but took care of the fish for free.

If we were really broke and too embarrassed to ask Louie for more credit, we could fill up for free at **Northampton County Area Community College**. It was a new school, commonly called "nack-ack" or "C-squared," then in temporary quarters on farmland in the northeast section of town.

Its best features were open admission, tiny tuition and—if you were creative with condiments—free lunch!

Vegetable soup was a cup of ketchup and relish diluted with hot water. Onion soup was made from onion slices and pepper in hot water with cracker crumbs, butter and grated cheese.

The free pizza was **Saltines** with ketchup, pepper and grated cheese. There was an unlimited supply of pickle slices, and we could make lemonade with lemons and sugar from the tea supplies.

Closer to Lehigh and right across the street from Louie-the-Greek, was the old **New Merchants Hotel**. Its first-floor bar did a thriving business, selling takeout beer to underage student drinkers.

Pennsylvania's liquor stores were owned by the state, and Liquor Control Board agents had reputations like redneck sheriffs. But, de facto, you could drink with impunity in Bethlehem if you were either 21 *or* a Lehigh student.

Lehigh had a well-deserved reputation as a big drinking school. Sunday dawn would reveal campus lawns strewn with empty kegs and cups, and roadways iridescent with beer, urine and vomit. The fine art of keg-tapping was the first lesson taught to new fraternity brothers, and there was a well-circulated story that Lehigh was banned from intercollegiate drinking competition because we had lost our amateur standing.

During the year I spent on the far side of town with the Webster family, I was isolated from campus life before and after classes. There were few college students in my neighborhood. If I craved some minimal social stimulation, I'd hang out at the laundromat, **McDonald's**, the pet department at the **Two Guys** discount store or the **Dennis Drugs** lunch counter.

The local people didn't know what to make of an apparently healthy, apparently adult, male human being who was on the street at 10 AM or 3 PM. As far as they were concerned, any man who wasn't crippled or retired should be shooting in Viet Nam or sweating "down the steel."

I tried explaining that college was like having a part-time job, going to classes, plus a full-time job, doing homework. One guy said he knew what I meant because he had a cousin who took some courses in the Army.

He had no idea what I meant.

Chapter 112
A few tips for other writers

Some sad rules of life in book publishing:

▶ The bigger the book, the more errors it will have, the more it will cost to produce, and the longer it will take to publish.

▶ When you try to correct errors, you may create more errors.

▶ If you strive for perfection, you'll never complete the book.

▶ No book is perfect—but do your best.

▶ Errors will be caught by readers, reviewers and nitpickers.

Specialization can help you get a job.
Versatility can help you keep a job!

I know a lot about electronics. My first job after college was as the assistant editor of a magazine that went to hi-fi equipment dealers. I sometimes filled in at other mags that the company published, dealing with health foods and art supplies. Later on, I worked for several advertising agencies. I was hired because I could write about hi-fi equipment, but *I kept my job* because I could also write about computers, light switches, motor oil, food, floor tile, wristwatches and bathing suits.

I can probably write about anything. What about you?

Experiment with different genres.

I've been writing nonfiction since I was a journalism major at Lehigh in the 60s. I never aspired to write "the great American novel." Or even a lousy un-American novel.

However, I've often been told that I have a great imagination—and maybe I was wrong to shun fiction.

As an experiment I wrote a novelized back story as the first half of a nonfiction book, **Internet Hell**. I think it turned out well and readers like it. I enjoyed the freedom of not needing to care about facts, truth and reality—but my training and experience as a journalist made unreality realistic.

I think all writers should experiment with genres outside their comfort zone. Try to write in an untried style. You might enjoy it, or even create something great.

Flexibility and versatility may help your financial situation.

When I first moved to Manhattan in 1970, I lived in a tiny-but-expensive room in a YMCA. The manager knew I worked for a magazine and asked for help writing a fundraising appeal. He liked my work—and lowered my rent!

Beware of ghosts.

I get bombarded with ads for ghostwriting services. I've written over 40 books with no ghosts.

If you need a ghostwriter (like **Donald Trump** does), you are a **customer**.

You are **NOT** an author, any more than someone who eats in a restaurant is a chef!

Beware of goofs.

You'll likely be horrified at the errors you'll find if you look at your book *without reading it*.

After reading your new masterpiece 183 times, LOOK at the pages—but *don't* read them. You'll probably be amazed, and maybe even horrified, at all the errors you detect when you are not concerned with content, meaning, grammar, spelling, punctuation and story-telling artistry. I aim my eyes at the three-o'clock position and make a clockwise scan of each page, but do what works best for you.

Some potential problems: Wrong typefaces or wrong fonts, (not necessarily the same thing) particularly when text is pasted-in from another source. Commas that should be periods—and vice versa. Straight punctuation that should be curly. Curlies that curl in the wrong direction. Missing spaces between paragraphs or sections. Bad justification in the last line of a page. Over-size spaces. Roman text that should be *italic*, and vice versa. Gray text that should be black.

Paul Simon sang about the 50 ways to leave your lover. I've found 50 ways to mess up my own books. How about you? These foibles and faults require *careful reading* to detect and fix—not just a look.

Here are a few:

o Paragraphs that accidentally merged
o Missing photo or illustration credits
o Credits for deleted photos or illustrations
o Chapters missing from the table of contents
o Inconsistencies such as **3pm** on one page and **3 P.M.** on another
o A topic not in the index because you added something after completing the index
o Inaccurate internal referrals such as "see comments on page 164"
o Words that shifted from the bottom of one page to the top of the next page
o Chapter names and page numbers in the table of contents that don't reflect changes made in the actual chapter name or the first page of the chapter
o Words that should have been deleted but were not
o Names that were changed in some places but not in all places
o Photos or illustrations accidentally flipped left-to-right
o Wrong ISBN or other information on the copyright page

Epilogue: What Was & What If?

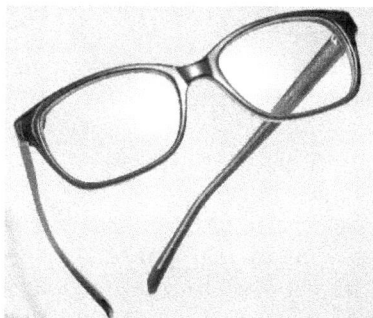

While writing my 2008 memoir, I spent time reading old love letters, appointment books, term papers, "little black books," yearbooks and autograph books, and looking at old pictures.

I Googled names and sent emails. I used social media and online media to find out what happened to friends, enemies and lovers from the past. Some people are still missing. Some stories were not written. Sometimes, I found only *my own words*.

Looking backward can be important, fun, surprising, revealing and intriguing. But playing "what if" can be addictive, unproductive—or even dangerous.

Historians get paid to contemplate how different life would be if the South had won the Civil War, if Germany had won World War II, if JFK, RFK and MLK had not been killed, and if one Supreme Court Justice hadn't awarded the presidency to Bush.

But personal retro-speculation can cause trouble. If you spend too much time rearranging the past in your mind, you can neglect the present and hurt your future.

In assessing my own life, I had to wonder about some decisions, indecisions and missed opportunities. A few weeks into my first semester in college, it was obvious that I was at the wrong college and headed for the wrong career. I didn't make either choice. **Elizabeth Clifford**, my well-meaning but misguided high school guidance counselor, picked both.

She decided that I should go to Lehigh University and prepare to become an electrical engineer, ignoring the evidence provided by my College Board scores. She knew I liked electronics, but the electronics that I liked centered on soldering irons and screwdrivers; and engineers used slide rules. I never figured out how to use the slide rule properly. Now I use computers.

This guidance counselor—entrusted to guide kids in some of the most important decisions of their lives—didn't know what engineers did, but she had decided that I should do what they do.

To guide me, Miss Clifford gave me an aptitude test that revealed I had a "99th percentile commonality" with chemical engineering students at Penn State.

I *hated* chemistry class. I resented memorizing atomic numbers of the elements. The chemistry labs in many sci-fi movies have huge periodic tables of the elements on the walls that the mad scientist could easily consult if he needed the atomic number for bohrium or zinc.

If important professional scientists could look at the big wall chart, why couldn't high school students? The best mark I got in chemistry was during the time when I stayed home with mononucleosis. The most fun I had with chemistry was mixing water with sodium bicarbonate and filling our basement with foam.

After one semester in college, I switched from electrical engineering to Lehigh's tiny but excellent journalism department—a spot that neither my guidance counselor nor I would have selected in advance.

But, looking back from 2024 to 1965 I realize that it seems to have been a great place to be. It even made this book possible. Who knew? Miss Clifford certainly didn't.

Sure, we all know that "shit happens." But so does serendipity. Lots of good things happen by accident. Even great people are born without planning. Teenagers are expected to choose their life path, and often their life mate, with very little information and very little experience.

My junior high school expected me to decide if I would start on the path to college or not, based on five-month courses in Spanish (called "Language Exploratory") and typing ("Business Exploratory").

But learning to say "*Mas salsa por favor, Señor Gomez*" with an authentic accent does not mean that a 15-year-old is either qualified or destined to become a doctor.

And being able to type 40 words per minute without peeking at the keys or making too many mistakes does not mean that a 15-year-old will become a good manicurist.

But that's what our school system assumed.

How can a 15-, 16-, or 17-year-old pick a career that will be right at age 30, 40, 50 or 60?

Or pick a mate who will be right at those ages?

I'm amazed at people who marry their high school sweethearts. I'm more amazed if they are still married 20 or 40 years later. How can a 16-year-old choose a 60-year-old spouse?

Strangely, it seems to work. The divorce rate for people married when they're under 20 is much lower than those who get married when they're between 20 and 24. Sadly, my high school classmates have had lots of divorces. But many married again. Eighteenth-century writer **Samuel Johnson** declared that second marriages are "the triumph of hope over experience."

The more often you've married, the more likely you are to have a divorce. The divorce rate for third marriages in the United States is over 70%.

While writing the memoir, it was inevitable that I thought about, fantasized about and played the "what-if" game about some of the high school sweethearts whom I didn't marry.

One time, as the book progressed, I nearly blacked out during a medical procedure. In my mind, I reached out and held the hand of a beautiful 16-year-old girl.

I later found a current picture of her. She had become a wrinkled old lady (and I was a wrinkled old man)—and one fantasy was destroyed forever.

But, I still have other fantasies.

The Three **BIG** Don'ts

After writing these rules, I disobeyed them.
I almost-sort-of-kinda-possibly fell in love with a former girlfriend.
It was a disaster.
Don't do as I did.
(And please don't tell my wife.)

❶ **Don't** focus on what could have been. Deal with what is. You probably can't change much.
❷ **Don't** try to manipulate the space-time continuum—even in your mind. You are not **Dr. Emmett Brown**. You do not have a **DeLorean** with a 1.21-gigawatt plutonium-powered flux capacitor. You might not be able to come *Back to the Future*.
❸ **Don't** seek a lot of information. The reality of the present can disrupt memories and fantasies of the past.

Enjoy your dreams!

MNM

[Delorean photo by DukeNukeIt. Thanks]

About The Author

Michael N. Marcus either is now or has been a journalist, author, editor, blogger, publisher, critic, maven, nitpicker, raconteur, gourmand, advertising copywriter, public relations practitioner, photographer, band manager, amateur attorney, golf ball SCUBA diver, recording engineer and founder of AbleComm ("the telecom department store").

He published a newspaper when he was in sixth grade, provided words for over 100 websites and blogs, was an editor at *Rolling Stone*, and wrote for many other magazines and newspapers. Michael specializes in making technology understandable, and often humorous. At least eleven of his books are bestsellers.

Born in 1946, Michael's a proud member of the first cohort of the Baby Boom, along with Dolly Parton, Candy Bergen, Donny Trump, Billy Clinton and Georgie Bush.

Electronics was always Michael's favorite hobby. He loved to build gadgets. The victim of a misguided guidance counselor, he went to Lehigh University to become an electrical engineer and was quickly disappointed to learn that engineering was mostly math—and slide rules were not as much fun as soldering irons. He got in big trouble for running intercom wire from his freshman dorm room to a friend's room two floors below, and when an inspector found a payphone in his suitcase. Following the advice of an older student from his hometown, Michael switched from engineering to journalism.

He recently learned of a parallel with comedian Garry Shandling. Garry went to college to study engineering—but became a writer and a funny guy.

Michael was one of a few literate people in his engineer-filled freshman dormitory and made money editing term papers.

While in college, he co-owned a band management company. One of its groups turned down the chance to record *Yummy Yummy Yummy, I've Got Love in My Tummy*, which became a hit for The Ohio Express.

Later, his college apartment had an elaborate and illegal multi-line phone system, a phone booth with a toilet in it, and an invisible phone activated by hand claps.

Michael lives in Connecticut with his wife Marilyn, the ghost of Hunter J. Marcus, their golden retriever, and a *lot* of stuff. Until a recent downsizing from a huge house to a right-sized apartment, he had *two* telephone booths (indoor and outdoor, of course), a "Lily Tomlin" switchboard, a teletype, three parking meters, a coin collector device from a New York City bus, lots of phones, books, tapes, tools, commercial artwork, cameras, CDs, DVDs, Coke containers, signs, and many black boxes with flashing lights.

He still has lots of media, cameras, gadgets, toy cars, bobble heads, tools and a collection of restaurant sugar lumps dating back to the 1930s.

Marilyn is very tolerant.

[Sugar photo from fellow collector Frank Kelsey. Thanks.]

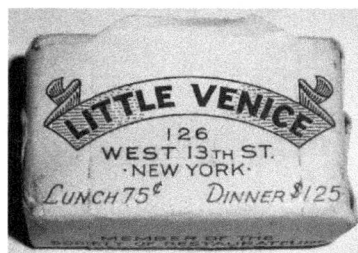

Some of Michael's other books

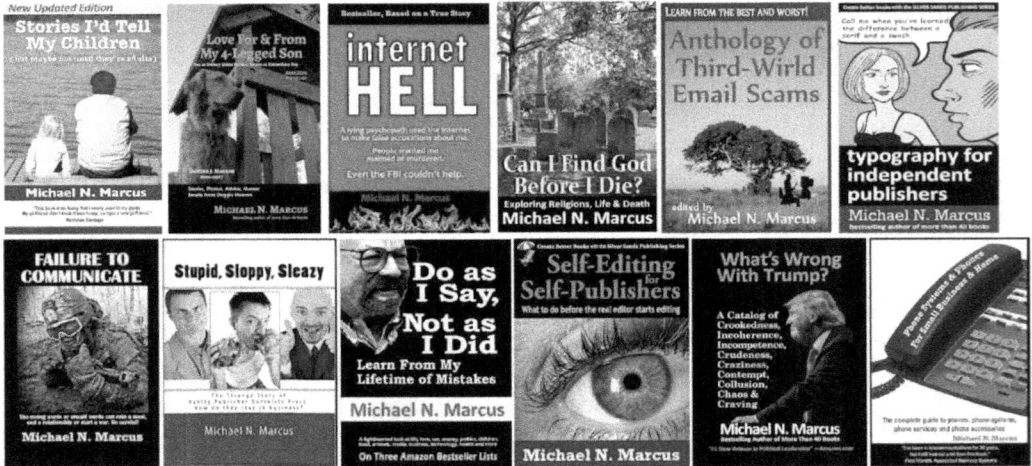

Michael's books are available at Amazon.com, Barnes & Noble, and wherever books are sold.

Signing Off
Which sign should we believe:
"One Lane Only" or "Use Any Lane"

Epigraphs
(some last words to ponder)

"Optima Dies Prima Fugit" ("The best days are the first to flee.")
• Roman poet Virgil (about 49 BCE), quoted by novelist Willa Cather in *My Antonia.* (1918)

"I went from adolescence to senility, trying to bypass maturity."
• Song writer, singer, professor Tom Lehrer

"I won't grow up. I don't want to wear a tie."
• Peter Pan (1953)

"Maturity is overrated and often counterproductive."
• The author (1977)

"...what we share from our teenage years is the dread that what happens now will forever determine what happens later."
• Professor Rachel Louise Snyder (2024)

"Age is just a number, kid."
• Joe Biden (2024)

"There's a certain point at which you don't want to hear *Happy Birthday*. You just want to pretend the day doesn't exist."
• Donald Trump (2024)

"Miami Beach is the waiting room for heaven."
• Unknown

"You know you're old when you look back more than you look ahead."
•The author (2009)

"Everyone's immortal when they're young."
• Mikael Andersson, Swedish union official (2024)

"Any author who writes for money is unworthy of being read."
• Winifred B. Shea, the author's 7th-grade English teacher (about 1960)

"Americans don't build monuments as well-made as the ancient Greeks built. ... our democratic ideas are the real monuments."
• Tressie Cottom, professor, author, *New York Times* columnist (2024)

"To a great degree, in older age, ambition falls away. ... We more easily accept the world as is, even as we doggedly keep trying to save it. ... Kitty Carlisle's mother said that the best thing about being older is that, every 15 minutes or so, it's time for breakfast again."
• Anne Lamott, *Washington Post* columnist

"What lies behind you and what lies in front of you, pales in comparison to what lies inside of you."
• Ralph Waldo Emerson, poet

"If you don't care what others think, you can accomplish a lot and have a lot of fun."
• The author (1962)

"Time is on my side, yes it is."
• Jerry Ragovoy (2004), popularized by the Rolling Stones

"The great thing about this age, you don't learn by your mistakes, you just keep doing the same stupid thing."
• Jay Leno (2024)

"If a professor leaves students laughing, they will walk away remembering."
• Dr. Ruth Westheimer, professor, author, sexpert (1984)

"Music is a powerful tool, a calming salve and one of the last things to go in a person's memory."
• "AA", in the *New York Times* (2024)

"It's always the wrong time for a vacation, so just go, and enjoy!"
• The author (1972)

"The more unhappy you are with life, the closer you are to death."
• Jesse Holmes on TV's *Life Below Zero* (2024)

"Life is a movie and you're the star. Give it a happy ending."
• Joan Rivers (1995)

"Those were the days, my friend. We thought they'd never end."
• Composed by Boris Fomin (1900—1948 CE) but credited to Gene Raskin, who put English lyrics to Fomin's Russian song *"Dorogoi dlinnoyu,"* with words by K. Podrevsky.

"A house is a thief."
• The author's mother

"The longer I live, the more beautiful life becomes."
• Frank Lloyd Wright

"After two days, fish and company start to stink."
• The author's mother

"We get old too soon and wise too late."
• Benjamin Franklin

"The Age Discrimination in Employment Act specifically forbids age discrimination against people who are age 40 or older. ... any boss who would rather put older employees out to pasture than benefit from their experience, is going to have a rude awakening in a few years."
• R. Eric Thomas, author and advice columnist for the *Washington Post* (2024).

"The older you get, the older you want to get."
• Keith Richards

"Age is an issue of mind over matter. If you don't mind, it doesn't matter."
• Mark Twain

"You are only young once, but you can stay immature indefinitely."
• Ogden Nash

"Anyone who stops learning is old, whether at 20 or 80. Anyone who keeps learning stays young. The greatest thing in life is to keep your mind young."
• Henry Ford

"One guy I talked to is a lifelong Republican, a good friend of mine, and he said: 'You know, my one parent had Alzheimer's, the other had dementia. It's sad to watch.'"
• Tim Ryan, former Democratic congressman

"Nothing is more effective for confronting those around you with the reality of yourself at any age—and all the prejudices and subconscious biases about women and age—than a bikini."
• Vanessa Friedman, fashion director and chief fashion critic for the *New York Times* (2024)

"The boomer fantasy is that we will die of a heart attack in our ninth or tenth decade, without ever having been sick a day, and while blissfully engaged in love making, skydiving or paragliding. Now, the truth: Most Americans who live beyond 85—there will be 8.5 million by 2030—will die after a period of extended mental or physical disability. Nearly half of those now over 85 suffer from dementia, of which Alzheimer's is the leading cause. Half will spend some time in a long-term care institution before they die."
• Susan Jacoby, in the *New York Daily News*.

"We can't control our genes, but we can exert a bit of control over our lives. Be careful, friends. The older we are, the less we can get away with. There's less time to heal, and maybe less strength to resist bad stuff."
• The author (2014)

"Many vast projects begin with half-vast ideas."
• Unknown

"Feeling tired all the time is not a normal part of aging."
• Dr. Trisha Pasricha, instructor at Harvard and columnist for the *Washington Post* (2024)

"I'm very pleased to be here. Let's face it, at my age I'm very pleased to be anywhere."
• George Burns

[Photo credits: Biden by Adam Schultz, Westheimer by Harald Bischoff, Rivers by Mike Hvozda, Leno by US mission to the European Union. Thanks]

www.ingramcontent.com/pod-product-compliance
Lightning Source LLC
Chambersburg PA
CBHW062058090426
42741CB00015B/3266